THE ORGANIZATION
OF PHONOLOGY

THE ORGANIZATION
OF PHONOLOGY

Stephen R. Anderson

Department of Linguistics
Harvard University
Cambridge, Massachusetts

ACADEMIC PRESS   New York   San Francisco   London

A Subsidiary of Harcourt Brace Jovanovich, Publishers

ACADEMIC PRESS, INC.
111 Fifth Avenue, New York, New York 10003

United Kingdom Edition published by
ACADEMIC PRESS, INC. (LONDON) LTD.
24/28 Oval Road, London NW1

Library of Congress Cataloging in Publication Data

Anderson, Stephen R.
     The organization of phonology.

     Bibliography: p.
     1.   Grammar, Comparative and general—Phonology.
2.   Generative grammar.   I.   Title.
P217.A6   415   73-18994
ISBN 0–12–785031–7

PRINTED IN THE UNITED STATES OF AMERICA

For Kitten, Thor, and Sigrid

My own subject, Phonetics, is one
which is useless by itself, while
at the same time it is the foundation
of all study of language, whether
theoretical or practical.

Henry Sweet

Contents

Preface

This book started as a revision of earlier work, but has been expanded in scope in the process of rewriting. I have incorporated in it some of the material on the nature of phonological representations and the history of phonology which I have found necessary to cover at the beginning of courses in phonological theory. This material does not seem to exist in any one place in convenient form, and, as so much of the rest of this book builds on these ideas, it seems appropriate to include at least some summary coverage of them. As a history of phonological theory, this material is very sketchy, since my concern basically has been to lay out problems, and the history of those problems serves more as a convenient expository framework than as a subject in itself.

This book is concerned primarily with making clear what constitutes a problem in phonological theory, what evidence is relevant to the solution of such problems, and what sorts of things count as solutions. In this enterprise, it accepts in large part the approach to phonology typified by Chomsky and Halle's "Sound Pattern of English." Most attention is devoted to the search for a formal system that allows adequate descriptions of the phonological systems of natural languages. Since this descriptive concern is primary, some readers familiar with the recent literature may well feel that not enough attention is devoted to topics such as naturalness, markedness, conspiracies, language acquisition, etc. These are, of course, all valid concerns, but it does not seem to me that they should replace the search for a framework for phonological descriptions which is adequate in purely descriptive terms. Some discussion of the relation between description and explanation in phonology will be found in the final chapter.

A number of examples from a variety of languages are discussed in various places here, and many of these are presented with insufficient supporting detail to be convincing in themselves *qua* analyses. In most cases, however, the examples have been discussed somewhere in print, and the skeptic can view some of the chapters as outlines for further reading. Where possible, I have tried to find examples from languages that are reasonably well described and/or well known, so as to lighten this chore somewhat. The examples are discussed here for the purpose of illustrating theoretical points, and as such are not generally intended as direct contributions to the scholarship of individual languages. The reader may sometimes find the laying on of other examples when one has already been examined an excess, but I have tried not to propose innovations or controversial mechanisms without at least two supporting examples, preferably from languages with quite diverse structures and genetic affiliations. This is based on the principle that anything happening only once or in only one place might as well not happen at all so far as the construction of a general theory is concerned. Phonology and morphology are related in ways that are not at all well understood (surely a euphemism, in light of the general ignorance which reigns in the field of synchronic morphology, with very few exceptions), and it is certain that an adequate view of morphology will include a range of idiosyncratic processes ranging from the fully suppletive to the fully productive. As long as the possibility exists that a given set of facts is a consequence of the morphological structure of a language and not a matter for phonology at all, the bearing of such facts on questions of theory will remain highly equivocal. Some of this risk is reduced if the problem is shown to be recurrent, however; this is even more true when processes of undeniably 'late' or 'low' levels can be invoked.

One further point that should be noted about the examples discussed in this book concerns systems of transcriptions. The distinction between slant brackets (/ · · · /) and square brackets ([· · ·]) is not generally the absolute one between underlying forms and surface phonetics, but rather a relative one. Forms enclosed in slant brackets may not be the deepest level of representation (or indeed very deep at all), but are rather those representations which are still to undergo further processes of significance to the discussion. Similarly, forms in square brackets are assumed to represent a level to which no further rules of interest apply. Thus, they may not be fully 'phonetic,' but are simply as detailed as necessary to support the associated discussion. Forms cited in other ways (usually in italics) are not mutually inconsistent, and are given in a wide variety of transcriptions. This is inevitable, given the diversity of descriptive traditions (and personalities) that have contributed data to this work, but it bears emphasizing that no particular phonetic or phonological details of such forms should be taken seriously unless explicitly discussed in the text. These transcriptions serve only to identify forms and to distinguish them from one another, where no further precision is necessary.

The book is organized into four parts. Part I introduces the concepts of representations and rules, and discusses the way rules can be seen as mediating between representations. The nature of phonetic structure is discussed first, and a characterization of this in terms of a two-dimensional matrix of binary specifications for a set of universally applicable parameters is accepted (though it is suggested later, in Chapter 14, that this conception needs revision). Then the notion of an abstract or phonemic level is introduced, on which the properties which distinguish any utterance from any other are represented directly. After a discussion of what has often been called the 'morphophonemic' level of representation, the ritual act is performed in which it is shown that the latter really serves the purposes of a phonemic level best, since the less abstract 'taxonomic' or 'autonomous' phonemic level simply gets in the way. This discussion is formulated in terms of the system of rules that must be assumed to relate one level to another, but some supporting discussion in terms of changing views on the nature of speech perception (and associated changes in conceptions of linguistic structure) gives some perspective. This part of the book owes a great deal to Morris Halle; as he has never gotten around to writing them down, I have given my own version here. Naturally he is not directly responsible for any of the things I have said.

In Part II, I deal with the formal problems of the structure and interrelation of rules discussed by Chomsky and Halle (1968) under the heading 'notational conventions.' The notion of disjunctive ordering among formally related rules is the central concern here, and I conclude that the account given by Chomsky and Halle of this notion in terms of formal abbreviatory devices (parentheses, variable feature coefficients, etc.) must be extended in ways which (though reasonably clear) are more elusive. Another problem of internal ordering which Chomsky and Halle solve through the introduction of simultaneously applied infinite schemata of rules is shown to be better approached through the iterative reapplication of simple rules.

One national problem that is not covered in detail is that of boundaries. Throughout this work I have assumed the existence of two distinct boundary elements which appear in phonological representations in a quasi-segmental way. One of these, '+', simply marks morpheme boundaries. It is assumed to be there when needed, and conveniently absent otherwise. This results (as in previous works) in a claim that processes may be restricted to occur only if a morpheme boundary is present, but cannot be required to apply only where one is absent. Thus, processes occurring within boundaries also occur across them. This theory seems in need of revision, along the following lines: since the point of phonological rules is to explain alternations, a rule should not apply unless it has this function. This means in outline that rules should only apply to a morpheme to specify the effects of other morphemes. This cannot be obtained by requiring (say) that all rules contain an instant of + and thus span two morphemes, since there are certainly cases of a rule which accounts for an alternation and yet applies entirely within the scope of a single morpheme. The interesting fact about such cases (e.g., the rules of glide formation and voiced stop deletion in Faroese, discussed in various places) is that, where the rule applies entirely withing the scope of a single morpheme, it does so under the influence of conditions created by the operation of other rules which (ultimately) reflect the effects of other morphemes. The form of such a condition on phonological descriptions, is not clear, but it seems to be an analog of Kiparsky's prohibition on absolute neutralization for context-sensitive rules.

In addition to +, I also assume a word boundary '#' (which may, however, occur word internally). This boundary does 'get in the way,' in that a rule cannot skip over it unless its presence is explicitly matched by some element of the structural description. With idiosyncratic exceptions, lexical items are flanked by this element, and phonological words are surrounded by double occurrences of it. Some instances of it, as noted, may occur internally within lexical items.

Perhaps the most important implication of Part II for future research is the suggestion that distinct formal properties are associated with rules of different types. There seem to be morpholexical rules, which specify phonological idiosyncracies of particular morphemes; phonological rules, which specify properties of strings in terms of their categorical phonological structure; and phonetic rules, which specify detailed values for features within the range of a single categorical value. Among the formal distinctions seem to be the facts that only morpholexical rules can perform exchange operations on distinct elements, exactly interchanging them in identical environments; and that the principle of disjunctive ordering is restricted to the phonological rules, and does not apply to phonetic rules. It is sometimes suggested that these and related formal distinctions can be made by dividing the rules into distinct components, and applying these components separately and in sequence. This does not seem likely to me, however. There are some cases in which clearly phonetic rules have to precede clearly categorial phonological ones; there are also cases in which morpholexical rules have to follow phonological ones. It seems most likely that these three sorts of rules are, to some extent, intermixed (though, of course, the morpholexical ones are mostly 'early' and the phonetic ones mostly 'late'). A highly articulated typology of rules seems more promising than an attempt to find boundaries between various 'components' in a phonological description. I have argued explicitly for this conclusion since the present work was completed (see, for example, my contribution to the Natural Phonology Parasession at the tenth meeting of the Chicago Linguistic Society.

Part III of the book deals with the problem of the ordering relation among phonological rules. It is shown that this cannot have the character of a linear list, as is frequently assumed, but must be conceived of in terms of a number of (potentially independent) pairwise relations between rules. The proposed theory of local ordering deals with the violations of linear ordering in terms of a set of principles of natural (née unmarked) ordering. Principles originally suggested by Kiparsky as governing historical change (including the maximizing of rule applicability, and the maximizing of rule 'transparency' or surface phonetic motivation) are shown to be important for the organization of synchronic phonology as well. Again, much work needs to be done in this area, refining and extending the principles of natural ordering.

Part IV is more speculative, and deals with three areas that seem to constitute 'current issues' in phonology: the interaction of several potential applications of a single rule in a single form (which it is suggested is governed largely by the same principles as those governing the interaction of distinct rules); the status of the segment and other issues of the structure of phonological and phonetic representations (which it is suggested have the character more of a musical score than of a string of discrete elements); and the relation between description and explanation in phonology (especially as related to the possibility that a single language may contain several processes with functionally similar effects). Very few answers are to be found in these chapters, though the rejection of some nonanswers may not be without interest. The issues taken up here are related to discussions in earlier chapters, but the point is to interest others in solving problems whose answers I would like to know.

Acknowledgments

Numerous people have contributed much to this work, and a list of all of them would be tedious and inadequate thanks. In addition to my faculty supervisors and colleagues at various times, I would like to express my gratitude to my students at Harvard and in Copenhagen (including those at the third Scandinavian Summer School of Linguistics) for their many interesting ideas and suggestions, and for listening. For reading portions of the present manuscript and giving me extremely useful comments, I should like to thank Janet Dean Fodor, Paul Kiparsky, Jørgen Rischel, Eli Fischer-Jørgensen, and Osamu Fujimura. My thanks also to Ellen Kaisse for preparing the indexes. If I had had as good advice on all of it, the book would have benefited greatly. Most of all, I am indebted to Morris Halle in general (for having, with Noam Chomsky, virtually created the field of inquiry to which this book is a contribution), and in particular for a critical reading of the manuscript, and for innumerable helpful conversations on various issues. I have no intention, however, of blaming any of these people for errors I have introduced despite their best efforts.

For financial assistance, I am indebted to the National Science Foundation (for support to various projects at Harvard and Brandeis Universities); the NDEA (for supporting my graduate work at the Massachusetts Institute of Technology, during which much of this work was done or at least begun); the American Scandinavian Foundation (for a grant from its Thor Thors Fund, which enabled me to spend the summer of 1968 in Iceland and the Faroes); the Language Research Foundation and its former director, Dr. Bruce Fraser (for supporting my work on phonology in ways and at times that were not always intentional); and The American Council of Learned Societies (for a postdoctoral fellowship which has allowed me to finish this book, while I was supposed to be working on another one). The support of the Massachusetts Institute of Technology (and its Research Laboratory of Electronics) and Harvard University in many areas is also gratefully acknowledged.

PART I

THE BASIC CONCEPTS OF PHONOLOGICAL STRUCTURE: REPRESENTATIONS AND RULES

CHAPTER 1

Phonetic Structure

A human language can be viewed as a more or less formalizable system of correlations between sound and meaning. Although everyone has at least some presystematic notion of what meanings are like, the concept of meaning has proven to be remarkably recalcitrant to precise definition and formulation, since individual meanings are not accessible to observation and comparison in any very satisfactory way. In the face of this difficulty, semantic research has often tended to dissolve into quibbles and self-doubts: fussy and self-conscious squabbling over the boundaries of the field, and indeed over the question of whether there is such a field.

The study of sound structure has been somewhat more fortunate, dealing as it does with the properties of events which, while transitory, are at least observable. As a result, much of linguistic research has centered on the regular patterns to be found in the speech events on the sound side of language. Though the physical properties of these speech events are thus the primary data of linguistic description, they are not in fact objects of the sort that can be directly held up to examination and compared with one another. While laboratory procedures allow us to record and thus to replicate individual speech events, the linguist's principal approach to them is through the medium of transcriptions — stable representations that attempt to capture as many aspects of the event as possible.

A phonetic transcription is, ideally, a complete and faithful record of the physical event it describes: every possible parameter of the speech event that can be observed, extracted, and quantified would be specified in a complete phonetic transcription. Since a speech event is not a particularly simple thing, this entails consideration of a vast range of factors. In addition, the event can be considered from several distinct perspectives: it can be characterized in terms of neurological, physiological, and aerodynamic events occurring in the speaker, the corresponding events taking place in the listener, or in terms of the acoustic events that relate these two sets. Indeed, for much of the early history of modern phonetics, this encyclopedic sort of coverage was the explicit goal—increasingly to refine one's observation so that no physical property of the speech event would escape unnoticed. As phoneticians became more and more sophisticated in the nineteenth and early twentieth centuries, they noticed more and more aspects of the utterance and were able to quantify and record them with considerable accuracy.

With such increasingly precise description, however, came the realization that much of it was irrelevant to the central tasks of linguistic science. Some properties of the speech event are clearly predictable in terms of others, while still other properties, though not constant throughout a given speech event, seem simply not to play any role in the functioning of language, the pairing of sounds with meanings. From among all of the possible parameters of the event, it is necessary for the linguistic phonetician to select the relevant ones, and within these, to isolate the independently variable ones. Insofar as phonetic description is taken to be an aspect of the theory of language, it is clearly essential to restrict it to those areas with a systematic role in language, but there is no obvious a priori way to distinguish these (seen simply as parameters of a physical event) from the irrelevant and predictable ones. Physical events are notoriously neutral.

For example, it is clear that speech is a continuum—that is, an utterance takes place over a stretch of time during every instant of which *something* is going on that is slightly different from what is going on either just before or just after. Accordingly, it would be possible to regard the speech event as infinitely divisible, and, indeed, to secure a complete and faithful record of the event, it would be necessary to do so. But from the point of view of the workings of the language, it is reasonably clear that we do not really want or need to do this. Corresponding to the presystematic notion of a sound in an utterance, the most accurate representation that we need to obtain in order to characterize the linguistic structure of the event adequately seems to be one that isolates a very few points within the utterance. Such a representation thus regards the utterance as a sequence of a finite number of discrete, homogeneously characterizable, atomic segments, rather than as a continuum. For instance, each segment is characterized in terms of a state of the vocal organs, and the transitions between these states are assumed to be predictable in terms of very general linguistic and physiological laws. Though much phonetic attention in the late nineteenth century was focused on these transitions between segments, as typified in the account of phonetics given in Ferdinand de Saussure's "Cours de linguistique générale," it was early seen that they are in large part either irrelevant to the functioning of speech, or predictable, and accordingly to be omitted from a linguistically oriented phonetic transcription.[1]

Another kind of idealization generally made by linguists has crept into the preceding—the notion that the individual segments of speech referred to above can be characterized in isolation from their surroundings. In fact, the vocal organs are all continually in motion, and at any given point in time, they are likely to be executing gestures associated not with one but with several of the segments of the utterance. That is, the organs do not simply adopt a static position, hold it briefly, and then move to another position, but rather, during the period associated with one segment, they are already moving into position for a segment to follow, perhaps at some considerable distance. Dramatic evidence of this is found in Öhman's (1966a) study of intervocalic stops in Swedish, for which he found that the cues to the identity of a particular segment may be spread out over a stretch of speech corresponding to several 'segments', and not recoverable from any one alone. This phenomenon of COARTICULATION is completely pervasive, and makes it impossible in any but the simplest of utterances to identify those aspects of the vocal configuration associated with just a given segment. This has not been indicated generally in phonetic transcriptions except where it becomes pronounced enough to modify the significant features of the segment affected (as in the nearly universal palatalization of a consonant

---

[1] It should be noted that phoneticians have once more directed attention to the possible role played by these real-time or transitional phenomena in recent work. Lisker and Abramson (1971) have, for example, explicitly denied that the activity of the larynx can be adequately characterized in steady-state terms, and have insisted that features of the relative timing of such gestures must be included in an adequate characterization of the speech event. Kim (1970), on the other hand, emphasizes the possibility of an account that relates voice onset time to glottal position. Öhman (1966b) has discussed the role of real-time relations between gestures in his stimulating study of Swedish accents. Similar questions have been raised by Ladefoged (1972). It is by no means clear that the present state of knowledge concerning the activity of the larynx and related structures in speech warrants an answer one way or another.

by a following or preceding high front vowel, due either to anticipation or lag, respectively, in the functioning of the articulatory apparatus).

It must be emphasized that there is very little basis in the physical event itself for the above abstractions involved in segmentation. Nothing whatsoever distinguishes one position of the utterance from other, immediately adjacent ones; nothing identifies one position as the articulatory basis of the segment, and another as part of the transition. The organs of speech are constantly in motion, and do not adopt rest positions during an utterance. Furthermore, there is no physical basis for associating some aspects of a given articulatory configuration with one segment and others with another, as coarticulation effects to be abstracted from the description of this particular segment. The validity of the segmental abstraction lies in the possibility of giving a set of principles from which transition and coarticulation phenomena can be deduced, and the utterance reconstructed from a sequence of mutually independent static points to its overlapping and continuous reality.

Even given the fairly plausible assumption that such an account of the utterance can be constructed in principle, it can still be asked what theoretical justification we have for making the segmental abstraction. The only justification that can be given is a pragmatic one; such a description, based on a segmental structure imposed on the event by the analyst, has been the basis of virtually every result of note that has ever been obtained in the field of linguistic phonetics or phonology. As such, it will continue to be employed until some deficiency is pointed out, in the form of a linguistically significant generalization that is essentially unstatable if the procedure of segmentation is adhered to. It is fairly clear what sort of situation would furnish such evidence, and it is interesting to note that some recent research in the area (appropriately enough) of suprasegmental phonology indicates a need for some revision of our notion of the segment.[2] By and large, however, phonetic segmentation is as satisfactory a means of representing an utterance as the standard sort of musical score is for representing the structure of an orchestral work. A musical performance is also a continuous event, with something going on at each point in time with a fair amount of overlap, but it is possible to divide the total performance into a number of discrete intervals, and to characterize each parameter (in this case, each instrument) indepen-

[2] See such works as McCawley (1970b), Leben (1971), and Halle (1971a) for some discussion of these problems in connection with pitch. The description of nasality in South American languages, such as those of the Gé family, seems also to present similar problems, since the correct statement of generalizations in this area sometimes appears to involve domains that are smaller than the segment. For further discussion of this problem, see Chapter 14.

dently at each interval. Whereas this is clearly an idealization of a fairly radical sort (i.e., a continuous event is represented as a sequence of points), the representation obtained is effective for characterizing the performance musically (although not, of course, physically). Indeed, a more complete characterization of the acoustic event that we perceive as an orchestral performance would only serve to obscure much of the musically significant structure in a welter of irrelevant detail.[3]

Given that an utterance is to be represented by a sequence of discrete segments, there is another important sort of idealization made in the linguistic study of sound that must be pointed out. Some of the observable characteristics of the utterance, even within the framework of the segment, are simply irrelevant. Any experienced psychologist who has ever tried to convince skeptical colleagues that his results are based on complete and comprehensive consideration of all the relevant facts knows that there are limitless parameters that could be specified in the determination of any event in the real world. When we describe what goes on linguistically when a particular person uses a particular linguistic form on a particular occasion, however, only a very few parameters suffice to characterize the utterance. Others, such as the loudness of the voice, the physical manifestations of the sex of the speaker, the movement of most of the facial muscles, the exact density of the transmitting medium, etc., play no role. Such irrelevancies should be excluded, but obviously we require a principled basis for deciding which ones to leave out, and such a basis is not provided by the brute facts themselves. What is the basis of the intuitions we have about which factors must be included and which factors can be omitted?

Of course, we want any proposed set of parameters for phonetic description to include every feature that can serve systematically to differentiate one utterance from another in any language. It is also necessary that the set of parameters include every feature in terms of which one language differs systematically from another, for otherwise linguists would be unable to characterize this distinction. For example, it is well known that the degree of aspiration of the voiceless stops in English varies systematically with context, but that in a particular context the degree of aspiration is always predictable (within certain limits). Accordingly, aspiration never serves (alone) in English to distinguish one utterance from another. In many other languages, however, the presence of aspiration is not predictable in this way, and can serve to distinguish

---

[3] The analogy is particularly apt, since the fact that the lines of an orchestral score need not be synchronized exactly may show us the correct view of problems involved in segmentation, referred to in the references of footnote 2.

utterances from one another. In Bengali and many other modern Indic languages for example, [p], [pʰ], [b], and [bʰ] are all distinct, and can appear in the same environment to distinguish words. Obviously, then, it is important to indicate aspiration in a linguistically adequate phonetic theory, since it sometimes (although not always) has a distinctive function.

But what about factors that never function distinctively in any language, and are always predictable? Here, too, it seems that an adequate phonetic theory may have to include such features, if the basis for predicting their value in a given utterance can vary from one language to another. Consider, for example, the question of whether stops are released or not. In English, stops followed by another obstruent are not released, while final stops are either released or not, in free variation. In Georgian, on the other hand, stops are released both in obstruent clusters and in final position; in French, they are unreleased in clusters, but released finally, whereas Korean stops are always unreleased both in clusters and in final position. Stop release does not function distinctively in any of these languages, and as far as we know, there is no language in which utterances can be distinguished solely in that one contains a released stop where the other contains an otherwise identical unreleased one. This does not affect the value of the above observations for a phonetic theory, however—the nondistinctive value of the parameter of release of stops is determined in different ways in all of these languages, and if phonetic descriptions did not take note of this fact, linguists would be unable to distinguish English, French, Georgian, and Korean (certainly an unfortunate result). Accordingly, we require that an adequate phonetic theory include the feature of stop release, as well as any other feature in terms of which languages can systematically differ from one another.

It is not the purpose of this work to defend a particular set of phonetic features as adequate for linguistic description. A list of the features employed here, with their definitions, may be found in the Appendix. It will be seen that this system is largely that of Chomsky and Halle (1968); most of the deviations from that framework are justified in the current literature.

We assume, then, that it is possible to represent every utterance in any language in terms of a language-neutral phonetic transcription, composed of a sequence of individual segments, for which each segment is characterized by a set of parameters (in the system employed here, these parameters are almost exclusively articulatory in definition). The set of parameters includes all and only those factors that can be shown to be independent variables in linguistic structures, either by having distinctive function or by differing systematically from one language to another. The specification of these parameters has two aspects, which must be distinguished. Primarily, we assume that each can be specified on a binary scale as either + or −. For some features, the values + and − will indicate the presence versus the absence of some articulatory property; for others, these will simply be opposed values of some property which is present in one way or the other in all sounds (the former represents a privative opposition in the sense of Trubetzkoy, while the latter represents an equipollent opposition, although no use will be made of the distinction between these two types of opposition).

Beyond this binary representation, however, it is clear that more is required if we are to achieve our goal of specifying all of the ways in which one language can differ from another. For instance, while velar stops are articulated in a fronted position before front vowels in both English and Icelandic, this palatalization is noticeably more pronounced in Icelandic then it is in English. If we were to indicate this by including another (independent) phonetic parameter, say by distinguishing FRONTED VELAR articulation from EXTREMELY FRONTED VELAR articulation, we would soon drown in a vast array of fine phonetic distinctions. More importantly, however, we would have obscured the necessary distinction between independent parameters and distinct values of the same parameter. Thus, we seek a way of indicating more than two distinct values for a given parameter.

This observation might be taken to mean that features are not specified in terms of binary values at all, but rather by integer- (or even real number-) valued scales. But this move would obscure the fact that those aspects of language structure that make reference to the values of the phonological parameters (i.e., the phonological rules) in general refer only to the presence or absence of a feature. Thus, we will assume that features have binary values, but that underlying these values is a specification of each parameter in more detailed terms, which is given on a continuous real-valued scale which we will arbitrarily assume to vary between 0 and 1. This scale is interpreted in such a way that values below some given point are interpreted as −F, while higher values are interpreted as +F. The dividing point for a given feature may well vary from language to language, and language-particular rules may well affect the detail values as well as the binary values of features. We will see, subsequently, some interesting differences between the rules specifying binary values and those interpreting or specifying these as real-number values, which we will refer to as detail rules. An example of the sort of thing referred to is the following. In the Breton dialect of Plougrescant [see Jackson (1961) for details], vowels can be distinctively either nasal or nonnasal. Thus, phonetic representations will specify some vowels as [+nasal], and others as [−nasal]. But among the oral vowels, some are more nasal than others: [−nasal] vowels immediately preceding a nasal consonant are slightly nasalized, though not so much as distinctively nasal vowels. We thus have at least the following three values (where the precise values, on a hypothetical scale, are irrelevant; only the relative values matter): [0nasal] (for oral vowels next to oral consonants); [.3nasal] (say) for oral vowels next to a nasal consonant; and [.7nasal] for distinctively nasal vowels. We can then say that any value over [.5nasal] counts as [+nasal], while values below [.5nasal] count as [−nasal]. We then have three values (at least) phonetically, but only two values in the slightly more abstract binary representation. Furthermore, some instances of the property in question (lowered velum) are treated as 'presence of F' (i.e., [+F]), while other instances of the property if low enough in value, are treated as 'absence of F' (i.e., as [−F]). We presume the reality of both sorts of phonetic representation in linguistic description.

CHAPTER 2

The Phonemic Insight and Its Development

The conception of phonetic representation developed in Chapter 1 satisfies our desire for a formal structure that eliminates dependent and irrelevant parameters. Such a phonetic representation, based as it is on a selection of parameters going beyond any individual language, is neutral and uniform in its application to utterances in any individual language. As soon as we investigate a particular language in any detail, however, we see that there is a vast range of systematic behavior, which such a transcription does not reveal. In every language, much of the detail of the phonetic transcription is predictable in terms of rules or principles specific to that language. Thus, although aspiration is distinctive in Bengali, and must clearly be indicated in any description of the sound structure of Bengali utterances, it is not distinctive in English. In English-particular terms, aspiration is as redundant and as unnecessary to specify as the position of the epiglottis, since it is a wholly automatic consequence of a set of general principles. Much of the study of sound systems has focused not on the construction of an adequate theory of universal phonetics, but rather on the question of what sorts of principles govern these predictabilities within each language, and on the construction of a level of representation more abstract than the phonetic in that it leaves out those properties that are predictable in a given language.

European Structuralist Phonology

FERDINAND DE SAUSSURE

In many ways the founder of modern linguistics, Saussure suggested a framework within which these questions could be raised and discussed productively. Much of his work, especially with respect to sound structure, shows a debt to Kruszewski, Baudouin de Courtenay, and their followers, but Saussure's work was the immediate source in which these insights were generally met for the first time by European and American scholars.[1] As is well known, Saussure distinguished, in the description of language, between the study of LANGUE and the study of PAROLE. LANGUE is similar in many ways to what most contemporary linguists, following Chomsky, prefer to call competence — the knowledge a speaker of the language has to have in order to be able to speak and understand the language, in order to distinguish sentences in the language from other formal (or phonetic) objects, etc. PAROLE (or performance), on the other hand, is the way in which the speaker puts this knowledge to use; it is the consequence of using particular mental, neurological, physiological, etc. mechanisms (which have their own limitations and properties, independently of their use in language) to implement his knowledge. Clearly, in describing the system of a language, the linguist is interested in studying langue; parole, on the other hand, is some different sort of empirical science, a branch of psychology, physiology, neurology, physics. If the system of langue can be isolated from the facts of parole, an important step will have been taken toward isolating the sort of properties that make a linguistic system what it is.

For Saussure, langue was a special sort of semiotic or sign system, and thus a static collection of signs as in other signaling systems. Each sign in a system, such as the Morse code, traffic lights, silver hallmarks, etc., can be seen as having two aspects: the SIGNIFIANT, or form of the sign, whose aspect differentiates the sign from other signs of the system and gives it its character as the individual sign that it is; and the SIGNIFIÉE, or content of the sign, the 'thing signified', or the information conveyed by the sign. In language, the sound system constitutes the system of the SIGNIFIANTS, and the function of the sound structure of any element of the language is to distinguish it from the other signs in the language. Saussure emphasized that what was important about the sounds of the language, the individual elements making up the signifiants

---

[1] For an extremely useful discussion of Baudouin de Courtenay's work and its influence on Saussure, see Jakobson (1971).

of signs in the semiotic system, is precisely the fact that they are different from one another. Seen in this light, the signifiant of any linguistic sign is not to be identified with its individual manifestations, or indeed with anything that is present in the speech event itself, but rather with its value in the system, which can be equated with the way in which it differs from all of the other signs in the system. This purely negative character of the sign, with the emphasis not on any positive property it may have, but rather on the fact that it is not some other sign, was elevated to the status of a methodological point of principle, and has come to underlie the notion of 'structural analysis' in many fields.

Applying this notion of the sign to the study of sound structure, we see that the kind of phonological representation that would be relevant to the system of langue would be one in which only those elements are distinguished that can serve to oppose one sign to another. Much of the wealth of phonetic detail that can be marked in a phonetic transcription, even one limited in the ways sketched above, does not serve such a function, and so would not be contrastively identified in a transcription of this latter sort. For instance, it was argued in Chapter 1 that the question of whether stops are released or not is a parameter that must be incorporated in an adequate phonetic descriptive system, but in English, stops can be either released or unreleased in final position in essentially free variation. Thus, two utterances of the English word *bit* as [bɪt] and as [bɪt˺] are both utterances of the same sign, and hence should not differ in their phonological representations.

Such a transcription, in which only those distinctions are marked that can serve to oppose one sign to another, has generally been referred to as phonemic in the work of a variety of traditions. The term PHONEME (Fr. phonème) was originally coined by Dufriche-Desgenettes in 1873 to serve as a substitute for the German term Sprachlaut 'speech sound', and at the time the word *phoneme* carried no particular connotations of minimal distinctiveness. Insofar as Saussure himself referred to phonemes in his published work, it was in an entirely distinct sense from that intended here—as a set of sounds with a unity established diachronically, rather than synchronically. Since Saussure, however, the word phoneme has come to be used generally to designate the minimal distinctive elements of sound structure in a transcription which distinguishes all and only the signs that are opposed within the system of langue.

This sense of the term should not be confused with the multitude of special conditions that have been imposed as defining criteria for the phonemes of a language within the context of particular theories of linguistic structure. Of course, as one's notions change as to what constitutes a possible linguistic system, what the relations are between sub-parts of the language, how the processes of speech production and perception operate, etc., this results in changes in the conception of the relation between phonemic and phonetic representations. These varying conceptions of phonemic analysis, however, differ not in the underlying definition of the phoneme, but rather in empirical and methodological hypotheses about the relation obtaining between the minimal elements of sound structure and phonetic 'reality'.

It is clear that all of the parameters of phonetic description are distinguished in a phonetic transcription, regardless of the language of the utterance. It is also clear that some of these phonetic parameters will never need to be distinguished in phonemic representations, since, for example, release of stops never functions (as far as is known) to distinguish signs. It is often the case, however, that some parameter that functions distinctively in one language, and hence is marked contrastively in phonemic transcriptions of that language, does not have any distinctive function in another language, hence is not distinguished phonemically in that language. In English, for example, the differences among the palatal, velar, and back-velar *k*-sounds [k_1], [k], and [q] in *keep, coop,* and *cop* ([$k_1$ijp], [kuwp], and [qap]) can never serve to distinguish words. The distinctions among these words are rather in terms of their vowels, and the variation in the initial consonant is a predictable consequence of the differing articulations of the following vowels. Accordingly, the differences among [k_1], [k], and [q] need not be indicated in a phonemic transcription of the English words *keep, coop,* and *cop.* In many other languages, however, one or more of these differences can serve to differentiate signs. In Serer, an African language [see Ladefoged (1968) for details], the difference between [k_1] and [k] serves (in part) to differentiate *cit* 'gift' ([k_1It]) from *kid* 'eyes' ([kɪd]), while the difference between [k] and [q] serves to differentiate *qene* 'this boy' ([qene]) and *qos* 'leg' ([qos]) from *kene* 'that' ([kene]) and *kor* 'man' ([kor]). Accordingly, the phonetic segments [k_1], [k], and [q] would have to be represented differently in a phonemic transcription of Serer, while they should all appear in the same form in a phonemic transcription of English.

One fundamental difference between alternative views of the phoneme, which has appeared in a variety of theoretical contexts, relates to the status of nondistinctive or subphonemic features in a phonemic transcription. The above definition of a phoneme ensures that differing segments in distinct phonemic transcriptions will never differ only in that one is marked one way for some subphonemic feature, whereas the other is marked the other way for the same feature. However, it does not force a decision one way or the other as to whether phonemes are marked at all for such features. One view, which has had numerous proponents over the years, would exclude all such predictable information from a phonemic transcription entirely. On this view, held by many of the linguists discussed subsequently, the phoneme is an incompletely specified entity — it has no characteristics whatsoever beyond those functioning distinctively in the language. Another view has also had its advocates, however — the view that the phonemes of a language are fully specified for all phonetic features, but are restricted in the range of variation that is possible. According to the first view, subphonemic variation is accounted for by specifying a set of principles by which noncontrastive information is added to the minimal distinctive core of (phonemically relevant) parameters, whereas according to the second view, nondistinctive features are specified by giving a set of principles that adjust or alter the (neutral or underlying) values of these segments, which are given in the phonemic representations. Of course, a third view is also possible, to the effect that the phonemes of a language have no phonetic properties, whatsoever, and are purely abstract, algebraic, theoretical entities with a correspondence to phonetic segments that is essentially arbitrary. This last possibility (which is arguably the position of Hjelmslev and Lamb) is not discussed at any length here since it has been adequately dealt with elsewhere (see Jakobson & Halle, 1956), but the distinction between the first two views will play an important part in the following discussion of the varying notions of phonemic transcription that have obtained in post-Saussurean linguistics.

Saussure was the first widely influential figure to emphasize the status of a description of utterances which indicated all and only the properties that served to distinguish one sign from another. His emphasis on the purely negative character of the sign, however, left much in obscurity concerning the actual nature of the relation between the phonetic reality of the speech act and the distinctive role of the sign in the system of langue. He was also little concerned with the practical problems of synchronic description, and gave little in the way of concrete hints or examples that would allow a linguist to commence the task of describing the sign system of a given état du langue. Moreover, there is no evidence that he was at all concerned with developing a notion of phonetic or phonemic 'representation' in a modern sense. His conception of the signifiant of the linguistic sign as an idealized internal 'sound-image' probably justifies our attributing to him the fully specified notion of the character of phonemic entities. Nevertheless, we can tell very little about the specific nature of the relation he envisioned between these entities and the concrete facts of phonetic performance, which was a part of parole for Saussure. Later writers have emphasized the fact that the systematicity of the relationship between phonemic and phonetic representation makes this as much a part of langue as the phonemic representations themselves.

POST-SAUSSUREAN STRUCTURALISM

A number of other European linguists in the early part of the twentieth century devoted considerable effort to an elaboration of Saussure's seminal ideas in an attempt to carry them out in practice as real descriptions of natural languages. Perhaps the most important group involved in this theoretical movement centered on the linguists of the so-called Prague school, including most prominently Trubetzkoy, Karcevskij, and Jakobson. Drawing on the work of Baudouin de Courtenay, Kruszevski, and the linguists of the Kazan and Moscow schools, they attempted to combine a serious concern for descriptive methodology with a sophisticated awareness of the theoretical issues that had been raised by Saussure and others. The most notable synthesis of the ideas of this group is Trubetzkoy's "Grundzüge der Phonologie," which combines a presentation of Praguean phonological theory with an outstanding survey of the relation of the theory to the facts of an impressive array of languages.

Following Saussure, Trubetzkoy begins by distinguishing the Sprechakt (parole) from the Sprachgebilde (langue). He observes that it is possible (and, indeed, necessary) to distinguish the study of speech sounds, which is a part of parole, from the study of speech sounds as composing the signifiants of the signs of langue. Phonetics is, for him, the study of sounds within parole, and is thereby associated with the physical and empirical sciences. Conversely, phonology is the study of sound systems within langue, and is properly the concern of linguistics, which is a social science. As Saussure had said, the system of phonemes or elements of the *signifiants* of particular signs exists for the purpose of distinguishing one sign from another; Trubetzkoy is more specific than Saussure, however, in emphasizing that the phonemic differences are to be associated with differences of meaning more or less directly through the medium of the sign. While Saussure naturally had wanted phonemic differences to be correlated with distinct signifiants of the sign system, and meaning differences to be correlated with distinct signifiés (where the sign is the union of a particular signifiant and signifié), he had not gone so far as to assert a direct correlation between phonemic and semantic differences. As will be seen below, Trubetzkoy's notion leads to important difficulties, but it had an advantage over Saussure's in being more precise and testable, and it was an adequate enough translation of

Saussure's intent to serve as the standard position of much later phonology.

Another and potentially more important shift of emphasis in Trubetzkoy's work concerned the basic character of the phoneme. While Saussure had thought of this largely as a negative entity, the existence of which consists in what it is not, Trubetzkoy related it more directly to the speech sound in the utterance. He interpreted Saussure to mean that a phoneme is characterized by those phonic properties that distinguish it from other phonemes, thus shifting the emphasis from the simple fact of its distinctive character to the properties on which this is based. Phonetics is to be maintained as a completely distinct science from phonology, but it is to be phonetic properties endowed with distinctive (and hence phonological) function that form the basis of the phoneme. The phoneme is thus identified with a collection of 'phonic norms' of phonetic properties. These 'phonic norms' are not to be identified with any statistical or computable facts about actual performances, but rather with the ideal elements of an abstract system (language).

There are three principal ways in which this conception departs from that of Saussure. First is the emphasis on the phonetic reality underlying the phoneme: the phoneme is the particular collection of (ideal) phonetic properties that define it, rather than being an arbitrary term in a sign system, that could be realized as well in any other way, as long as its distinctness from the other terms of the system is preserved. In other words, phonemes are not complete abstractions, but are rather specified in terms of the same kinds of parameters that specify (universal) phonetic representation. Second, the phoneme is construed as a partially specified entity: since it is exactly the set of distinguishing phonological properties that compose the phoneme, it does not contain any specification for redundant, nonphonological, subphonemic properties. And third, the system of phonemes has a significant degree of internal structure. Indeed, much of Trubetzkoy's book is devoted to clarifying the kind of internal structure than can exist within phonemic systems. This structure rests on the fact that the same small set of (phonological) distinctive features can be combined in various ways, and any one of them can appear as a constituent of more than one phonemic element. Thus, /p/ is opposed to /b/ in exactly the same way as /t/ is opposed to /d/, /s/ to /z/, etc. — in terms of the presence versus the absence of the feature (or parameter) of voice. Thus all of these oppositions are parallel, while the opposition of, say, /d/ to /n/ resides in an entirely different property of distinction, namely nasality. Oppositions can be classified in terms of the number and type of distinctive feature differences on which they rest; the fact that some segments are more closely related than others and form natural classes, can be expressed in terms of shared features, etc. This kind of structure, going beyond the arbitrariness and negativity of Saussure's conception of phonemic oppositions, became the basis for much productive discussion of the phonological systems of natural languages.

One of the most important aspects of Trubetzkoy's conception was the 'naturalness' of the relation between the phonemic and phonetic representations of an utterance. The phoneme, since it can be equated with a particular set of phonological properties, is an ideal entity with real and identifiable characteristics. The features that identify a phoneme are identifiable in the phonetic representation as well. The attempt to provide some sort of analog to this extreme notion of naturalness in the face of a much more abstract conception of phonemics has been a concern of much recent discussion in phonology [see Postal (1968) and Kiparsky (1968b)]. Since the distinctive properties of a particular phoneme are, for Trubetzkoy actually present in the sound, not only is the set of properties underlying the phonemic system fixed by a naturalness condition, but also the relation between the two representations (phonetic and phonemic) becomes for Trubetzkoy a very restricted one. Aside from the fact that the phonetic representation indicates a large number of additional properties (those not functioning distinctively in the language in question) that are not present in the phonemic representation, in addition to the fact that phonetic representation may specify something about the ways in which the phonic norms are realized in sound by a particular speaker on a particular occasion, no essential difference between the two representations is possible. For example, if voicing is a distinctive feature in some language, it is not possible for an entity which is phonemically a voiced dental stop (/d/) to be sometimes voiced ([d]) and sometimes voiceless ([t]), depending on the environment. The character of [t] as voiceless dictates its assignment to /t/ rather than /d/ in all occurrences, since the distinctive character of /t/ (namely, voicelessness) is found in it. Thus it is not possible to say that German *Land* is phonemically /land/, in both [lant] (*Land*) and [landə] (*Lande*). A particularly rigorous set of constraints on possible relations between the phonemic and phonetic representations arose more or less naturally from the act of identifying the phonemic character of a sound with a subset of its phonetic properties, and these constraints characterized (implicitly or explicitly) much later work by the linguists of the Prague School, as well as the American 'neo-Bloomfieldians', who elevated them to the status of dogma. Much effort was expended in the 1930s, 1940s, and 1950s in either justifying or circumventing these restrictions. This is discussed in the following, in the context of American linguistics.

American Structuralist Phonology

FRANZ BOAS

Despite the importance of William Dwight Whitney, American linguistics as a distinctive approach to language is generally felt to have begun with Boas. Boas' primary concerns were ethnological, rather than linguistic, and his interests in describing the vast range of American aboriginal languages were, to some at least, distressingly practical. His theoretically oriented works were largely concerned with stressing the extent to which individual languages constitute self-contained and perfectly complete systems, despite a considerable degree of deviation from the familiar languages of Europe.

In the field of sound structure, Boas really had very little to say. He stressed the claim that there is a potentially infinite class of possible sounds that can be produced by the vocal organs, but that each language makes a very restricted choice of a set of these to distinguish. There is very little in his work to suggest any articulated notion similar to that of the phoneme, however, and neither Boas' theoretical writings nor the descriptive grammars of the "Handbook of American Indian Languages" and other Boas-influenced works pay significant attention to problems of delimiting those sound distinctions that function distinctively in a language from those that do not.

It is also questionable whether Boas ever accorded any recognition to phonological representation on more abstract levels than that of classical phonemic theory. A notion rather like that of the morphophonemic representation (discussed below) seems implicit in his discussions of 'euphonic processes', which can have the effect of changing one sound into another under the influence of the surrounding sounds. Indeed, an examination of the "Handbook" grammars suggests a highly articulated theory of these processes—each grammar discusses euphonic changes under a number of classifications, such as anteactive versus retroactive changes, processes of vocalic harmony, assimilations, etc. The grammars often contain statements suggesting the view that phonological theory specifies a restricted range of possible 'euphonic processes', and the business of description in any given language is to specify the way in which each of these universal rule schemata is instantiated in the language under consideration. Statements about 'euphonic processes' in these grammars generally do not take the form 'Language L has a rule that turns x into y in the environment A ____ B', but rather take the form 'The metathesis rule in Language L applies only under the following conditions.' This sort of account of phonological processes seems to offer a hopeful approach to problems of evaluation of grammars that have been discussed recently under the heading of 'markedness' in phonology (discussed briefly in Chapter 15). It is by no means clear, however, that Boas and his students meant to imply any theoretical statements about the organization of language and the role of universals in a grammar by their descriptive practice. It is at least equally plausible that they meant simply to provide a relatively uniform descriptive format, for pragmatic rather than principled reasons. The same is no doubt true of Boas' approach to 'levels' in phonological description; there is no reason to believe he had any notion of assigning systematic status to any level of representation more abstract than that of 'broad phonetics'. First, it is clear from his practice that Boas' descriptive statements were never intended to account for any deviation between 'basic' forms and 'phonetic' forms except that required by alternations. In his treatment of *c* in Dakota (Boas & DeLoria, 1939), the possibility of deriving *all* instances of *c* from *k* is ignored, and *c* is only related to *k* in cases where a morpheme appears in two shapes, one with *k* and one with *c*. It is certainly true that his grammars contain statements according to which one segment becomes another in a certain environment, but a statement of the form '*x* becomes *y* in the environment *A* ＿＿ *B*' can equally be read as 'where one would otherwise expect *x* in a form, *y* is found if it is in *A* ＿＿ *B*'. There are no doubt substantial problems that would arise if such purely distributional statements are taken seriously and formalized, especially insofar as two statements interact with one another. Since there is no evidence that Boas ever attempted such a formalization, however, there is no reason to believe that he was aware of them, and accordingly that he drew the proper conclusions from them. Such efforts as that of Postal (1964) to show that Boas attributed systematic status to a level of representation approximately like that of systematic phonemics (described subsequently) seem essentially misconceived in this way. Though he undoubtedly had a strong influence upon the next generation of American linguists, especially by emphasizing the internal consistency and autonomy of 'exotic' languages, Boas cannot be said to have significantly influenced the development of the conception of phonological structure.

EDWARD SAPIR

The first notable American linguist to articulate a distinct conception of phonemics was Sapir, a student and colleague of Boas. Particularly in his emphasis on the psychological basis of the phonemic system of a language, Sapir falls somewhat outside the mainstream of later American thinking about phonological structure. Sapir's phoneme was not an idealization based on a subset of the objective phonetic properties of a segment, but rather a fully specified phonetic element, endowed with a particular psychological value through its relation to the other terms of the system, and underlying the actualized phonetic segments through the sound mechanics of the language. An important feature of Sapir's phonemes was that, although fully specified segments, they were not simply arbitrary: the phonemes of a language were all selected from the phonetic segments that occur in the language. That is, the phonetic segment inventory could be divided into two classes: the phonemes, and the variants. Thus some elements were basic, forming the phonemic pattern, and appearing in 'psychological phonetic' representations as well as in actual speech; while others did not occur in the phonemic system, but were simply ways in which particular phonemes might be realized under appropriate circumstances in which, for some reason, their basic form did not appear.

The system of phonemes for Sapir, just as for Trubetzkoy and the Prague School linguists, had a significant internal structure. But unlike Trubetzkoy's kind of internal structure, which rested on the phonetically based defining distinctive features that made up a phoneme, Sapir's notion of internal structure was much more abstract. Simply knowing the phonetic facts about two segments did not necessarily tell one anything about their relations within the system of phonemes. These relations were based entirely on other properties in the grammar of the language. Two phonemes that alternated in the same form in different environments were thereby closer in the phonemic system; similarly, two phonemes with common distributional properties, such as 'occurrence as the second member of a consonant cluster', etc., were thereby considered to be close. As McCawley (1967) has pointed out, there is no evidence that Sapir ever went through a language and tried systematically to set up the phonemic system on this basis, but there is no doubt from his theoretical works that this was what he intended. Accordingly, the same phonetic contrast in two different languages could have very different phonemic values. In English, for instance, [Θ] and [ð] are quite close together, as shown by alternations such as *bath / bathe, breath / breathe,* etc., while in Spanish they are quite far apart. In Spanish they share essentially no properties with one another, while [Θ] is quite close to velars such as [k] (because of alternations like *dico / dice*), and [ð] is close to [d] (of which it is essentially the intervocalic variant).

An apparent contradiction in Sapir's notion of phonemics is immediately explained by this observation. How can it be, if the phonemes of a language are phonetically specified elements, that two languages with phonetically distinct segments can still have identical phonemic systems (a situation for which Sapir gives several examples, both hypothetical and real)? The answer, of course, is that while the elements themselves may be defined in phonetic terms, their relations within the system are not—these are defined in terms of other facts of the grammar, as was just pointed out.

An alternative resolution can be based on the possibility of interpreting the notion of distinctive feature in a relative, rather than an absolute fashion. Is the voiced member of a voiced / voiceless pair a segment with a specific degree of voicing, or is it simply the member of the opposition with more voicing? Can the same feature be said to distinguish [p] from [b] in both English and French? If so, there is no need for two segments to be physically identical in order to have identical specifications. There are a few remarks in Sapir's work that suggest this sort of basis for the features defining segments on the phonemic level, although the characteristics of segments in purely phonetic representation were certainly specified in absolute and physically objective terms. If the features characterizing segments in phonemic and phonetic representations did indeed differ in this way for Sapir, it is clear that the conception suggested above of the phoneme as simply a phonetic segment embedded in a system of phonemic relations determined by the rest of the structure of the language would stand in need of revision. While it is entirely clear that for Boas all segments in all kinds of representations (i.e., both the inputs and the outputs of the 'euphonic laws', insofar as these were distinct) were of the same formal phonetic character, the question of whether Sapir's phonemes were homogeneous with phonetic segments perhaps requires further research.

LEONARD BLOOMFIELD

A significantly different conception of the phoneme appears in Bloomfield's work. Bloomfield's early training was as a Germanist, and his early theoretical writings were heavily influenced by the then-popular psychological views of Wundt. Impressed by the developing climate of positivistic thought in the 1920s and 1930s, however, Bloomfield altered his position fairly radically, leading the movement toward a totally operational empirical linguistic science. Accordingly, the emphasis in Sapir's work on the psychological status of the phoneme is completely absent in Bloomfield: the phoneme must either be an observable property of the speech event, or serve as nothing but a descriptive convenience for the linguist.

In an early review (Bloomfield, 1922), he mentions such phoneticians as Jones, Sweet, Passy, Boas, Saussure, and Sapir as having arrived at the essential concept of the phoneme: the notion of DISTINCTIVE FEATURES. By this, he is referring to the observation that only some sound features serve within a given language to distinguish words. Among these various writers, however, there was certainly no unanimity of opinion, and for some of them the phoneme (insofar as this term was used) was clearly closer to its original sense of mere Sprachlaut than anything else. Bloomfield's own conception is rather like that of Trubetzkoy: the phoneme is a bundle of distinctive features found in all of the phonetic segments that represent it. An important difference from Trubetzkoy is in the kind of distinctive features Bloomfield could employ—Trubetzkoy was quite explicit about the relative basis of his features. The same feature (say fortis / lenis) might serve in one language to distinguish [t] from [d], and in another [tʰ] from [t], while the same phonetic distinction (say [t] versus [d]) might be interpreted phonologically as fortis / lenis in one language and as voiced / voiceless in another. Bloomfield, on the other hand, confined his features (in theory, at least) to absolute, physically measurable parameters.

An important aspect of the fact that the parameters defining Bloomfield's phonemes were purely phonetic was his rejection of phonetic representation in the traditional sense. In his view, the only real representation of the physical event in objective terms which deserved any sort of recognition was a perfect laboratory record of the physical properties of the event. Any sort of phonetic transcription could be nothing but a limited and highly imperfect approximation. The particular features indicated in a phonetic transcription were bound to be selected in an unscientific and arbitrary way, dictated by the range of phonetic phenomena the particular investigator happened to have encountered in his partial experience with other languages. Such an ad hoc and anecdotal record can have no systematic status, according to Bloomfield. Only the instrumental record of the laboratory can have significance, at least in considering the speech event as a physical occurrence. From the point of view of language function, on the other hand, another kind of representation can play a role: one which indicates all and only those features of the speech event that function distinctively in the language. This is the phonemic representation. In the overall antimentalist context of Bloomfield's thought, it would of course be impossible for the psychological value of a physical difference to affect its role in a scientific theory—only its role in evoking differential behavior could be taken into account. A phonemic transcription was partly a theory about the way people behave linguistically, and as such could contain nothing beyond the observable.

In addition to these empiricist principles, however, there was another strong reason for Bloomfield's phonemes to have an absolute phonetic basis: the phonemic transcription was not intended to supplement the phonetic transcription, but to replace it entirely. Bloomfield is quite clear about his views on the generally pernicious and unscientific character of phonetic transcriptions. But if the phonemic representation is to be the only one included in the grammar, it is clearly the only place in which relevant information about the absolute phonetic facts of a language could be captured.

In his actual practice, and to some extent in his theoretical writings, Bloomfield deviated in two principal ways from this concept of the phoneme. One was quite explicit—in addition to phonemic representations, he also developed a notion of morphophonemic representation, of the sort discussed below. In a paper such as his classic presentation of Menomini phonology (Bloomfield, 1939), he employs a vastly more abstract level of representation, related to phonemics only through the operation of a large and complex set of rules, which add, delete, permute, and otherwise alter segments in radical ways. This work is obviously (and consciously) modeled on the descriptive technique of Pāṇini. The abstract level of representation here has a different sort of status from the phonemic, however. While the latter is in some sense a real and important aspect of the language, morphophonemic representations and rules are quite explicitly nothing but a descriptive device invented by the linguist to keep things straight, and to organize his data. Morphophonemic representations have no direct behavioral correlates (unlike phonemic representations), and hence cannot be anything but a convenient fiction.

In contrast to the supplementary character of morphophonemics, another deviation from the strictest interpretation of his theoretical principles affected Bloomfield's practice in phonemicizing. Most notably in connection with the reduced vowels of American English, but also in dealing with other languages, Bloomfield takes a somewhat puzzling attitude toward neutralizations of phonemic distinctions. He never writes [ə] or [ɨ] for English reduced vowels, but rather some full vowel, such as [i], [ɛ], [a], etc. Which vowel he writes is generally determined by the vowel that appears in some other form of the word, where reduction does not take place: thus, he might write [harmonij] *harmony*, with [o] for the second vowel because of [harmonik] *harmonic*. In many cases, it seems as if the spelling alone has led to a choice of a particular reduced vowel. In other languages, such as Ojibwa, his choice for a reduced vowel symbol is always motivated by the value of the same vowel when unreduced. In a letter to Hockett (quoted in Hockett, 1970, p. 375) he suggests that such a transcription is better "because it tells the reader what unreduced vowel is involved." It is interesting that he does not extend this principle to other sorts of cases: for example, although he discusses the neutralization of voicing in syllable-final obstruents in German in several places, nowhere does he suggest phonemic transcriptions such as [rund] / [rundes] as opposed to [bunt] / [buntes]. A form such as [rund] is only suggested as a 'hypothetical base form', not a phonemic form. It is frustratingly difficult to tie down Bloomfield's exact views on the status of transcriptions showing distinct elements in different forms in positions of neutralization: for example, in the letter to Hockett cited above, he goes on to say that "[t]his is not a question about the language: it is a question about the clearest and most convenient way of telling about the language." In any event, such a practice is clearly inconsistent with the notion that phonemes are sets of phonetic features present in the utterance itself: there is nothing in a particular occurrence of the reduced vowel to identify it as reduced [o] in *harmony*, but as reduced [i] in *hardily* (see *hardy*). Some of Bloomfield's colleagues and students felt this to be an anomaly in his work, and criticized him for it. Hockett describes himself as "(beginning) to evolve an understanding of all this that differed from Bloomfield's; . . . (partially in that) I supposed that when things sounded the same, they had to be the same phonemically, however different the 'same' words or morphemes might sound in other arrangements" (Hockett, 1970, p. 369). Whatever Bloomfield's precise view on the phonemic status of neutralizations, he was regarded as advocating an 'illicit' intrusion of 'morphophonemic' information.

POST-BLOOMFIELDIAN PHONOLOGY IN AMERICA

In the 1930s, 1940s, and 1950s, numerous other linguists, many of them students of Sapir and/or Bloomfield, participated in the development of phonemic theory in America. Among those who participated in this effort to specify as precisely as possible the relation between phonemic and phonetic entities, and the exact character of phonemic analysis, were (in no particular order) Bloch, Twaddell, Harris, Hockett, Chao, Swadesh, and others. While it is a serious oversimplification to represent all of these by a single, uniform position, there was certainly a substantial community of views as to the aims and methods of phonemic analysis, and together they evolved a position which has since come to be known (following Chomsky, 1964) as that of TAXONOMIC PHONEMICS. Unlike earlier writers, they were concerned to set out exactly what they meant by phonemic and phonetic representations, and the character of the relation obtaining between them. Much of what they had to say concerned itself with the practical problem of discovering the phonemic system of a language, but, at the same time, was intended to define the notion of such a system by giving an explicit set of procedures, which, if followed correctly, would yield it automatically without involving subjective decisions on the part of the analyst.

One problem to which much attention was given was the precise ontological status of the phoneme. Was the phoneme, as Sapir had said, a psychologically real, ideal phonetic segment, which was realized by a particular speech sound? Was it, rather, as Bloomfield had suggested, a subset of the phonetic properties of the speech sound itself? Or was it simply an artifact of the description, a label applied to some speech sounds and not to others? One point of view adopted in this period by many was the notion that the phoneme differed from the phonetic segment in that the phoneme was a class of segments, displaying (an undefined amount of) phonetic similarity, and appearing in complementary distribution. This last requirement meant that two phonetically distinct segments which belonged to the same phoneme must have the property that they never appeared in exactly the same environment, or that if they did, the distinction was never the basis of a contrast between two linguistic forms (i.e., the two segments were in free variation in the environment). This allowed segments to be taken as representatives of the same phoneme, even when there was no specific phonetic material that they (and they alone) shared. Consider the following situation. In most positions in some language, the nasal consonants [m], [n], and [ñ] contrast with one another. In the position before velar obstruents [k], [g], and [x], however, while both [m] and [ñ] appear, [n] does not; instead [ŋ] appears in this position. Clearly, we have three contrasting phonemes to deal with here: /m/, /n/, and /ñ/, and /n/ assimilates to the point of articulation of a following velar. But there is no obvious phonetic material that the various representatives of /n/ (namely, [n] and [ŋ]) share to the exclusion of /m/ and /ñ/. There is therefore no way of describing this situation if the phoneme is to be taken as an invariant set of phonetic properties. Since [n] and [ŋ] appear in complementary distribution, however, and are phonetically 'similar' (both are nasal consonants), the definition of the phoneme as a set of phonetic segments allows us to say the right thing. Various authors took different positions on such questions as phonemic overlapping (can a given phonetic segment represent phoneme $/P_1/$ in one environment, but a distinct phoneme $/P_2/$ in another environment?), the role of 'grammatical prerequisites' (what use can be made of nonphonetic information such as boundary signals and morpheme-class membership in determining the phonemic value of a segment?), but the criteria of phonetic similarity and complementary distribution came to define the class of segments belonging to the same phoneme. Two segments were ideally shown to belong to different phonemes by the presentation of a minimal pair—two forms which were linguistically distinct, and differed only in that one had segment [P₁] in the position where the other had segment [P₂].

One question that had arisen was what it meant for two linguistic forms to be linguistically distinct. As will be remembered, Trubetzkoy had suggested that this obtained if they had distinct meanings. Thus, phonemic distinctions were to be all and only those that were correlated with differences of meaning. But there are obvious problems with this definition, which proves both too strong and too weak. On the one hand, there are homophonous forms in most languages—cases in which a difference in meaning is correlated with no phonetic difference at all. Conversely, there are cases in which a phonetic difference which is clearly distinctive elsewhere does not correspond to any meaning difference: these are optional variants, such as the two pronunciations of forms like *economics* ([ékənamiks] versus [íjkənamiks]), *ration* ([réjšən] versus [rǽšən]), *advertisement* ([ædvə́rtɨsmənt] versus [ædvərtájzmənt]), etc. One would certainly want to claim that [e] and [ij], [ej] and [æ], [ɨ] and [aj], etc. belong to distinct phonemes, but here they do not correspond to differences in meaning, despite the fact that they are minimal pairs (except for stress, in some cases). Basing phonemics on meaning differences, in any case, was a procedure regarded as highly suspect in the absence of a purely operational definition of meaning.

Accordingly, a more operational criterion of distinctness came to prevail: the difference between utterances that were repetitions and utterances that were felt to contrast, according to the intuitions of native speakers. It was largely taken for granted that native speakers would agree that, e.g., the two pronunciations of *ration* are not repetitions of one another, though both mean the same thing; and that, e.g., *pear* and *pair* would be identified as repetitions, despite the fact that they mean different things. Thus, phonemics could take account of [rǽšən] versus [réjšən], and did not have to try to find a difference between [pɛr] *pair* and [pɛr] *pear*. This notion of contrast was generally assumed by taxonomic phonemicists, although it should perhaps be noted that it, too, falls down in both directions. On the one hand, it is well known that native speakers often feel there is a difference in two forms, where no objective phonetic difference exists, if their morphological composition is different. Thus, many speakers feel there is some difference between, say, *bard* and *barred,* though no difference exists for most speakers. Another example of this sort of thing is given by Sapir

(1949), who describes his Sarcee informant as insisting on a difference between two forms both pronounced [dìníh]. The difference turned out to reside in their morphophonemic sources—in one form, the final [h] was a purely 'inorganic' segment, added after an otherwise final vowel; while in the other, the [h] was the phonetic reflex of morphophonemic [tʰ]. A different sort of failure of this notion of contrast has recently been noted by Labov (1972): he cites several instances in which informants claimed two forms were repetitions, when in fact there turned out to be a consistent phonetic difference between them. For example, in dealing with a dialect lacking preconsonantal [r], he found many informants who insisted that such words as *sauce* and *source* were homophonous. On examining spectrograms made from recordings of these informants, however, Labov found clear acoustic differences (in the quality of the vowel) which kept the two words apart. This, as he says, is the 'maximal failure of the minimal pair.'

In any event, one thing is thoroughly clear about all notions of phonemic analysis in this period: whether (like Bloomfield and others) you denied the significance of a phonetic representation or not, you had an absolute faith in the proposition that whatever distinguished one phonemic element from another was located in the phonetic event alone, and that analyses like Bloomfield's of vowel reduction phenomena were illicit. It was generally considered inconceivable that anything else could be true, on the basis of generally held views on the nature of the linguistic behavior, and the process of speech perception. According to the prevailing model of the perceptual process, the listener's task was somewhat analogous to that of a voice-operated typewriter—presented with a stream of phonetic data as input, his task was to divide it into segments, and assign each segment a phonemic identity. This phonemic output could then serve as the input to further processors, which divided it into morphological elements, and so on, but clearly the work of these higher level processors could not be performed until they were provided with an input in the form of a phonemic transcription. That being the case, the conversion from raw phonetics to phonemes had to be carried out entirely on the basis of information present in the phonetic signal itself, with no reference to anything else. Insofar as phonemes were real elements of the linguistic system, then, such a view of the organization of speech perception naturally implies a very tightly constrained relation between phonetic and phonemic elements.

This relation was the basis of the frequently heard objections to 'mixing levels' in analysis (the importation of higher-level morphological information into phonemic descriptions), and also for most of the conditions placed on phonemic discovery procedures. These have been characterized by Chomsky (1964) under the four headings of linearity, bi-uniqueness, invariance, and local determinacy. There is some question as to the extent to which individual writers actually accepted all of these constraints (some, for instance, would explicitly reject invariance, and many analyses violate linearity), but the essential features of all taxonomic phonologists are the following, which follow directly from the position just sketched on linguistic organization: (1) the requirement that two utterances have distinct phonemic representations if and only if they contrast (in the sense sketched above); and (2) the requirement that in order to convert a phonetic representation to a phonemic one (or vice versa), all of the information necessary to determine the phonemic (respectively, phonetic) correspondent of a given element be present in the phonetic (respectively, phonemic) representation alone. This last condition implies the requirement that all of the statements relating phonemic representation to phonetic representation apply simultaneously, that is, it can never be the case that one statement requires information which is only provided by the operation of another statement. This condition of simultaneous application, which was generally adhered to in taxonomic analyses, is directly contrary to the kind of phonemic–phonetic relation expressly envisioned by Sapir (and, less explicitly, by the grammarians of the "Handbook of American Indian Languages,") which allowed some rules to apply to the output of other rules. Another condition which follows from these, of course, is a prohibition on analyses like Bloomfield's account of vowel reduction; since no information is present in the phonetics alone to identify a given reduced vowel as belonging to one phoneme rather than another, all occurrences of the reduced vowel must be assigned the same phonemic value.

CHAPTER 3

Morphophonemic Representation

A concept of phonemic structure similar to that described at the end of the preceding chapter came to dominate nearly all thinking and descriptive work in phonology by the mid-1950s (with the possible exception of the English Prosodic school; for some discussion, see Langendoen, 1968). Almost as soon as it was articulated, however, it was seen to be inadequate for the description of the total phonological structure of natural languages. Virtually any language can be seen to have some properties of a systematic nature that cannot be captured in a strictly taxonomic description. Consider, for example, the following facts about obstruents in Korean, for which initially and medially these contrasts are found:

(1) [p] [t] [č] [k]
 [pʰ] [tʰ] [čʰ] [kʰ]
 [p*] [t*] [č*] [k*]
  [s]
  [s*]¹

---

¹ The segments written p*, t*, č*, k*, and s* are produced with glottal constriction, but without the ejection or implosion characteristic of glottalized consonants in most languages. Refer to Kim (1970), Kagaya (1971), and references given therein for details.

In final position, however, only [p¹], [t¹], and [k¹] are found. As all of the segments in (1) contrast medially and initially, there is no difficulty about establishing them as distinct taxonomic phonemes; the status of the final segments, however, is more problematic. Consider the following Korean words, each of which is the objective case form of a noun[2]:

(2)   a. [nadɨl]   'a grain (obj)'
        b. [natʰɨl]   'piece (obj)'
        c. [nasɨl]   'sickle (obj)'
        d. [naɟɨl]   'day (obj)'
        e. [načʰɨl]   'face (obj)'

Clearly the material [-ɨl] in each of these forms represents the objective case ending, and the roots [nad-], [natʰ-], [nas-], [naɟ-], and [načʰ-] are easily isolated. These roots are phonemically /nat-/, /natʰ-/, /nas-/, /nač-/, and /načʰ-/. A problem arises when the roots appear in isolation, however, as they do in the subjective form of the above nouns; in this case, each of the roots above is pronounced [nat¹]. Now what is the phonemic representation of a given instance of phonetic [nat¹] to be?

According to the principles of taxonomic phonemics, all of these instances of [nat¹] must be treated as phonemically identical, for the important point is that there is nothing present in the phonetic representation alone from which it is possible to discover that this particular instance of [nat¹] is, say, the word for 'piece' (and hence related to [natʰɨl]). Let us assume the final segment [t¹] is assigned to the phoneme /t/: then any instance of phonetic [nat¹] must be treated as phonemic /nat/, regardless of which of the words in (2) it is related to. But in that case, the phonemic representations alone are clearly insufficient for representing the full range of phonological properties of a given root. For given a particular root /nat/, it is still necessary to have more information in order to predict the form in which it will appear in the objective case, in addition to any other environment in which it is followed by a vowel. This information has a perfectly systematic character: whatever segment appears in place of the [t¹] before the objective ending [−ɨl], the identical segment will appear when that root is found in a position before any other vowel-initial element, whether a suffix or the second element of a compound. That is, the variation shown in (2) is not an idiosyncratic fact about the objective case, but rather a system-

---

[2] It should be noted that the unaspirated plain stops are represented by voiced segments in intervocalic position: [b], [d], [j], and [g] are clearly to be identified with the phonemes /p/, /t/, /č/, and /k/.

atic reflex of the idiosyncratic properties of the roots involved. Accordingly, the phonemic representation /nat/ is an inadequate form in which to display the sound structure of any one of these roots: some representation must be found that allows us to differentiate the final segments of roots which are phonemically /nat/ from one another, so that we predict that while the root for 'piece' appears with the final segment [tʰ] before vowels, the root for 'sickle' appears with the final segment [s], despite the fact that both have final [t¹] in isolation.

The kind of 'dictionary representation' that we want in this case is, of course, quite simple to construct. Let us assume that such representations are enclosed in [] . . . [] brackets. Then we could have the forms in (3):

(3)　　　　　　　　　　a.　[]nat[]　'a grain'
　　　　　　　　　　　　b.　[]natʰ[]　'piece'
　　　　　　　　　　　　c.　[]nas[]　'sickle'
　　　　　　　　　　　　d.　[]nač[]　'day'
　　　　　　　　　　　　e.　[]načʰ[]　'face'

Such dictionary representations are related to phonemic representations by a simple rule: when obstruents appear in position before another obstruent or in final position any labial is represented by /p/, any velar by /k/, and any coronal element by /t/.[3] Elsewhere (i.e., before sonorants, including vowels), each dictionary element corresponds to a distinct phonemic element in an obvious way.

Such a dictionary (or morphophonemic) representation, was posited by many linguists at a fairly early point. Apparently, since Sapir's notion of phonemics was not subject to the constraints of taxonomic theory, he had no need for a distinct level of this sort—information of the kind we have been considering could perfectly well be part of the phonemic representation in Sapir's work. Indeed, a frequent criticism of Sapir in the work of his followers [as in the review of Sapir's "Selected Writings" (Harris, 1951)] was his 'mixing' of morphophonemic and properly (i.e. taxonomic) phonemic information. Beginning with Bloomfield, however, such an additional representation was required if the entire sound structure of a language was to be elucidated. Indeed, Bloomfield's paper on Menomini (Bloomfield, 1939) together with Swadesh and Voegelin

---

[3] Important questions are being begged here about the way in which elements of dictionary representations are specified. We assume they are specified in phonetic terms, and that it makes sense accordingly to talk about 'coronal' elements in such representations. These would, of course, be []t[], []tʰ[], []t*[], []s[], []s*[], []č[], []čʰ[], and []č*[] in Korean.

(1939), marked the beginning of serious descriptive work employing morphophonemic entities as well as phonemes in a linguistic description.

Morphophonemes, however, could not be given the kind of operationalist definition that appealed to the positivism of the period. It is not possible to recover morphophonemic information directly and unambiguously from the speech event itself. Accordingly, the morphophoneme was never regarded as a legitimate or 'real' entity within taxonomic theory, but rather as a pure descriptive artifact, a convenient fiction devised by the linguist to shorten his description. Thus, no effort was made to impose any sort of condition of naturalness on the elements of a morphophonemic representation: these could be literally anything at all, with any arbitrary set of rules to specify the correspondance between morphophonemic and phonemic entities. A failure to appreciate this arbitrariness has occasionally led to misinterpretations of early morphophonemic analyses. For example, Lightner (1970) criticizes Swadesh and Voegelin's analysis of some alternations in English. To account for the alternation in *leaᴦ / lea*v*es, wi*ᴲ*e / wi*v*es, kni*ᴲ*e / kni*v*es,* etc., Swadesh and Voegelin set up a morphophonemic element []F[], defined as /v/ before *plural,* etc., and /f/ elsewhere. Lightner correctly observes that this []F[] cannot be identified with []f[] (because of nonalternating forms such as *belief / beliefs, cuff / cuffs,* etc.) or with []v[] (because of *cove / coves, infinitive / infinitives,* etc.), but then goes on to claim that Swadesh and Voegelin must have meant []F[] to be, say, []f[] with some additional diacritic features, such as [+pharyngealized]. Obviously, such an unnatural solution is to be rejected, since there is nothing whatever to motivate a particular phonetic property as underlying the diacritic distinguishing []F[] from []f[]. But to suggest that Swadesh and Voegelin meant this is to misconstrue the nature of their morphophonemic elements. An item such as []F[] was not intended to have *any* phonetic interpretation directly, but only through the medium of the phonemic interpretation of the formula defining it. []F[], in other words, is a purely arbitrary element, standing for /f/ in some environments and /v/ in others, but without any phonetic interpretation of its own. Such a case is atypical of early morphophonemes only to the extent to which it is possible to give a coherent phonetic definition of the class of alternants represented by the formula in question. Other early morphophonemic elements often abbreviated alternations between elements with no discernible phonetic coherence, the only condition being that the elements were in complementary distribution, the fact that one occurred in some environments, while the other occurred in distinct ones. Since it was nothing but a linguist's device, there was no reason whatsoever to expect a morphophoneme to have a coherent and natural definition. In-

deed, some writers seemed to feel that the very fact that many morphophonemes do have coherent definitions (such as Swadesh and Voegelin's
[]F[]) rendered them suspect: this coherence could only be due to an
illicit intrusion of diachronic considerations into synchronic analyses.

Whatever suspicions individual linguists may have harbored about its
status, the morphophonemic representation was firmly established as a
part of a full linguistic description through work by linguists such as
Bloomfield, Swadesh, Voegelin, Hockett, Trubetzkoy, and others. The
organization of a grammar was then seen as involving three stages of
representation concerned with sound structure: morphophonemic, phonemic, and phonetic. Two sets of statements established the corre-
spondences between the morphophonemic and phonemic levels, and
between the phonemic and phonetic levels. These two sets of statements
were taken to be totally distinct, just as the three kinds of elements
(morphophonemes, phonemes, and phonetic segments) were totally distinct.

Before long, however, it was noticed that this organization of a phonological description had unfortunate consequences. Various linguists (e.g.,
Hamp, 1951) suggested that there were cases in some languages for
which a set of statements relating morphophonemic representations
directly to phonetics could capture generalizations about the phonological structure of the language more successfully than if the taxonomic
phonemic representation is required to be an intermediate step in the
description. The most forceful demonstration of this point was given by
Halle (in an unpublished paper read at the Winter meeting of the
Linguistic Society of America in December 1957), the facts of which are
discussed in Halle (1959). This discussion dealt with the facts of voicing
assimilation in Russian obstruents. The basic generalization about
voicing in obstruent clusters in Russian is the following: an obstruent
has the same value for the feature [voice] as a following obstruent.[4]
This results in alternations between voiced and voiceless segments in
some words, depending on whether a given obstruent is followed by a
sonorant, a voiced obstruent, or a voiceless obstruent. From stems

---

[4] Actually, this is oversimplified. The segment [v], phonetically an obstruent, is anomalous in its behavior, since it assimilates to become [f] before a following voiceless obstruent, but does not cause preceding voiceless obstruents to become voiced when it is the
last member of a cluster. For details, see Andersen (1969). Lightner's (1965) observation
that [v] is generally derived from underlying /w/, a nonobstruent, is surely correct, but its
relevance is not clear. Since [v] functions both as an obstruent (in undergoing assimilation)
and as a sonorant (in not producing assimilation) in the same rule, it will not do to represent it as /w/ and only convert it to [v] after the assimilation rule has been applied.

which appear as /dat^y-/, /god-/, and /žeč-/, combined with the endings /-l^{y}i/ and /bɨ/, we have alternations such as those in (4):

(4)		I	II	III
	a.	[]dat^y+l^{y}i[]	/dat^{y}l^{y}i/	[dat^{y}l^{y}i]
		[]dat^y+bɨ[]	/dad^{y}bɨ/	[dad^{y}bɨ]
	b.	[]god+l^{y}i[]	/godl^{y}i/	[godl^{y}i]
		[]god+bɨ[]	/godbɨ/	[godbɨ]
	c.	[]žeč+l^{y}i[]	/žečl^{y}i/	[žečl^{y}i]
		[]žeč+bɨ[]	/žečbɨ/	[žejbɨ]

The forms in column I of (4) are morphophonemic representations, those in column II are (taxonomic) phonemic representations, and those in column III are phonetic representations. The operation of the principle of voicing assimilation can be seen in (4a) and (4b): a morphophonemic voiceless obstruent, such as t^y, is replaced by the corresponding voiced obstruent in phonemic representation, if a voiced obstruent (such as b) follows.

In (4c), however, something else happens. Despite the fact that the (morphophonemically voiceless) segment č is followed by the voiced segment b in the second form, it is unaffected: it is replaced by phonemic /č/ both before b and before l^y, rather than becoming /ǰ/ before b. The reason for this is not hard to find: while most of the voiced and voiceless pairs of obstruents in Russian contrast (e.g., t contrasts with d, t^y contrasts with d^y, p contrasts with b, etc.), there are three segments for which this is not the case. Thus, both [x] and [γ] exist, but they are never in contrast, since [γ] appears only before voiced obstruents, while [x] never appears in that environment. Similarly, [č] and [ǰ], [fs] and [dz], appear phonetically, but with voiced and voiceless elements in complementary distribution. There is, accordingly, no basis for establishing distinct phonemic entities /x/ and /γ/, /č/ and /ǰ/, /fs/ and /dz/: both members of each pair must be assigned to the same phonemic element. Accordingly, the morphophonemic rule of voicing assimilation has to make a change in (4a), converting t^y into /d^y/, since /t^y/ and /d^y/ are phonemically distinct, but need do nothing to č, since [č] and [ǰ] correspond to the same phonemic entity /č/. But then the voicing assimilation rule has not been completely stated, as a principle relating morphophonemic to phonemic representations: we need an additional voicing assimilation principle to turn phonemic /č/ into phonetic [ǰ] before a voiceless obstruent (as well as /x/ into [γ], and /t͡s/ into [d͡z]).

Thus, because of the properties of phonemic representation, a phonological description incorporating such a level needs two distinct voicing assimilation rules: a morphophonemic rule, applying to all obstruents except *x*, *č*, and *t͡s*; and a phonemic rule, applying *only* to /x/, /č/, and /ts/. Except for the classes of segments they apply to, both rules operate identically: they perform the same change, and have the same restrictions (nonapplication before *v*). As a result, we have effectively lost the generalization about voicing assimilation in Russian. Nowhere in the grammar of Russian, on this model, is there a single unified statement of the voicing assimilation principle; rather, this rule is distributed between two rules which are in principle completely distinct and independent. There is, apparently, no way to remedy this situation. It is clearly impossible to put all of the weight of the voicing assimilation rule on the morphophonemic statement: since *č* and *ǰ* do not contrast, the principles defining the phonemic level require that we not assign them to distinct phonemic entities, and so the morphophonemic statement cannot perform assimilation for such segments. It is also impossible to effect all of the assimilation by the phonemic → phonetic rule. To do this would require that we assign distinct representations, e.g., to the [dʸ] of [dadʸbɨ] (assigning it to /tʸ/, since it is related to the [tʸ] of [datʸlʸi]) and the [d] of [godbɨ] (assigning it to /d/, since it is related to the [d] of [godlʸi]), ignoring the difference in palatalization. But this step is also contrary to the principles of the phonemic level: given a particular instance of [d] (or [dʸ]), it would then be impossible to tell on the basis of information present in the phonetic representation alone whether to assign it to /d/ or to /t/ (respectively, /dʸ/ or /tʸ/). It is thus precisely the principles defining the taxonomic phonemic level that are responsible for the problem here; they require the description of Russian to contain a level of representation such that it is impossible to state the principle of voicing assimilation in a unified way.

If Halle's example is at all typical, it demonstrates a serious deficiency in the theory of taxonomic phonemics. If principles such as voicing assimilation in Russian are indeed real generalizations about phonological structure, then it is clear that some generalizations cannot be stated in terms of taxonomic phonemes (which, as we have seen, was the motivation for the development of a level of morphophonemes), but the positing of such a level is also a positive hindrance to capturing some generalizations. This would, of course, be a powerful argument that the level of taxonomic phonemics must not only be supplemented, but abandoned altogether. If, on the other hand, Halle's example were to turn out to be completely isolated, we might well argue that, indeed, voicing assimilation in Russian is not a unified generalization, and should properly be treated as the combined consequence of two completely independent rules. This conclusion would follow from the general desirability of imposing conditions on grammars that are as strong as possible. The constraints defining the notion of taxonomic phonemic representation are, indeed, of a highly restrictive sort: if, in fact, it were possible to maintain the claim that every correct grammar of a natural language provided a level of description that satisfied them, this would place heavy restrictions on the class of possible grammars allowed by linguistic theory and, furthermore, constraints with a great deal of persuasiveness on the basis of a priori views on the nature of speech communication. In the face of one single counterexample to this claim, we would certainly prefer to see it as showing something about the structure of the example itself, rather than about phonology in general. We might look for other evidence (such as facts of historical change, or metrical patterning, or orthographic traditions, or other evidence from outside the grammar itself, as is discussed elsewhere in this volume) that, indeed, the opposition between [č] and [j] has a different status in the language than that between, e.g., [t] and [d].

Unfortunately for our general knowledge of phonological systems, Halle's example does not appear to be at all isolated. Several similar examples are discussed in Chomsky (1964); and a similar argument can be constructed for any number of common situations. Consider, for example, the following set of facts typical of numerous languages. A language has only two nasal consonants, [m] and [n], that contrast in most positions (initially, finally, intervocalically). Before an obstruent, however, there is a different range of phonetic segments: [m] can appear before any obstruent, but [n] can only appear before dentals. Before labials, only [m] appears, and before velars, [m] and [ŋ] appear. What, then, is the status of this [ŋ]? Since it only appears before velars, where [n] does not appear, it does not contrast with [n]; and since (ex hypothesi) [m] contrasts with [ŋ] before velars, it cannot belong to the same phoneme as [m]. Therefore, [ŋ] must represent /n/. Now what of [m] before a labial? This could represent either a basic *m* or an assimilated *n*. But from phonetic evidence alone, there is no way of distinguishing the two sources, and all instances of [m] before labials must be assigned the same phonemic representation (let us say /m/). Now consider the following hypothetical forms:

(5)

	I	II	III
a.	[]bum+ar[]	/bumar/	[bumar]
	[]bum+ti[]	/bumti/	[bumti]
	[]bum+bum[]	/bumbum/	[bumbum]
	[]bum+gəl[]	/bumgəl/	[bumgəl]
b.	[]ban+ar[]	/banar/	[banar]
	[]ban+ti[]	/banti/	[banti]
	[]ban+ban[]	/bamban/	[bamban]
	[]ban+gəl[]	/baŋgəl/	[baŋgəl]

Here we see that the rule assimilating *n* to the position of a following obstruent has been divided into two parts, as in the Russian voicing assimilation rule. Thus, assimilation before a labial (as in [bamban]) is a morphophonemic rule, while assimilation before a velar (as in [baŋgəl]) is a phonemic → phonetic rule. Nowhere in the grammar can there be a single rule to the effect that *n* assimilates to a following obstruent, if the conditions of the taxonomic phonemic level are to be maintained. This example is somewhat oversimplified for clarity, but is clearly typical of a wide range of familiar cases. A real example of this form is found in Spanish [see Harris (1969) for discussion]. In general, whenever an assimilation process produces a wider range of phonetic segments than contrast in other positions, a similar argument can be constructed that the imposition of the constraints defining the taxonomic phonemic level of representation leads to a loss of important generalizations about the language.

Accordingly, we are led to reject the taxonomic phonemic level as a systematic stage in phonological descriptions. We are left, then, with a model of phonological structure that incorporates only the two levels of morphophonemic and phonetic representation, and that utilizes a single set of statements to relate the two. Henceforth, unless explicit indication appears to the contrary, the terms PHONEME and PHONEMIC are used in this work to refer to the level previously called MORPHOPHONEMIC. This is because the level of morphophonemics is just as much a phonemic level in the sense in which that notion was introduced above as is the level of taxonomic phonemes — it is a representation of those sound properties of the utterance which are not completely predictable in terms of the general principles of the language, and which can serve to distinguish one utterance from another within the language. The strong constraints on the relationship between phonemic and phonetic representation, which were motivated in the taxonomic model by the particular view of the process of speech perception associated with that theory, are absent; but those constraints were logically independent of the notion of PHONEMIC in any case. The rejection of a taxonomic phonemic stage in descriptions is therefore a retrograde step, since it results in a loosening of the constraints on possible grammars (and hence in a reduction of the empirical content of linguistic theory), but it is apparently one that is dictated by the realities of natural language structures.

But what of the considerations that motivated linguists to posit a taxonomic phonemic level in the first place? Basically, there were three, although they were not altogether independent. First, as mentioned, there was a particular view of the process of speech perception, which saw this process as a completely passive one, taking speech events as input and performing only the functions of segmenting and classifying the physical data. Such a process was visualized as no more than a simple table look-up procedure, and was restricted to information present in the event itself. If this were, indeed, the way the (first stage of the) speech perception process operates, it would be reasonable to expect that language would be organized in a way closely conforming to the constraints of taxonomic phonology, where the phonemic entities correspond to the distinct classifications that can be assigned to a speech segment by the perceptual processor. But research in speech perception in the past twenty years or so has tended to disconfirm this purely passive view of speech perception in several respects. More recent views, such as the analysis-by-synthesis model suggested by Halle and Stevens (among others[5]), and the motor theory of speech perception,[6] suggest a much more active view of this process, with the perceptual mechanism actively generating hypotheses about the signal being processed, and then comparing these with the actual signal. In this case, the plausibility of the taxonomic model vanishes. There is no reason, on such assumptions, to expect that only information directly present in the speech signal itself could play a role in such hypothesis-generation and testing.

A second motivation for taking the taxonomic phonemic level to be a

---

[5] For further information, see Halle and Stevens (1962), Stevens and House (1970), and other references cited therein.

[6] For a discussion, see Liberman *et al.* (1963, 1967), and others cited therein.

valid requirement was the heavily procedural bias of most linguistic theorizing, especially in America, during the 1940s and 1950s. A linguistic theory was supposed to give an explicit account of the way in which the system of a language could be discovered and confirmed by a field worker with no previous knowledge of the language. The field worker, armed with nothing but raw phonetic data, and bringing no particular hypothesis about the language, was of course always an idealization of a radical sort, but he was the ideal, whose operations in arriving at the grammar of the language it was the business of linguistic theory to describe. Obviously, such a field worker is limited in the same ways as the perceptual mechanism considered above; he can do nothing but arrange and classify his phonetic data, on the basis of information in the speech event itself. His categories can be based only on phonetic information, together with the information that certain utterances contrast while others are free variants of one another. In such a linguistic theory, a level of taxonomic phonemes seems inevitable. But as a motivation for points of linguistic theory, this view suffers serious problems. The task of linguistic theory is, presumably, to describe languages, not linguists, and the typical situation in which language appears is in its use by a fluent native speaker, who knows it completely, rather than in the attempts of a linguist who knows nothing about it and is attempting to arrive inductively at a grammar. Correspondingly, it is the situation of the fluent speaker or listener that the grammar should attempt to describe, and in that case, there is no reason to make the strong assumption that the structure of any given utterance is discoverable wholly without additional knowledge of the language. Indeed, the facts of actual language use would seem to indicate exactly the opposite—that the speaker makes constant use of the full range of his knowledge about all aspects of the language in speaking and understanding utterances.

A third motivation for taking taxonomic constraints as defining the phonemic level is less a prioristic, and consists in an important condition of adequacy for grammars. It is clearly a fact that some utterances contrast with one another, while others are free variants (although, as has been seen above, this notion of contrast is not necessarily a simple one). It is clearly necessary, if a linguistic description is to give an account of the phonological structure of a language, that it make it possible to distinguish contrasting utterances from utterances that are variants. Now clearly it is impossible to determine whether or not two utterances contrast simply by examining their phonetic representations: free variants may perfectly well have distinct phonetic representations, without thereby being in contrast. For instance, [buwt^h] and [buwt^1] are free variants in English. As argued above, they are distinct in phonetic representation, but do not contrast. On the other hand, it is possible to determine whether or not two utterances are in contrast by examining their taxonomic phonemic representations, since one of the important defining properties of that level is precisely the requirement that all and only contrasting utterances have distinct phonemic representations. Thus, both [buwtʰ] and [buwtˀ] are phonemically something like /buwt/, and hence it can be seen that they are free variants; but [buwt] and [bowt] are phonemically /buwt/ and /bowt/, which are distinct, and thus it can be seen that they contrast and are not free variants of one another. Phonemic representations in our sense do not have this property, as is readily seen; while phonemic identity is a guarantee of free variant status, phonemic distinctness does not guarantee contrast. Thus, as in the example mentioned on page 27, [baɹd] can be either *bard* 'poet' or *barred* 'marked with or possessing bars'; in the former case, its phonemic representation is presumably simply /bard/, while in the latter, it is /bar # əd/. Though these phonemic representations are distinct, the two forms have the same range of variation. The feeling of many speakers that these two ought to contrast (though they cannot, of course, identify a particular instance of phonetic [baɹd] as either *bard* or *barred* with any reliability) is presumably based on this phonemic distinction, but does not affect the fact that they do not, in fact, contrast phonetically.

This is a more serious objection to the rejection of the taxonomic phonemic level than the other two. If a grammar is genuinely unable to distinguish contrast from repetitions, it has seriously failed to give an adequate description of the language. As Postal (1968) has pointed out, however, it is completely fallacious to construe this observation as a motivation for a particular level in linguistic theory. So long as it is possible to determine from the grammar whether or not two utterances contrast, this objection is met—whether or not the grammar provides a distinct level of representation at which exactly contrasting utterances differ. The reason for this, of course, is the fact that a grammar is not simply a set of representations, but is also a set of rules that relate the phonemic representations to the phonetic representations. Given that the representations do not simply exist in the grammar independently of one another, there is a natural way to explicate the notions of contrast and free variation, even without a particular level of representation on which this information is specified. Clearly, any two phonetic forms which are specified identically are not in contrast. The problem arises only when we have two distinct phonetic forms. We can then say (following Postal, 1968), that two distinct phonetic forms are variants if the rules of the grammar assign them to the same phonemic representation, for some well-formed phonemic representation in the language.[7] If two distinct phonetic forms are not variants, they are taken as contrasting. It is a requirement of such an operation that in order to determine whether or not two forms contrast, we consult not a single level of representation, but rather the rule-governed relation between phonemic and phonetic representations; but if we take seriously the notion that this rule-governed relation is indeed the central part of the grammar, this seems perfectly natural. Accordingly, the need to give an account of the difference between contrast and variation cannot be seen as a valid motivation for a taxonomic level of phonemic description.

But if we abandon these criteria for a phonemic representation, what basis have we for establishing the phonemic forms of a language? In fact, we have already seen an indication of a domain of fact that is apparently relevant in establishing the distinctive sound properties of elements in a language — the range of variation in shape that they undergo in various environments. In considering the Korean obstruents, we saw that there is a general principle in the language which determines, in large part, the shape of obstruents in final and preobstruent position (as unreleased stops). Given a particular morpheme, such as []nac^h[] 'face', which appears in isolation as [nat^1], we can then ask what features of sound structure are characteristic of this element, and distinguish it from other elements of the language. Clearly, the fact that the final segment is an unreleased stop in final position is not a distinctive property of this form — the only distinctive thing about the final segment of the form in isolation is that it is a coronal obstruent. On the other hand, when it appears before a vowel, as in [nac^{h}ɨl], all of the features of being an aspirated alveopalatal affricate are properties of this form. Accordingly, if we represent the element in question as phonemically /nac^h/, its variation in shape (i.e., the fact that it is [nac^h-] in some environments, but [nat^1] in others) will be completely accounted for by general facts of the Korean language: in particular, the rule that states 'obstruents are replaced by the corresponding unreleased stops when they appear before other obstruents or word boundary'. Otherwise we would either have to assign two distinct phonemic representations to []nac^h[], or assign it the representation /nat/, together with a specific statement about this mor-

---

[7] Hans Basbøll has pointed out to me that there are some problems of detail in formalizing this notion in a satisfactory way. These do not, however, affect the point that a grammar can provide an account of contrast and variation even without employing a taxonomic phonemic level of representation. Given problems of the sort alluded to above (page 28) with the notion of contrast, it would not be surprising if substantial indeterminacies arose in its formulation.

pheme (as well as others, but still referring to particular morphemes rather than simply to sound structure): 'when /nat/ represents the morpheme 'face', final /t/ is replaced by /cʰ/ if a sonorant follows.' Our goal in choosing /nacʰ/ as the phonemic form of this item, then, was to give a characterization of its sound structure from which all of the facts about its range of variants in different environments could be predicted solely in terms of general facts about the sound structure of Korean. In other words, insofar as possible, we would like to choose a single representation for a form from which it is possible to derive all of its occurring shapes by phonological rules. Insofar as this is possible, and the representation we have chosen does imply all of the distinct phonetic forms the element takes, we will have isolated those facts about the element's sound structure which are genuinely distinctive of that element. All other properties of the phonetic forms, and all ways in which these differ from the phonemic form, are to be taken as distinctive not for this item, but rather as automatic consequences of general facts of the language. From this it follows that phonemic forms will be as much as possible like phonetic forms, deviating from them only due to general properties of the language and the need to describe variations which the form undergoes in various environments. This requirement that phonemic representations be as much like phonetic representations as possible, specifying the way the morpheme would be pronounced in all positions if general rules of the language did not dictate otherwise, has been called the requirement of naturalness by Postal (1968).

In order to give real content to this statement it would be necessary to specify what the general rules of the phonological structure of a language are. In other words, it is necessary to know when a particular property should be assigned to the operation of a phonological rule, and when it should be associated with the underlying representations of particular morphemes. This might be accomplished by assigning a 'cost' to any given phonological rule, and by providing a procedure for determining when the cost associated with the rule was outweighed by a corresponding reduction in the 'cost' due to complexities in the phonemic representations of particular morphemes that could be eliminated if the rule were accepted. Such research on evaluation procedures occupied much early discussion in the field of generative phonology (see Chomsky & Halle, 1965, and references therein for discussion), but it has proved extremely difficult to provide an absolute criterion of the sort suggested. Some remarks on this topic appear in Chapters 6 and 15, but in all too many places in the subsequent discussion, it will be necessary to rely on the reader's agreement as to what constitutes a valid general property of the languages discussed.

Once we require a phonemic representation to come as close as possible to an optimal form from which all morphological variation can be predicted, we see that an interesting consequence follows: it may turn out to be the case that the phonemic form which meets this condition, and which we accordingly accept as the underlying form, is one that never occurs in exactly that phonetic shape in any phonetic form. Many early writers on language had given descriptions in which the variant phonetic forms of some item are derived from a single form by rules of the language (including Pāṇini, most European traditional grammars through the nineteenth century, Whitney, Boas, and the linguists of the "Handbook of American Indian Languages", Sapir, Bloomfield, etc.), but many of them had imposed a constraint on such descriptions that the 'basic form', from which the others were to be derived, be one of the actually occurring shapes of the element in question.

An example of the effects of such a constraint may make it clearer. In Sanskrit, two aspirates may not (with very few, onomatopoetic exceptions) appear in the phonetic shape of a root (including the reduplicated syllable, if any). Thus, while there are forms with initial aspirates (such as *bhavati* 'he is'), medial aspirates (such as *bibheti* 'he fears'), and root-final aspirates (such as *bodhati* 'he wakes'), there are no forms with aspirates in both initial and final positions in the root (i.e., there is no **bhodhati*). It is also the case that aspiration is lost in certain positions (finally and before obstruents, in general), so that a root like /kṣudh/ (as in *kṣudhyati* 'he is hungry'), when it appears before the -*s* of the future ending, loses its aspiration (as well as being devoiced, by a general assimilation) and becomes *kṣotsyati* 'he will be hungry'. Now there is a class of roots for which there is an additional complication: when a root-final consonant loses its aspiration under this latter influence, the (previously unaspirated) initial stop of the root becomes aspirated. Thus, when the root of *bodhati* appears before the future ending, it becomes not **botsyati,* but *bhotsyati* 'he will wake'.

Whitney described this phenomenon in terms of a shift of aspiration. Thus, he establishes a basic form for this root /budh/, and then applies a rule that says 'before obstruents and word boundaries, root-final aspiration is moved to the initial stop of the root.' Such a rule is not stated quite that generally, however: Whitney's discussion includes a list of the specific roots to which it can apply, implying that there are other roots which would not undergo it.[8]

---

[8] This seems to be the thrust of Whitney's remarks: his tone does not suggest that he is simply giving a list of all of the forms which could possibly meet the 'structural description' of his rule. This is undoubtedly because, as Whitney knew, there were various roots in ear-

This analysis has at least two deficiencies, however, beyond the fact that it treats aspiration shift as an idiosyncratic fact not derivable from phonological structure. The aspiration shift rule in question can of course only apply within the root, and cannot be responsible for the behavior of reduplicated syllables. In reduplication, both aspirated and unaspirated initials are reduplicated as unaspirated, in contrast to the usual process, which involves simply copying the initial. This is true regardless of the nature of the root final: whether it is aspirated, as in *bubodha* from /b(h)udh/; unaspirated, as *cachanda,* from /chand/; or nonobstruent, as *babhūva,* from /bhu/. Clearly, some principle is necessary to account for this failure of aspiration in reduplication; equally clearly, it cannot be the rule of 'aspiration shift'. If we accept that the generalization in both cases is 'aspiration is lost when another aspirate stands in the same syllable or in the following (nonsuffixal) syllable', as has been assumed since the first discussions of the phenomena in question, we should have a common explanation, or the generalization will be lost.

Second, the rule deleting aspiration in root final stops when they occur before an obstruent or word boundary is needed in any case, to deal with roots such as those of *kṣudhyati / kṣotsyati, pṛchati / prakṣyati,* etc. But in this case, another important generalization is missed—the grammar contains a rule that eliminates aspiration in some environments, and the aspiration shift rule must state that exactly where the aspiration would be lost by this rule, it is shifted to root initial position in some roots. The overlapping nature of the two rules remains unexpressed, as long as they are treated as completely distinct processes.

An alternative analysis is, of course, readily available, and it is this analysis which has figured in most recent discussions of the topic. If we represent roots which show a shift of aspiration, such as the root /bhudh/ for *bodhati / bhotsyati,* with aspirates in both the initial and the final position, a straightforward formulation results. Any roots which do not show this alternation in early Sanskrit can be represented with plain initial and aspirated final; by classical times, we assume that a morpheme structure condition had arisen allowing only aspirates from

lier Sanskrit which did not undergo aspiration shift because their initials were not originally aspirated. In classical Sanskrit, however, it appears that even roots of original *DVDh* form were reanalyzed as shiftable, just like the roots of original *DhVDh* form. For some discussion, see Wackernagel, Debrunner, and Renou (1957). Various accounts of this reanalysis could be given, some of which would be consistent with Whitney's (and Pāṇini's) aspiration-shift analysis rather than with that accepted here. They would still have to overcome the objections below, however. I am grateful to Paul Kiparsky for calling my attention to this fact.

among the stops in initial position when the root terminated in an aspirate (and the initial was not followed by another consonant, as in, e.g., /kṣudh/). Now we can have two rules: one which removes root final aspiration before an obstruent or word boundary, and another, which deaspirates a stop in a root if another aspirate follows within the root. Thus, *bodhati* will be phonemically /bhaudh+ati/, and only the second rule will be applicable, giving (together with the rules for coalescence of vowels) [bodhati], while *bhotsyati* will be phonemically /bhaudh+sya+ti/. To this form, the second rule will not apply, and so the initial aspiration is preserved; the rules of voicing assimilation and vowel coalescence give [bhotsyati].

In this analysis, the peculiarities of the aspiration shifting forms have been represented in their phonological structure, and it is not necessary for the rules to refer to any morpheme specifically. That is, both the cluster rule and the initial deaspiration rule can be stated in terms of phonological structure alone. The deaspiration rule has a single statement which covers both the root-initials and the reduplicated syllables. Furthermore, the relation between the two rules can now be expressed: the initial aspiration is preserved just in case some rule has applied to make the initial deaspiration rule inapplicable. Thus, the environment of the cluster deaspiration rule no longer has to be stated independently in two distinct places. For these and other reasons, this analysis should be preferred as a part of the synchronic grammar of classical Sanskrit.

Why, then, did Whitney (whose grammar is often taken as a model of insight and precision) reject this analysis? It is probable that this is because it violates the constraint discussed above, that the phonemic forms be possible phonetic forms in the language. The phonemic form /bhudh/, containing aspirates in both initial and final positions, is not a possible form in Sanskrit (because the initial deaspiration rule would, of course, reduce it to /budh/), and so Whitney could not have accepted it as a phonemic form from which the other forms can be derived. He is forced, therefore, to take this root to be /budh/, and to characterize it as undergoing the aspiration shift rule in those environments in which it would otherwise undergo final deaspiration. This constraint must have a systematic status; he is certainly aware of the analysis suggested above (since he includes it in a note as the historical explanation of the synchronic situation), but he chose not to use it because it would violate the constraint on possible underlying forms.

Although we would like to maintain a maximally natural relation between phonemic and phonetic forms, we see no reason to require that all limitations on possible phonetic forms (some of which are, of course, consequences of the rules of the grammar) will also serve as constraints on the phonemic forms of the language. We would accept, therefore, the analysis of Sanskrit aspiration which posits (phonetically nonoccurring) /bhudh/ as the phonemic form of the root in *bodhati / bhotsyati,* since this analysis seems to optimize the prediction of the phonetic forms a root takes in various environments in terms of generalizations about the phonological structure of the language alone. Such a conclusion—that the phonemic forms of roots can be phonetically nonoccurring items—is of course no novelty. It was perfectly familiar to Bloomfield (in his morphophonemic work, of course, and in several analyses given to illustrate exactly this point in *Language,* pp. 218–219), and to Sapir.[9]

But does the acceptance of such abstract underlying forms mean that phonemic forms are *totally* abstract, bearing no direct relation to phonetic forms except the accidental correspondence established by the rules of the grammar? This conclusion would mark a return to totally abstract positions such as those of Hjelmslev and Lamb, which have been more than adequately criticized by Jakobson and Halle (1956), Postal (1968), and other authors. But such a step is by no means entailed in our acceptance of such analyses as suggested in the preceding. For even if our phonemic forms are not themselves occurring phonetic forms in the language, they are composed of elements that are phonetically possible segments in the language; that is, the phonemes are not simply abstract elements in an arbitrary formula, but are intended to have an explicit phonetic interpretation. Insofar as the actual pronunciation of the morpheme varies from this ideal pronunciation in one way or another, this is a consequence of general facts about the phonological structure of the language, even if it should turn out to be the case that some such a principle should intervene in every single environment in which the morpheme actually occurs. The phonemic representation is intended to present the ideal phonetic form of the element in question, the form it would take if no other principle of the language were to dictate otherwise. We require justification for every deviation between phonetic and phonemic form: in order to justify a rule that will establish such a dif-

---

[9] It has sometimes been suggested that Sapir, too, adhered to the constraint that the phonemic form of a morpheme had to be one of its occurring phonetic shapes. That this is not so can be seen from the example of Southern Paiute discussed in Sapir, (1949). Here, the informant transcribed phonetic [-βa] as *pa.* Sapir is quite clear that this is a shape in which this morpheme never occurs—it is always either spirantized, as in this form, or nasalized, or geminated, depending on the character of the preceding stem. Interestingly enough, this element can occur as [-pa], after a geminating stem ending in a voiceless vowel (which induces secondary degemination), but Sapir says explicitly that this [-pa] is not to be identified with the phonemic *pa* written by the informant for phonetic [-βa]. This latter is a nonoccurring form of the morpheme in question.

ference between the two representations of the form, we must show that the cost of the rule is outweighed by the savings it results in in terms of prediction of generalities of the phonological structure of the language.

Having accepted this view of the relationship between phonemic and phonetic representations, there is a further issue for which it is necessary to establish a position. This is the question of the extent to which phonemic segments are specified for all of the features specified in phonetic representations. The first work to accept the general position on phonological structure taken here, Halle's fundamental work on Russian (Halle, 1959), accepted the notion that the phonemic elements were to be specified only for those features that were not predictable in terms of the phonological rules of the language. As we have suggested above, some early writers such as Trubetzkoy and Bloomfield took this view of the phoneme, while others, such as Sapir, Saussure (apparently), and Whitney took the opposite view, that phonemes were fully specified phonetic segments. It seems likely that in taking over the position of partially specified phonemes, Halle was in fact adhering to one of the principles that had motivated work in taxonomic phonemics — the desire to establish the phonemic level as one indicating all and only the contrastive features of an utterance. Obviously this position precludes the overt indication of values for features that are predictable. But the same objection can be raised against this position as was raised against the claim of taxonomic phonemics (that the phonemic level had to differentiate all and only those utterances that are in contrast). Once we recognize that a grammar contains rules, as well as representations, there is no longer any reason to expect that facts about which features are distinctive and which are predictable will be a defining property of a particular level. So long as it is possible to determine from the grammar as a whole whether or not a value for a given feature in a given form is distinctive, the need to give an account of distinctiveness will have been satisfied. This means that in addition to the phonological rules which specify the range of shapes a morpheme may take on in various environments, we also need a set of statements to characterize the range of well-formed phonemic representations. Such a set of statements was incorporated in the description in Halle (1959), and in other works of the same sort, in the form of a set of morpheme structure rules, the function of which it was to fill in the values of the unspecified features. It was noticed early, however, that the use of unspecified features and blank-filling rules led to formal problems in constraining analyses. A discussion of these issues, based on Stanley (1967), can be found in Chapter 15. Stanley suggested that the formal problems could be avoided if phonemic representations were taken to be composed of fully specified segments, and the morpheme structure rules were replaced with a set of well-formedness conditions that defined the set of phonemic representations, but without performing the function of filling in any feature specifications. In addition to the technical difficulties discussed by Stanley, this approach also resolves another problem with incompletely specified phonemic forms: it is often the case that feature values are interdependent. Thus, in many languages (including English), a cluster of nasal + obstruent will always have the same point of articulation for both segments. Clearly, the position features in both segments are not independently variable, and in a theory that requires us to eliminate all predictable feature values, one or the other must be left unspecified for position. But there is no formal basis for choosing one rather than the other of the two segments as the one with predictable values—it is indeterminate whether we should specify the position of the nasal or of the obstruent. But in a fully specified representation, of the sort we are suggesting, such an indeterminacy does not arise: the well-formedness conditions simply specify that no morpheme is well formed if it contains a cluster of nasal followed by nonhomorganic obstruent. Other such situations crop up in numerous places in many languages. In order to avoid them, as well as Stanley's difficulties, and to preserve the condition that phonemic forms be phonetically natural, we will accept the position that the elements of such forms are fully specified for all features.

Just as it was possible to give an account of contrast and free variation within a theory whose phonemic level was not defined by these properties, it is also possible to give an account of distinctive versus redundant features in a theory of the type accepted here. Both accounts involve the observation that a grammar is more than a set of representations: it also includes the rules that define and relate these representations. In the case of distinctive versus redundant features, it is easy to see what is required. A particular feature in a particular form is distinctive if and only if the rules of the grammar would characterize another representation, which was identical with this one except that it contained the opposite specification for just this feature, as a well formed phonemic form in the language. In the case of covariant features, as will be seen, this account claims that neither (or none, if more than two are involved) of the features *alone* is distinctive, for neither can be replaced by its opposite without altering anything else. Only the combination has a distinctive value, which varies as a whole. This account of distinctiveness diverges somewhat from traditional ones, but seems to yield a perfectly satisfactory basis for the distinction between the distinctive and the redundant aspects of a phonological form.

Thus the notion of phonemic representation developed in this chapter is carried through the remainder of this book. Such a representation is a phonetically fully specified and maximally natural form, which deviates from the occurring phonetic forms only insofar as such is dictated by the need to optimize predictability of variation and to capture generalizations about phonological structure. It is related to the phonetic form through a set of rules, of two types: one set (which will appear in various places below), the morpheme structure conditions, specifies the range of well-formed phonemic representations. The other set — the phonological rules proper — specifies the variations in shape morphemes undergo in various environments. The relation between the two levels is not constrained by conditions like those of taxonomic phonemic theory, although it is desirable for us to discover other constraints that can be put on this relation, since such constraints increase the substance of our linguistic theory.

CHAPTER 4

Phonological Rules and Their Justification

We argued in the preceding chapter that the primary reason for incorporating phonological rules in a linguistic description was the need to describe alternations in shape which a morpheme undergoes in various environments. That is, instead of simply listing all of the forms in which a given morpheme can appear, we set as our goal a description in which each morpheme has a single underlying phonemic form (perhaps, but not necessarily, identical with one of its phonetic forms), to which various phonological rules can apply in appropriate environments. In such a case, the variation is no longer treated as a property of the individual morpheme, but is shown to follow from generally valid principles of the sound structure of the language.

A bit of reflection will convince us immediately that it is impractical to expect this goal to be met with respect to the variations in shape evidenced by every morpheme in every natural language. A certain amount of overt listing of alternatives is necessary for cases in which the variation in a given morpheme is not, in fact, a consequence of the structure of the language as a whole, but is rather an isolated and idiosyncratic fact about a particular element. A good example of this sort of situation is the range of shapes of the verb 'to be' in English (and in many other languages). The shapes *am, are, is, was, were,* and *be* have no obvious phonological relation to one another, and it is clear that whatever base form we establish, the rules required to derive all of these forms from it will be of incredibly tortuous complexity. More important than the sheer complexity, however, is the fact that these rules would have absolutely no general validity: they would have to be restricted (overtly or covertly) so as to prevent their applying to other elements of the language (such as the noun *bee*), and would in fact describe nothing at all beyond the behavior of this one morpheme. Thus, even if it were possible to formulate rules in strictly phonological terms to cover these facts, to do so would be to miss the point: the behavior of the verb *be* is not, in fact, a consequence of the phonological structure of English, but is simply an arbitrary fact about this particular element of the language. Much better than any set or rules deriving the observed forms from a common phonemic form would be a simple, suppletive list:

(1)　　[]be[]　=　/æm/　in the context:　＿＿ 1sg. pres.
　　　　　　　=　/ar/　in the context:　＿＿ (2sg. or) pl. pres.
　　　　　　　=　/iz/　in the context:　＿＿ 3sg. pres.
　　　　　　　=　/wəz/　in the context:　＿＿ 1 or 3sg. past.
　　　　　　　=　/wər/　in the context:　＿＿ (2sg. or) pl. past.
　　　　　　　=　/bij/　in the context:　＿＿ (nonfinite forms)

The exact form of a set of rules like (1) is irrelevant: the point is that such a treatment assigns all of the variation to the particular morphological and syntactic element []be[], rather than associating it with some phonological conditions.

Of course it would be possible, in principle, for all of a speaker's knowledge of the sound structure of the elements of his language to be characterized by a gargantuan list with a form like that of (1), giving explicitly each of the elements that could possibly occur in phonetic representations of utterances in the language. It would be impossible, we should note, to characterize a speaker's knowledge of the syntactic structures of his language in this way, in light of the recursive (and therefore potentially unlimited) nature of the syntactic system he knows. A language contains a finite number of distinct lexical items, however, and each of these occurs in a finite number of morphological environments; thus, it is at least possible that these could simply be memorized as a list. If this were a true description of the nature of phonological knowledge, the linguist could simply give up and go to the beach: a list like (1) is by its nature unstructured, and accordingly any systematic properties a linguist found in the language would simply be artifacts of his descriptive technique. In fact, speakers appear to reduce the burden on memory by memorizing only those elements, for most items in the list, which are necessary to distinguish them from one another, and generalizing properties of the list in the form of phonological rules that allow most morphological variation to be treated in terms independent of particular items.

Such generalizations about the elements of the language can be taken to have the canonical form of implicational expressions like (2):

(2)   *If a linguistic form has the properties x_1, x_2, . . . , x_i,*
        then it is also to be assigned the properties
        y_i, y_2, . . . , y_j.

Psychological and behavioral evidence for generalization of this sort, while rather nebulous, is nonetheless quite convincing. Thus, speaker behavior does not in general have the random, atomistic, isolated, and unstructured character of items on a list. When speakers learn a new form, they do not simply enter it independent of the ones they already know, but rather they extend to it properties of the other elements of the vocabulary. Mistakes do not consist of completely unrelated substitutions, but rather in replacement of a form by another that is closely related to the original in terms of the systematic properties of the other forms of the language. When languages change, a very frequent form of such change is the extension of a preexisting generalization to include a larger class of forms than previously. Another frequent form of change is the introduction of some completely new property, not in a single item of the language, but in a whole class of systematically related items. Such kinds of 'evidence' could be extended without difficulty, and all such behavior is inconsistent with the denial of the reality of rule-like statements about regularities of language. The items in the phonetic repertoire of a language have the character of a structure, not an inventory; and more importantly, this structure is based on elementary units that can be revealed by an analysis based on phonetic properties. That is, the groups of elements that function together, and the properties referred to in the rules of the language [statements like (2)], are in large part defined not by arbitrary designations, but by the possession of common properties in terms of the system of features employed in phonetic representation. The identity of the features employed in phonetic and phonemic representations is of course a consequence of the principle of naturalness referred to in Chapter 3, but it is an important empirical result that the same set of properties also functions in defining the regularities of correspondance and variation in a language's phonological system.

Given a set of facts about the variation that some element(s) of a language displays, it is important to have some basis for saying that this particular set of facts should be explained by positing a phonological rule, rather than a suppletive list such as (1). Let us therefore consider a particular example and examine the sort of evidence that can be adduced for a phonological rule. We can consider the formation of the plurals of nouns in English. As is well known, there is a small class of irregular items, such as *ox /oxen, child / children, sheep / sheep,* etc., the plural forms of which are obviously idiosyncratic. Such elements must obviously be treated suppletively, and we will not otherwise discuss them: it is the so-called regular plural formation that we are interested in. This appears, of course, in three basic shapes: as [-ɨz], in words with final consonants from the set [s, z, š, ž, č, ǰ]; as [-s] after words with final voiceless consonants other than those just listed; and elsewhere as [-z]. Clearly, we could describe these facts in either of the ways we have been considering: either as suppletive forms from a list, or as phonologically determined variants of a single basic form.

In the model of morphological description by allomorphy statements, which prevailed in the United States in the 1940s and 1950s, it was generally assumed that such a description should have the former, list character. Insofar as the variant allomorphs of a morpheme were phonemically distinct (and [-s], [-z], and [-ɨz] are clearly phonemically distinct in taxonomic terms), they were to be described by listing them, and associating each item on the list with a specification of the environment in which it could appear. Such a description, then, would presumably have the form of the three statements in (3), disregarding the irregular items:

$$(3) \quad []\text{PLURAL}[] \;=\; /\text{-ɨz}/ \quad \text{in the context:} \quad \begin{bmatrix} +\text{coronal} \\ +\text{strident} \end{bmatrix} \; \underline{\quad\quad}$$

$$=\; /\text{-s}/ \quad \text{in the context:} \quad \begin{bmatrix} -\text{voice} \\ (\text{elsewhere}) \end{bmatrix} \; \underline{\quad\quad}$$

$$=\; /\text{z}/ \quad \text{elsewhere}$$

A description of this sort, whatever its exact form, correctly states the facts about the distribution of the shapes of the regular plural formation in English. It states them as properties explicitly associated with this particular morpheme.

Alternatively, we could describe these same facts in terms of a common underlying form and a set of phonological rules. Let us pick one of the forms as basic: say [-z], in part because that seems to be the 'elsewhere' case, and we have as yet no motivation for choosing any other particular form. If the regular plural is then /-z/, we can account for the other shapes in terms of the two rules in (4):

$$(4)^{1} \quad \text{a.} \quad \emptyset \longrightarrow \text{ɨ} / \begin{bmatrix} +\text{coronal} \\ +\text{strident} \end{bmatrix} \; \# \; \underline{\quad\quad} \; z \; \#$$

$$\text{b.} \quad z \longrightarrow [-\text{voiced}]/[-\text{voice}] \; \# \; \underline{\quad\quad} \; \#$$

This description also accounts for the facts correctly: a plural form such as /##čərč#z#/ is converted by (4a) into /##čərč#ɨz#/, to which (4b) cannot apply and which is the correct form; a form like /##buk#z#/ is not affected by (4a), but is changed into /##buk#s#/, the correct form, by (4b); while a form like /##leg#z#/ is unaffected by either (4a) or (4b), and remains in this (correct) form.

How are we to choose between these two formulations? Both seem equally good, on the face of it. Both describe the facts correctly, both capture the relevant generalizations about the phonological nature of the environments in which the variants occur, and both are of approximately equal complexity, insofar as it makes sense to compare them in these terms. It might be thought that the second formulation [as phonemic /-z/ together with the rules (4)] better expresses the phonological coherence of the class of alternants. That is, it would complicate rules (4) if the alternants were, say, /-lar/, /-in/, and /-s/ (appearing in the same environments), while the description in (3) could describe this situation just as well as the actually occurring facts. But this is the whole question: we are trying to decide, in choosing between (3) and (4), whether the alternation of shapes of the regular plural is a phenomenon whose coherence is to be found in phonological structure, rather than simply in morphemic identity; to make the decision on the basis of a presystematic intuition that (4) is more phonologically coherent would be circular. It seems clear that, on the basis of nothing but the facts presented thus far, there is no systematic basis for a choice between (3) and (4). We must, accordingly, look for some additional facts in order to determine whether the plural forms should be treated as phonologically determined or not.

Such additional data are not hard to find. The variations in the shape of the plural affix remind us of several other morphemes in English. Consider, for example, the regular 3sg. pres. ending of verbs. Just as we

---

[1] The formalism employed here should be fairly transparent. I assume that all phonological rules are ultimately stated in terms of features, rather than segments, and accordingly that terms like 'ɨ', 'z', etc., in rules like (4) are to be regarded as abbreviations for the set of features which characterize these segments. The import of the rule, of course, is as follows: $A \rightarrow B \mid X$ ____ Y means that wherever the string XAY occurs in a phonological form, the A is to be replaced by B. Sometimes this may involve only a partial replacement, as when the specification [+voice] is changed to [−voice] by (4b), leaving all of the other features of /z/ intact. I also assume conventions of word-boundary placement as in Chomsky and Halle (1968): each lexical category, such as a noun or verb, is bounded at each end by word boundary (#). Similarly, each larger category dominating such a lexical category is bounded by #. In the case at hand, this means that the plural form of a noun will have two instances of # initially, one after the stem word, and one after the whole item, including the plural ending. Thus, /##boy#z#/, etc.

have the alternants [-ɨz], [-s], and [-z] in the plurals *churches, books,* and *legs,* we also have the same alternants in the verb forms *watches, looks,* and *sees.* Furthermore, the principle governing the distribution of these forms is exactly the same in both cases: the [-ɨz] form appears after words ending in a coronal strident consonant, the [-s] form appears after words ending in voiceless consonants other than these, and the [-z] form appears elsewhere. Let us see how we could incorporate these additional facts into our two alternate descriptions.

In the case of the description based on (3), the description of the 3sg. pres. form is exactly analogous: in addition to (3), we need to add (5) to the grammar of English:

(5)   []3sg. pres.[] = /ɨz/   in the context: $\begin{bmatrix} +\text{strident} \\ +\text{coronal} \end{bmatrix}$ ——

= /-s/   in the context: $\begin{bmatrix} -\text{voice} \\ (\text{elsewhere}) \end{bmatrix}$ ——

= /-z/   elsewhere

Now the important thing to note about the statement in (5) is that, while it is certainly no more complicated than (3), it is also completely independent of it. That is, just as the variation in (3) is treated as a property of the morpheme []PLURAL[], the variation in (5) is treated as an idiosyncratic fact about the morpheme []3sg. pres.[]. Nowhere does the fact that these two elements show exactly the same variation find expression: given the facts of (3) it is no easier and no harder to add the facts of (5) to the description than it would be if (3) were not there, or if (3) were completely different. That is, this description treats the facts of (3) and of (5) as totally independent.

Things are rather different with the description of the plural morpheme based on (4), however. Given the rules of (4) to describe the plural, we need do very little to incorporate the facts of the 3sg. pres. verb ending into our description — all we need is (6):

(6)   []3sg. pres.[] = /-z/

Here we need say nothing about the variation in shape of this ending, but can simply assign it the single underlying form /-z/, just like that of the regular plural ending. The rules in (4) are already a part of the grammar, and we can use them to explain the facts about the 3sg. pres. ending. Thus, this description is much simpler, given the facts as they are, than it would be if the plural and 3sg. pres. endings were completely independent, as (3) and (5) claim. We can make use of the rules established for the one to account for the other.

When we go a little further, we find other facts of the same sort. Two other elements in English show the same range of variants as the plural and 3sg. pres.: the possessive *'s*, as in *Wallace's, Dick's*, and *Ed's;* and the reduced form of the auxiliary verbs *is* and *has*, *'s* as in *Alice's coming, Dick's coming, and Jane's coming too*. Both of these elements show [-ɨz] after coronal stridents, [-s] after other voiceless obstruents, and [-z] elsewhere. To incorporate these facts into a discription based on (3) and (5), two further allomorphy statements of the same form would be needed, each of which would again be completely independent of the other, and also of (3) and (5). Thus, the fact that these four elements all show exactly the same range of variation would remain unexpressed in such a description: each would be treated in complete isolation from the rest. In the description based on (4) and (6), however, all that is necessary is to specify the possessive as /-z/, and to provide rules for reducing *is* and *has* to /-z/ in certain positions (which are needed in any case). The fact that all of these elements show the same range of variation is treated here as systematic, rather than accidental: the rules which account for one form can be used to explain the variation found in the others. All that is now idiosyncratic and particular about the morphemes involved is the fact that they all incidentally consist of underlying /-z/: the fact that this leads to the same consequences in all cases follows automatically. The description would actually be complicated if it were not so.

One final set of facts remains to be considered in this example. The endings of the past and participial forms of weak (or 'regular') verbs show an alternation that looks rather like that we have seen in the other elements: the ending [ɨd] after the dental stops *t* and *d*, the ending [-t] after voiceless stops other than *t*; and otherwise the ending [-d]. We could, of course, incorporate these facts into the description based on (3) and (5) by simply adding (7):

(7)   []PAST[], []PARTICIPLE[] = /ɨd/ in the context: *t* or *d* ____

  = /t/ in the context: [−voiced] ____
  (other than /t/)

  = /d/ elsewhere

But the point is, we could equally well incorporate any other set of facts instead. The obvious coherence of all of these facts is going begging.

The description based on (4) can do better. We need only modify the rules given there, so that (4a) will insert a reduced vowel between any two 'similar' coronal obstruents, leaving (4b) the same. We can then take the regular past and participle ending to be /-d/, and the other variants will then be given by the same rule that accounts for the variants of the

/-z/ endings. The revised set of rules is given in (8):

$$(8)^2 \quad \text{a.} \quad \emptyset \longrightarrow \dot{\imath} \; / \; \begin{bmatrix} +\text{coronal} \\ +\text{obstruent} \\ \alpha\text{strident} \\ \beta\text{del. rel.} \end{bmatrix} \# \underline{\hspace{2em}} \begin{bmatrix} +\text{coronal} \\ +\text{obstruent} \\ \alpha\text{strident} \\ \beta\text{del. rel.} \end{bmatrix} \#$$

b. $[+\text{obstruent}] \longrightarrow [-\text{voice}] \; / \; [-\text{voice}] \; \# \underline{\hspace{2em}} \#$

We see, therefore, that the description of plural inflection based on phonological rules, rather than on allomorphy statements, allows us to express the coherence of this set of elements in a natural way. When we consider the fact that the whole range of fully productive noun and verb inflection in English is covered by this set of rules, it is obvious that this coherence is not simply an artifact. The phonological generalizations expressed in (8) are, first, that in inflectional processes two consonants cannot come together if they are too much alike [in the sense made precise by rule (8a)]; and, second, that clusters resulting from inflection are homogeneous with respect to the feature of voicing. From the evidence just considered, it is clear that the variant forms assumed by inflectional endings (and also by the contracted auxiliaries) are governed by these generalizations, which are facts about sound structure, rather than by unique, individual, and idiosyncratic statements about each.

The point of this example has been to illustrate the kind of justification that can be given for describing some aspect of morphemic variation by phonological, rather than morphological rules. In comparing the two descriptions alone, it is often impossible to decide between the two alternatives without additional facts. The decision can be made, however, if we can find additional facts for which the two descriptions make distinct predictions. In this case, positing rules like (4) [or (8)] to explain the plural ending makes the implicit prediction that, if other endings are found with phonemic shapes satisfying the environments of the rules, they will show the same alternations. The allomorphy statement, on the other hand, since it treats the facts about the plural as individual properties of that element, makes the prediction that if any other element is found to show the same variation, it must be purely coincidental, since that element is unrelated to the plural. The fact that several additional elements, forming an obviously coherent class, show alternation that can be predicted in terms of the rules for the plural endings therefore strongly confirm the phonological basis of the original alternation.[3]

---

[2] The meaning of the notation '[αstrident]', etc. is discussed in Chapter 7. For the moment, it is sufficient to note that as employed in rule (8a), it means that the two segments which are given this specification must agree in stridency, and also in the feature of delayed release. That is, both must be strident or both nonstrident; and both must be spirants or affricates, or both must be stops.

³ As noted above, we have given no justification for our choice of this particular analysis, which takes the sibilant endings to be phonemically /-z/ and the weak past ending to be /-d/. It is clear that accounts could be constructed on the assumption that these endings are /iz/ and /-id/, /-s/ and /-t/, or some other form which does not occur phonetically. To the best of my knowledge, the first explicit attempt to decide this question is Bloomfield's (1933, pp. 210 ff). Bloomfield observes the similarity between the inflectional endings and the reduced auxiliaries, and suggests that an account based on the shapes /-iz/ and /-id/ is ·to be preferred. The reason he gives of course, is that on this account, instead of a rule like (8a) which inserts an i in certain environments, this analysis involves a rule which deletes i in the complement of those environments. Bloomfield then suggests that this rule is necessary in the grammar in any case, to perform the operation of reducing the auxiliaries (which obviously have syllabic underlying forms). Unfortunately, this motivation for Bloomfield's analysis will not stand. As Zwicky (1970) and others have recently shown, the conditions for contraction of auxiliaries are by no means simple, and involve numerous strange restrictions on the syntactic environment of the elements involved. These restrictions are unrelated to the operation of rule (8a), and to attempt to combine the auxiliary reduction rule with (8a) will lead to an enormous increase in complexity of the total rule system. I think, therefore, that this justification for preferring the syllabic variants of the affixes as the phonemic forms must be discarded. For some discussion, see Shibatani (1972). There is also, I think, some reason to prefer a nonsyllabic form. As is well known, when both regular plural and possessive endings are attached to the same form, the latter has no phonetic realization: *the boys' books.* This cannot be due to a morphological rule which says '*poss* → ∅ / *plural* ____', since the possessive occurs perfectly regularly with those irregular plural forms which do not have the sibilant ending: *the children's books.* Thus, it seems reasonable to posit a rule which deletes the regular possessive ending when it follows the regular plural ending. Now notice that if we assume the nonsyllabic shapes for both endings, the grammar of English already contains a rule which will accomplish this: the rule of geminate reduction (see Chomsky & Halle, 1968), which deletes one of a pair of identical consonants. This rule does not apply between a word final sibilant and one of the endings (that is, we have *kisses,* not **kiss'*), because of the intervening word boundary (#). The conventions suggested above for the placement of this element, however, would suggest that the plural and the possessive are separated by simple morpheme boundary (+), rather than word boundary, since the word including the plural and the possessive does not dominate any lexical element that is not dominated by the word including just the plural. That is, the natural underlying structure of *boys'* is /##boy#z + z#/. It is argued in Chomsky and Halle (1968), and accepted here, that + does not impede the operation of rules, and accordingly the independently needed rule of geminate simplification will account for the reduction of possessive after the regular plural if we assume both have the shape /-z/ (or /-s/). A parallel use of geminate reduction cannot be made if we assume the syllabic variants, for obvious reasons. The choice, then, would seem to be between /-z/ and /-s/; and this choice I resolve in favor of /-z/ because of the choice of /-s/ would require us to formulate rule (8a) so as to add the epenthetic vowel to the stem (that is, before the boundary) rather than to the ending if rule (8b) is to work correctly. This conclusion I find counterintuitive, but without real evidence beyond that. I assume throughout, of course, that whatever choice is made for the sibilant endings, the analogous choice should also be made for the dental preterite. Despite the intrinsic interest of these questions, it is important to point out that their resolution has no bearing on the argument given in the text. Since any of the possible choices of phonemic forms leads to a comparable set of rules, the account given could have been based equally well on any of the alternative analyses. Some further discussion and argument in favor of the nonsyllabic representations will be found in Anderson (1973).

We have presented this choice as if it were a strictly binary one, between a purely phonological account on the one hand and a purely morphological one on the other. Indeed, this is probably true on one level: the grammar contains, on our view, morphological rules (to deal with alternations such as the verb *be*; the alternants of the plural morpheme, now /-en/ / *ox* ____ ; /-ren/ /*child* ____ ; Ø/*sheep* ____ ; etc., and /-z/ elsewhere; and in general with the range of irreducible forms in which morphemes occur) and phonological rules (to deal with the phonetic variants of a single phonemic shape, such as the three forms taken by /-z/ in various environments), and a given rule presumably belongs to one or the other type. But this dichotomy does not rest on very firm ground until we give an account of the kind of information which can be used by 'phonological' rules. Obviously, we cannot limit such information to the segmental content of the morphemes making up an utterance; we have already had occasion, in discussing the example above, to make use of information about the placement and type of boundaries between elements,[4] and we can ask how much more information is available for defining the operation of rules. We assume here, on the basis of work by Postal (1968, and references cited therein), that the input to the phonological rules is a matrix provided with a significant amount of syntactic information: at least, boundary elements such as morpheme boundary (+) and word boundary (#); and a bracketing of the string into immediate constituents, together with an indication of at least major lexical category (N, V, Adj., etc.) membership. The question of whether additional syntactic information is necessary appears to be open: there do not appear to be any rules of segmental or intraword suprasegmental phonology that make use of categories such as NP, VP, etc. It would seem reasonable to require that only information about lexical category, together with the position and degree of boundaries, plays a role in defining the input string. The question of more specific reference in phonological rules to particular grammatical categories, individual morphemes, etc. will arise at various places below, but has not been well studied. It should be emphasized that the decision to allow phonological rules to have access to some kind of information, such as that just described, is not based on a priori considerations of what kind of information could possibly play a role, but rather on the presentation in the literature of specific phonological problems that appear to require refer-

---

[4] It was the issue of whether this sort of information could be employed in phonological description that was debated under the name of 'grammatical prerequisites to phonemic analysis' in taxonomic discussion. See Pike (1947, 1952).

ence to such information in order to state an apparently significant generalization. The fact that many questions in this area have not yet been resolved should not be taken as a point of theoretical inadequacy, but rather of empirical indeterminacy: appropriate examples for making the decision have not yet been presented or sufficiently established.

CHAPTER 5

The Interaction
of Phonological Rules

It will be observed from some of the examples that have been discussed up to this point that the generalizations captured by a given phonological rule cannot be treated in complete isolation from the other rules of the language. That is, rules interact with one another; and it is often only with reference to the effect of some other rule that a rule can be said to express a correct generalization at all.

For an example of rule interaction, let us consider the following case. In most of the Turkic languages, the vowels of affixes (and of roots, as well, in many cases) are subject to a principle of vowel harmony. Accordingly, some of the features of such vowels are predictable in terms of the features of other vowels in the word. Most typically, this harmony operates with respect to the feature [±back]: if a word contains one back vowel, all of the remaining vowels of the word are back; and, conversely, one front vowel implies that all of the other vowels are front. In Chapter 12 some of the issues involved in the description of such vowel harmony processes are considered in more detail; for the moment, let us assume that the language simply contains a process which assimilates the backness of any vowel to that of the preceding vowel:

(1)[1] $[+\text{syllabic}] \longrightarrow [\alpha\text{back}] \;/\; \begin{bmatrix} +\text{syllabic} \\ \alpha\text{back} \end{bmatrix} C_0 \underline{\hspace{1cm}}$

[1] As will be discussed briefly below, the abbreviation C_0 stands for 'any number of consonants, 0 or more'.

Such a rule will convert suffix vowels into the corresponding vowels with opposite values of the feature [back] if they do not agree with the backness of the preceding vowel. For the sake of simplicity we assume that the rule operates progressively from left to right across the word (an assumption that is examined in Chapter 9).

Now in most of the individual Turkic languages, there are factors which complicate this basic principle. In some dialects of Modern Uighur[2] for example, the following facts are of note: first, there is no vowel *ɨ* to serve as the back equivalent of *i*, and in fact the vowel *i* occurs in both front and back vowel words. Historically, this is of course the result of a merger of *ɨ* and *i*. Synchronically, however, *i* is a neutral vowel, in that it does not participate in the harmony process. We could express this by revising rule (1) so that it applies only to vowels other than *i*, and bypasses syllables containing *i* in searching for a harmonic environment:

$$(2)^3 \quad \begin{bmatrix} +\text{syll} \\ \begin{cases} -\text{high} \\ +\text{round} \end{cases} \end{bmatrix} \longrightarrow [\alpha\text{back}] \; / \; \begin{bmatrix} +\text{syll} \\ \alpha\text{back} \\ \begin{cases} -\text{high} \\ +\text{round} \end{cases} \end{bmatrix} (C_0 i)_0 C_0 \underline{\hspace{2em}}$$

This statement includes the behavior of the vowel *i*, but is still not sufficient to provide for the facts of Uighur vowel harmony. There is another front vowel that sometimes occurs in back vowel words: *e*. The distribution of *e* in back vowel words is rather limited, however: in each case, it is unstressed, followed by exactly one consonant, and the following vowel is *i*; furthermore, there are no forms in which either *a* or *ä* (its front counterpart) appears in this environment, but most such forms with *e*, including all of those in which it functions as a back vowel harmonically, are related to other forms having the vowel *a* (or, if a front vowel word, the vowel *ä*) in place of the *e*. There is, for example, a root appearing generally as *al-* 'take' which appears as *el-* when followed by a suffix with initial *i*, e.g., *eliš* 'the taking', *elin-* 'be taken (stem)', etc. Further, there is no word *ališ*, *äliš*, *alin-*, *älin-*, etc. (unless the initial

---

[2] Also known as East Turki. See Pritsak (1959) and Poppe (1965) for more information on this interesting language. Many irrelevant complications in the statement of vowel harmony and related processes in Mod. Uighur have been ignored in the following account; they do not, I believe, obscure its basic correctness.

[3] The use of braces in this rule indicates that it is satisfied if either of the terms in braces is present. The term '$(C_0 i)_0$' means 'skip over as many syllables whose vowel is *i* as possible.'

vowel is stressed). Clearly Modern Uighur has a rule of Umlaut, according to which *a* and *ä* are replaced by *e* in this environment:

$$(3)^4 \qquad \begin{bmatrix} +\text{syll} \\ +\text{low} \end{bmatrix} \longrightarrow \begin{bmatrix} -\text{back} \\ -\text{low} \end{bmatrix} / \#C_0 \begin{bmatrix} \underline{\hspace{2cm}} \\ -\text{stress} \end{bmatrix} C \; i$$

It is the interaction of this rule with the vowel harmony rule that is of interest to us here. This interaction can be observed when we add a harmonizing suffix to a stem within which rule (3) has applied: we get *elinmaq* 'to be taken (verbal noun)' by adding the nominalizing suffix *-maq / -mäq* to the stem *elin-*, underlying /al+in/. From a stem whose underlying vowel is *ä*, however, such as *bär-* 'give', a parallel formation gives suffixes with front vowels: *berilgän*, from /bär+il/ plus *-gan / -gän*.

Elements of the form $\#C_0 \breve{e} CiC_0$-, then, are apparently exceptions to the principle of vowel harmony, in that their harmonic behavior cannot be predicted from their surface form. Given a particular stem with the shape $C_0 \breve{e} CiC_0$, it is not possible to tell whether it will take front or back vowel affixes, unless one considers other forms of the same root that indicate whether the vowel of the first syllable is /a/, /ä/, or /e/. Taken in conjunction with rule (3), however, the generalization expressed by rule (2) is valid: if we 'subtract' the effect of rule (3), and distinguish underlying /a/ from /ä/ and /e/, vowel harmony is predictable on the basis of these representations: back-harmonic $C_0 \breve{e} CiC_0$ is really $/C_0 \breve{a} CiC_0/$, while front-harmonic forms have underlying front vowels. Vowel harmony as expressed by a rule like (2) is not a valid statement about phonetic forms in isolation; only by considering it in its interaction with the Umlaut rule can we arrive at a correct statement of vowel harmony.

We must now begin to inquire about how the interaction of rules should be formalized in phonological theory. Within taxonomic phonemic theory, of course, more than one rule could apply to a given form: in general, in fact, one rule would have to apply for each phonemic segment, specifying its phonetic realization. But here the interaction among the rules is particularly simple. Given the constraint that the information required to determine the phonemic (respectively, phonetic) element corresponding to any given phonetic (respectively, phonemic) element must be entirely phonetic (respectively, phonemic), rules must be related in a particular way. No rule should apply so as to destroy any informa-

---

[4] For most Modern Uighur dialects, this rule applies only in initial syllables. In others it has been generalized to apply in medial unstressed syllables as well. In the latter case, the $\#C_0$ can be omitted from the rule.

tion which may be required by any other rule, and further, no rule can make use of any new information which another rule has supplied. These conditions can most satisfactorily be met if we apply all of the rules simultaneously, that is, to the same representation. Thus, all rules have exactly the same information to go on, and no rule can be said to apply 'before' another rule, in the sense that the other rule presupposes information which is only provided by the operation of the first rule.

By discarding the strong constraints imposed in taxonomic theory on the phonemic level, we are no longer automatically assured a priori that this mode of application is appropriate. We are by no means, however, assured of the opposite, that this mode of operation is *not* appropriate. For example, an analysis of Russian involving a unitary voicing assimilation rule is, as we saw in Chapter 3, inconsistent with the requirements of a taxonomic phonemic level; nonetheless, this analysis is perfectly consistent with the simultaneous application of phonological rules. If we say 'obstruents take on the voicing of the last member of an obstruent cluster of which they are members' (making reservations for the peculiar behavior of *v* noted above), this rule can perfectly well be applied simultaneously to all phonemic elements in a given representation.

A somewhat more complicated case is presented by examples such as that of Modern Uighur just discussed. While the Russian example involves only one rule, this involves at least the two rules of vowel harmony and Umlaut. Let us see what happens if, instead of applying the rules simultaneously, we apply them one after another; that is, apply one to the representation created by applying the other. If we apply vowel harmony first to /al+in+mʌq/,[5] this will yield /al+in+maq/; applying Umlaut to this will yield the correct [elinmaq]. If we had applied the rules in the opposite order, however, we would first have converted /al+in+mʌq/ to /el+in+mʌq/, and vowel harmony could not now apply correctly; instead *[elinmäq] would result.

Arguments similar to that of the preceding paragraph are occasionally found in the literature to support the conclusion that rules must apply in an order. [An example that comes perilously close is found in Chapter 10 of Mathews (1972).] But notice that no such result follows from this example: the correct results could equally well have been obtained by applying the rules simultaneously to the phonemic representation /al+in+mʌq/, without involving any intermediate step. The only thing shown by an example of this form is that, if the rules are to apply in an

---

[5] The symbol ʌ is employed here to indicate the harmonizing vowel that is either *a* or *ä*, depending on the stem. This device is used simply to avoid taking a stand on issue of the underlying backness of such vowels, not to imply an incompletely specified segment.

order, it can make a difference which order they apply in. Such an example, then, is counterevidence against a procedure of applying the rules one after another, but in a completely random order: any ordered application of rules (2) and (3) must ensure that rule (2) precedes. But, while this example is certainly consistent with ordered application of the rules, it does not by any means require it. Neither of the rules involved presupposes any information which is only provided by the other; it is simply the case that one of the rules (Umlaut) must apply so as not to destroy some information needed by the other.

Now if it were generally possible to apply the rules of a grammar simultaneously, this would presumably be an important positive step, since it would place very narrow constraints on the way rules can interact, and accordingly limit the class of possible grammars. Such a requirement would be a substantive addition to linguistic theory. Unfortunately, there are numerous examples which show it to be incorrect, and which demonstrate the need to apply rules in an order in at least some cases. We have already considered two such examples in the preceding: the cases of the deaspiration in Sanskrit, and of epenthesis and devoicing in English inflection. In each of these cases, one of the rules cannot be stated in a general form unless it is allowed to make use of information provided by the other, a situation which is formalizable by having the 'presupposing' rule apply not to the underlying form, but to the representation created by the operation of the other. In the case of the Sanskrit rules, the rule which must apply first is the one deaspirating stops before another obstruent or finally ("cluster deaspiration", or *DaC* as it will be called in some places below), and the rule which must apply second is the one which removes initial aspiration if root-final aspiration remains (Grassmann's law, or GL). This is because, as noted above in the discussion of this example, Grassmann's law can only be stated generally if by the time it applies all of the root-final aspirates that are to be deaspirated are identifiable, so they can be excluded from serving as environments for the rule. In other words, Grassmann's law must 'know', at the time it applies, which root-final aspirates will be turned into plain stops by cluster deaspiration. If both rules are to apply to the same representations, the environment of cluster deaspiration will have to be built into Grassmann's law, as a negative condition, as well as appearing as a separate rule. This is obviously to miss the generalization.

A similar situation obtains in the rules for English inflection (4.8). Here it is the voicing assimilation rule that must apply after the epenthesis, because final obstruents meeting the conditions for (4.8b) only assimilate to the voicing of a preceding obstruent if they will remain adjacent to it in the output. That is, if epenthesis (4.8a) breaks up a cluster, there is no assimilation, and we always have a voiced segment in the inflectional ending. Thus, we have [čərčɨz], not *[čərčɨs], where we would expect the latter if the rules applied either in the order (4.8b)–(4.8a), or simultaneously. Again, information provided by one rule (epenthesis) is crucial to the operation of the other (voicing assimilation).

We can conclude from these examples, then, that the premise underlying the hypothesis of simultaneous application is false: that no rule makes crucial use of the effects of another. We can suggest, therefore, that the rules apply in a sequence, with each rule applying to the output of the preceding one. This mode of operation allows a given rule to have access, not to the underlying representation, but to a representation which has already been affected by the operation of other rules. There are, however, a vast range of alternatives consistent with this and it will be our business in much of what follows to examine several of these and to refine our notion of rule interaction.

One possibility, for instance, can be (and was, above) discarded: it might be the case that the rules apply in a sequence, but one whose specific order is random. That is, the rules apply randomly until no more can apply. In order for this to be the case, it would have to be the case that the rules of a grammar are such that all possible orderings of rules give the same result (assuming that each underlying form has a unique phonetic form). We have already seen that this condition, which is quite close in effect to that of the simultaneous mode of application, is not satisfied in natural languages: the rules of East Turki, which were consistent with simultaneous application, were not consistent with random sequential application. We can therefore forget about this possibility.

If, therefore, a specific order of application must be provided for the rules, we can now inquire into the question of whether this order is a property of specific grammars of specific languages, or whether rather it is predictable or specifiable in general terms within linguistic theory. For the observation that the order must be nonrandom does not entail the conclusion that it must be language-particular; it might well be that some set of general principles could be established such that, given a set of rules, it is possible to specify their order of application without reference to the specific facts of the language.

In order to disconfirm this possibility, it is not, of course, adequate simply to point to cases where no apparent principle can be found to account for the observed ordering relation. The fact that one has not yet been found hardly shows that it could not exist. The strongest form of counterevidence to such a theory would come in the form of two distinct grammars, each containing the same rules, identical in all relevant respects except that one order of the rules is necessary in one grammar, and the other order is necessary in the other. If this were to be shown, it would be impossible to maintain the claim that order is never an explicit property of particular grammars.

In fact, cases of this sort apparently exist, and have been reported from time to time in the literature. An excellent example is found in Keyser (1963). Keyser discusses some low-level phonetic facts about American English dialects, and shows that these can be interestingly explicated by positing phonological rules, which differ slightly in form and order from dialect area to dialect area. He discusses, among other things, the pronunciation of the /ai/ and /au/ diphthongs in several areas. These can be assumed to be systematically /ai/ and /au/ in all areas, but show interesting phonetic variations, depending on the one hand on the following consonantism, and on the other on the second element of the diphthong. Four sets of forms are presented in (4):

(4) a. Charleston: [fa·ɨv] 'five' [daun] 'down'
              [twɐɨs] 'twice' [ɐut] 'out'
     b. New Bern: [fa·ɛv] [dæ·un]
              [twa·ɛs] [æ·ut]
     c. Winchester: [fa·ɛv] [dæ·un]
              [twɐɨs] [ɐ·ut]
     d. Roanoke: [faiv] [dæun]
              [twɐis] [æut]

We assume the underlying forms of these words are /faiv/, /daun/, /twais/, and /aut/, respectively.[6] Ignoring the variations in vowel length and in the quality of the second elements, it is apparent that a small set of principles governs the quality of the nuclear vowels. One of these principles is illustrated in (4a), the dialect of Charleston: here there is apparently a principle backing /a/ in diphthongs to [ɐ] when a voiceless consonant follows:

(5) $a \longrightarrow ɐ$ / _____ $\begin{bmatrix} +\text{sonorant} \\ +\text{high} \end{bmatrix}$ [−voice]

This rule is no doubt a part of the general process of laxing of diphthongs and other vowels before voiceless segments, but can be considered in isolation here.

---

[6] These 'underlying forms' may well not be the phonemic forms, but rather a relatively late stage of derivation. It is possible, for instance, that a synchronic rule of vowel shift is involved in the derivation of these diphthongs (see Chomsky & Halle, 1968) from sources such as /i:/ and /u:/. This is irrelevant to our discussion, however.

In the forms in (4b), from New Bern, on the other hand, we do not see the operation of rule (5), but we do see that the vowels in the *au* diphthongs are systematically distinct from the vowels in the *ai* diphthongs: here there is apparently a fronting rule:

(6)   a ⟶ æ / _____ u

Now in the dialect of Winchester (4c), the effects of *both* rules can be seen. The significant form to notice here is [ɐ·ut], where both (5) and (6) could apply. Since the vowel quality is [ɐ], as produced by rule (5), we must assume either that (5) applies first, and removes the vowel from the domain of (6), or that (5) applies to cancel the output of (6), being applicable to either *a* or *æ*. Either assumption is possible; let us accept, with Keyser, the position that (5) and (6) apply only to *a*, and accordingly that (5) precedes (6) in Winchester.

Both (5) and (6) can also be seen to apply in the data from Roanoke (4d), as well. But there is a significant difference: *out* is pronounced [æut] in Roanoke, showing that here rule (6) takes precedence over rule (5), the opposite situation to that obtaining in Winchester. Apparently, then, rules (5) and (6) apply here as well, but in the opposite order. There are certainly other differences between the two dialects, but none that appear germane to the operation of the two rules in question: the point is that one rule prevails (in cases where both are applicable) in the one dialect, while the other rule prevails in the other dialect. This is exactly what is meant when we say that the two rules apply in different orders in the grammars of the two dialects.

Other examples of the same sort have been cited at various times in the literature. A particularly clear case is found in Vogt's (1970) discussion of Catalan, based on data from Fabra (1912, 1914). In Catalan, clitic pronouns can appear either before or after the verb. In all cases except after a verb ending in a consonant, they lose their vowel: thus, /me/, /nos/, /lo/, /los/, /ne/, etc. become /m/, /ns/, /l/, /ls/, /n/, etc. Now in case they are preceded by a vowel (i.e., when they appear after a vowel-final verb), they retain this form. In other cases, however, an epenthetic vowel is inserted to 'support' clusters in initial position or finally after a consonant. Vogt shows clearly that the underlying forms of the pronouns must be taken to be those with full vowels, and gives the epenthesis rule, which can be stated as follows:

(7)   Ø ⟶ ə / # _____ [−syllabic] (#) [−syllabic]

This rule requires some refinement, in order to restrict it to clitics, final clusters (which cannot be more than two consonants in length) and initial clusters whose second element is an obstruent, but we will ignore that here. Rule (7), then, converts /m/ to /əm/ before a consonant initial verb, converts /ls/ to /əls/ anywhere, etc. The interesting forms are those of the pronoun /vos/. In positions in which the vowel is lost in this form, standard Catalan does not show the expected [əvs], with truncation and epenthesis, but rather [us]. This is due to the operation of a rule turning *v* to *u* before consonants, a rule which is independently needed in Catalan to explain alternations like (8):

(8) a. [bláu] (masc.)   [bláβə] (fem.)   [bláus] (pl.)   'blue'
     b. [bíu]   [bíβə]   [bíus]   'alive'
     c. [jəlíu]   [jəlíwə]   [jəlíus]   'frigid'

In (8a,b) we see stems ending in *v* (/blav/, /biv/), which are distinct from stems like that in (8c) (/jeliw/) in the feminine forms. Given a rule of vocalization, such as (9), we can easily explain the appearance of [us] as the reduced form of /vos/:

$$(9) \qquad \begin{bmatrix} +\text{cont} \\ +\text{voice} \\ +\text{labial} \end{bmatrix} \longrightarrow u \ / \ \underline{\qquad} \begin{Bmatrix} C \\ \# \end{Bmatrix}$$

/vos/ is reduced to /vs/ by the rule of truncation, and then /vs/ becomes /us/ by rule (9). At this point, the form will no longer meet the conditions for the application of rule (7), and we will get [us] rather than [əus]. In order for this explanation to hold, it is of course necessary that rule (9) precede rule (7) in the grammar.

While these are the facts obtaining in standard Catalan, things are slightly different in Barcelona: the rules (7) and (9), as well as the truncation rule and all of the other rules of standard Catalan hold here, but with one difference. The reduced form of /vos/ initially is not [us], but [əus]. A ready explanation for this is available, of course: In Barcelona Catalan, rule (7) applies before, rather than after rule (9). Thus, /vos/ becomes /vs/ by truncation, which becomes /əvs/ by rule (7), and then [əus] by rule (9). This seems a natural account of the rather minor difference between the two forms of the language, and again presents us with two grammars which are identical in all relevant respects except for the ordering of two rules.

Examples such as those just discussed argue that it must be possible for grammars of particular languages to contain explicit ordering restrictions, since there are evidently cases in which no unitary principle can predict the order in which the rules will apply. To argue that order is sometimes an independent variable, however, is not to claim that it is never possible to predict the order of rules in a grammar from their form and effects. Much of our discussion in the chapters to follow will be devoted, in fact, to the investigation of principles for predicting the 'natural' order for a given set of rules. It will be shown that there are cases in which it is not only possible to predict order, but indeed necessary to do so, since no single explicit ordering statement can account for all of the facts. But again, to observe that some orderings are predictable is not to show that all orderings are, any more than the opposite is true. Several recent papers (e.g., Vennemann, 1971; Koutsoudas, Sanders, & Noll, 1971) have claimed that phonological theory can predict all ordering relationships in a grammar. This seems much too strong; and indeed, it is not particularly plausible, in the face of the full range of arbitrary and ad hoc facts presented by virtually any natural language when taken in its entirety. It is only when one focuses on a narrow collection of facts, chosen specifically for their general and interesting nature, that such a claim has even surface plausibility.

It is worth noting in passing that the observation that the rules of the grammar apply in an order, with the output of one serving as the input to the next, makes extremely reasonable our assumption that the same set of features characterizes both underlying and surface representations. If the output of one rule is the input of another, it is clear that the inputs and outputs of rules form a homogeneous class. Of course, it is possible that the grammar contains a set of rules at the very end which turn all of the features employed in phonemic and later representations into features from a distinct set; but in a grammar of this type, this would be a distinct complication. The most natural situation would be if such a set of rules were not necessary, and the same set of features characterized both phonemic and phonetic forms. Thus, the assumptions that the rules apply in an order and that the same set of features characterizes all levels of representation are complementary. In a grammar the rules of which all apply simultaneously, on the other hand, there is no reason for there to be any overlap between phonemic and phonetic features, since no rule's output is ever part of another rule's input. Indeed, this might be cited as another part of the complex motivation for the position of taxonomic phonemics: the desire to avoid 'mixing levels' entailed a strict separation of phonemic and phonetic features, at least in systematic status, and this nonoverlap between the two sets suggests rules which apply simultaneously (or, rather, the equivalent constraint that no rule provide information which is necessary for another rule, and thus that all information needed to determine the operation of any rule be present in the input representation alone).

We can accept the following model of the phonological component of a grammar, then: such a grammar contains two levels of representation, the phonemic and phonetic (as characterized in Chapters 1 and 3); there is a set of morpheme structure conditions which define the set of well-formed phonemic representations; and there is a set of phonological rules which convert phonemic representations into phonetic forms. The phonological rules apply according to the following principle, the hypothesis of linear order:

(10)   *The rules apply in an order, with each rule applying to the form produced by the application of the previous rule. The grammar specifies an arrangement of rules in a linear list; and each rule applies after all of the rules which precede it on the list, and before any of the rules which follow it on the list. No rule appears more than once on the list.*

It must be emphasized that this principle is an empirical hypothesis, and that there are many ways in which it could be falsified. The evidence we have provided so far suggests such a principle, but, needless to say, it is also consistent with many other hypotheses. Among the ways in which (10) could prove to be false are the following:

1. It might turn out to be the case that there are some rules in natural languages that cannot be ordered with respect to one another. This should be kept distinct from the case in which the order of some pair of rules makes no difference: in that case, (10) can be trivially satisfied by any order. Rather, we are imagining a case in which information needed for two distinct rules is present in the same level of representation, and either rule, by its application, will destroy the information required by the other. In such a case, obviously, no order of application will yield the correct results. We consider the possibility of such a situation arising in natural languages in Chapter 7.

2. It might be the case that some rule R_1 provides information required by some other rule R_2, and hence must precede R_2 in the ordering; but also, some information which R_2 needs is no longer present after R_1 applies, either because R_1 destroyed it, or because R_1 must apply after some R_0 which destroyed it. In this case, the problem is that no single level of representation is adequate to define the operation of R_2. A case of this sort has been suggested recently in the literature (see Kisseberth, 1971), but the facts are not yet sufficiently well established to demonstrate conclusively the need for rules of this type. If they do prove to be necessary, one would hope that restrictions can be placed on

the range of representations which a rule can 'consult'; perhaps only the underlying phonemic form, in addition to the immediately preceding stage of the derivation, could be relevant. Much more investigation of this possibility remains to be carried out.

3. Less radically, it might turn out to be the case that for any single form, an order can be provided for the rules that will give the correct result, but the required order for some forms is distinct from that for others. That is, R_1 may precede R_2 in some derivations, but follow it in others. Or it might be that R_1 precedes R_2, and R_2 precedes R_3, but R_3 precedes R_1. These and other situations would all be inconsistent with the single linear order suggested in (10); we will argue below that such cases do indeed exist, and that they motivate a fundamental revision of (10).

We will, however, accept the model of phonology incorporating (10) as a temporary framework for examining certain theoretical problems. In the following chapters, we will discuss a number of problem areas, some of which suggest revisions of this model, and some of which simply fill it in with further detail.

PART II

FORMAL ASPECTS
OF PHONOLOGICAL THEORY

CHAPTER 6

Formal Resemblances
among Rules
and Descriptive Simplicity

In Part I, we established the notions of representations in phonology and of rules to relate one representation to another, but we have so far said nothing principled about the form these rules are to take. In presenting rules above, we have employed without discussion a notation which represents a highly developed and articulated theory of rule operation (that of Chomsky & Halle, 1968). It will be our purpose in the following chapters to examine the details of this theory, and to propose elaborations and corrections to it where necessary.

The basic form of a phonological rule is clear: it must specify the class of strings (phonological representations, taken as concatenated sequences of segments and boundary elements) to which the rule applies, and it must specify the change the rule makes in them. It consists, therefore, of a structural description (SD) and structural change (SC). We could write such a rule in the general form (1):

(1) $$X \, A \, Y \longrightarrow X \, B \, Y$$

In such a formulation, A, B, X, and Y stand for arbitrary substrings (perhaps null) of a phonological string. The rule specifies that the class of representations meeting the SD of the rule are those containing $X \, A \, Y$ as a substring; and that the structural change that is to be performed is the replacement of A in the input string by B in the output. We could also write the same operation as (2):

(2) $A \longrightarrow B \mid X \underline{\qquad} Y$

This is exactly equivalent to (1), and we can regard rules written in form (2) as representing rules of form (1). The only reason for preferring form (2) is that, in general, we restrict the change made by a given rule so that it affects only one segment, and the formulation (2) makes that clearer. There are cases, however, in which this restriction does not hold. Examples are rules of metathesis; rules specifying the coalescence of two segments into one, including rules where a segment is deleted with compensatory lengthening of another segment; and some assimilation processes. Accordingly, a formulation more like (1) will be used for such cases. An example will appear in the discussion of Finnish consonant gradation below, and other rules in various places.

We assume that the elements in the SD and the SC of a rule, unlike the segments in a phonological representation, are only partially specified. That is, a given element in the SD of a rule is specified by the minimal number of features necessary to restrict the rule's operation to the appropriate segment or class of segments. Any representation containing elements which satisfy the SD of the rule as a submatrix, then, is subject to the rule. The SC of a rule similarly specifies the minimal number of features that must be altered in the input string in order to yield the appropriate output. Features not mentioned in the SC of the rule are assumed to be unaffected by its operation, and to be the same in both input and output, with one exception. This exception arises through certain formal properties of the feature system, by which certain feature specifications are incompatible with one another: for example, a segment cannot be simultaneously [+high] and [+low], since the tongue body cannot be both raised and lowered from a neutral position simultaneously. It must be emphasized that this is not a fact about particular languages, but about the feature system itself, and the definition of the feature system must contain specifications of such incompatibilities. They are to be strictly distinguished from language particular incompatibilities: for instance, in many languages, there are no [−low] vowels that disagree in the features [±back] and [±round]. This is not a fact about the feature system, however, because there are, of course, many languages that do have [−low, +back, −round] vowels, for instance. Incompatibilities due to the structure of the feature system, such as the impossibility of [+high, +low], we assume to be corrected by a convention reflecting these universal facts. Thus, when a rule makes a segment

[+low], we assume that it is also specified as [−high] without the rule's needing to mention this fact explicitly. In a language whose nonlow vowels agree in backness and rounding, however, we shall assume that it is, nonetheless, necessary for a rule which makes vowels [−back] to specify further that they are [−round] (if any [+round] vowels would fall under the rule), since this is a language particular fact. In Chapter 15 we consider ways in which such language particular redundancies might be incorporated into the statement of rules, but for the present we will assume the position just given.

It has often been argued (e.g., Halle, 1962; Chomsky & Halle, 1965; Chomsky, 1967) that linguistic theory must provide not only a framework in which all possible processes that might be found in a natural language can be expressed, but also some way to decide, given two or more distinct accounts of some linguistic fact or process, which is the most natural, in the sense of embodying the most linguistically significant generalizations. It is necessary, then, to have a way of comparing the degree of generality of two (or more) rules or sets of rules. If we can give a principled basis for choosing, in any such case, one of the descriptions over the others, such that our choice is consistently confirmed by additional evidence where such is available, our theory can be said to have captured a fundamental aspect of the structure of natural languages: namely, what makes them natural. There are, of course, fundamental issues of method that are unjustifiably assumed to be decided here: it is assumed for one, that agreement can be reached on what is a linguistically significant generalization; for another, that such agreement, when reached among linguists, corresponds in some interesting sense with what is indeed natural in language; and so on. We accept here the desirability of giving a principled basis for choosing, from a set of alternative possibilities, that description which maximizes the degree of significant generalization: it is hoped that, where the notion plays an important role below, the reader's judgments on these issues will coincide with ours (and that both reflect real properties of human languages).

To some extent, the use of a feature system for the statement of representations and rules helps us to accomplish the goal of providing such a basis for comparison of the degree of generality of two formulations. Since the features in such a system are defined on the basis of the properties that play a role in language structures, they admit of a fairly straightforward definition of the degree of generality achieved in the specification of a class of segments which plays a part in a rule: of two given classes, the one which is definable in terms of the smaller number of such features is the more general. There are, of course, a number of problems with this measure of generality: all features are not strictly comparable, and some are more general than others. Nonetheless, this definition appears to make many choices correctly, and it serves as a useful first approximation. On the basis of it, we can go on to define at least part of the notion of the generality of a rule: of two proposed rules, the one statable in terms of more general classes (and hence, by the above definition, the one formulated in terms of the smallest number of feature specifications) is the more general. Again, numerous problems arise when we try to compare sets of rules on the basis of simply counting features: are two rules, containing a total of n features, more or less general than a single rule containing n features? How do we compare a rule using an additional feature with a rule using an additional notational device of the sort to be discussed below? Are features specified by variable coefficients (as will be discussed in Chapter 7) more or less general than features specified by constant coefficients ($+$ or $-$)? But again, this definition of generality serves as a useful first approximation to the definition of naturalness of a rule or set of rules. As has frequently been pointed out, it is of course only applicable to the comparison of alternatives for the formulation of some subpart of a grammar, such that each formulation accounts for the same range of basic data; it makes no sense to speak of using a procedure of this sort to compare, say, the naturalness of a grammar of English with that of grammar of Abaza.

In addition to expressing the naturalness of a set of segments in a phonological formulation, we want to be able to express the extent to which a set of strings, which are found in distinct rules, are naturally related. For example, if a language has two or more rules according to which segment a is replaced by b in several distinct environments, we want to express the extent to which these environments form a coherent or natural class. That is, given the two sets of rules in (3), we want to express the sense in which we feel that (3b) is more natural than (3a):

(3)   a. $a \longrightarrow b \mid c \underline{\quad} d$ b. $a \longrightarrow b \mid c \underline{\quad} d$
                $a \longrightarrow b \mid e \underline{\quad} f$ $a \longrightarrow b \mid c \underline{\quad} e$
                $a \longrightarrow b \mid g \underline{\quad} h$ $a \longrightarrow b \mid c \underline{\quad} f$

In (3b), the process '$a \rightarrow b$' applies after a c, and before any of d, e, or f; in (3a), on the other hand, there is no relation among the environments. The environments of (3b) are, in that case, more coherent and hence more natural.

This fact can be explicated on the basis of the formal resemblance among the rules. If we had some way of saying that the c in (3b) only 'counts' once, since the same element is repeated in the same position in each rule, and then counting features, the rule set (3b) would be evaluated as more natural than (3a). To express this, we introduce the following NOTATIONAL CONVENTION, defining the notation of curly brackets: If two adjacent[1] strings (representing formally specified rules) in the grammar Σ_1 and Σ_2 differ from one another only in that $\Sigma_1 =$ 'As_1B', while $\Sigma_2 = $ 'As_2B', where A and B are arbitrary strings of symbols (perhaps null), and s_1 and s_2 are arbitrary (nonnull) strings, the pair $\Sigma_1\Sigma_2$ can be abbreviated as '$A\{{}^{s_1}_{s_2}\}B$'. The notation extends in the obvious way to more than two strings. Given the rules in (3), then, we can abbreviate them by means of this convention as in (4):

(4) a. $a \longrightarrow b \ / \ \begin{Bmatrix} c \underline{\quad} d \\ e \underline{\quad} f \\ g \underline{\quad} h \end{Bmatrix}$ b. $a \longrightarrow b \ / \ c \underline{\quad} \begin{Bmatrix} d \\ e \\ f \end{Bmatrix}$

We call the expressions in (4) RULE SCHEMATA, and regard them functionally as abbreviations for the rule sets in (3). If, however, we perform the feature counting operation in terms of which we are to evaluate complexity on the schemata in (4), rather than on the sets of 'elementary' rules in (3), we will (ex hypothesi, correctly) evaluate (4b) as more general than (4a). This notational convention, then, makes the claim that a certain formal resemblance between adjacent rules (their sharing a subpart) contributes to the generality of a set of rules. We could, of course, make up any number of other notational conventions, allowing us to combine rules on the basis of virtually any formal property: the choice of the specific definition given for the curly brackets notation above makes some specific predictions, and it is necessary to confirm that these are correct before we can accept the notational device as a systematic part of linguistic theory. If we do not find preferences for rules that can be abbreviated in this way over otherwise similar rules that cannot, but instead find a preference for rules of the form (5a), this might induce us to abandon the definition given above in favor of one that allows us to abbreviate (5a) as (5b):

(5) a. $a \longrightarrow b \ / \ x \underline{\quad} y$ b. $a \longrightarrow b \longrightarrow c \longrightarrow d \ / \ \begin{Bmatrix} x \underline{\quad} y \\ e \underline{\quad} f \\ g \underline{\quad} h \end{Bmatrix}$
      $b \longrightarrow c \ / \ e \underline{\quad} f$
      $c \longrightarrow d \ / \ g \underline{\quad} h$

---

[1] 'Adjacent' here means 'constituting successive rules in an ordering permitted by principle (5.10).' When this principle is modified below, it will be necessary to provide a sense of adjacency for the curly bracket and other notations.

As an example of rules employing the curly bracket notation as defined above, let us consider the well-known process of consonant gradation in Finnish. As a result of this rule, the following changes take place in stops at the beginning of a noninitial short closed syllable:

(6)   a.   Geminate stops (*pp, tt, kk*) are simplified to single stops (*p, t, k*).
      b.   Single stops assimilate completely to a preceding liquid or nasal with which they agree in point of articulation (i.e., *mp, nt, ŋk, rt, lt* become *mm, nn, ŋŋ, rr, ll*, but, e.g., *lk* does not become *ll*).
      c.   Except as provided in *b*, single stops are affected as follows: *p* becomes *v*; *t* becomes *d*; *k* becomes *j* after *h* or after a liquid before *e*; *k* becomes *v* between two high rounded vowels; and *k* becomes Ø elsewhere.

From the effects of the rule as given in (6), a certain amount of detail can be abstracted in order to arrive at a view of the gradation process itself. In particular, the complex reflexes of gradated *k* can be ascribed to a set of rules which are distinct from the primary process. Let us suppose, then, that the gradation rule converts *p, t,* and *k* into voiced segments; continuant for *p* and *k*, and noncontinuant for *t*. They thus become β, *d*, and γ, and later rules perform the following operations:

(7)   a.   Gamma-adjustment:

$$[\gamma] \longrightarrow \left\{ \begin{array}{l} [\beta] \ / \ \begin{bmatrix} +\text{high} \\ +\text{round} \end{bmatrix} \underline{\qquad} \begin{bmatrix} +\text{high} \\ +\text{round} \end{bmatrix} \\ [j] \ / \ \left\{ \begin{array}{l} [h] \ \underline{\qquad} \\ [l] \ \underline{\qquad} [e] \end{array} \right\} \\ \text{Ø} \end{array} \right\}$$

      b.   Beta-adjustment:
$$[\beta] \longrightarrow [v]$$

We could then distinguish two kinds of gradation behavior: either the stop becomes a voiced segment of some kind [as in (6b) and (6c)], or it disappears. If the assimilations in (6b) are treated as a special case of the same voicing process that produces (6c) [after the rules in (7) have applied to its immediate outputs β, *d*, and γ], we will need an assimilation rule, such as (8)[2]:

(8) Sonorant assimilation:

$$
\begin{bmatrix} +\text{cons} \\ -\text{obst} \\ \alpha\text{coronal} \end{bmatrix} \begin{bmatrix} +\text{obst} \\ +\text{voice} \\ \alpha\text{coronal} \end{bmatrix}
$$

$$
\begin{array}{cc} 1 & 2 \\ \Rightarrow \quad 1 & 1 \end{array}
$$

Having posited rules (7) and (8) to account for much of the effect of gradation, there are two distinct possibilities for an account of the remaining parts of the rule. The first, and perhaps most obvious possibility, is to write two rules, one of which makes single stops voiced (and, if noncoronal, continuant), and the other of which deletes one of a pair of identical stops. Such a pair of rules is given in (9):

(9) a. $\begin{bmatrix} -\text{cont} \\ -\text{voice} \end{bmatrix} \longrightarrow$

$\begin{bmatrix} +\text{voice} \\ \langle+\text{cont}\rangle \end{bmatrix} / [-\text{obst}] \begin{bmatrix} \underline{\hspace{1cm}} \\ \langle-\text{cor}\rangle \end{bmatrix} [+\text{syll}][-\text{syll}] \begin{Bmatrix} [-\text{syll}] \\ \# \end{Bmatrix}$

   b. $\begin{bmatrix} -\text{cont} \\ -\text{voice} \end{bmatrix} \longrightarrow \emptyset / \begin{bmatrix} -\text{cont} \\ \alpha\text{cor} \end{bmatrix} \underline{\hspace{1cm}}_{\alpha\text{cor}} [+\text{syll}][-\text{syll}] \begin{Bmatrix} [-\text{syll}] \\ \# \end{Bmatrix}$

A number of remarks are in order to explain these rules. First, the use of angle brackets ($\langle$ and $\rangle$) means that either all of the material within such brackets in the rule is present or else all of it is absent; thus, rule (9a) makes the affected segments [+cont] if and only if they are [−cor]. Second, the specification [−obst] in the segment preceding the stop affected in (9a) ensures that only single stops undergo the rule; in clusters following an obstruent other than a homorganic stop, no gradation takes place, and in clusters with a homorganic stop, the degemination case applies instead. The specifications

$$
\text{`}[+\text{syll}]\,[-\text{syll}] \begin{Bmatrix} [-\text{syll}] \\ \# \end{Bmatrix},
$$

---

[2] This rule seems most naturally stated in a transformational format, resembling (1) above rather than the usual (2). No special significance should be associated with this fact, since, as noted, (2) can be regarded as an alternative expression for (1) in any case. The use of the terms [αcoronal], as usual, means that the segments affected by the rule must agree in this feature. It is a fact of Finnish phonology that agreement in point of articulation can be achieved by agreement in the feature [±coronal] alone, since there are no clusters of [−coronal] consonants that disagree in the feature [±anterior].

indicate the structure of a short closed syllable; long vowels in Finnish are represented as a sequence of two identical vowels, and any syllable is closed by a cluster or a word-final consonant.

An alternative view of Finnish gradation has been presented in several papers by McCawley (1964, 1966, 1967a). McCawley argues that the gradation rule is a unitary process, and should not be split up into two rules, as (9) claims. Instead, McCawley proposes that a single gradation rule should exist: voice all stops at the beginning of a noninitial short closed syllable. This would then necessitate additional rules to (a) devoice stops in nongradating positions (i.e., after *s* and *k* in *tk*); (b) delete a voiced stop after a homorganic voiceless one; and (c) convert *b* and *g* into continuants. The entire set of rules would then look like (10). [Recall that (7) and (8) apply after (10), just as they apply after (9)]:

(10)   a.   Gradation:

$$[-\text{cont}] \longrightarrow [+\text{voice}] \:/\: [\text{seg}] \:\underline{\quad}\: [+\text{syll}][-\text{syll}] \left\{ \begin{matrix} [-\text{syll}] \\ \# \end{matrix} \right\}$$

b.   Voiced stop adjustment:

$$\begin{bmatrix} +\text{obst} \\ +\text{voice} \end{bmatrix} \longrightarrow \left\{ \begin{matrix} \text{i.} \;\; [-\text{voice}] \:/\: \begin{bmatrix} +\text{obst} \\ \left\{\begin{matrix} +\text{cont} \\ -\alpha\text{cor} \end{matrix}\right\} \end{bmatrix} \begin{bmatrix} \underline{\quad} \\ \alpha\text{cor} \end{bmatrix} \\ \text{ii.} \quad\;\; \emptyset \quad\; /\: [+\text{obst}] \:\underline{\quad} \\ \text{iii.}\; [+\text{cont}] \:/\: \begin{bmatrix} \underline{\quad} \\ -\text{cor} \end{bmatrix} \end{matrix} \right\}$$

Both analyses [(9)–(8)–(7) and (10)–(8)–(7)] give identical results, but they are not completely equivalent. The analysis with rule (10) claims that gradation is basically the same process in all positions; the analysis with the rules in (9) claims that gradation of geminates is distinct from the gradation of nongeminates. It is important to find some basis for choosing between the two accounts, and this will have to be on the basis of additional data, since both sets of rules account for the primary data of gradation equally well.

One minor difference in favor of rule (9a, b) involves the qualification that gradation only takes place in noninitial syllables. Both rules in (9) are dependent on the character of the segment preceding the stop being affected, and hence each requires there to be a preceding segment. But since there are no initial clusters in Finnish, and since an initial vowel would of course be the initial syllable, the fact that gradation only applies in noninitial syllables follows naturally from other aspects of the formulation of the rule. In (10), on the other hand, this is not the case: it is necessary to include the specification 'after [+segment]' (i.e., after anything, so long as there is some segment there). This remains an arbitrary complication of the rule: in some sense, the restriction to noninitial syllables is explained in rule (9) in a way that it is not in rule (10).

If we perform our feature counting operation on the two possible accounts, we see that the tentative evaluation measure discussed above gives the result that (9) is more general than (10). For the curly brackets notation discussed above allows us to collapse the two rules of (9) into the schema (11):

(11) $\begin{bmatrix} -\text{cont} \\ -\text{voice} \end{bmatrix} \longrightarrow$

$$\begin{Bmatrix} \begin{bmatrix} +\text{voice} \\ \langle +\text{cont}\rangle \end{bmatrix} / [-\text{obst}] \begin{bmatrix} \underline{\hphantom{xx}} \\ \langle -\text{cor}\rangle \end{bmatrix} \\ \emptyset \qquad / \begin{bmatrix} -\text{cont} \\ \alpha\text{cor} \end{bmatrix} \begin{bmatrix} \underline{\hphantom{xx}} \\ \alpha\text{cor} \end{bmatrix} \end{Bmatrix} [+\text{syll}]\,[-\text{syll}] \begin{Bmatrix} [-\text{syll}] \\ \# \end{Bmatrix}$$

The formulation (11) involves 14 features (assuming $\emptyset$ and $\#$ each count as 1). The formulation in (10), on the other hand, involves 18 features. As was mentioned above, feature counting arguments can seldom be taken absolutely literally, but here the complicating factors seem about equally distributed between the two accounts: the comparability of $\emptyset$, $\#$, and feature specifications does not arise, nor does the difference between $[\alpha F]$ and $[+F]$ or $[-F]$, since each rule makes the same amount of use of these devices. In this case, it seems that feature counting must be taken seriously if it is correct anywhere. And the fact that the account involving rule schema (11) involves four fewer features than the account involving the rules of (10), a difference of about 25%, leads us to prefer rule (11).

But so far we have given no empirical evidence for the correctness of the feature-counting procedure. Is there anyplace we can look to confirm it? Clearly the data of gradation itself cannot provide such confirmation, for both accounts deal accurately with this range of facts. There is, fortunately, an additional source of evidence to which we can turn to make a decision in this case. As we will see many times in the subsequent chapters, otherwise valid phonological rules do not always apply to all of the forms in which we would expect to see their operation. It is often necessary to exempt some small and (at least from the synchronic point of view) generally arbitrary set of forms from the operation of a given rule, and for this purpose we assume the grammar to contain rule exception features which can be associated with morphemes in the lexicon. The use and limitations of such features are briefly discussed below, but for now we can accept Halle and Chomsky's suggestion that they are associated with an entire morpheme, and have the effect of preventing the rule in question from altering any segment which is part of a morpheme so marked. We assume the existence of a distinct exception feature (potentially) for each rule of the grammar, and this assumption will occasionally play a role in arguments. That is, if two processes have distinct classes of exceptions, we can take this as evidence that they are in fact two distinct rules in the grammar.

The relevance of exceptions to the treatment of consonant gradation in Finnish is the following: partially assimilated loan words from other languages are often subject to the normal rules of Finnish phonology, including the rules of consonant gradation. Now it is a fact that every word in the language, regardless of the extent to which it is felt to be foreign, is subject to consonant gradation in those forms where the rule would affect a geminate. Thus, *Kalkutta* 'Calcutta' appears as *Kalkutan* in the genitive, where the final *-n* results in a closed syllable, and hence in a gradation environment. Thus, gradation of geminates in roots of all kinds is absolutely exceptionless. Gradation of single stops, on the other hand, has numerous exceptions (especially in nursery words and in the loan vocabulary). Thus, e.g., *auto* 'automobile', *pupu* 'bunny rabbit' have genitives *auton, pupun,* in place of the expected **audon, *puvun*. It is apparent, then, that Finnish words can be marked as exceptions to gradation of single stops, but not of geminates. To state this generalization, however, it is necessary that the rule of gradation for single stops be distinct from that affecting geminates. This is, of course, the case in the analysis based on rule schema (11): some forms are exceptional with respect to the part of it that appears as (9a), but none with respect to the (9b) part. In the analysis based on (10), however, no such statement can be given, since the gradation of geminates is dealt with by the same rule that affects single stops. Either one must include a special rule, which only the exceptional forms undergo, which reverses the effect of gradation in single stops, or one must leave the generalization about exceptions unstated. This is an important flaw in the analysis based on (10), and confirms the feature-counting evaluation measure in preferring (11) to (10) as a description of consonant gradation in Finnish. That is, whereas either of the two is a possible account, given only the data of gradation itself, we can tell when we consider the distribution of exceptions that an analysis distinguishing gradation of geminates from other cases of gradation is to be preferred. This is also the choice made by our tentative evaluation measure by number of features: the data from Finnish thus provide some support for the correctness of the evaluation, at least in cases as limited as this.

We must note, however, that if the rules of gradation in Finnish were stated as in (9) there would be a serious flaw in the analysis. The reason is that both (9a) and (9b) apply in exactly the same environment, and accordingly an analysis expressed as (9) would be missing an important generalization: that both gradation of single stops and gradation of geminates apply at the beginning of a non-initial short closed syllable. When the same statement appears more than once in different parts of the grammar of a language, we can usually suspect that something is being missed. (9a) and (9b) are obviously related, and the fact that they apply in the same environment is no accident. If we were forced to state the environment separately as a part of (9a) and as a part of (9b), however, we would be claiming that this environment was an idiosyncratic fact about each rule, and thus independent of the other rule. This duplication and loss of generality might well lead us to prefer an account like (10); recall that the principal insight underlying this rule set was the claim that gradation was a single unitary process. This is obviously expressed in the fact that the environment only appears once.

The solution to this problem is not, obviously, far to seek: once we have abbreviated (9) as (11), the 'two-rule description of gradation no longer has stated the environment in two distinct places. That is, the duplication of statement is precisely what is eliminated in the application of the curly-bracket notation in forming (11) from (9). The notational convention of curly brackets, then, predicts that duplication of statement only counts against an analysis when it cannot be eliminated by the application of the collapsing process. This process is formally defined on the basis of adjacency in the set of rules and a precise formal resemblance: the claim is thus that exactly when these conditions are met, a grammar can have two rules that partially duplicate one another without being subject to the usual loss of generalization that follows from multiple statement of the same fact. The curly brackets notation is thus essential if the description of gradation as two distinct rules [(9), or its schematic form (11)], which we have seen to be preferred on all other grounds, is even to be a possible analysis.[3]

---

[3] We have, of course, ignored the fact that the environment in both parts of (9) contains another use of curly brackets, in the term 'before nonsyllabic or word boundary'; and also that the notation has been employed in (10) to abbreviate the various fates of voiced stops in various environments. If the rules in question were expanded to the full set of statements eliminating all abbreviatory devices, similar points could be made in favor of the other uses of curly brackets; we have concentrated on this one instance of the notational convention for convenience and clarity. Additional data about Finnish consonant gradation can be found in such standard handbooks as Fromm and Sadeniemi (1956), Sauvageot (1949), etc.; and in Karttunen (1971).

Some writers (most notably McCawley, 1970a) have criticized the use of curly brackets in phonological statements, asserting that they are merely ways of concealing the places in a set of rules where a generalization is in fact being lost. Now evidence against the correctness of the curly brackets notation is rather hard to come by (as is evidence in its favor). This is because, unlike the other notational conventions to be discussed below, it makes no claims about the way grammars must be organized, but simply about the degree of generalization or naturalness of a set of rules. Kiparsky (1968a) has tried to argue from facts of historical change that the curly brackets notation is confirmed by the fact that rules abbreviated by it tend to function as a unit in historical change, but his examples are not unequivocal, and there is little of a strictly necessary character that can be adduced in favor of the use of curly brackets in phonology.

McCawley (1970a) has asserted that, in every case where curly brackets have appeared in phonological statements, one of the following is true: either the rules can be shown to be incorrect on other grounds, and in the correct set of rules no curly brackets appear; or the feature system or other aspects of the formalism underlying the analysis can be shown to be wrong, so that the terms which are disjoined in the curly brackets are expressed by a unitary term when the deficiency is corrected; or in fact the rules so abbreviated have nothing to do with one another, and should not be related in a single schema. Evidently McCawley does not actually go through the hundreds of instances of curly brackets that have appeared in the literature to demonstrate his point, but it is clear that each of his criticisms is valid for at least some examples. The case of Finnish gradation just considered, however, is not obviously vulnerable on any of these counts (it is, of course, *possible* that the rules given above are incorrect, but we know of no evidence which suggests this). Notice, by the way, that the facts which led us to a two rule analysis of gradation implied that a reanalysis, though it need not preserve the rules of (9), must separate two kinds of gradation. In that case, if the curly brackets are to be eliminated, it must either be shown that it is indeed an accident that both rules apply in the same environment, or the analysis must eliminate this environment from one of the rules. Neither prospect seems too hopeful. It is also unlikely that a different view of the feature system would allow us to collapse the two terms in curly brackets into one: these are phonetically quite different effects, and the argument above has been directed toward the proposition that they must be kept distinct. An argument based on the claim that the two parts of gradation are in fact unrelated to one another seems implausible in the extreme.

We conclude, therefore, that there are at least some valid instances of rules abbreviated by the curly bracket notation, since it was necessary to apply this in order to make (9) [in the form (11)] a possible analysis of consonant gradation. It is, nonetheless, true that heavier restrictions probably ought to be placed on its use than has been the practice in the past. Mere adjacency and formal resemblance are obviously not enough to guarantee relatedness among rules, as is claimed by the purely formal statement of the notation. Suppose, for example, that a language has an Umlaut rule such as (12):

$$(12) \qquad [+\text{syll}] \longrightarrow [-\text{back}] / \underline{\quad} C_0 i$$

Suppose further that the language syncopates certain medial vowels, by a rule such as (13):

$$(13) \qquad [+\text{syll}] \longrightarrow \emptyset / VC \underline{\quad} CV$$

If these two rules happen to be adjacent in the grammar of the language, the curly bracket notation permits their abbreviation as the schema (14):

$$(14) \qquad [+\text{syll}] \longrightarrow \begin{Bmatrix} [-\text{back}] / \underline{\quad} C_0 i \\ \emptyset \quad / VC \underline{\quad} CV \end{Bmatrix}$$

Now let us suppose that, as a result of a historical change, the Umlaut rule becomes restricted to nonlow vowels:

$$(15) \qquad \begin{bmatrix} +\text{syll} \\ -\text{low} \end{bmatrix} \longrightarrow [-\text{back}] / \underline{\quad} C_0 i$$

We would now be extremely surprised if the syncope rule were also to reflect the same restriction, with medial low vowels remaining, but nonlow vowels continuing to syncopate. Yet this is exactly the prediction made by the curly brackets notation, insofar as it makes any prediction at all. Clearly the Umlaut and syncope rules have nothing to do with one another, and the fact that they both apply to vowels is a fortuitous resemblance that does not alter that fact. Yet the curly brackets notation as it stands makes no distinction between a case of this sort and one such as the Finnish example where the rules are clearly related as weakening processes. Combinations of such processes as degemination of double stops, voicing of single voiceless stops, spirantization of voiced stops, and disappearance of spirants are bound together, functioning as units in large numbers of languages,[4] and it is impossible to deny a connection among them: exactly the fact that they are all 'weakening' processes. It would seem reasonable to restrict the use of curly brackets to cases of this sort, where some general relation can be found between the items disjoined in the resulting schema. Such a restriction, however, must await a much more sophisticated typology of phonological processes than is available to us at our present stage of knowledge of phonological structures. As was mentioned above, the grammarians of the "Handbook of American Indian Languages" seemed to have some such notion of phonological typology in mind; another effort in that direction [according to Jakobson's (1971) interpretation] was Kruszevski and Baudouin de Courtenay's work on alternations. Some further remarks are made on this subject in Chapter 15, but we have no substantive proposals to make here. The formulation and testing of such typological proposals, on the basis of data available from large numbers of languages, remains, no doubt, the most important descriptive task facing future researchers in phonology.

---

[4] For a survey of lenition processes of this sort in a number of widely scattered languages, see Ultan (1970).

CHAPTER 7

Formal Resemblances among Rules and the Organization of Grammars

The case which we considered in Chapter 6, like those dealt with earlier, involved rules that applied in an order, according to the principle (5.10). Thus, despite the fact that the subparts of (6.11) are combined by the device of curly brackets into a single schema, the subparts of the schema function independently, and the second subpart (gradation of geminates) is formulated the way it is on the assumption that, at the point at which it applies, the first subpart will already have applied. Once the first part of the rule applies, the only voiceless stops remaining in clusters with homorganic noncontinuants will be part of a geminate, and thus nothing more need be specified to limit the effects of the rule to geminates. The rules could, of course, be so written as to be consistent with some other principle of application, but to do so would be an unnecessary complication, given the motivation that has already been established for a principle of ordering.

The facts that we have given so far do not, of course, establish that *all* rules need to be ordered, or even that all rules *can* be ordered: they only indicate the need for a partial ordering. The principle (5.10), then, is a hypothesis which suggests that in every case in natural language, the required partial ordering can be extended to a complete linear ordering. It is important to consider the sort of evidence that would argue against this proposal.

It is pointed out by Chomsky (1967) that such a claim would be imme-

diately falsified if the following situation were found to obtain in any natural language: suppose the language contains the forms /XAY/ and
/XBY/, such that /XAY/ is realized phonetically as [XBY], and /XBY/
is realized phonetically as [XAY]. Assuming no other relevant complications, this language could be assumed to have phonological rules performing the operations in (1):

(1) a. $A \longrightarrow B \;/\; X \;\underline{\quad}\; Y$

b. $B \longrightarrow A \;/\; X \;\underline{\quad}\; Y$

Obviously, there is no way of ordering these rules with respect to each
other. If (1a) precedes (1b), both /XAY/ and /XBY/ would be neutral-
ized in phonetic [XAY], while if the order is reversed, both will appear
as [XBY]. If examples with this formal character exist in natural languages, they constitute exceptions to a principle of strict linear application, such as (5.10).

The sort of process that is involved can be exemplified in Dinka, a
language of Sudan.[1] In this language there is a complex set of vowel alternations that distinguish singular forms of nouns from plural forms.
Nouns with a long vowel in their singular form have plurals that are
produced by replacing the vowel by the corresponding short vowel:

(2) a. pɛɛi 'moon'; plural pɛi
b. čiin 'hand'; plural čin
c. agəək 'monkey'; plural agək

On the other hand, there is a class of nouns whose singular forms
display short vowels, which form their plurals by lengthening the vowel:

(3) a. pal 'knife'; plural paal
b. atuel 'club'; plural atueel
c. nin 'sleep'; plural niin

Thus, we apparently have the two rules in (4):

(4) a. $\begin{bmatrix} +\text{syll} \\ +\text{long} \end{bmatrix} \longrightarrow [-\text{long}] \;/\; \begin{bmatrix} \underline{\quad\quad} \\ \text{PLURAL} \end{bmatrix}$

b. $\begin{bmatrix} +\text{syll} \\ -\text{long} \end{bmatrix} \longrightarrow [+\text{long}] \;/\; \begin{bmatrix} \underline{\quad\quad} \\ \text{PLURAL} \end{bmatrix}$

---

[1] This example was brought to my attention by M. Halle. Further information about
Dinka can be found in Nebel (1948).

Here we have two rules of the required type, which cannot be ordered in either way with respect to one another.

We note, of course, that the two rules are very similar to one another: they differ only in the values of the coefficients of the feature 'long'. Wherever (4a) contains '+long', (4b) contains '−long', and wherever (4a) contains '−long' (4b) contains '+long'. Independently of ordering considerations such as those that confront us with rules such as those in (4), it was proposed by Halle (1962) that sets of rules with this sort of formal resemblance were frequent in natural language, and that they expressed a generalization. Accordingly another notational convention was defined, based on this resemblance, to capture the similarity between such rules in the same sort of way that the curly braces notation operates. Whenever two rules have the property of identity except that some instances of '+F_i' in one are matched by '−F_i' in the other, they can be abbreviated into a schema by introducing a variable feature coefficient. Such a variable is assumed to take the two values '+' and '−', and to abbreviate a pair of rules, with one obtained by substituting the value '+' for each instance of the variable and the other obtained by substituting '−' for the variable. An algebra of a simple kind is defined over such variables, such that '− − = +', and '− + = −'; they are usually designated in phonological descriptions by Greek letters. Using this convention, the rules in (4) could be combined into the schema in (5):

(5)
$$\begin{bmatrix} +\text{syll} \\ \alpha\text{long} \end{bmatrix} \longrightarrow [-\alpha\text{long}] \; / \; \begin{bmatrix} \underline{\hspace{2cm}} \\ \text{PLURAL} \end{bmatrix}$$

This schema is expanded, by applying the convention just described, into the pair of rules in (4).

The convention of variable coefficients for feature values was originally suggested as a way of capturing the similarity between rules like (4a) and (4b). It was thus a part of the procedure for evaluating alternative formulations as proposed parts of grammars. It filled that function by allowing rules to be collapsed into a schema if they could be formulated in such a way as to have the precisely defined formal property which defines the notation, but not otherwise. This function of evaluation, of course, is completely independent of the actual mode of application of the rules in question. Despite being collapsed into a single schema, the two rules (4) were taken to be individual parts of a grammar of Dinka, just as the two parts (6.9a) and (6.9b) were taken to be separate parts of the grammar of Finnish as far as their operation was concerned.

The significant point made by Chomsky (1967) about these cases was the following: if every case of rules in natural languages which violate the principle of linear ordering were formally similar to that in (4), it would be possible to accommodate them within the theory of grammar by a fairly simple move. Let us modify principle (5.10); instead of saying that all rules are arranged in a linear order, and apply one after another (*conjunctively*), let us say that

(6)   *The rules of a grammar are arranged in a linear order, with each rule applying to the output of the previous rule in the list, except that if two adjacent rules are abbreviable by the convention of variable feature coefficients, they are not applied sequentially, but rather both are applied simultaneously to the representation created by the rule before them on the list. Neither applies to the output of the other, and the next rule on the list applies to the result of their simultaneous application.*

This principle, of course, will give us the right result in the case above. If rules of the form (1) are applied simultaneously, rather than in sequence, the problem of ordering them disappears: only one of the pair can apply to any given form, and the other rule cannot now come afterward to eliminate the effects of the first rule.

The principle (6), of course, is not formally as simple as (5.10). A homogeneous procedure no longer governs the application of all of the rules of the grammar. But the important point to note is this: under principle (6), it is still the case that grammatical theory specifies exhaustively the mode of application of all of the rules of the grammar, and does not leave this as a variable for individual cases in particular languages. That is, given a set of rules, it is never indeterminate how to apply them: if they satisfy the formal requirements of the variable-feature-coefficient notation, apply them simultaneously, and otherwise (even if, for example, they satisfy the curly brackets notation), they are to be applied in sequence. This principle makes the important claim that all and only the exceptions to the principle of linear application of rules will turn out to have a very specific formal property, namely, abbreviability by the convention of variable values for feature coefficients. This use of notational conventions, then, is completely different from the original purpose for which they were devised. Besides stating that sets of rules showing certain formal structural properties express unified generalizations, we are now claiming that these same formal resemblances are also the basis of part of the organization of the grammar. The way the rules are to be interpreted and applied, and not simply the way they are to be evaluated, is to be determined by conventions of notational abbreviation based on purely formal properties.

This important hypothesis, unfortunately, is still in need of definitive verification. The problem is not the existence of cases that are exceptions to linear ordering, but are not abbreviable by the variable-coefficient convention; nor is it cases that are so abbreviable, but which must be applied sequentially rather than simultaneously. Some cases of the former sort are discussed below, and are argued to fall under other generalizations about the organization of grammars. Cases of the second sort apparently do not exist. The problem is rather that the need for such a revision of (5.10) has not been conclusively demonstrated by facts from real languages.

A case such as the Dinka example above cannot be used to show the need for nonsequential application of some rules, because it is not clear that we are indeed dealing with a set of phonological rules. In (2) and (3) above, we do indeed have variations in the shapes of morphemes (between singular and plural forms), but this variation depends solely upon the category PLURAL, and not on any aspect of the phonological environment. There is, thus, no reason to treat this variation as the consequence of phonological rules, rather than as lexically determined morphological variation. Since the plural forms of nouns do not contain any phonological material that is not also present in their singulars, there is no phonetically motivated basis for stating the process in the form of a phonological rule. Futhermore, if such rules were written, it would not be possible to give justification for them such as was provided for the rules dealing with plural forms in English: there are no other elements of Dinka which show a variation in shape that the proposed rules [(4) above] could be used to account for. In short, there is nothing whatever to motivate the phonological rules involved. When we see furthermore that by no means all Dinka nouns form their plurals by switching the length of the root vowel (many undergo a completely different set of changes in vowel quality or replacement of a suffix, or even show completely suppletive forms), it seems perfectly plausible that we are dealing with a case of morpholexical variation, rather than with a phonological rule. The fact that the alternation is somewhat systematic (in those forms in which it occurs) shows that it should not be treated as purely arbitrary suppletion, such as the forms of English *be*; but we saw above in Chapter 4 that there is no a priori reason why morpholexical statements [such as the account (4.5) of English plurals] cannot be perfectly systematic. The important difference between processes dealt with by phonological rules and those dealt with by statements of morpholexical alternation is that the former are asserted to be general facts about the sound structure of the language, regardless of the identity of the particular morphemes that are involved, whereas the latter are asserted to be idiosyncratic properties of particular morphemes.

As we are concerned in this work primarily with the operation of phonological rules, processes of the other sort cannot furnish evidence for our hypotheses. The Dinka case seems to be a nearly paradigmatic instance of a nonphonologically conditioned alternation, and thus need not cause us to modify a position such as (5.10). The other cases that have been adduced in the literature in support of the existence of segmental phonological 'exchange rules' are either of this same sort,[2] or else are suspect on independent, factual grounds.[3] Some authors have objected that 'exchange rules' could not possibly appear in grammars, because they would have to have been added at some point as historical changes. The addition of such a rule would (it is claimed) radically impair intelligibility between the generation of speakers with the rule and

[2] For example, the cases presented in Chomsky and Halle (1968, Chapter 8), involving morphological categories such that some element A marks category I for some items, while another item B marks category II; but for other items, A marks category II, while B marks category I. An example of the same sort is discussed by Gregersen (1972) for Luo and related languages; again, the exchange rule in question is morpholexical rather than phonological in nature. Besides these examples, Wang (1967) has claimed that exchange rules are quite common for tones in Asian languages. We do not have access to the data on which he bases this assertion, and so restrict our claim to segmental phenomena.

[3] These include the following: Bever (1967) proposes a rule of this sort in Menomini, with a strictly phonological environment. His analysis of the phonemic structure of the forms involved, however, is by no means obvious, and alternative accounts are not hard to construct; see Goddard (1972) for the motivation for a nonphonological account of the morphological categories for which Bever's rule was devised. Chomsky and Halle (1968) deal with the most celebrated instance of this sort of rule, the English vowel shift. A number of other writers have questioned both the existence and the precise formulation of this rule, however, and it cannot be regarded as conclusively established in the form of an exchange rule. Some further cases are discussed by Wolfe (1970), but they are also faulty. One involves a drum-signaling system, and it is certainly not obvious that the formal properties of phonological rules will be duplicated in such systems. Another relies on a particular interpretation of orthographic variations in Old Prussian texts, but so little is definitely known about this language that little can be based securely on it. The most convincing case deals with a rule of vowel shift in Czech, but as Anderson and Browne (1973) show, the rule involved here is not an exchange rule either, since the product of one part of the rule (the raising of *e:* under stress) is not the same segment as the input to the other part (the *i:* which is lowered being phonemically distinct from simple *i:*). The only remaining case in the literature appears to be a rule interchanging *o* and *ɔ* in Icelandic, proposed in Anderson (1972b), but this rule too is suspect, despite the evidence provided there for its existence, since it does not really function to account for alternations in morpheme shape, but rather serves to rationalize other such alternations. This note is intended only to point out that no firmly established examples have been able to withstand detailed scrutiny to date.

the previous generation, without it. This argument seems completely spurious on all counts: for one thing, it assumes that rules must be added in precisely their synchronic form as historical changes, but it is well known that rules can also arise in synchronic grammars as a result of restructuring (among other things); for another it assumes that any such rule would make it impossible to identify individual elements, but the amount of redundancy that is found in language is sufficient to ensure that any but the most radical change would still leave plenty of additional cues from which morpheme identity could be recovered at least in enough cases to make it clear to hearers that a process of exchange was taking place; and for a third reason, it ignores the fact that precisely such radical losses of intelligibility have occasionally occurred in history, as between antagonistic social or age groups, or at the time of migrations, acculturations, and other social upheavals. Although we cannot conclude that exchange rules are impossible a priori, this does not guarantee that they do exist, either, and it is important to find empirical evidence. So long as this cannot be firmly established, linguistic theory should probably choose to retain a hypothesis such as (5.10), rather than modifying it to (6), since (5.10) makes the (possibly correct) claim that exchange rules are not possible in natural language, for whatever reason.

Regardless of whether or not exchange rules should be recognized as a systematic class of exceptions to the principle of linear ordering, with the variable feature coefficient notation delimiting a class of cases where simultaneous application prevails, there are other cases which show that neither (5.10) nor (6) can be maintained unchanged. Consider, for example, the well-known rules for the assignment of stress in Latin words. Monosyllables (e.g., *rḗs*) are, of course, stressed on their only syllable; bisyllabic forms (e.g., *tóga*) are stressed on the penultimate syllable; while trisyllabic and longer forms have two different treatments. If the penultimate vowel is short and followed by, at most, one consonant, stress falls on the antepenultimate syllable (e.g., *cōnfíciunt*), while words whose penultimate vowel is either long (e.g., *inimícus*) or followed by a cluster (e.g., *impedīménta*) receive penultimate stress. There are, then, three principles for stress assignment:

(7)[4] a. $V \longrightarrow [+\text{stress}] / \underline{\hspace{1em}} C_0 \begin{bmatrix} V \\ -\text{long} \end{bmatrix} C_0^1 V C_0 \,\#$

b. $V \longrightarrow [+\text{stress}] / \underline{\hspace{1em}} C_0 V C_0 \,\#$

c. $V \longrightarrow [+\text{stress}] / \underline{\hspace{1em}} C_0 \,\#$

---

[4] The notation C_0 stands again for 0 or more consonants; the notation C_0^1 stands for from 0 to one consonant(s).

Rule (7a) applies to trisyllabic and longer forms with short penult; (7b) applies to all other forms that are bisyllabic or longer; and (7c) applies only to monosyllables. Clearly all three of the rules in (7) cannot be allowed to apply sequentially, or simultaneously. If this were to happen, all bisyllabic and longer forms would have stress not only on the correct syllable, but also on all following syllables. From the later development of these vowels in the Romance dialects, however, we can see that posttonic vowels did not bear stress, and so the set of rules in (7) must be constrained in some way to prevent the assignment of stress to more than one vowel in a word. If the rules apply in sequence, we could do this by requiring that each rule apply only to vowels that are not preceded by a stressed vowel. In this way, application of any one of the rules would preclude the application of the others. But in order to do this we must introduce a significant degree of complexity into the statement of the rules. We are furthermore claiming that such complexity is indeed a complication of the Latin stress rule: that is, that Latin would be simpler in some sense if the complication were missing, and the rules were as they are in (7). But we know from the study of large numbers of other languages that this is not likely to be the case. When a language has one stress treatment for one class of words and another for another it is almost invariably the case that the rules operate so that any given word undergoes only one rule. The mutual exclusivity of a set of stress assignment rules like (7) should not be treated as a complication in the rules themselves, but rather as a systematic property of such a set of rules.

Just as the device of variable feature coefficients was defined originally to capture evaluation properties of a set of rules, and was later argued to define a class of cases whose organization in the grammar is unusual, a notational convention has been familiar from earliest work in generative phonology that appears to delimit the class of cases like (7). Where two strings are identical, except that the first contains an additional subpart that is not present in the second, they can be abbreviated by the use of parentheses as in (8):

(8)   a. i. $X \longrightarrow Y \,/\, A \rule{1cm}{0.4pt} BC$

           ii. $X \longrightarrow Y \,/\, A \rule{1cm}{0.4pt} C$

       b. $X \longrightarrow Y \,/\, A \rule{1cm}{0.4pt} (B)C$

The two rules in (8a) are abbreviated as (8b). It is worth noting that the notation, if it is to be well defined, must require that the order of the rules in the expanded form be uniquely specifiable; we require, therefore, that in order for the parentheses collapsing operation to be performed, the rules in question be ordered as in (8), with the longer rule preceding.

Once again, then, we have a formal criterion which identifies certain sets of rules as having special properties. The parentheses notation, like the others considered so far, was originally conceived as capturing properties that were relevant to evaluation, but Chomsky (1967) proposed that this formal resemblance could also be used to specify an organizational property of grammars. We could, that is, replace (6) [or (5.10), if simultaneous application of variable-coefficient rules is unnecessary] by

(9)   *The rules of a grammar are arranged in a linear order with each rule applying to the output of the previous rule in the list, except: (i) if two adjacent rules are formally related in such a way that the parentheses notation is applicable to them, then they apply* DISJUNCTIVELY, *in that the applicability of the first (or longer) rule precludes the applicability of the second, regardless of whether the structural description of the second rule is satisfied; [and (ii) if two adjacent rules are formally related in such a way that the variable feature coefficient convention is applicable to them, they are applied simultaneously rather than in sequence].*

The principle of disjunctive order which is included in (9) is an important hypothesis about the organization of grammars. The claim is presented that, while rules may not always apply in exactly the same ways, it will always be possible to tell how a set of rules is to be applied simply by inspection of the formal nature of the rules themselves. If true, this furnishes an important kind of evidence for the reality of notational conventions. In the case of the curly brackets notation, it was necessary to go outside the grammar itself, to the facts of historical change for example, to confirm the reality of the relationship between rules which the notation claimed existed. In the case of the parentheses notation, however (and the variable feature coefficient notation as well, perhaps), it is possible to obtain confirmation from within the grammar itself. We have suggested that this formal relationship is associated with a particular ordering property, and we can therefore examine any set of rules that are abbreviable by parentheses and ask whether it is appropriate to apply them disjunctively. In many cases, of course, it will turn out that it does not matter whether we apply such a set of rules disjunctively or conjunctively, since the environments will be mutually exclusive and only one of the rules could apply in any event. What we require is that disjunctive ordering be correct in each case where it makes a difference. Our set of rules for Latin stress, for example, bear the appropriate formal property, and can be abbreviated as

$$(10) \qquad V \longrightarrow [+\text{stress}] \,/\, \underline{} C_0 \left(\left(\begin{bmatrix} V \\ -\text{long} \end{bmatrix} C_0^1 \right) V C_0 \right) \#$$

We predict, therefore, that the rules represented by (10), namely (7), should apply disjunctively, and of course that is exactly what we saw above to be necessary. We do not, therefore, need to build into the statement of the Latin stress rule any explicit mention of the fact that only one stress is assigned to any given word; this follows from our general hypothesis of disjunctive ordering.

A notation which is clearly related to the parentheses convention just discussed has appeared in several rules up to this point. This is the 'subscript–superscript', or simply 'subscript' notation. This convention has also been widely used in phonological descriptions, though with little explicit justification. According to the definition of the notation, the term $(X)_m^n$, where 'X' is an arbitrary string, and m and n are nonnegative integers with n greater than m, is to be regarded as an abbreviation for a set of $(n - m + 1)$ terms. The first of these is obtained by replacing $(X)_m^n$ by n consecutive instances of X, the second by substituting $n - 1$ instances of X, and so on, with the last term having m instances of X. The notational content of $(X)_m^n$ is 'from m to n X's'. Plainly, this notation is definable in terms of the parentheses notation: the expression $(X)_3^5$, for example, could be written as $XXX(X(X))$. Since there is no reason to believe that these two formulations have distinct properties of any kind, we will henceforth avoid the use of expressions of the form '$(X)_m^n$', except as unsystematic abbreviations for the form with parentheses.

A variant of this notation, however, is not so easily reduced to parentheses form. This is the case with expressions of the form $(X)_n$, where no upper limit is specified. The notational content of such an expression is 'n or more instances of X', but since no upper limit is specified, we have no upper bound to the potential length of the expanded expression. Since words in natural languages, and hence rules that operate on them, are always in fact of finite length, we could of course always select some arbitrarily large number as the upper bound of such an expression. To make such a choice would be meaningless, however—why 1,000,000 rather than 1,000,117? Clearly, whatever the upper bound to such an expression, it is not a fact about the rule in which the term appears, but about other properties of the language that impose limitations on the length of its forms. We can say, therefore, that the notation $(X)_n$ has a

54473

quasi-independent status, since we cannot actually write another expression in terms of simple parentheses that is equivalent to it. This notation stands for a potentially infinite set of expressions, each with one more instance of X than the following. The ordering property of this set of expressions is the following: of two expressions in such an infinite schema, the expression with more instances of X precedes the one with fewer instances of X. Thus, while we cannot actually write the 'first' term of the expansion, we can always tell which of several alternative possibilities should be taken as ordered earliest.

That this device defines a schema with ordering properties similar to those of the parentheses notation will not come as a surprise. To see this, we can consider the rule which assigns stress in Tahitian, for example (see Tryon, 1970, for details). In this language, there are no consonant clusters, but there are numerous instances of vowel clusters. Words can also be of considerable length. Stress is assigned in the following way: if a word contains a cluster of two adjacent vowels, or a long vowel (= a sequence of two identical vowels), stress is assigned to the first vowel in the first such cluster in the word. If there is no vowel cluster (or long vowel), stress is assigned to the penultimate syllable. No stress appears on monosyllables (these forms are almost exclusively pronouns, particles, and prepositions). While this process appears at first glance to present a problem in formulation, it turns out that the principle at work is really quite simple: put stress on that nonfinal syllable which is furthest from the beginning of the word, and which is preceded only by vowel moras separated by consonants. This can be formulated as (11):

(11) $\qquad V \longrightarrow [+\text{stress}] \ / \ \#C_0 \ (V \ C)_0 \underline{\qquad} C_0V$

In order for this rule to work correctly, two things are necessary: first, it is necessary that the term '$(V \ C)_0$' be taken to mean 'as many $(V \ C)$ sequences as it is possible to find'; second, it is necessary that *only* this longest term of the expansion of the rule schema (11) apply, and not the other applicable but shorter subrules. If they were to apply, we would encounter the opposite of the problem faced in Latin: here we would stress not only the correct syllable, but also all of the preceding syllables. This would, of course, have the wrong result. This example demonstrates the disjunctive character of the $(X)_n$ notation, because clearly such an unbounded notation is needed here and equally clearly its terms must be disjunctive. The need for the $(X)_n$ notation follows from the fact that, in principle, any number of syllables can precede the stressed syllable, but a particular condition must be imposed on each of them: that it consist of exactly one vowel, followed immediately by a consonant. If there are no vowel sequences in the word, all of its syllables will meet this condition, and the rule will skip all the way to the end to give penultimate stress. If there is some vowel sequence in the word, on the other hand, the first vowel in such a sequence will fail to meet the condition, and so cannot be included in the left hand part of the environment. The result of this will be that the rule can only skip as far as the first element of this sequence, correctly.

The discussion thus far in this chapter has followed the program of attempting to provide purely mechanical, formal definitions for the sets of circumstances in which the simplest form of the linear ordering principle is violated. We have discovered that the members of some sets of rules are mutually exclusive, and have suggested that applying them disjunctively is the appropriate way to resolve this; and we have further hypothesized that a mechanical procedure can be given for deciding when to apply rules disjunctively. But this leaves no principled basis for the disjunctive application of rules with no particular formal resemblance to one another, and it is an important part of the hypothesis (9) that such rules will always apply conjunctively. It is necessary to inquire whether this is in fact the case.

There exists a certain amount of evidence, to which we turn now, that a purely formal approach to the specification of disjunctive ordering is inadequate. An instructive example of this is found in the rules which determine the quantity of vowels in Middle English.[5] At this stage of the language, as in Modern English, there was a rule which shortened a stressed vowel which was followed by two or more syllables. For example, a word like *sori* ([sɔːri]) which has a long vowel in the first syllable (from Old English *sārig*), had a trisyllabic plural form *sorie* ([sɔriə]), with a shortened vowel in the first syllable. The rule which performs this shortening can be formulated as

$$(12)^6 \qquad \begin{bmatrix} +\text{syll} \\ +\text{stress} \end{bmatrix} \longrightarrow [-\text{long}] \ / \ \underline{\hspace{1cm}} \ CVC_0V$$

(trisyllabic shortening)

---

[5] For details of these rules, see the standard handbooks, such as Wright (1928), Moore (1951), Brunner (1963), Luick (1914–1921), and specialized treatments, such as Dobson (1962).

[6] The rule is formulated in this way, with C rather than C_0 after the vowel in question, because there was a distinct rule which applied to shorten vowels before clusters, regardless of the number of following syllables.

Another rule in Middle English resulted in the lengthening of stressed vowels in open syllables. Thus, OE forms like *bacan, hara,* etc., with short vowels, became ME *bāken, hāre* with long vowels by virtue of the fact that the stressed syllable is open. One might write a rule such as (13) to deal with this:

(13)
$$\begin{bmatrix} +\text{syll} \\ +\text{stress} \end{bmatrix} \longrightarrow [+\text{long}] \; / \; \underline{\quad} \; CV$$

This is by no means the whole story of the open syllable tensing rule, however. The operation of rule (13) was accompanied by a change in quality as well, initially affecting only the nonhigh vowels, but eventually extending to include high vowels as well. The mid-vowels *e* and *o* when lengthened in open syllables were lowered to $\bar{\varepsilon}$ and $\bar{ɔ}$; while the high vowels *i* and *u* were lowered in this position to $\bar{e}$ and $\bar{o}$. This results in ME alternations such as *wik* 'week, sg.': *wēkes* 'id., pl.': *sun,* 'son, sg.': *sōnes* 'id., pl.', and similar pairs with mid-vowels (our attention will be confined here to forms with basic high vowels, simply because the orthography indicates the quality change for these vowels, but not for the words with basic mid-vowels). This quality shift is confined to long vowels produced by this rule,[7] and it must be incorporated into the formulation of the rule. We can thus replace (13) by (14):

(14)[8]
$$\begin{bmatrix} +\text{syll} \\ +\text{stress} \\ \langle -\text{high}\rangle \end{bmatrix} \longrightarrow \begin{bmatrix} +\text{long} \\ -\text{high} \\ \langle +\text{low}\rangle \end{bmatrix} \; / \; \underline{\quad} \; CV$$

The question before us is, how are rules (12) and (14) to be ordered with respect to one another? To determine this, we must of course find forms to which both could apply. Consider the alternations in (15):

(15)   a. *ēvel* 'evil'; gen. *iveles* (see OE *yfel, ifel*)
         b. *sēker* 'secure'; adv. *sikerli* (see OE *sicor*)

---

[7] This is shown by numerous forms in which an underlying long vowel is not affected by rule (14). Any form with a long high vowel, for instance, is of this sort.

[8] The angled brackets here represent a discontinuous environment: thus, the rule makes all vowels [−high], and if they already were [−high], it also makes them [+low]. This device will not be examined here.

It should be noted that the process expressed by (14) was confined (in this form) to certain northern dialects of ME. For this reason, and because alternations like those in (15) were uniformly leveled out by the generalization of one or the other vowel in the later history of the language, it is not generally possible to infer details of the process from standard Modern English forms, as is attempted by Stampe (1972).

    c. *bēsi* 'busy'; *bisines*
    d. *sōmer* 'summer'; pl. *sumeres* (see OE *sumor*)
    e. *stērop* 'stirrup'; pl. *stirropes*

The vowels in the initial syllables of these words are in open syllables in both the disyllabic and the trisyllabic forms, but in the trisyllabic forms, they are short, rather than long as would be predicted by rule (14). This point argues that (14) cannot apply after (12), for if it did the vowels would be lengthened, wiping out the effect of trisyllabic shortening. Indeed, this would be the case with every form in which trisyllabic shortening applies. But it is also not possible to apply (12) to the output of (14); since, while this will yield the correct value for the feature [±long], it would give incorrect derived vowel qualities. Sample derivations of the trisyllabic forms are given in (16) under each of the possible orderings of (12) and (14) with respect to each other:

(16)		*bisines*		*sumeres*	
underlying	/bisi+nes/			/sumer+es/	
(12)	/bisi+nes/			/sumer+es/	
(14)	/bēsi+nes/			/sōmer+es/	
(14)		/bēsi+nes/			/sōmer+es/
(12)		/besi+nes/			/somer+es/
Output:	*[bēsines]	*[besines]		*[sōmeres]	*[someres]

All of these outputs are incorrect. There would thus appear to be no possible order in which (12) and (14) can apply. Observe that we cannot simply mark these roots as exceptions to (14) (the quality change for which is the principal difficulty), since the same roots in shorter forms must undergo this rule: *bēsi, sōmer,* etc. In fact, the class of exception would be exactly 'form to which trisyllabic shortening applies', and this is the traditional treatment of the phenomenon in the handbooks. Another possibility is to restrict rule (14) explicitly to dissyllabic forms. But this complication to (14) looks just like the kind of complication which we could have added to the Latin stress rules to prevent more than one of them from applying to the same form: both this solution and the 'exception feature' solution are simply ways of coding the fact that (12) and (14) are disjunctive. Of course, given the finite character of phonology, we can probably always do something of this sort; but to do so is surely to miss a generalization about the relation between the two processes. We are thus apparently confronted with a case in which disjunctive ordering obtains between two rules that are not abbreviable by a notational convention that enforces such ordering.

If we accept this conclusion, it would seem to follow that the property of disjunctiveness can be stated ad hoc for any pair of rules in the grammar of any natural language, at least in the cases where it is not predicted by a notational convention. But this is surely the wrong conclusion: among the thousands of rules that have been proposed for the many languages that have been examined in the course of the development of generative phonology, no other pair (except as will be noted below) has ever been presented as disjunctively ordered unless a notational similarity enforcing such order obtained. From this we would surely like to conclude that formally unrelated rules apply conjunctively.

An alternative to stating disjunctiveness ad hoc for every pair of rules in every language would be to extend the principle of one of the notational conventions to include cases such as the one just discussed. This might seem a reasonable move; the environments of (12) and (14) are related by the parentheses notation, since one is a substring of the other:

(17) $\qquad \cdots / \underline{\qquad} CV(C_0V)$

Furthermore, the rule corresponding to the longer of the two environments in the expansion of (17) takes precedence, as we suggested was universally the case with rules abbreviated by the parentheses notation. Notice also that, while the structural changes performed by the two rules are not identical, as they would have to be in order to allow the parentheses notation as presently defined to be appealed to, they have a very definite functional relation: both serve primarily to specify the value of the feature of length. The rules are evidently related (in the general sense of 'related' that was appealed to in Chapter 6 in connection with the subrules of Finnish consonant gradation). We might suggest, then, that the parentheses notation could be modified, so as not to require total identity of strings (except for the addition of extra material to one of them), but rather to require that (a) the structural changes of the two rules be 'related'; and (b) the structural descriptions be collapsable by the present convention for the use of parentheses.

Although this suggestion would preserve the formal and strictly mechanical character of the property of disjunctive ordering, it cannot, unfortunately, be maintained. Other examples suggest that disjunctive ordering or its equivalent is required even where this lessened requirement is not satisfied. For example, consider the assignment of stress in Indonesian (see Verguin, 1955, for details). Stress in this language falls generally on the penultimate syllable of the word; but if the penultimate vowel is ə, stress falls instead on the final syllable. There are evidently two rules involved here:

(18)   a. $V \longrightarrow [+\text{stress}] / ə C_0 \underline{\quad\quad} C_0 \#$

                 b. $V \longrightarrow [+\text{stress}] / \underline{\quad\quad} C_0 V C_0 \#$

These two rules cannot be collapsed by parentheses, although collapsing may be possible if one employs the 'angle brackets' extension of the parentheses notation introduced in Chomsky and Halle (1968). They must clearly be applied disjunctively if we are to avoid stressing penultimate ə's. This can be achieved by requiring the vowel following a penultimate vowel which is to receive stress to be unstressed, but this is obviously nothing but a way of coding disjunctive application. It is also possible to assign stress correctly by stressing all penultimate vowels, and then applying a rule of stress jump:

(19)

$$
\begin{bmatrix} ə \\ +\text{stress} \end{bmatrix} \quad C_0 \quad V \quad C_0 \quad \#
$$
$$
\quad\quad 1 \quad\quad\quad\; 2 \quad\; 3 \quad\; 4 \quad\; 5
$$
$$
\Rightarrow \begin{bmatrix} 1 \\ -\text{stress} \end{bmatrix} \quad 2 \begin{bmatrix} 3 \\ +\text{stress} \end{bmatrix} 4 \quad 5
$$

But rule (19) is not particularly appealing. It makes the claim that penultimate ə's go through an intermediate stage of derivation at which they are stressed, and there is no evidence whatsoever for this suggestion. The rule itself does not account directly for any facts in the language: it serves simply to patch up some incorrect results of the too-general (18b). But this function seems better served by the plain statement in (18a), together with the requirement that the rules of (18) operate disjunctively.

In both cases above, we are confronted with the following situation. Two rules specifying closely related changes apply in environments such that all of the cases satisfying the environment of one rule also satisfy the environment of the other, but not vice versa. This is extremely similar to the sort of situation that called for the use of disjunctive order in connection with rules abbreviable by parentheses. Recall the Latin stress rules: every word in the language has a final syllable, so any word meeting either of the other two analyses will also satisfy the final stress case. Of the remaining two, one case only requires that the word have a penultimate syllable, while the other requires both an antepenult and a *short* penult. Clearly, then, any word satisfying the antepenult rule will also satisfy the penult rule. In the Indonesian case, the penultimate stress rule simply requires that a word have two syllables; while the final stress rule requires in addition that the penult be the vowel ə. Here too, any word satisfying the final stress rule will also satisfy the penult rule, but not vice versa. And in the Middle English case, both rules require that the vowel in question be followed by CV; they differ in that the trisyllabic shortening rule requires that this sequence be followed by another syllable in addition. Clearly, any form satisfying trisyllabic shortening also satisfies the tensing rule, but not vice versa.

We suggest, then, that this notion be made the basis of a principle of disjunctive ordering, rather than trying to maintain a purely mechanical comparison of the rules' formulations as the basis for this organizational property. Given two rules, if the domain of one is a proper subset of the set of forms to which the other can apply, we can refer to the former as the 'more specific' rule. We can then say that if two rules are adjacent, and specify changes that are related, then for any given form, if the more specific of the two is applicable, this precludes the application of the other. Obviously there is much to be made precise here, in specifying the nature of the relation which must obtain between the rules, and in formalizing the notion of 'more specific rule'. We have no concrete proposals to make concerning these issues, however, and leave them to further research. Several other examples have been discussed by Kiparsky (1972a) in which disjunctiveness based on the precedence of the more specific rule is required if the grammar is to operate correctly. This device provides a way of formalizing the notion of 'elsewhere' in phonology, as Kiparsky points out: of a set of related rules, the case which applies if none of the other conditions are met need have no environment specified (beyond, perhaps, one common to the entire set): all of the other rules in the set will then be more specific than it, and accordingly, it will only apply if none of these more specific rules apply.

It may well turn out that all of the cases subsumed under Chomsky and Halle's theory of disjunctive ordering, based on formal resemblance alone, also fall under the principle just suggested. It would of course be sufficient to confirm the hypothesis if all of those cases in which disjunctive ordering makes a difference fell under it, and there do not appear to be any counterexamples to this claim. We may note as an aside that this modification of the theory of disjunctive ordering appears to make it virtually identical with the corresponding principle which governs much of Pāṇini's grammar.[9] It can also be noted that it provides a solution to a

---

[9] See Kiparsky and Joshi (1971) and Staal (1968) for some discussion of Pāṇini's meta-theoretical assumptions in this area.

minor difficulty in the formalism of the theory of exceptions. It is well known that even the most general rules can have some exception: there are a very few words which, for one reason or another, have exceptional stress in Latin, for example. These words are presumably entered in the dictionary with their exceptional stress. But now a problem arises: not only is it necessary to stress these words individually in the lexicon, but it is also necessary to prevent them from undergoing the regular stress rules. This can be done, of course, by simply marking them [−STRESS RULES] (or whatever the exception feature for the stress rule is to be called), but this leaves something unexplained. Why should it be the case that all and only the forms that have their stress assigned idiosyncratically are also exceptions to the stress rules? But this fact follows automatically from the assumption of the principle of extended disjunctive order just proposed. Since the assignment of stress on an item-by-item basis is clearly a process related to stress assignment in general, the disjunctiveness of the two follows from the fact that idiosyncratic specification of stress is always more specific than assignment of stress by a general rule. Thus, there is no need to mark these forms [−STRESS RULES]; this property will follow automatically from the principle of disjunctive order, if we assume that lexical assignment of stress constitutes a rule.

One more problem deserves mention here, though no solution to it will be attempted. It has been pointed out recently (see, e.g., Bever, 1967; Johnson, 1970; Howard, 1972) that there is an interesting indeterminacy in the theory of disjunctive ordering. While this theory specifies the conditions under which the application of one rule precludes the application of some other, it was only meant to cover cases in which the domains of the two rules overlapped to some extent. Cases have been illustrated, in the works just mentioned, that demonstrate the fact that, when one part of a disjunctive schema applies to one part of a form, it does not preclude the application of the other part of the schema to some completely unrelated portion of the same form.[10] Proposals have been made for formalizing the relation that must exist between the two environments in question in order for disjunctive ordering to obtain [the first such proposal was that of Bever (1967); others appear in the works mentioned above], but we know of none that is completely satisfactory and strongly supported in detail by empirical facts. As can be imagined, the examples that would provide crucial evidence are not easy to find in

[10] The problem arises when the substring of the form analyzed by the more specific rule overlaps with, but does not properly include, the substring analyzed by the less specific rule.

a matter of such fine detail as this. Accordingly, we leave the issue unresolved at this point, except to note that disjunctive ordering is presumed not to obtain if the portion of the form analyzed by the SD of the longer (or more specific rule) is totally disjoint from the portion analyzed by the SD of the shorter (or less specific) rule.

CHAPTER 8

Mirror-Image Rules
and Disjunctive Ordering

In addition to the devices discussed in the previous chapter, there is another formal resemblance between phonological rules which has been proposed and defended as the basis for a notational convention. This is the so-called NEIGHBORHOOD or MIRROR-IMAGE RULE, first proposed by Bach (1968) and later discussed by Langacker (1969). The mirror-image notation makes the claim that a pair of rules related by symmetry represents a generalization over an unrelated pair of rules of otherwise identical complexity. The examples adduced by Bach and Langacker are mostly of the form familiar from traditional grammars ('x is replaced by y when adjacent to a z'): process $X \rightarrow Y$ applies if the segment X has a Z on either side. The rules involved are

(1)   a. $X \longrightarrow Y \mid Z$ _____

  b. $X \longrightarrow Y \mid$ _____ Z

Bach's paper proposed an abbreviation for such rules: delete the dash specifying the location of the affected segment in the environment altogether, and write the set of rules (1) as the schema in (2):

(2) $X \longrightarrow Y \mid Z$

More generally, when Z is a string of symbols $z_1 z_2 \cdots z_n$, (2) is an abbreviation for the set of rules (3):

(3)   a. $X \longrightarrow Y \,/\, z_1 z_2 \cdots z_n$ ____

                 b. $X \longrightarrow Y \,/$ ____ $z_n z_{n-1} \cdots z_1$

Let us now consider some of the consequences of Bach's choice of a notation. Since the dash is deleted from the schema, it must obviously be possible to reconstruct its position uniquely in the rules to which the schema expands. Since Bach's cases involve environments that appear on only one side of the affected segment at a time, this causes no problems: the convention expanding (2) as (3) deals adequately with these cases. Notice, therefore, that Bach's notation claims that mirror image rules will be restricted to rules of the form

(4) $X \longrightarrow Y \,/\, A$ ____ B

together with their symmetrical equivalents, WHERE B IS NULL. This restriction does not figure in any other theoretical statements in phonology, and it would be quite interesting if it turned out to be true. Second, note that it is necessary for a decision to be made by the theory as to whether a rule set abbreviable as (2) is to be expanded as (1) or as (5):

(5)   a. $X \longrightarrow Y \,/$ ____ Z

                 b. $X \longrightarrow Y \,/\, Z$ ____

Since there is no way of specifying a choice between (1) and (5) in the notation (2), it must be made universally as part of the convention for the notation, just as the location of the blank in the rule must be chosen universally, as a consequence of the formal properties of the notation Bach has selected. It may well seem superfluous to point out these things, but it is useful to note that while, as mentioned in Chapter 6, a notational convention can be devised to abbreviate virtually anything, the choice of notation once made has testable empirical consequences that are forced by its formal properties. Bach's notation is a good example of this, since it claims that the cases of mirror-image rules that will be found in natural languages will be limited to cases with the form (and internal order of subrules) of (3).

The type of example on which Bach based his proposal was the following. In English, and many other languages, the backness of velars is determined by the backness of the adjacent vowels.[1] Thus, after front vowels, velars are front, and after back vowels they are back, unless the velar is also followed by a vowel, in which case this vowel determines the backness of the velar. This situation can be described by the rules in (6):

(6)   a. $\begin{bmatrix} +\text{obst} \\ +\text{high} \end{bmatrix} \longrightarrow [\alpha\text{back}] / \begin{bmatrix} +\text{syll} \\ \alpha\text{back} \end{bmatrix}$ ____

       b. $\begin{bmatrix} +\text{obst} \\ +\text{high} \end{bmatrix} \longrightarrow [\alpha\text{back}] /$ ____ $\begin{bmatrix} +\text{syll} \\ \alpha\text{back} \end{bmatrix}$

These rules are abbreviated as (7), using Bach's notation:

(7) $\begin{bmatrix} +\text{obst} \\ +\text{high} \end{bmatrix} \longrightarrow [\alpha\text{back}] / \begin{bmatrix} +\text{syll} \\ \alpha\text{back} \end{bmatrix}$

In this case, the order of expansion makes a difference to the operation of the set of rules, since whichever rule comes second will override the effect of the first if the velar in question is between two vowels. Since the order in (6), which is the one required by Bach's notation, is the one that gives the correct results, the example is perfectly consistent with the claims of the notation.

Consider the rule of glide formation in Icelandic, however, discussed in Anderson (1969a). This rule converts high vowels into glides when they are adjacent to another vowel; it consists of the two parts:

(8)   a. $\begin{bmatrix} -\text{stress} \\ +\text{high} \end{bmatrix} \longrightarrow [-\text{syllabic}] /$ ____ $[+\text{syll}]$

       b. $\begin{bmatrix} -\text{stress} \\ +\text{high} \end{bmatrix} \longrightarrow [-\text{syllabic}] / [+\text{syll}]$ ____

The rules must apply in this order, since a sequence / · · · iu · · · / should become [· · · ju · · ·], and not [· · · iw · · ·]. The rules in (8), however, are not in the appropriate form of (1) for Bach's notation, but rather in the other order [that of (5)]. We must conclude from this, therefore, that order of subrules in a mirror-image schema is not always the same, and that Bach's notation must be revised to allow an idiosyncratic specification of order of expansion. We can observe in passing

[1] In fact, the facts are more complex than this, but this example will serve for illustration. See Ohala (1971) for details.

that the rule of Icelandic glide formation is consistent with the spirit of Bach's notation, which claims that segments following the affected segment take precedence over segments preceding it in determining the application of a rule, i.e., that regressive changes are commoner than progressive changes. It is the formal nature of the operation being performed by the rule which requires the order of expansion to differ in the two cases. This asymmetry is rather pronounced in connection with most sorts of phonological rules (with the exception of vowel harmony processes, perhaps). Whatever the status of this generalization, it is left completely unexpressed in current phonological theory.

The consequence that the formal nature of the operation performed by the rules in (8) requires the order of their expansion to be different from the one Bach would predict follows from the assumption that neighborhood (mirror-image) rules are ordered conjunctively. We can note that if the rules were applied disjunctively, we could still obtain the correct results for the velar fronting rule (7) if we applied its subparts in the opposite order from that given in (6). If the rules in (8) applied disjunctively, they would still have to apply in the same order, however. We will proceed below to examine the question of whether neighborhood rules should be ordered conjunctively or disjunctively.

Before doing that, however, we must examine the other aspect of Bach's claim, namely, that specified material appears on only one side of the environment of mirror-image rules. Let us consider the rule of glide insertion in Faroese, discussed in Anderson (1972c). In Faroese, whenever two vowels (or diphthongs) come together at morpheme boundary, either directly through affixation, or through the deletion of an intervocalic consonant, a glide is inserted, whose character is determined by the surrounding vowels. The possible combinations are given in the following table:

(9)

V_2 \ V_1:	[i]	[ej]	[oj]	[uj]	[u]	[iw]	[ew]	[e]	[ø]	[o]	[a]
[i]	j	j	j	j	w	w	w	j	j	j	j
[u]	j	j	j	j	w	w	w	w	w	w	w
[a]	j	j	j	j	w	w	w	—	—	—	—

Only [a], [i], and [u] have been considered as possible V_2 because these are the only vowels that appear in unstressed position, and the second member of such a sequence is invariably unstressed. The [w] glides which are inserted before [u] after [e], [φ], [o], and [a] are turned into [v] by the operation of an independently needed rule which need not concern us here.

Clearly the principle at work in determining the quality of the inserted glide is the following: it is *homorganic* with the preceding segment, regardless of the following, if the preceding segment is [+high]; if the preceding segment is [−high], it is homorganic with the following segment, if that is [+high]; and if neither preceded nor followed by a [+high] vowel or glide, the hiatus is not broken by any glide. This process (which must be limited as discussed in Chapter 14 below; hence the + in the rules below though we will later discard this formulation of the restriction) can be described as the two rules in (10):

$$
(10) \qquad \text{a.} \quad \emptyset \longrightarrow
\begin{bmatrix} -\text{obst} \\ -\text{cons} \\ -\text{syll} \\ +\text{high} \\ \alpha\text{back} \end{bmatrix}
\bigg/
\begin{bmatrix} -\text{cons} \\ +\text{high} \\ \alpha\text{back} \end{bmatrix}
+ \underline{\quad\quad} \; [-\text{cons}]
$$

$$
\qquad \text{b.} \quad \emptyset \longrightarrow
\begin{bmatrix} -\text{obst} \\ -\text{cons} \\ -\text{syll} \\ +\text{high} \\ \alpha\text{back} \end{bmatrix}
\bigg/ \; [-\text{cons}] \; \underline{\quad\quad} +
\begin{bmatrix} -\text{cons} \\ +\text{high} \\ \alpha\text{back} \end{bmatrix}
$$

These two rules are clearly related by the neighborhood convention, since they are symmetric, but they contain an environment on each side of the dash, and hence are not collapsable by Bach's device.

We see, then, that both of the claims made by the original choice of a notation for mirror-image rules are false: the place of the affected segment is not always at the end of the string, but may be embedded within it, as shown by the Faroese rules; and the order of expansion of a pair of mirror-image rules is not unique. In light of these objections, let us formulate a new notation for mirror-image rules, to replace that of (2). Let us define the schema (11) as an abbreviation for the set of rules in (12):

$$
(11) \qquad X \longrightarrow Y \; \% \; A \underline{\quad\quad} B
$$
$$
\qquad\qquad (\text{where} \quad A = a_1 a_2 \cdots a_n \quad \text{and} \quad B = b_1 b_2 \cdots b_m)
$$

$$
(12) \qquad \text{a.} \quad X \longrightarrow Y \; / \; A \underline{\quad\quad} B
$$
$$
\qquad\qquad \text{b.} \quad X \longrightarrow Y \; / \; \overline{B} \underline{\quad\quad} \overline{A}
$$
$$
\qquad\qquad (\text{where} \quad \overline{A} = a_n a_{n-1} \cdots a_1 \quad \text{and} \quad \overline{B} = b_m b_{m-1} \cdots b_1)
$$

Using this notation, it would not be possible to specify a preferred order of expansion (that is, to choose universally between (12a)–(12b) and (12b)–(12a) as the order in which the rules must appear in order to be collapsed), since A and B are taken to be any strings, and hence formally indistinguishable. Thus, this notation allows either order of expansion to be specified as part of the formulation of the rule: if it were desirable to collapse the rules (12a) and (12b), but in the opposite order, this result could be obtained by writing, instead of (11), the schema (13):

(13) $$ X \longrightarrow Y \mathrel{\%} \overline{B} \underline{\hspace{2em}} \overline{A} $$

Using this notation, we can now write the Faroese glide insertion process as (14):

(14) $$ \emptyset \longrightarrow \begin{bmatrix} -\text{syll} \\ -\text{obst} \\ -\text{cons} \\ +\text{high} \\ \alpha\text{back} \end{bmatrix} \mathrel{\%} \begin{bmatrix} -\text{cons} \\ +\text{high} \\ \alpha\text{back} \end{bmatrix} + \underline{\hspace{2em}} [-\text{cons}] $$

We have not yet discussed explicitly the question of whether the sub-parts of a mirror-image schema should be applied conjunctively, as was the case with curly brackets schemata, or disjunctively, as was the case with the notations discussed in Chapter 7. In none of the cases that have been discussed so far has it been necessary to require that the rules apply conjunctively: that is, there have been no cases yet in which the application of the second part of the schema is based on the effects of the first part. In each case the operation of each subpart is independent of the other. On the other hand, neither the English nor the Icelandic case require disjunctive ordering, either: each can be satisfactorily formulated on either assumption. The Faroese case, however, does require that the rules be applied disjunctively. If they are not, a sequence such as / · · · i+u · · · / will become, by the operation of (10a). / · · · i+ju · · · /, and then (10b) will be able to apply as well, giving / · · · ij+ju · · · /. This result is incorrect; the only instances of geminate glides that arise in the language are those that come from the second element of a diphthong followed by an inserted glide. Some further discussion of Faroese rules which depend on this fact are included in Chapter 11, below. It is sufficient to note here that rules (10a) and (10b), abbreviated as (14) must be applied disjunctively in order to give the correct results.

On this basis, we might suggest that another clause be added to the hypothesis of linear ordering, to the effect that mirror-image rules are also exceptions to linear ordering in that they fall under the principle of disjunctive ordering just as do rules abbreviable by parentheses, variables, etc. It is difficult to find further cases which support or refute this contention, since most real-language examples of such rules are of the extremely simple sort exemplified by Bach's cases. There do appear to be a few cases which furnish further evidence, however, and these will now be discussed.

In Acoma, a Keresan language (see Miller, 1965, for details), there is a highly complex system of accentual alternations. As part of this system, the following process is described:

> §22.2 A short accented syllable before or after a glottalized sonorant usually loses its accent. If both of the syllables are short, either syllable (usually the first) may lose the accent, but never both (Miller, 1965, p. 85).

Miller then gives several examples, showing accent loss before or after *m̓*, *n̓*, *w̓*, and *y̓*, and instances where accented short vowels would be expected both before and after such a segment, but the rule in question has eliminated one of the accents. Some morphemes are evidently exceptions to the process; the irregularities in some others are fairly clearly due to the operation of other rules. Basically, we have the following rules:

$(15)^2$

a. $\begin{bmatrix} +\text{syll} \\ -\text{long} \\ +\text{accent} \end{bmatrix} \longrightarrow [-\text{accent}] / \underline{\hspace{1cm}} \begin{bmatrix} -\text{obst} \\ -\text{syll} \\ +\text{gl. const.} \end{bmatrix}$

b. $\begin{bmatrix} +\text{syll} \\ -\text{long} \\ +\text{accent} \end{bmatrix} \longrightarrow [-\text{accent}] / \begin{bmatrix} -\text{obst} \\ -\text{syll} \\ +\text{gl. const.} \end{bmatrix} \underline{\hspace{1cm}}$

From Miller's statements and examples, there is evidently some uncertainty as to whether the order of expansion should be (15a)–(15b), or (15b)–(15a), but it is clear that the two rules [abbreviable as (16)] must be applied disjunctively.

(16) $\begin{bmatrix} +\text{syll} \\ -\text{long} \\ +\text{accent} \end{bmatrix} \longrightarrow [-\text{accent}] \% \underline{\hspace{1cm}} \begin{bmatrix} -\text{obst} \\ -\text{syll} \\ +\text{gl. const.} \end{bmatrix}$

Another example of a mirror-image process that must apparently apply disjunctively is to be found in the ancient Italic dialect Oscan (for

---

[2] Further research into the exact phonetic nature of the Acoma accents is called for before a more precise description than the cover symbol [±accent] can be provided.

information on Oscan and Umbrian, see Buck, 1904). In Oscan, there was a rule which inserted an epenthetic or '*anaptyctic*' vowel in clusters of noncoronal obstruent and sonorant consonant. Such a rule can also be found in Latin, where it is responsible for the italicized vowels in, e.g., pōc*u*lum (from *pōclom), stab*u*lum, stab*i*lis (from *stablom, stablis), The vowel of the following syllable, clearly, determines the quality of the anaptyctic vowel. Latin evidently had a rule such as (17):

$$(17) \quad \emptyset \longrightarrow \begin{bmatrix} +\text{syll} \\ \alpha\text{low} \\ \beta\text{high} \\ \gamma\text{back} \end{bmatrix} \Big/ \begin{bmatrix} +\text{obst} \\ -\text{cont} \\ -\text{cor} \end{bmatrix} \underline{\quad\quad} \begin{bmatrix} -\text{obst} \\ +\text{cons} \\ +\text{lateral} \end{bmatrix} \begin{bmatrix} +\text{syll} \\ \alpha\text{low} \\ \beta\text{high} \\ \gamma\text{back} \end{bmatrix}$$

In Oscan, however, this rule was considerably generalized: the sonorant can be either *r* or *l* or a nasal, the obstruent need not be a stop; and most importantly for our purpose, the rule applies in either direction. Thus, we have *ar*ʌ*getud* (cf. Lat. argentum), *Memer*ɛ*keis* (from Mamercius), *Mulu̯kiis* (from Mulcius), with anaptyxis applying in the opposite of the Latin direction, as well as *sak*ʌ*rater* (from sakrater) and *puk*ʌ*lat-ui* (from puclat-o), where the rule applies as it does in Latin.

We could, thus, formulate Oscan anaptyxis as follows:

$$(18) \quad \text{a.} \quad \emptyset \longrightarrow \begin{bmatrix} +\text{syll} \\ \alpha\text{low} \\ \beta\text{high} \\ \gamma\text{back} \end{bmatrix} \Big/ \begin{bmatrix} +\text{syll} \\ \alpha\text{low} \\ \beta\text{high} \\ \gamma\text{back} \end{bmatrix} \begin{bmatrix} -\text{obst} \\ +\text{cons} \end{bmatrix} \underline{\quad\quad} \begin{bmatrix} +\text{obst} \\ -\text{cor} \end{bmatrix}$$

$$\quad \text{b.} \quad \emptyset \longrightarrow \begin{bmatrix} +\text{syll} \\ \alpha\text{low} \\ \beta\text{high} \\ \gamma\text{back} \end{bmatrix} \Big/ \begin{bmatrix} +\text{obst} \\ -\text{cor} \end{bmatrix} \underline{\quad\quad} \begin{bmatrix} -\text{obst} \\ +\text{cons} \end{bmatrix} \begin{bmatrix} +\text{syll} \\ \alpha\text{low} \\ \beta\text{high} \\ \gamma\text{back} \end{bmatrix}$$

These rules can, in turn, be collapsed to the schema (19):

$$(19) \quad \emptyset \longrightarrow \begin{bmatrix} +\text{syll} \\ \alpha\text{low} \\ \beta\text{high} \\ \gamma\text{back} \end{bmatrix} \% \begin{bmatrix} +\text{syll} \\ \alpha\text{low} \\ \beta\text{high} \\ \gamma\text{back} \end{bmatrix} \begin{bmatrix} -\text{obst} \\ +\text{cons} \end{bmatrix} \underline{\quad\quad} \begin{bmatrix} +\text{obst} \\ -\text{cor} \end{bmatrix}$$

The crucial cases for our discussion here, of course, are those in which both rules in (18) could apply: that is, forms containing a cluster of the general form -RCR-. Fortunately, a few such forms are found in the corpus of Oscan: we have *an*ʌ*friss,* from anfriss with medial *-nfr-*, and

*Her*ɛ*kleis*, from Herkleis, with medial -*rkl*-. The interesting fact to note, of course, is that -V_1RCRV_2- becomes -$V_1RV_1CRV_2$-, and not -$V_1RV_1CV_2RV_2$-. Thus, of the two parts of the mirror-image schema (19), evidently only the first part applies if both are applicable. This is just what we would expect if the subparts of such a schema apply disjunctively.

Based solely on such facts, we would be justified in adding to the principle of linear ordering the condition that rules related by the mirror-image notation apply disjunctively. But the evidence is not, unfortunately, unequivocal on this point. Just as the examples we have dealt with above argue for disjunctive application of such schemata, other examples argue with equal force for the conjunctive application of mirror-image schemata. The first such case to be noted is really representative of a large class of similar cases, distributed in a wide variety of languages. It is probably the case that the most typical kind of mirror-image rule is a process by which some feature of the articulation of a consonant is transferred to an adjacent vowel as a nondistinctive secondary feature: e.g., vowels are nasalized next to a nasal, pharyngealized next to a pharyngeal consonant, etc. In general, such a process consists simply in marking the vowel with some absolute degree of nasality, pharyngealization, etc. Thus, a vowel may become, say, [.5 nasal] in the environment '% ____ [+nasal]', etc. Such a rule would not, of course, provide any evidence relevant to our concern in most cases, since once a vowel has become [.5 nasal] by the application of one part of the rule, it does not matter if the value [.5 nasal] is also assigned to it by the other part of the rule. Thus one could not tell whether the two parts of the rule had affected the vowel conjunctively or not. In some cases, however, the rule operates differently. According to Keller (1959, p. 45) in the Mayan language Chontal:

> Vowels contiguous to glottalized consonants, glottal stop, or the allophone of the phoneme /b/ which has glottal quality [this is an implosive segment which appears in syllable-final position -SRA] may be laryngealized. The laryngealization is more pronounced between two such consonants than when contiguous to just one.

An example is the form *ʔahpək'əb*, where all three vowels are nondistinctively laryngealized, but the feature is said to be more prominent on the last syllable, where the vowel occurs between (ejective) *k'* and (implosive, because syllable final) *b*. The possibility that more than one degree of a given feature must be specifiable in the output at least of the lowest level of phonetic rules of a language was mentioned in Chapter 1, and the two different degrees of laryngealization reported by Keller for Chontal are clearly to be accounted for in terms of two distinct numeric values for the feature of [glottal constriction]. Let us assume that the scale for this feature runs from 0 (the equivalent of classificatory [-glottal constriction], if nothing else intervenes) to 1. We can arbitrarily locate the first and second vowels of ʔahpəkəb at the phonetic value of [.4 glottal constriction], and the third vowel at [.8 glottal constriction].[3] We could then describe the facts under consideration with rules (20):

$$(20)^4 \quad \text{a.} \quad \begin{bmatrix} +\text{syll} \\ x\text{glottal constriction} \end{bmatrix} \longrightarrow [x + .4\text{gl. con.}] \;/\; [+\text{gl. con.}] \underline{\quad\quad}$$

$$\text{b.} \quad \begin{bmatrix} +\text{syll} \\ x\text{gl. con.} \end{bmatrix} \longrightarrow [x + .4\text{gl. con.}] \;/\; \underline{\quad\quad} [+\text{gl. con.}]$$

It is not possible to determine uniquely a correct ordering for the two rules in (20), which are abbreviable as the mirror-image schema (21):

$$(21) \quad \begin{bmatrix} +\text{syll} \\ x\text{gl. con.} \end{bmatrix} \longrightarrow [x + .4\text{gl. con.}] \;\%\; [+\text{gl. con.}] \underline{\quad\quad}$$

Obviously, in order to obtain the value [.8gl. constr.] for the vowel which is adjacent to glottalized segments on both sides, it is necessary for the effects of the two parts of this schema to be additive, and hence for the rules to be applied conjunctively. This example, then, and many others like it involving secondary features, can be taken as evidence for conjunctive application of mirror-image schemata.

Another example of apparently conjunctive application of mirror-image schemata is again typical of a class of rules in several languages. Consider the quality of vowels in unstressed closed syllables in Old Irish (see Thurneysen, 1961 for details). Consonants in Old Irish were apparently of at least two, and perhaps three, contrasting qualities: 'neutral', '*i*-quality', and '*u*-quality'. Let us assume that the latter two were [+high], and furthermore, [−back] (palatalized) for the *i*-quality, and

---

[3] The exact choice of values is of little consequence for the structure of this argument; all that matters is that the third vowel has a higher value than the first two. I have assumed that the maximal value achieved is still less than the maximum theoretically possible (1), as seems reasonable for a nondistinctive feature, and that the relation between the two values is simple and additive. If this second assumption, in particular, is incorrect, it would require a more complex arithmetic function in rules (20) and (21), but there is no reason why such an account should be impossible.

[4] The coefficient x here is taken to be a variable ranging over numeric values for feature coefficients, just as α was a variable ranging over categorical values. The rule, then, has the effect of incrementing the numeric value of the feature, whatever it may have been, by .4.

[+back, +round] for the *u*-quality. Neutral consonants we take to be [−high]. While it is not possible to determine the quality of unstressed vowels in closed syllables precisely, we can tell that there was some difference in quality both from the later history of these vowels, and from the way they were written. This difference depends entirely on the quality of the surrounding consonants. Between two neutral consonants, the vowel (written *a*) probably had a schwa-like quality. If next to an *i*-quality consonant, it was somewhat raised and fronted; if next to a *u*-quality consonant, it was somewhat raised and backed, as well as rounded. The point is that the influencing consonant could be on either side, and the effect of two influencing consonants was cumulative. Thus, for example, the orthography represents a vowel between two neutral consonants as *a*; between a neutral and a *u*-quality consonant as *o*; and between two *u*-quality consonants as *u*. Things are somewhat more complex when *i*-quality effect is taken into account too, but the outlines of the process are again clear. We have to do with a vowel which is basically [-high, -low], and most importantly, [0high]; the rule is a mirror-image process that increments the value for [high] by some amount when the vowel is adjacent to a [+high] consonant, and has a similar effect on the features [back] and [round]. To write the rule in the present state of our knowledge of Old Irish phonetics would be folly (a discussion of the facts will be found in section 102 of Thurneysen, 1961), but the important aspects of it can be determined from our available facts. The rule must be mirror-image, and it must apply conjunctively, for the effects of two applications are cumulative. Similar rules for determining vowel quality in terms of the quality of adjacent consonants can be found in many other languages, including especially the Caucasian languages with their notoriously rich consonant systems and minimal vowel systems. A good example is Oubykh (discussed in H. Vogt, 1963). Oubykh has somewhere around 85 consonants, and two vowels (each of which appears long and short). The two vowels, however, have a wide range of allophones, and in fact there are as many vowels phonetically as in most other, more familiar languages. The rules governing these allophones are very similar to those we infer for unstressed vowels in Old Irish; and again, appear to be mirror-image and conjunctive. Similar conclusions might be reached on the basis of the effect of palatalized consonants on adjacent vowels in Modern Russian.

One more example of conjunctive mirror-image rules can be found in the rules which determine the quality of unstressed mid-vowels in Breton (discussed in meticulous detail by Falc'hun, 1951). The Breton (oral) vowel system contains three mid-vowels: a front, unrounded one (e); a front, rounded one (œ); and a back, rounded one (o). Each of these, in turn, has three variants in stressed position (in the Léon dialect described by Falc'hun): a close variant (é, œ́ ó) occurring when the vowel is lengthened (by a 'weak' voiced consonant following); a very open variant (ê, œ̂, ô) (essentially, before velar and uvular continuants); and a moderately open variant (è, œ̀, ò) (elsewhere, i.e., before clusters and 'strong' consonants). These phonetic variants, while quite noticeable, are nondistinctive, and are clearly produced by a relatively simple pair of rules applying to vowels in stressed position. Unstressed vowels, on the other hand, generally have the moderately open quality in all positions. They are never lengthened, regardless of the following consonants, and the very open quality before velar or uvular continuants only occurs exceptionally (in the ending *-er*, for example). We could represent all of these vowels as [−high, −low], with the three qualities distinguished numerically as [.4high, 0low] (close); [0high, 0low] (moderately open); and [0high, .4low] (very open).

Now the important fact for us is not the quality of the stressed mid-vowels, but the influence this has on adjacent unstressed vowels. As Falc'hun (1951, p. 21) says:

> Un *e*. œ, ou *o* accentué tend à communiquer son degré d'aperture à une voyelle inaccentuée de même timbre dans une syllable voisine.

He then goes on to give several examples of assimilations of quality from all three types of vowels in both directions. The mirror-image rule involved apparently is like (22):

$$(22)\quad \begin{bmatrix} +\text{syll} \\ -\text{high} \\ -\text{low} \\ \alpha\text{back} \\ \alpha\text{round} \end{bmatrix} \longrightarrow \begin{bmatrix} x\text{high} \\ y\text{low} \end{bmatrix} \% \begin{bmatrix} +\text{syll} \\ +\text{stress} \\ -\text{high} \ (=x\text{high}) \\ -\text{low} \ (=y\text{low}) \\ \alpha\text{back} \\ \alpha\text{round} \end{bmatrix} C_0 \underline{\quad\quad}$$

To approximate a statement of this rule, we have had to devise notations ad hoc (in particular, the value '[$-F_i$ $(=xF_i)$]', which might also be expressed '[xF_i, $x < .5$]', if [$.5F_i$] is the boundary between [$+F_i$] and [$-F_i$]), but the content of the rule is clear, as is its mirror-image character, from Falc'hun's statement and his examples. Now the important fact is that a stressed mid vowel can be both preceded and followed by vowels of the same basic quality, and when this happens, the vowels in both adjacent syllables are assimilated. Thus, we have [bè|lèyèn] 'priests', in which all three vowels are open because the stressed vowel (the second) is followed by the 'strong' consonant *y*, which prevents it from lengthening; and [mé||lénét], with all three vowels close, because the stressed vowel (again, the second) is lengthened and opened by the following *n*. The assimilation only applies to vowels that agree with the stressed vowel in backness and rounding; it is mirror-image, since it applies in either direction; and it must be conjunctive, since it can apply both progressively and regressively from the same vowel.

These examples, which seem to require conjunctive ordering just as firmly as the first class of examples required disjunctive ordering, might cause us to give up in despair as far as predicting the way in which mirror-image schemata should apply, and by extension, to give up on predicting all instances of disjunctive ordering on the basis of formal similarities between rules. In the case of mirror-image rules, at least, it seems that rules bearing this formal resemblance to one another can apply in either way, and the choice is an idiosyncratic fact about the particular rule.

But there is, it seems, a more interesting generalization to be extracted from these examples, and one which has a great deal of potential importance for phonological theory. The cases supporting disjunctive application differ systematically from those supporting conjunctive order in that the disjunctive cases all involve rules which alter the categorial value $(+ / -)$ of features, while the conjunctive sets all involve rules which specify the numeric detail value of a feature on an arbitrary, quasi-continuous scale, without thereby affecting the categorial value distinctively.[5] On this basis, therefore, we might suggest that there is a basic distinction between rules of these two types (although this does not necessarily imply that they are divided into two sets, with all of the categorial rules ordered before any of the numeric detail rules), and that the conventions governing the one type are not necessarily valid for the other. Specifically, it might be the case that disjunctive ordering is a property that is restricted to categorial rules. In that case, we could list mirror-image rules with the other cases that fall under the convention of disjunctive ordering, and the fact that some mirror-image rules are conjunctive would follow from the general fact that numeric detail rules are not disjunctive. In order to investigate this further, naturally, it is necessary to inquire about rules that fall under the (extended) principle of disjunctive ordering developed in the previous chapter, but which apply to the detail values of features. Obviously, if stress rules count as rules specifying detail values, this will be disconfirmed: the initial use of disjunctive order was in connection with the rules for assigning primary

[5] This observation was first suggested to me by Allan Timberlake.

stress in English, and there is no reason to suspect that this principle was in error. Stress, however, is a feature that behaves differently in many ways from other features, and it would be advisable to examine some cases of segmental phonological rules of this sort before making (or discarding) any generalizations. As no cases of the required form are presently known to us, however, we leave this matter open for future research.

CHAPTER 9

Infinite Schemata
and Iterative Rules

Thus far, we have been assuming a theory of what it means to apply a rule to a form, without making that theory explicit. In Chomsky and Halle (1968), a formal procedure is suggested, in terms of which questions of this nature may be raised and discussed. Their suggested algorithm is approximately as follows: to apply a rule to a form, the string in question is scanned for positions in which the structural description of the rule is satisfied. Such segments as the rule can affect are then designated, and all of the changes are then carried out at the same time. The rule is not then permitted to apply to its own output.[1] The question of the adequacy of simultaneous application at all possible places in the string will be examined in Chapter 13; at this point, we are merely concerned with the claim that rules cannot reapply to their own output.

The principle of nonreapplication of rules has never been explicitly argued for, to our knowledge, and it has always been assumed that rules obviously cannot be allowed to apply freely to their own output. However, we will see that this assumption leads Chomsky and Halle to propose a device for formalizing certain processes which produces more problems than it solves.

The processes in question are those that apply 'all the way across' a

---

[1] Except by some extra principle, such as that of the transformational cycle.

long form, such as the following. Consider a language with a simple alternating stress principle: stress the first, third, fifth, seventh, etc. syllables. In a case such as this, there does not seem to be any way to state a single rule which will apply in all and only the correct positions in a string of arbitrary length which is, at the outset, without stress. Rather, there seems to be a (potentially) unlimited set of such rules: stress the first syllable, stress the third syllable, stress the fifth syllable, etc. There is no unified statement, in terms of the devices we have discussed so far, which covers all of these cases.

Chomsky and Halle (1968) approach such problems by introducing a new notational operator, $(X)^*$, which is defined approximately as follows:

(1)   The string '$X(Y)^*Z$' is a schema representing the potentially infinite set of strings 'XZ', 'XYZ', '$XYYZ$', etc., with each one obtained from the preceding one by the addition of another instance of the substring Y.

Thus far, this notation seems indistinguishable from the notation $X(Y)_0Z$. The difference, however, is the following: while we have seen that $X(Y)_0Z$ has to be applied disjunctively, with only the longest expansion applicable being applied, Chomsky and Halle define the subrules expanded from $X(Y)^*Z$ as being applied simultaneously,[2] with all applicable expansions being applied. Using this notation, we can then write a rule for the simple alternating stress case:

(2) $[+\text{syll}] \longrightarrow [+\text{stress}] / \# \; C_0(VC_0VC_0)^* \underline{\hspace{1cm}}$

This rule will stress every odd-numbered syllable at the same time.

A real-language example with which this notation is exemplified is the slightly more complicated rule of alternating stress in Southern Paiute (see Sapir, 1949). In this language, every even mora receives stress (where long vowels are represented as consisting of two identical moras, while short vowels consist of a single mora), except that final moras are

---

[2] Actually, Chomsky and Halle make an inexplicable move, and define ALL infinite schemata as being applied simultaneously. This has the consequence of making the notation '$X(Y)_0Z$' exactly equivalent to '$X(Y)^*Z$', and also of making impossible the statement of, e.g., Tahitian stress given in Chapter 7, where disjunctive application of an '$X(Y)_0Z$' schema was necessary. We will assume that the need for a disjunctively applied infinite schema notation has already been demonstrated, and that Chomsky and Halle are in error with regard to the application of $X(Y)_0Z$.

not stressed, and a bimoric word receives stress on its first mora. The rule is given, making use of the new notation, as (3):

(3) $V \longrightarrow$
$$[+\text{stress}] \ / \ \# \ \langle \ C_0V(C_0VC_0V)^* \ \rangle \ C_0 \underline{\quad\quad} \langle \ [+\text{seg}]_0 \ \rangle \ C_0V \ \#$$

The rule contains angled brackets, which are to be interpreted as a discontinuous variant of the parentheses notation. Schema (3), then, abbreviates the two rules

(4)   a. $V \longrightarrow [+\text{stress}] \ / \ \# \ C_0V(C_0VC_0V)^*C_0 \underline{\quad\quad} [+\text{seg}]_0 C_0V \ \#$

b. $V \longrightarrow [+\text{stress}] \ / \ \# \ C_0 \underline{\quad\quad} C_0V \ \#$

where (4b) is the rule for bimoric forms, and (4a) is the rule for longer forms.

Notice that, in defining two different forms of the infinite schema notation, we have provided an option as to whether disjunctive ordering should apply in such a case, or whether simultaneous application of all possible subrules should be made. Thus, we are giving up, at least covertly, the claim that formal considerations will predict disjunctive order in all cases. This fact alone would be enough to suggest that a reexamination of the bases for the ( )* notation is in order. But what are our alternatives? If rules apply in Chomsky and Halle's manner, we seem to have none. But suppose we allow rules to reapply to their own output. Then we could write a rule which said simply: stress a vowel which is two moras from either the beginning of the word or another stressed vowel. This rule could not stress all of the necessary vowels at once, but by 'working its way across the word', it could achieve the same effect. Taking the complications of the Southern Paiute case into account, such a rule could be written as (5)[3]:

(5) $[+\text{syll}] \longrightarrow [+\text{stress}] \ / \ \left\{ \begin{matrix} \# \ (C_0V) \\ \begin{bmatrix} V \\ +\text{stress} \end{bmatrix} C_0V \end{matrix} \right\} C_0 \underline{\quad\quad} C_0V$

Such a rule is no more complex than Chomsky and Halle's account, and there is no reason to believe that similar accounts cannot be constructed

---

[3] Actually, under the assumptions about rule application which will be adopted in Chapter 13, the second part of this rule could be reformulated, so as to result in the environment

$$\left\{ \begin{matrix} \# \ (C_0V) \\ \begin{bmatrix} V \\ -\text{stress} \end{bmatrix} \end{matrix} \right\} C_0 \underline{\quad\quad} C_0V.$$

for related processes. If this is indeed the case, we would be able to eliminate the ( )* notation altogether.

But there are stronger reasons for wanting to eliminate the ( )* notation from phonological theory than those already given. Let us consider another example of a process that works its way across the word. In Takelma (see Sapir, 1922), there is a process of Umlaut, which affects the vowel *a* in nonstem syllables when followed by *i*. Thus, a form which is underlyingly /alxīxamis/ 'one who sees us' (see [alxīxam] 'he sees us' for the vowel of the element -*am*- '1 pl. obj.') is phonetically [alxīximis], with the underlying nonstem *a* of the third syllable Umlauted to *i*. Now there are two interesting facts to be noted about this rule: first, it can apply to any number of syllables, so long as all have the vowel *a* and the last is followed by *i* (and they meet the other condition to be noted below). Thus, from underlying /ikūmanananink^h/ 'he will fix it for him', we get [ikūmininininink^h], with all three *a*'s Umlauted. Second, the rule only applies if the consonants separating the *a* to be Umlauted from the conditioning *i* are all voiced. Parallel to [lohōnininin] 'I caused him to die for him', with two *a*'s Umlauted by the *i* of the final syllable, we have [lohōnananhi], where Umlaut is blocked by the presence of the voiceless consonant *h*. This restriction on the intervening consonantism applies to all of the vowels to be affected, and not just the last one; thus, in [alsegesak^{h}sinik^h] 'we keep nodding to one another', from /alsegesak^{h}sanik^h/, only the *a* of the penultimate syllable is affected. The *a* of the antepenult cannot be affected, because the voiceless consonants -*k^{h}s*- intervene between it and the following vowel.

An iterative formulation (one in which the rule is taken to apply to its own output) would capture Sapir's description of a "regressive assimilation of nonradical -*a*- to an -*i*-, caused by an -*i*- in an immediately following suffixed syllable, whether the -*i*- causing Umlaut is an original -*i*-, or itself Umlauted from an original -*a*-" (Sapir, 1922, p. 24):

$$(6) \qquad a \longrightarrow i \ / \ \left[\underline{\hspace{1.5em}}_{-\text{STEM}} \right] \begin{bmatrix} -\text{syll} \\ +\text{voice} \end{bmatrix}_0 i$$

In order to write this in a grammar without iterative rules, however, it would be necessary to formulate it as:

$$(7) \qquad a \longrightarrow i \ / \ \left[\underline{\hspace{1.5em}}_{-\text{STEM}} \right] \left(\begin{bmatrix} -\text{syll} \\ +\text{voice} \end{bmatrix}_0 a \right)^* \begin{bmatrix} -\text{syll} \\ +\text{voice} \end{bmatrix}_0 i$$

Now notice the term inside the ( )* in rule (7). The important fact about this term is that it is not in any way arbitrary: this stands for exactly a syllable which will, by the operation of the rule, become $C_0 i$. In other words, the syllables which can intervene between an affected vowel and a vowel which causes Umlaut are precisely those which will, through the application of the rule, be converted into syllables that could have served as environments for the rule in the first place. The formulation in (7) forces us, therefore, to state the restrictions on the operation of the rule twice; and further to miss completely the generalization that the conditions on each vowel are exactly the same as those on the vowel immediately before the *i* that causes the Umlaut. In the iterative formulation, (6), on the other hand, this fact is used crucially: it is precisely because the rule creates new instances for the application of its simple form that it applies to more than one syllable.

An even better example of the duplication and loss of generality induced by the use of ( )* is furnished by the alternating stress principle of Tübatulabal, a Uto-Aztecan language not too far removed from Southern Paiute [see Voegelin 1936 for a description of the language]. Main stress in Tübatulabal is said by Voegelin to be determined by a complex interaction of phonological, morphological, and syntactic factors, and we will assume it is already marked. The application of the alternating secondary stresses, however, is determined by the following rules:

(8) a. If a vowel preceding a stressed vowel is long (= two moras), it takes secondary stress.

b. If a vowel preceding a stressed vowel is short, it is skipped over, and stress falls on the preceding vowel.

c. A glottal stop which is nonepenthetic (i.e., which is present in underlying forms) counts as a vowel for the purpose of (8b): that is, a vowel followed by a glottal stop followed by a stressed syllable is stressed, even if short.

d. If a vowel should receive stress by any of the above rules, and is long, it is stressed on its first mora; if a vowel, either short or long, should receive stress by any of the above rules, and is separated from the preceding vowel only by a glottal stop, the stress falls instead on the preceding vowel.

e. "Stressed vowel" in the above statements refers to a vowel with primary stress, a vowel with secondary stress derived from a previous application of one of the above principles; or a vowel which has inherent, or lex-

ically marked, secondary stress. If one of the above
processes would otherwise skip over such a lexically
marked vowel, this does not happen; but rather stress
assignment starts again from the inherently stressed
vowel.

This description is formulated, as was Voegelin's, on the assumption
that stress is assigned by an iterative process, which reapplies to its own
output to assign stress progressively further to the left. The factors in (8)
can be expressed in the rule

(9) $[+\text{syll}] \longrightarrow$

$$[+\text{stress}] \, / \, \underline{\qquad} \left(\text{?} \left(\begin{bmatrix} +\text{syll} \\ -\text{stress} \end{bmatrix} \right) \right) C_0 \left(\left\{ \begin{bmatrix} +\text{syll} \\ -\text{long} \\ -\text{stress} \end{bmatrix} \right\} \right) C_0 \begin{bmatrix} +\text{syll} \\ +\text{stress} \end{bmatrix}$$

The application of this extremely complicated process can perhaps be
better seen through the examples in (10):

(10) a. ïmbïŋwïbaʔat 'he is wanting to roll string on this thigh'
          2   2 1   (the ʔ here is epenthetic, and hence does not
                                count as a mora)
      b. yu:udu:yu:udat 'the fruit is mashing'
            2   2   2   1
      c. pïtïpïtï:dinat 'he is turning it over repeatedly'
              2 2   1
      d. kuʔudzubil 'the little one' (VʔV counts as one unit)
            2   1
      e. na:adïʔi 'the cat (obj)' (ʔ counts as a mora)
            2   2 1
      f. tïkapïganan 'the one who was eating'
            2   2   1
      g. (a:dawï:k) tïkapïganayin (he saw) the one who was eating'
            2   1   2   2   2 1 (the element /-pigana-/ has fixed
                                            stress on the last V)

As we see, the rule (9) is applicable before stresses assigned by prior instances of its application, as well as before primary stresses and lexically
marked stresses. The iterative application of rule (9) is of course contrary to the principle of simultaneous rule application; is it possible to
reformulate this process as a single infinite schema? Such a reformula-

tion is possible, but at a tremendous cost:

(11) $[+\text{syll}] \longrightarrow$

$$[+\text{stress}] / \underbrace{\left(\left(? \left(\begin{bmatrix} +\text{syll} \\ -\text{stress} \end{bmatrix} \right) \right) C_0 \left(\left\{ \begin{bmatrix} +\text{syll} \\ -\text{long} \\ -\text{stress} \end{bmatrix} \right\} \right) C_0 V C_0 \right)^*}_{A}$$

$$\underbrace{\left(? \left(\begin{bmatrix} +\text{syll} \\ -\text{stress} \end{bmatrix} \right) \right) C_0 \left(\left\{ \begin{bmatrix} +\text{syll} \\ -\text{long} \\ -\text{stress} \end{bmatrix} \right\} \right) C_0 \begin{bmatrix} +\text{syll} \\ -\text{stress} \end{bmatrix}}_{B}$$

Observe that the A part of this rule simply restates the highly complex environment of the B part, allowing this environment to appear any number of times between a vowel to be stressed and a stress center. The principle of simultaneous application has forced us to state the conditions in (8) twice, while the iterative formulation states them only once. Clearly, the effect of the iterated term A is precisely to say 'two moras [in the Tübatulabal sense, defined by (8)] before a stressed vowel'.

We have seen that if we adhere to the simultaneous theory of rule application, we are forced to employ a notation like that of ( )* for iterative processes. This notation has the consequence of making disjunctive ordering unpredictable for a class of rules [by allowing an infinite schema to be written either with the disjunctive ( )$_0$ or with the simultaneous ( )*]; it also has the consequence of forcing us to state the conditions for such processes twice. This is not immediately obvious in a simple case like that of Southern Paiute, but when complex and idiosyncratic conditions occur, as in Tübatulabal stress or Takelma Umlaut, it becomes clear. For these reasons we clearly want to replace this notation with the device of iterative application of rules.

But once we abandon the use of ( )* in favor of iterative rules, we see that another desirable consequence follows. Notice that the point about each of the above examples was that it made use of its own effects to establish further environments for its application. It is clear that it is only possible to formulate an unbounded process iteratively if it has this character: each application sets up the possibility of another application. With the device of ( )* available, on the other hand, it is possible to formulate unbounded processes that do not have this character. For instance, it is no harder to express a process which is like the Takelma rule above except that it converts any number of a's preceding an i to o:

(12) $a \longrightarrow o \ / \ \underline{\hspace{1cm}} \ (C_0 a)^* C_0 i$

The interesting fact about this proposed rule is that its application to one vowel does not thereby create the conditions for its application to the preceding vowel. It could not, therefore, be formulated as an iterative rule. In terms of ( )*, however, it is no harder to express than the occurring rule (6).

Now it appears to be the case that the only real examples of unbounded processes in natural languages have the character of (6), and not of (12): that is, such rules are so constructed as to operate across arbitrarily long sequences if and only if they have the effect of creating new environments for their own operation. If we were to abandon the ( )* notation in favor of iterative reapplication of rules, we would have made the hypothesis that this is the only kind of unbounded process that can exist. By making it impossible to express (12), we build into the theory of phonology the claim that such a process could not be a part of a natural language. This claim appears to be correct, and is strong enough to be worth trying to capture.

Among published analyses, there is one rule which has been proposed that appears to be a counterexample to the claim just made. In their survey of Latvian morphophonemics, Halle and Zeps (1966) establish a rule by which the vowel *æ* is replaced by *e* if followed by *i* or *j*. Furthermore, this rule can apply to any number of *æ*'s, so long as an *a* or *u* does not intervene. Thus, we have the alternation *æcætu* 'I would harrow' / *ecesi* 'you will harrow'. This rule could be formulated as

(13)
$$\text{æ} \longrightarrow \text{e} / \underline{\quad} (C_0\text{æ})^* C_0 \begin{bmatrix} -\text{cons} \\ +\text{high} \end{bmatrix}$$

Rule (13) would appear to contradict our hypothesis, since the vowel which *æ* becomes is not the same as the vowel which caused it to be changed. There is, however, an important fact about the Latvian vowel system which has not yet been mentioned, and which eliminates rule (13) as a counterexample to our suggested limitation on unbounded processes: there are no underlying mid-vowels in Latvian, and the only source of the vowel *e* is the operation of the rule in question. We could therefore formulate the process as one which raises low front vowels to mid when they are followed by a nonconsonantal *nonlow* front segment, rather than saying 'nonconsonantal, high, front':

(14)
$$\begin{bmatrix} +\text{syll} \\ -\text{back} \end{bmatrix} \longrightarrow [-\text{low}] / \underline{\quad} C_0 \begin{bmatrix} -\text{cons} \\ -\text{back} \\ -\text{low} \end{bmatrix}$$

Rule (14), then, can apply perfectly correctly (if applied iteratively), with the same effects as (13).

We will assume, then, that the device of ( )* is not available to phonological theory, and that rules are allowed to apply to their own output. The same conclusion has recently been argued for on independent grounds by a number of other writers (including Howard, 1972; Johnson, 1970; Palacas, 1971; and others), and now seems well established. It is still necessary to determine, however, if there are any limitations on iteration of rules: are there any rules which must be prevented from applying to their own outputs? An obvious candidate for such status would be an exchange rule, exchanging *a* and *b* in some environment. If such a process were allowed to reapply to its own output, it would presumably 'go on spinning' indefinitely: converting *a* into *b*, and then back into *a*, and then back to *b* again, and so on. This consequence ought certainly to be prevented. We could propose, therefore, that a limitation similar to that imposed by the principle of disjunctive order for parentheses schemata be applied: no rule can apply to a domain which is entirely included within a domain in which it has just applied. This would prevent a rule from applying over and over again to the same segment or group of segments under the influence of the same conditioning factor. The uses of iterative application which were discussed earlier in this chapter would be unaffected by this restriction.

In addition to this general limitation on iteration, however, it is clear that rules must in some cases be marked as (idiosyncratically) prevented from reapplying to their own output. An example of such a situation is provided by a syncope rule of Nitinat (described in Swadesh & Swadesh, 1932). According to this rule nonfinal short vowels in a class of derivational affixes[4] are deleted when followed by a single consonant or underlying consonant cluster (a) in final position; (b) before a word suffix; or (c) before a short stem–suffix vowel or before glottal stop plus any stem–suffix vowel. The important restriction is to vowels before underlying clusters: this prevents the rule from syncopating a vowel followed by either a suffix–final consonant plus a following stem–suffix consisting of exactly a consonant, or before a cluster formed by syncope. The restriction against application before clusters formed over a stem–suffix boundary is presumably related to an independent rule inserting a vowel in such environments, which would cause the vowel in the preceding suffix to be nonfinal. The remaining restriction against applying the rule before clusters formed by syncope is clearly equivalent to

---

[4] STEM-SUFFIXES, as opposed to WORD SUFFIXES; this distinction is a crucial one in Nitinat and other Nootka dialects, and can be represented as a difference between suffixes preceded by simple morpheme boundary + and those preceded by word boundary #.

preventing the rule from reapplying to its own output. The rule could be given as (15), provided it can be marked as noniterative:

$$(15) \qquad \begin{bmatrix} +\text{syll} \\ -\text{long} \\ -\text{ROOT} \end{bmatrix} \longrightarrow \emptyset \ / \ \underline{\hspace{2em}} \begin{bmatrix} C_1 & \begin{Bmatrix} \# \\ +\breve{V} \end{Bmatrix} \\ ? & +V \end{bmatrix}$$

Even quite low-level rules may have this noniterative character. Thus, Hallberg (1972) reports that in Swedish, the rule of voicing assimilation (as opposed to tenseness assimilation) in obstruent clusters can only affect one segment. A cluster such as /-gdt-/, then, undergoes assimilation of its middle element, but this does not then produce further assimilation of the cluster-initial consonant which would result in a uniformly voiceless cluster.

It may be possible to suggest general principles which would permit us to predict what rules are allowed to reapply iteratively and what rules are prevented from applying in this way. Thus, it seems extremely unlikely that a language with a rule like that of Nitinat syncope would allow the rule to reapply so as to delete all of its unstressed vowels. In other cases, the choice seems much less obvious, however, and we have no general suggestions to make concerning the formal properties of rules that are prevented from reapplying. We assume provisionally that rules are simply marked individually for their status. While such a division may well seem to induce a completely arbitrary division of the set of possible rules, it is clear that this is a pseudoissue. After all, the difference between a rule that can reapply and one that cannot is no more arbitrary than the difference between a rule that contains a parentheses–star term and one that contains no such term. Such a device seems inevitable to delimit processes with potentially unlimited scope from those with limited scope. In line with the suggestions that will be made about ordering statements in Chapters 10–13, it is presumably unnecessary to mark a rule in either way (that is, for reapplication or for nonreapplication) if it performs a change that could not possibly require this choice to be made. Furthermore, it may be possible to make use of principles of natural ordering obtaining between pairs of rules to predict the behavior of an individual rule, as suggested for another class of cases in Chapter 13. It is to the investigation of such ordering principles that we now turn.

PART III

THE ORDERING RELATION
AMONG PHONOLOGICAL RULES

CHAPTER 10

The Ordering Relation

Thus far, we have assumed that the ordering relation which governs the operation of a set of phonological rules can be characterized by giving the rules in a linear list: first the rule at the top of the list is applied, and then the next rule on the list, and so on, without ever returning to a rule that has already been passed. When the last rule on the list has been applied, the derivation is assumed to terminate, and the resulting form is taken to be the output in phonetic terms. Such a list defines the relative ordering of any pair of rules on it, in the sense that, given two rules, *A* and *B*, we can always tell unambiguously from the list whether *A* precedes *B* or vice versa.

We could regard the ordering relations between pairs of rules, however, not as defined by the list, but rather as defining it: that is, we might take the pairwise relations between rules as primary, rather than the overall organization of the entire set. This seems a reasonable point of view, given the nature of the ordering relationship. When we argued, in Chapter 5, that it was appropriate to apply the rules of phonological description in a sequence, the reason for this was the observation that a rule may require information which is supplied by another rule. This relation is essentially one obtaining between two rules at a time: either rule *B* requires some information supplied by rule *A*, or the other way around (or, of course, the two are completely independent). When the complete set of rules is considered, a given rule may well bear ordering relations to several other rules, or indeed to all of the other rules; but these ordering relations are, in origin, facts about individual pairs of rules. The linear list is a derivative representation, from which the individual pairwise relations are recoverable.

The point of this shift in emphasis is to show that the linear list organization of the rules, far from being a sort of null-hypothesis about ordering, equivalent to the claim that the rules are ordered, is in fact a very strong claim about the ordering relation in phonology. There is absolutely no a priori reason why a set of pairwise relations between elements of a set should be organizable into a linear list of this sort. It is trivially easy to imagine alternative situations: suppose that we have established three rules of the phonology of some language, A, B, and C. Now suppose that there is a set of forms within which both A and B apply, and in which A must precede B. Suppose further that another set of forms supports the relation 'B precedes C'. Now consider a third set of forms, to which only A and C apply. If the rules of the grammar are organized in a single list, it is clear ex hypothesi that this list must have first A, then B, and then C. Thus, the list predicts that in the third set of forms A will have to precede C. Yet the facts which led us to establish the list did not give us any direct information about the interaction of A and C, and it is certainly logically possible that the third set of forms could be such as to support rather the relation 'C precedes A'. In this case, of course, there would be no linear order consistent with all three of the observed pairwise restrictions. The arrangement of rules into linear lists, then, embodies the prediction (which is clearly an empirical one) that this sort of situation cannot possibly arise in natural languages.

It is easy to see why the assumption of linear ordering has been made: in fact, most of the ordering relations with which we are familiar do have this property (e.g., the relations 'greater than' and 'less than' between natural numbers). A certain amount of study has been devoted to the characteristics of ordering relations within the study of formal logic, and we can give a set of mutually independent conditions such that, if a relation R defined over some set $X = x_1, x_2, \ldots$ satisfies these conditions, R is a linear ordering. Given a particular relation, then, we can confirm or disconfirm the hypothesis that it is linear by investigating the extent to which it satisfies these conditions:

(1) a. Connectedness: For all x_i, x_j in X, either $(x_i \; R \; x_j)$ or $(x_i \; R \; x_i)$.

    b. Irreflexivity: There is no x_i in X such that $(x_i \; R \; x_i)$.

    c. Antisymmetry: If x_i and x_j are in X, and $(x_i \; R \; x_j)$ and $(x_j \; R \; x_i)$, then $x_i = x_j$.

   d. Transitivity: If x_i, x_j, and x_k are in X, and $(x_i \; R \; x_j)$
                         and $(x_j \; R \; x_k)$, then $(x_i \; R \; x_k)$.

These requirements can be interpreted in terms of an ordering relation defined over a set of phonological rules as follows:

(2) a. Connectedness: For any pair of rules A and B, either A
                          must precede B, or B must precede A.
     b. Irreflexivity: No rule precedes itself.
     c. Antisymmetry: If some rule both precedes and follows
                          another rule, it must be the same as that
                          other rule.
     d. Transitivity: If A precedes B, and B precedes C, then
                          A must precede C.

We can now proceed to consider the extent to which phonological rules in natural languages, in fact adhere to the conditions in (2).

   Condition (2a) does not bear directly on the issue of whether it is possible to arrange the rules in a linear order, but rather on the question of whether this order must be unique. If conditions (2b–d) are satisfied, it will always be possible to arrange the rules in at least one linear order, but it may well be the case that more than one is possible. If two rules were absolutely unrelated to one another, there would be no basis for assigning either the order 'A precedes B' or 'B precedes A'. Now suppose that A and B both bear exactly the same ordering relations to the other rules R_1, R_2, etc. Then we could have either of two lists: R_1, R_2, . . . , R_i, A, B, R_j, . . . , R_n; or R_1, R_2, . . . , R_i, B, A, R_j, . . . , R_n. Thus the ordering would not be unique. There are, of course, numerous cases in natural languages of rules that would appear to be counterexamples to the claim of a unique order for every set of rules, in the form of rules which simply do not interact with one another. If, for example, two rules are so formulated as to make it logically impossible that any form which meets the analysis of one of them could ever meet the analysis of the other, then it could never be the case that either rule provides information which is necessary for the operation of the other. Although either or both might be ordered crucially with respect to other rules, the two could never apply in the same derivation, and thus a particular order imposed on them could never have any directly observable consequences.

   Condition (2a) claims that the order of any two rules will always be unique, and thus that the total ordering of the rules (whether linear or not) will also be unique. Since there is no particular reason to believe this, and it has apparently never been explicitly defended, we can eliminate (2a) from consideration and take (2b–d) as defining the weaker claim of partial linear ordering:

(3)   *The rules of the grammar can always be arranged in at least one linearly ordered list.*

Of the three remaining conditions, we have already argued that one is incorrect. In Chapter 9, we claimed that rules must, in at least some cases, be allowed to reapply to their own output. Any rule that applies in this way, however, will thereby violate requirement (2b), irreflexivity, by requiring the rule in question to precede itself. While a violation of (2b) is more important conceptually than violations of (2a) as a counterexample to linear ordering, the damage done to the spirit of the linear ordering principle is still minimal. If (2c) and (2d) were maintained, we could arrange all of the potential applications of any given rule into a contiguous block, and discuss the ordering of this block with respect to other rules (or to similar blocks of identical rules). This would allow the same rule to appear more than once on the list of rules, but the various occurrences of a given rule would all bear the same ordering relationships to all of the other rules of the grammar, and it would be largely an issue of terminology to say that principle (3) was being violated.

Apparent counterexamples to (2c, d) ("ordering paradoxes") have arisen from time to time in work on a variety of languages. Many of these have been dealt with by reformulations of otherwise well-motivated rules, redefinitions of features, and other ad hoc devices which allowed the requirement of linear order to be maintained, though sometimes at the cost of counterintuitive claims about the structure of the language in question. Some such cases will be analyzed in the immediately following chapters, and it will be shown that the correct solutions to these problems do indeed constitute counterexamples to (3). The existence of such cases, then, will constitute positive counterevidence to the principle of linear ordering, and as such will force us to conclude that the notion of ordering which is relevant for phonology is not, in fact, analogous to such ordering relations as those that hold among the natural numbers, etc. It will therefore be necessary to suggest alternative principles governing the application of rules, in order to accommodate the facts of the so-called 'paradoxes'.

Attempts have already been made, of course, to introduce such additional principles into the theory of generative phonology. The most extensively investigated proposal of this sort is the principle of the TRANSFORMATIONAL CYCLE, whereby the rules are organized linearly, and apply in a linear order first to each of the innermost constituents of the syntactic bracketing. The entire list is then reapplied, in the same linearly specified order, to constituents at the next highest level of bracketing, and this procedure is repeated until the highest order of brackets is reached. Such a principle has found its most extensive support in the analysis of English stress begun in Chomsky, Halle, and Lukoff (1958), and continued in Chomsky and Halle (1968) and Halle and Keyser (1971) (although the cyclic description of English stress has also been attacked, e.g., by Ross, 1969). Numerous attempts have been made to apply this device in segmental phonology, but those analyses which have been based on this assumption have generally been shown to be incorrect in one way or another. An essential difference between the cyclic theory and the theoretical devices that will be suggested below is that the cyclic theory embodies a claim that the (at least partially syntactically motivated) constituent structure of a string can influence the order in which the rules apply; while the devices to be advocated below do not allow such an effect and claim that differences in rule ordering arise from other causes, specifically the phonological makeup of the string. Stress assignment rules are in general more intimately connected with syntactic structure than are other phonological rules [indeed, it has recently been suggested by Bresnan (1971) that the cycle which is required for the assignment of stress within the sentence as a whole can be identified with the syntactic transformational cycle], and these may well be subject to additional, syntactically determined principles such as that of the cycle. This is a special fact about stress assignment rules, however, and an adequately articulated phonological theory need not imply similar conclusions for other types of rules. Some work on Arabic by M. Brame (1970) and on Klamath by Kisseberth (1972a) have suggested motivations for segmental cycles in these languages, but these results appear somewhat tenuous at present, and cyclic analyses will be disregarded in what follows.

The first example of a genuine counterexample to linear order, unconnected with the principle of the cycle, which we will consider is the following. Both Old Icelandic and Modern Icelandic are subject to a rule of *u*-Umlaut, which is responsible for alternations between *a* and a rounded vowel. In Old Icelandic this vowel was phonetically [ɔ] (written o), while in Modern Icelandic it is [ö], (written *ö*). Details of the formulation of this rule can be found in Anderson (1969b, 1972b), as well as in later discussion below in Chapter 11. The rule is responsible for alternations such as the following:

(4) a. *barn* 'child'; dat. pl. *börnum*
     b. *svangt* 'hungry neut. nom. sg.'; neut. dat. sg. *svöngu*
     c. (ég) *kalla* 'I call'; (við) *köllum* 'we call'

The appearance of *ö* is governed by the vowel of the immediately following syllable: if this is *u*, *ö* appears; otherwise *a* appears. The Umlaut process can be described by analyzing the roots in (4), and others like them, with underlying /a/, which may be affected by the following rule:

(5) $$a \longrightarrow ö \ / \ \underline{\qquad} \ C_0 u$$

There are two classes of exceptions to this statement, apparently: some instances of *u* do not cause Umlaut of a preceding *a*, and some instances of *ö* are not followed by *u*. The non-Umlauting *u*'s can all be shown to be the product of an epenthesis rule which is discussed in Chapter 12, and hence are not present at the stage of the derivation to which rule (5) applies. The apparently unconditioned *ö*'s, on the other hand, can be argued to be followed by *u* at the relevant stage of the derivation. The *u*'s in question are then deleted by syncope processes (see Anderson, 1969a).

Rule (5) interacts with another rule which is responsible for the syncope of certain vowels in stem-final syllables before vocalic inflections, as in the forms in (6):

(6)   a. *hamar* 'hammer';   dat. sg. *hamri*
      b. *fífill* 'dandelion';   dat. sg. *fífli*
      c. *morgunn* 'morning';   dat. sg. *morgni*

The exact formulation of this rule is not relevant here; a first approximation could be given as follows:

(7) $$\begin{bmatrix} +\text{syll} \\ -\text{stress} \end{bmatrix} \longrightarrow ∅ \ / \ C \ \underline{\qquad} \ C + V$$

Further conditions need to be put on the relation between the consonant following the syncopated vowel and the structure of the preceding syllable; there is also a class of (recently borrowed) words which are simply exceptions to (7). Nonetheless, (7) will suffice for the following discussion.

To determine the relative ordering of rules (5) and (7), let us examine some forms to which both can apply:

(8)   a. *ketill* 'kettle' (underlying /katil+r/; see dat. sg. *katli*)
          kötlum (underlying /katil+um/);   dat. pl.

b.   *regin* '(the) gods' (underlying /ragin+Ø/; see gen. pl. *ragna*)

   rögnum (underlying /ragin+um/)   dat. pl.

c.   *alin* 'ell of cloth' (underlying /alen+Ø/)

   ölnum (variant of *álnum*)   dat. pl.

In the derivation of these dative plural forms, we can see that the syncope rule [rule (7)] must precede the Umlaut rule [rule (5)], since it is only after rule (7) has deleted the vowel of the stem–final syllable that the environment of rule (5) is satisfied.

The interaction of rules (5) and (7) can also be seen, however, in forms such as those in (9), consisting of a root plus one of the stem-forming suffixes -*ul*, -*un*:

(9)   a.   *böggull* 'parcel, package' (underlying /bagg+ul+r/; see *baggi* 'pack, bundle');

   böggli (underlying /bagg+ul+e/)   dat. sg.

b.   *jökull* 'glacier' (underlying /jak+ul+r/; see *jaki* 'piece of ice');

   jökli (underlying /jak+ul+e/)   dat. sg.

c.   *þögull* 'taciturn' (underlying /þag+ul+r/; see *þagga* 'to silence');

   þöglan (underlying /þag+ul+an/)   masc. acc. sg.

d.   *jötunn* 'giant' (underlying /jat+un+r/, perhaps from deeper /et+un+r/; see *eta* 'to eat[1]')

   jötni (underlying /jat+un+e/, from /et+un+e/)   dat. sg.

In these cases, the *u* of the stem-forming suffix causes Umlaut in the root, even though it is itself deleted by syncope. If this is to be the case, then it cannot be that the syncope rule precedes the Umlaut rule absolutely, as seemed to be suggested by the forms in (8).

The facts just cited seem to require that the rule of *u*-Umlaut [rule (5)] both precede syncope [as shown by (9)] and follow it [as shown by (8)], in direct contradiction of the principle of antisymmetry (2c) given above [since rules (5) and (7) are clearly not the same rule]. In order to reconcile these facts with the notion of linear ordering, we would have to argue either (a) that one of the rules involved appears twice in the grammar — once before and once after the other rule — or (b) that one of the rules involved does not, in fact, play a role in one or the other set of derivations. There seems no reason to suggest that the syncope involved

---

[1] N. B.: giants eat people.

in the forms in (8) differs from that in (9); nor is there motivation for claiming that the Umlaut observed in (8) differs in character from that in (9). The basis for splitting either of the rules (5) and (7) into two distinct statements, therefore, is completely lacking. Next, we can examine the possibility that one or the other does not apply in one of the sets of forms. It seems clear that syncope is involved in both sets; similarly, the presence of a paradigmatic *a* / *ö* alternation in the forms of (8) shows that Umlaut does indeed apply to these forms. The only alternative would seem to be the following: since the paradigms of the forms in (9) show the vowel *ö* in all forms, one might argue (along the lines of Kiparsky, 1968b), that their underlying representations should contain this vowel as well. Although the vowel *ö could* be produced from *a* by Umlaut in these forms (assuming the ordering problem can be solved), it might be argued that such a derivation should be prohibited in a case like this, where it is not required to account for any intraparadigmatic alternation.[2] Of course, if the forms in (9) have the vowel *ö* in their underlying forms, rule (5) does not need to apply to them, and no ordering problem arises. The rules can simply be applied in the order required by the forms in (8): first syncope, then Umlaut. The forms in (9) undergo only syncope.

To deny that the forms in (9) are derived from representations with underlying /a/ is not particularly appealing, however. As pointed out in (9), these forms are related derivationally to other forms in which the vowel /a/ is clearly indicated for the root. It is obviously desirable to derive both *jökull* 'glacier' and *jaki* 'piece of ice' from the same root; since it seems unlikely that a satisfactory rule of 'reverse *u*-Umlaut' can be constructed to derive *jaki* from a root /jök/, we seem to be forced to derive both from /jak/, with *jökull* undergoing *u*-Umlaut. The ordering problem thus seems unresolvable.

In fact, the evidence of rhyme in Old Norse Skaldic verse provides clear and compelling evidence that forms showing *ö* throughout their paradigms, such as those in (9), should nonetheless be derived from underlying forms with /a/. Whereas these facts do not apply directly to Modern Icelandic, of course, the rules of *u*-Umlaut and syncope are in all relevant respects identical in the two stages of the language, and the ordering paradox which concerns us arises in Old Icelandic as well as in Modern Icelandic. Evidence for the abstract derivation at one point in

---

[2] It should be pointed out that Kiparsky, in the paper cited above, did not argue for as strong an antiabstractness position as this; the presence of related derivational forms in which the vowel alternation *a* / *ö* shows up would be enough to support the derivation of *ö* from *a* according to his theory.

time is therefore applicable, at least inferentially, to other stages, since the formal properties of the two sets of rules are identical. In Anderson (1972c), it is shown that the Skaldic rhyme scheme, which was rigidly adhered to in a vast corpus of highly original poetry, cannot be stated unless certain abstract derivations are allowed. The rhyme is stated, not as a constraint on the surface forms of rhyming words, but as a formula which may be satisfied at various stages of a derivation, similar to those discussed by P. Kiparsky (1971a) and Halle (1971). This argument shows conclusively that it is necessary to derive forms like those in (9) from underlying representations containing the vowel /a/.

If this is so, the data just discussed constitute an inescapable violation of the principle (2c) above. How are we to account for such a case? In order to propose a solution, we must first discuss briefly a principle that has been suggested by P. Kiparsky (1968a) in discussing historical change. Kiparsky observed that historical change can be described as various sorts of change in grammars, rather than directly as changes in surface forms. Some changes can be seen as the addition of a new rule to the grammar of an earlier stage of the language, some as the loss of a rule, and others as simple changes in the lexical representations of various items in the language. Still other changes, however, seem to consist in the replacement of one grammar by another which contains essentially the same set of rules and representations, but in which the order of some pair of rules is reversed: where rule *A* preceded rule *B* in the grammar of the initial stage, rule *A* follows rule *B* in the grammar of the innovating stage.

More important for our purposes, however, than the discovery that historical change can consist in the reversal of rule orderings, was the observation that certain such changes have a different status than others. Let us consider two of the possible relations that may obtain between a pair of rules [examples and further discussion will be found below and in Kiparsky (1968a), as well as in the related discussions of Chafe (1968) and Newton (1971a)]. If one of these, rule *A*, converts forms that would not otherwise meet the structural description of the other, rule *B*, into forms that can undergo rule *B*, we can say (with Kiparsky) that rule *A* FEEDS rule B. If, on the other hand, rule *A* has the effect of altering forms that would otherwise undergo rule *B* so that they no longer meet rule B's analysis, then we can say that rule *A* BLEEDS rule *B*. If neither of these relations obtains, we can say that *A* and *B* are NEUTRAL with respect to one another. Given a pair of rules, either or both of the possible orders in which they can be applied may be feeding; similarly, either or both possible orders may be bleeding, or neutral. Kiparsky's observation about historical change in rule orderings, then, was this:

where a feeding order is possible, change tends to operate so as to establish it, and not to destroy it; and where a bleeding order is possible, change tends to operate so as to destroy it, and not to establish it. Thus, change may proceed from an original bleeding order to a new neutral or feeding order, or from an original neutral order to a new feeding order; but would not be expected from an original feeding order to anything else or from an original neutral order to a bleeding order. These observations, based on a study of a number of known cases of historical change involving shifts in order of a pair of rules, suggest that rules most naturally apply in such a way as to maximize their applicability within the language: where a rule would not previously have been allowed to apply to some class of forms, a change may result in widening its scope to include those forms.

The notions of FEEDING and BLEEDING ORDERS were introduced with reference to pairs of rules, and much later discussion has assumed that, given a pair of rules, it can be determined whether one or the other of their possible orderings is feeding, bleeding, or neutral. But it is not hard to see that the notions of feeding and bleeding order can only be defined for a pair of rules in relation to a form (or class of forms). The same ordering that is feeding for one class of forms may be bleeding for another. Consider the two rules (5) and (7) above (*u*-Umlaut and syncope in Icelandic). For the forms in (8), the operation of rule (7) brings new forms under the analysis of rule (5), by eliminating the vowel which formerly intervened between root *a* and a following *u*. The order syncope-Umlaut, then, is feeding for this class of forms. The order Umlaut-syncope, however, is neutral, for while it does not allow syncope to feed Umlaut, neither of the rules bleeds the other. Consider now the forms in (9). For them, the order syncope-Umlaut, which is feeding for the forms in (8), is bleeding, for it allows syncope to remove the *u* that could otherwise cause Umlaut. The order Umlaut-syncope, which is neutral for the forms in (8), is also neutral for the forms in (9), since again neither rule either feeds or bleeds the other in this relationship for these forms.

Now recall that the order of application that was desired for the forms in (8) was the order syncope-Umlaut, which we have just seen to be feeding for these forms, and the order which was desired for the forms in (9) was Umlaut-syncope, which we have just seen to be neutral (as opposed to bleeding) for these forms. This suggests that the notions of feeding and bleeding order may play a role in synchronic phonology, as well as in the theory of historical change. To deal with the forms in (8) and (9), we needed a principle which could differentiate between the two classes on a systematic basis. Let us define a notion of NATURAL ORDER for a pair of rules, and say (as a first approximation, to be amplified in later chapters) that where only one of the two possible orders for a given pair of rules is feeding, the feeding order is the natural one; and that where only one of the two possible orders is bleeding, the other order is the natural one. In all other cases (i.e., when both possible orders are of the same type) no natural order is (yet) defined.

We could say, then, that the basis for dealing with the forms in (8) and (9) is an ordering statement to the effect that rules (5) and (7) apply in the natural order, whichever that is for the form in question. The grammar, then, contains ordering statements of two sorts: for some rules, a specific statement such as 'Rule A precedes rule B' appears. For others, however, the statement is of the type 'Rules A and B apply in the natural order for any given form.' Still other rules, which have no forms in common and hence do not interact, may be related by no ordering statement at all. We will call this theory, in which rules may be related either by an explicit ordering or by a natural ordering statement, the theory of LOCAL ORDERING, as opposed to linear ordering. By a relatively simple move, we can immediately account for Kiparsky's observations about historical change in the theory of local ordering. Suppose that we take the case in which rules apply in the natural order as the typical one, and say that only in case this is not true does the grammar need to contain a statement about the ordering of a given pair of rules. Natural orderings, then are treated on a par with pairs of rules that do not interact: in neither case does the grammar of the particular language need to say anything about their interaction. In the one case, this is because there is nothing to be said; in the other case it is because it is given by general principles rather than being a language-particular fact. In the great majority of cases, the natural order for a pair of rules turns out to be the same for all forms in the language, and so it will not be possible to distinguish empirically between an explicitly given order which is natural (as assumed by the theory of linear ordering), and an unstated one which is predicted. We assume that the order is never stated in the grammar unless it is unpredictable. Now we can see that the kinds of change Kiparsky discussed are exactly analogous to any other instances of the simplification of grammars: just as change can result in the deletion of some feature specification from the statement of a rule, so it can also result in the deletion of an ordering statement from the grammar. When that happens, a previously unpredictable ordering is resolved in favor of a natural ordering. This principle admits exactly the class of changes discussed by Kiparsky, and treats them as formal simplification through the elimination of ordering statements from the grammar.

The theory of local ordering just outlined predicts the existence of a class of violations of principle (2c), antisymmetry, of rather precise form. That is, exactly where two rules are such that the order which is natural for some forms in the language is not natural for other forms, a reversal of ordering can take place if the two rules are allowed to be related naturally. This is exactly correct for the Icelandic example discussed above, which therefore constitutes evidence for this theory. If this example were completely isolated in the languages of the world, we would naturally hesitate to make fundamental revisions in the theory of phonology to accommodate it. There are, however, a number of other examples that give further confirmation to the theory of local ordering, some of which will be discussed below.

A reasonably clear case is found in the rules that determine the nasality of vowels in Sundanese.[3] The basic rule involved is a simple process of progressive nasalization, which applies (iteratively) to nasalize an arbitrarily long sequence of vowels preceded by a nasal consonant and separated only by ʔ or *h*:

(10) $$[+\text{syll}] \longrightarrow [+\text{nasal}] \ / \ [+\text{nasal}] \left(\begin{bmatrix} -\text{cons} \\ -\text{syll} \\ -\text{high} \end{bmatrix} \right) \underline{\hspace{1.5cm}}$$

The effects of this rule can be seen in forms like the following:

(11)
a.	*maro*	[mãro]	'to halve'
b.	*maneh*	[mãnẽh]	'you'
c.	*mandi*	[mãndi]	'to bath'
d.	*ɲiar*	[ɲĩãr]	'to seek'
e.	*ɲaian*	[ɲãĩãn]	'to wet'
f.	*niis*	[nĩʔĩs]	'to take a holiday'
g.	*miasih*	[mĩʔãsih]	'to love'
h.	*kumaha*	[kumãhã]	'how?'
i.	*ɲahokən*	[ɲãhõkən]	'to inform'
j.	*bəŋhar*	[bəŋh̃ãr]	'to be rich'

There are no nasalized vowels in underlying forms in Sundanese, and all of the nasalization in (11) must be regarded as the product of rule (10) (with the exception of the [h̃] of *bəŋhar*, which is nasalized by a separate

---

[3] These rules are discussed in Anderson (1972a) in more detail. The facts of Sundanese, especially with respect to nasalization, are presented in a series of classic papers by Robins (1953a, b, 1957, 1959). In the following I have substituted ə for the IPA symbol used by Robins for a mid–back unrounded vowel.

rule). Normally the process of nasalization is stopped by a word boundary or any "supraglottally articulated consonant" (Robins, 1957, p. 90).
An important exception to this principle, however, is illustrated by the
class of forms in (12):

(12)   a. *moekən*   [mõẽkən]   'to dry';   pl. *maroekən* [mãroẽkən]
       b. *ɲaur*   [ɲãũr]   'to say';   pl. *ɲalaur* [ɲãlaũr]
       c. *niis*   [nĩʔĩs]   'to cool oneself';   pl. *nariis* [nãriʔĩs]
       d. *ɲaho*   [ɲãhõ]   'to know';   pl. *ɲaraho* [ɲãrahõ]

The plural forms of these words are produced by the addition of the infix
-ar- / *-al-* after the first consonant of the root. The distribution of the two
alternants is predictable by a rule given by Robins. The nasalization of
these forms is apparently unlike that of the forms in (11), in that (a) the
sequence of nasalized vowels in, e.g., *ɲaraho,* is interrupted by a nonnasal vowel; and (b) the propagation of nasality is apparently not
stopped by the (supraglottally articulated) *r* or *l* of the infix. That it is
indeed nasalization by the root-initial consonant, and not by the plural
infix itself, is shown by the fact that no nasalization appears in a root like
dahar [dahar] 'to eat', plural (*di-*)*dalahar,* where the root initial is nonnasal.

Problem (a) above, the nonnasal character of the vowel which immediately follows the infix, is resolved by positing a rule of denasalization
which applies after the nasalization process:

(13) $[+\text{syll}] \longrightarrow [-\text{nasal}] \;/\; \begin{bmatrix} +\text{cons} \\ -\text{nasal} \end{bmatrix}$ ___

This rule was first suggested in a preliminary version of Howard (1972),
and will be assumed here on the basis of its high degree of phonetic plausibility. The second problem is not as easily resolved, however. Why
should not the consonant of this infix impede nasalization, when others
do? In Anderson (1972a), it is suggested that this is due to the fact that,
at the stage of the derivation to which nasalization applies, the infix is
not in fact present inside the form, but is rather in a position before the
root, as a prefix. It is argued there that a rule of infixation applies, to
move the infix into its medial position. The class of infixes is specifiable
in terms of syllable shape; this rule can be given as (14):

(14)   + V   C   #   (C)   V
           1   2   3   4   (5)   6 $\Rightarrow$ 4   (5)   2   3   6

If the infix is only moved into place [by rule (14)] after the nasalization rule has applied, then there is no longer any problem with the presence of the consonant *r* or *l* in the middle of the sequence of nasalized segments. Note that the details of rule (14) are irrelevant to our argument; if this (phonological) rule were not accepted, some other (morphological) process would still be required to insert the infixes into the root. Whatever the infixation rule looks like, it is this rule which we suggest follows nasalization.

For this explanation to hold, it must be the case that the rule of nasalization precedes the rule of infixation. There is evidence, however, that this cannot be the case in all forms. A minor difficulty is the fact that the vowel *a* of the infix itself is nasalized, which could only come about after the infix has been moved into place, so that this vowel comes to stand after a nasal in forms like (12). This difficulty could be avoided simply by generalizing rule (13) to an alpha rule like (15), since (13) / (15) is known to apply after (14), regardless of the operation of rule (10):

$$(15) \qquad [+\text{syll}] \longrightarrow [\alpha\,\text{nasal}] \; / \begin{bmatrix} +\text{cons} \\ \alpha\,\text{nasal} \end{bmatrix} \underline{}$$

This cannot, however, be the explanation of a further set of facts. In addition to *-ar-* / *-al-*, Sundanese contains other infixes, which are presumably also placed by the operation of (14). Among these we find the element *-um-*, which itself contains a nasal. In the form *dumǝhǝs* [dumә́hә̃s], from the root *dǝhǝs* [dǝhǝs] 'to approach (a superior)', we see that the sequence of vowels following the nasal of the infix is nasalized. This cannot be due to the operation of a rule like (15), for (15) can only affect a vowel which is immediately preceded by a consonant, and hence only one of a sequence of vowels. This property is essential if (13) / (15) is not to denasalize several vowels in the plural forms in (12). The natural explanation is that rule (10) is responsible for the nasalization here, as well as elsewhere. But in order for this to be the case, rule (10) must apply after infixation.

In the theory of local ordering, this example has a ready explanation. If we assume that the rules of nasalization and infixation are allowed to apply in the natural order (that is, there is no ordering restriction stated in the grammar of Sundanese for this pair of rules), the correct results will be obtained. In the plural forms in (12), the order nasalization–infixation is neutral, while the opposite order would be bleeding. For these forms, then, the order nasalization–infixation is natural. For the class of forms like *dumǝhǝs,* however, the order infixation–nasalization is feeding, while the order nasalization–infixation would be neutral. For such a form, then, the order infixation–nasalization is natural. Exactly the correct derivations are predicted:

(16) a. *nariis*   b. *dumǝhǝs*

underlying:	/ar # niʔis/	underlying:	/um # dǝhǝs/
(10)	/ar # nĩʔĩs/	(14)	/# dumǝhǝs/
(14)	/# narĩʔĩs/	(10)	/# dumɔ̃hɔ̃s/
(15)	/# nãrĩʔĩs/		
output:	[nãriʔĩs]		[dumɔ̃hɔ̃s]

This example, then, provides further confirmation for the theory of local ordering suggested above.

A number of interesting examples are provided in a discussion of the phonology of Modern Greek dialects by Newton (1971a) (further data can be found in Newton, 1967b). Newton suggests, for example, that in the dialect of Lesbos there is a rule of palatalization, and a rule of vowel-dropping (which deletes short high vowels in unstressed syllables). There is also a rule of epenthesis, which breaks up certain final consonant clusters by inserting a vowel /i/. These rules convert /exun/ 'they have' and /exi/ 'he has' to [ex,in] and [ex,], respectively. In the derivation of [ex,in], vowel dropping first deletes the vowel /u/, yielding /exn/; this is then subject to epenthesis, becoming /exin/, which is then palatalized to [ex,in]. In this derivation, palatalization cannot apply until after epenthesis, which in turn cannot apply until after vowel dropping. In the derivation of [ex,], on the other hand, palatalization applies first, changing /exi/ into /ex,i/; only then does vowel dropping apply to produce [ex,]. In these two derivations, two different orders of vowel dropping and palatalization are required; it will readily be seen that these two different orders follow for their respective form classes if we adopt the principle of local ordering and impose no explicit constraint on the order of the two rules. This example, then, and the others discussed by Newton,[4] are further evidence for the theory of local ordering in that they constitute violations of the requirement of antisymmetry which can be resolved according to the principles of natural orders.

The cases illustrated above, and others like them, have the property that one class of forms requires one order for the rules *A* and *B*, and

---

[4] All of the examples discussed in Newton (1971a) are of this type, or of the type to be discussed in the next chapter, with one exception. They can thus be formulated naturally within the theory of local ordering. It is noteworthy that the one example which cannot be formulated adequately within this theory (Newton, 1971a, pp. 44–45) is a hypothetical one, not attested in any real dialect.

another class requires the other order, but in each case the order that is required is the one which is natural for the forms in question. A further set of cases exists in which again one set of forms requires one ordering of the rules and another set of forms requires the opposite order, but where only one of the required orderings is a natural one. The other ordering is one which obtains in a class of forms for which there is no natural ordering: that is, a natural ordering is defined for only some of the forms in the language, and in these, the rules apply in that order; but in the forms for which there is no natural ordering, some ordering restriction must be given, and this happens to be the opposite of the (natural) ordering obtaining in the other class of forms. An example of this sort is found in the African language Kasem.[5]

An interesting class of nominals, called "class *C*" by Callow, take the suffixes /+a/ 'singular' and /+i/ 'plural'. These include forms such as the following:

(17)   a.   *bakada* 'boy';   pl. *bakadi*
       b.   *sada* 'grass mat';   pl. *sadi*
       c.   *fala* 'white man';   pl. *fali*
       d.   *bakala* 'shoulder'; pl. *bakali*

If such a form would otherwise end in two identical vowels, one of these is truncated, as in the forms (18a, b). In Callow's data, however, the only instances of truncation are with the vowels *a* and *i*; round vowels, such as those in the forms (18c, d), from class *D*, are not truncated:

(18)   a.   *kambia* 'cooking pot';   pl. *kambi*
       b.   *pia* 'yam';   pl. *pi*
       c.   *kuu* 'bone';   pl. *ku:du*
       d.   *voo* 'leaf';   pl. *ku:du*

Given these facts, we could formulate a truncation rule as follows:

(19)
$$
\begin{bmatrix} +\text{syll} \\ -\text{round} \\ \alpha\text{high} \end{bmatrix} \longrightarrow \emptyset \;/\; \underline{\hspace{2em}} \begin{bmatrix} +\text{syll} \\ -\text{round} \\ \alpha\text{high} \end{bmatrix}
$$

Identity of highness is sufficient to insure that two ([-round]) vowels are identical, since the vowel *e* is always secondary, and thus only *a* and *i* need to be distinguished.

[5] Kasem is described in two articles by Callow (1965, 1968). An analysis of Callow's data is presented by Chomsky and Halle (1968), and this analysis is refined and extended by Anderson (1969b) and Howard (1969, 1970).

Another rule discussed by Chomsky and Halle, and by Howard, is that deleting a stem final velar in plural formations. Chomsky and Halle note only the deletion before /+i/, and formulate the rule in purely phonological terms. Howard notes that the rule also applies before the affix /+du/ 'plural' of the *D* class, and in fact there is no other plural suffix exemplified in Callow's data before which stem-final velars do not delete. Howard prefers to separate the two deletions, however, for the following reason: there is a rule in the language which lengthens stem-final vowels before a single consonant in a following suffix. Class *D* nominals (whose endings are /+u/ in the singular and the already-noted /+du/ in the plural) with final velars would appear to meet the conditions for the application of this rule if velar elision precedes lengthening, but forms such as *kasugu* / *kasudu* 'bundle(s) of millet stalks' show that it does not apply. Accordingly, velar elision in class *D* nominals should follow lengthening. The lengthening rule, however, must follow other rules which in turn must follow the elision of velars before the /+i/ of class *C*. This makes it impossible (for Howard) to collapse the two cases. We should note, however, that the vowel lengthening rule and the elision of velars before /+i/ do not interact with one another, since both can never apply in the same form: obviously, if the suffix following the stem has the shape /+i/, it cannot begin with a single consonant. Because of this, Howard's ordering problem does not arise in the framework adopted here, in which such arguments for ordering from transitivity are rejected. We shall write the velar elision rule in the (partially morphological) form (20), and require simply that 'vowel lengthening precedes velar elision':

$$(20) \qquad \begin{bmatrix} +\text{cons} \\ +\text{high} \\ -\text{cor} \end{bmatrix} \longrightarrow \emptyset \,/ \underline{\qquad} +[\text{PLURAL}]$$

The alternatives of separating (20) into two rules or writing a rule involving the term 'before *i* or +C' do not appear attractive.

Another rule of Kasem phonology creates the glide *w* from underlying /u/ before another vowel. This rule always applies before *i* or *e*, never before *u* or *o*, and before *a* only if this *a* is followed by another consonant. Thus we could give the rule as (21):

$$(21) \qquad \begin{bmatrix} +\text{high} \\ +\text{back} \end{bmatrix} \longrightarrow [-\text{syll}] \,/ \underline{\qquad} \begin{bmatrix} +\text{syll} \\ -\text{round} \\ {}_a\langle +\text{low}\rangle \end{bmatrix}\, {}_b\langle[-\text{syll}]\rangle$$

condition: if *a*,   then *b*

The combination of rules (20) and (21) is responsible for such alternations as that found in *buga* / *bwi* 'river(s)': the root is here /bug/, which is unchanged before the singular /+a/, but which loses its final velar before the plural /+i/. The resulting /bu+i/ then becomes [bwi] by glide formation.

We must also discuss two other processes having to do with the treatment of vowel sequences. First, there is a rule rather like that involved in the vowel contraction associated with Sanskrit *guṇa*, which contracts sequences /ai/ and /au/ to single vowels, /e/ and /o/, respectively:

(22)
$$\begin{bmatrix} +\text{syll} \\ +\text{low} \end{bmatrix} \begin{bmatrix} +\text{syll} \\ +\text{high} \end{bmatrix}$$
$$1 \qquad 2 \quad \Rightarrow \begin{bmatrix} 2 \\ -\text{high} \end{bmatrix}$$

This rule plays a part in deriving alternations such as *laŋa* / *le* 'song(s)', *naga* / *ne* 'leg(s)', etc. The roots are here /laŋ/ and /nag/, which remain unchanged before the singular /+a/; before the plural /+i/, however, they lose their final velars, becoming /la+i/ and /na+i/. These intermediate forms are in turn converted into the outputs *le* and *ne* by rule (22).

With the rules developed thus far,[6] it is possible to eliminate the vowels *e* and *o* from underlying representations in Kasem, and to reduce the underlying inventory to /a,i,u/.[7] Knowing this, we can approach the highly problematic set of forms in (23):

(23) a. *koga* 'back';   pl. *kwe*
      b. *čoŋa* 'path';   pl. *čwe*

The roots in (23) are apparently /kog/ and /čoŋ/, as shown by the singulars. Taking the effects of (22) into account, we can reduce these to /kaug/ and /čauŋ/, which are preserved before the /+a/ of the singular with only (22) applying. Before the plural /+i/, we expect the final velars to drop, giving /kaui/ and /čaui/. The forms *kwe* and *čwe*, however, seem

---

[6] Not quite. The contraction rule (22) is responsible for most instances of *e* and *o*, but some final *o*'s, such as that of *vo:do* 'leaves' cited above, are the result of a further process assimilating final *u* to the height of a preceding *o*.

[7] Each of the five phonetic vowels of Kasem actually occurs in two harmonic variants, which we have disregarded here. These are differentiated, as is typical in African languages, by a feature such as [±advanced tongue root], which defines two classes for the vowel harmony rule. However, the harmony involved is irrelevant to the operation of the rules discussed here.

to represent /kuai/ and /čuai/. To explain this, Chomsky and Halle propose a rule of metathesis, which they support with several other examples and which is further supported by Howard:

$$(24) \qquad\qquad \begin{array}{ccc} [+\text{syll}] & [+\text{syll}] & [+\text{syll}] \\ 1 & 2 & 3 \end{array} \Rightarrow 2 \quad 1 \quad 3$$

In other words, the first two of three consecutive vowels are metathesized.

Consider now the form *pia* 'sheep', pl. *pe*. The plural looks like /pai/, and seems to be related to singular by metathesis. Chomsky and Halle suggest that this would follow naturally if we took the root to be /pia/, with the usual class *C* endings /+a/ and /+i/. In the plural form /pia+i/, metathesis will apply, giving /pai+i/, to which truncation [rule (19)] applies, giving /pa+i/, which reduces to the correct /pe/ by rule (22). But what of /pia+a/? We would expect metathesis to give /pai+a/, from which **pea,* rather than *pia.* Instead, we wish only to apply truncation in this form, without metathesis. But we cannot apply truncation first, apparently, since truncation must *follow* metathesis in the derivation of *pe.* Chomsky and Halle resolve this difficulty by imposing a not particularly elegant restriction on the metathesis rule: the rule does not apply if $2 = 3 = a$. With this restriction, /pia+a/ does not, of course, go to /pai+a/, and so is available for truncation to /pi+a/. While this device allows the correct forms to be produced, there is no basis for limiting the restriction to cases where $2 = 3 = a$; we could equally well constrain it simply by prohibiting metathesis if $2 = 3$. But then it is clear that there is a generalization being missed: if $2 = 3$, then the rule of truncation would apply to reduce the three vowel sequence to two. In other words, metathesis of a three vowel sequence is blocked exactly where the sequence is one that truncation could reduce to two vowels, a reduction that would of course render the sequence ineligible for metathesis. In that case, it is clear that Chomsky and Halle's restriction is nothing but a device to get around what is really an ordering problem: truncation should be allowed to apply first to /pia+a/, but to /pia+i/ only after metathesis.[8]

---

[8] Notice now that the discussion above could equally well have started from a posited root /pai/ for the word 'sheep'; in this case, the metathesis rule would have to apply in the singular, giving /pia+a/ from which *pia* by truncation, while truncation would have to apply first to /pai+i/, giving /pa+i/ from which *pe* by rule (22). In fact, Howard prefers to take /pai/ as the root in this case, in order to state a morpheme-structure constraint on underlying vowel sequences. We do not agree with his views on the range of such sequences in Kasem, and merely note that the structure of the argument here is identical, regardless of which form is posited.

It is crucial to note that our analysis rests on the claim that the restrictions on metathesis are identical with the conditions for truncation. Howard (1970) suggests that this may not be so, however. We have noted above that truncation does not apply if the two vowels in question are [+round]; Howard argues that metathesis is nonetheless blocked in this case. He suggests that this is shown by forms such as *naboo* / *nabo:do* 'cattle yard(s)', *voo* / *vo:do,* which are nouns of Callow's class *D.* If the roots here are taken to be /nabau/ and /vau/, the derivations proposed are the following: /nabau+u/ does not metathesize (because $V_2 = V_3$, even though truncation cannot apply); contraction [rule (22)] applies, giving /nabo+u/, from which the vowel assimilation rule mentioned in footnote 6, page 154 gives *naboo*. The derivation of *voo* follows the same lines. In the case of /nabau+du/, on the other hand, only rule (22) applies, giving /nabo+du/; the vowel lengthening and assimilation rules which we have mentioned then give *nabo:do* (and, similarly, *vo:do*).

These observations are indeed correct if the roots in question are /nabau/ and /vau/. There are reasons to suspect, however, that this is not the case. First, we must note that there are instances of metathesis which rule (24) cannot account for:

(25)　　a.　*godo*　'cloth';　　pl. *gwa:du*
　　　　b.　*bolo*　'valley';　　pl. *bwa:lu*
　　　　c.　*sono*　'one who is loved';　　pl. *swa:nu*
　　　　d.　*fogo*　'die, dice';　　pl. *fwadu*
　　　　e.　*jogo*　'breechcloth';　　pl. *jwadu*

In the plural forms, we assume the ending to be the basic /+du/ of class *D.* In (25a–c), the *d* of this affix undergoes assimilation to a preceding sonorant and subsequent geminate reduction (processes illustrated elsewhere in the language), so the roots can be taken to be /gaud/, /baul/, and /saun/, as suggested by the singulars. In the case of (25d, e), a stem-final velar would be elided by rule (20) above in the plurals, so these roots seem naturally to be /faug/ and /jaug/. In all of the plurals, the root vowels must metathesize from / · · · au · · · / to / · · · ua · · · /; once this has happened, glide formation will apply in all the plurals [giving / · · · wa · · · / by rule (21)], since all of these instances of /a/ are followed by consonants as required. Vowel lengthening will then apply to (25a–c), since the vowel is followed by a morpheme beginning with one consonant; vowel lengthening cannot apply to (25d, e), because its environment is not satisfied until after the operation of velar elision, and as we noted, lengthening cannot follow velar elision (by an absolute ordering restriction).

The metathesis involved in (25) is different from that produced by rule (24), since it cannot apply to the sequence / · · · ai · · · /, as (24) can. This is shown by the form *sio | se :du,* from the root /sai/. In /sai+u/, metathesis (24) applies, giving /sia+u/ from which *sio* arises by (22). /sai+du/ will yield /se+du/ by (22), from which *se :du* by regular lengthening. This is only possible, however, if the SECOND METATHESIS process under discussion does not apply here. In fact, it seems to apply only to the sequence / · · · au · · · /. Howard states this as metathesis of / · · · au · · · / before two consonants, but it will be noted that all of the two consonant sequences before which it applies have the following property: they are all simplified, either by assimilation and subsequent degemination, or by velar elision. (No instances of class *D* nouns ending in a labial with vowel *o* are given by Callow.) In addition, metathesis of exactly the sequence /au/ before two consonants has no apparent phonetic motivation. The process in question seems more likely to be a morphological one, which can be formulated as follows[9]:

$$(26) \qquad \begin{bmatrix} V \\ +\text{back} \end{bmatrix} \begin{bmatrix} V \\ +\text{back} \end{bmatrix} + [\text{PLURAL}]$$
$$1 \qquad 2 \quad 3 \qquad 4 \quad \Rightarrow 2\ 1\ 3\ 4$$

But now, given this rule, we can return to the proposal to derive *naboo | nabo :do* and *voo | vo :do* from the roots /nabau/ and /vau/. If this analysis is accepted, it becomes difficult to explain why /vau+du/ gives *vo :do,* etc. We should rather expect metathesis (26) to apply, yielding *vwa :du,* since the environment for its application is met. Suppose, however, we take the stems to be /nabua/ and /vua/. Then the plurals /nabua+du/ and /vua+du/ will metathesize by (26), giving /nabau+du/ and /vau+du/ from which *nabo :do* and *vo :do* are derived by familiar processes. In the singulars, /nabua+u/ and /vua+u/, metathesis (24) applies, giving /nabau+u/ and /vau+u/: these cannot, of course, undergo truncation since their vowels are round, and so give rise to *naboo* and *voo* as required. But now we see that these stems are not, in fact, evidence for a restriction on the operation of metathesis (24). Howard's contention that (24) is constrained in ways distinct from the operation of truncation, then, is unsubstantiated.[10]

[9] Notice that the alternations *yua | ywe* 'hair(s)' and *nanjua | nanjwe* 'fly | flies' suggest that metathesis rule (24) cannot similarly be limited to the plural. These class *C* nouns have apparently metathesized from /yau+i/ to /yua+i/, etc. in the plurals; but if this is the case, they must also have metathesized in the singular from /yau+a/ to /yua+a/, etc.

[10] Howard has, in fact, indicated (personal communication) that he is aware of an alternative to the argument presented in Howard (1970). I presume the above line of reasoning is approximately what he means.

The system of rules at which we have now arrived appears to cover all of the facts of Kasem that are available. There are some peculiar features to this set of rules, however, that demand some explanation. First, why should a language have both of the metathesis processes we have posited for Kasem in the rules (24) and (26)? And second, why should both the second metathesis of (26) and the velar elision rule of (20) be conditioned by the presence of PLURAL morphemes? It seems not unreasonable to seek the answers to both questions in the process of historical change. Two aspects of these processes seem to have phonetic plausibility: the elision of velars before the class *C* plural ending, and the first metathesis rule. It is not surprising that velars should be elided before *i*: we can imagine a sequence of steps in which velars are first fronted, then converted to glides ([j]), and then absorbed into the following vowel. We can suggest, therefore, that the velar elision rule entered the grammar originally in essentially the form given by Chomsky and Halle: as a purely phonological rule, deleting velars before $+i$. Similarly, the metathesis rule has the effect in most cases of altering vowel sequences so that an open vowel is surrounded by two close vowels, a more natural sequence than an open vowel followed by two closed vowels. This rule too, then, we can suggest arose first in the phonologically conditioned form (24). But now, in both cases, the alternations produced by the rules of velar elision and metathesis differentiated singulars from plurals, as marks supplementary to the segmental affixes. We may suggest, therefore, that both rules were morphologized, in the sense that they were reinterpreted as producing marks of the grammatical category PLURAL, and were then extended into plural categories which did not meet their original structural description. This resulted in the alteration of the environment for velar elision from a phonological to a morphological one, and in the introduction of 'second metathesis', rule (26). Such a change in the status of a rule is exactly the sort of thing which is familiar from studies of historical morphology in Indo-European languages by scholars such as Kuryłowicz, Watkins, and others. In the absence of historical data on Kasem, or further information from other classes of nouns, this account must remain entirely speculative, but it seems reasonable in light of our present evidence and expectations about historical change.

In sum, all of the facts seem consistent with an analysis on which we can remove the restriction on metathesis (24) by making use of the rule of truncation. This is only possible, however, if we can resolve the ordering dilemma, which (it will be recalled) came from the fact that it was necessary for (19) to precede (24) in some derivations, but follow it in others.

Let us consider what natural orders can be defined between the pair of rules (19) and (24), whose ordering presents this paradox. For the form *pe*, from underlying /pia+i/, the order metathesis–truncation is feeding, since truncation cannot apply until metathesis has produced the sequence /aii/. The opposite order, truncation–metathesis, is a neutral order; and therefore the natural order is seen to be metathesis–truncation for forms of this type. In the case of underlying /pia+a/, however, the situation is different. The order which is natural for /pia+i/, metathesis–truncation, is here a bleeding order, since truncation could apply to the underlying form, but is kept from doing so if metathesis applies first. The opposite order, truncation–metathesis, is also a bleeding order, for here the application of truncation prevents the application of metathesis. Both orders of the rules are thus bleeding for these forms, and we have no way of defining a natural order.

In this case, therefore, though there are two classes of forms with respect to the rules in question, a natural order is defined for only one of these. In this class, the natural order is indeed the one which obtains. In the other class, since there is no natural order, and it makes a difference which way we apply the rules, the grammar will have to contain some sort of statement to enforce the ordering truncation–metathesis. If such a statement is construed absolutely, it would contradict the observed natural ordering in the other class of forms. Suppose, however, that we differentiate between two kinds of stated orderings: some, which are to be taken as governing the operation of the rules in question for all forms in the language, we can call ABSOLUTE ordering restrictions. In addition to these, we can identify others as defining the relative order of a pair of rules only in derivations where the principles of natural ordering do not provide a basis for a choice between the two possibilities. Such CONTINGENT ordering restrictions, then, are ignored where a natural order is defined, and only come into play where there is none. This allows us to solve the Kasem problem: we can say that the grammar contains the restriction: 'Truncation precedes metathesis (contingently).'

The notion of a contingent ordering restriction follows naturally from the notion of allowing rules to apply in the natural order, whichever that is for a given form. Some rule pairs will be such that a natural order is defined for all forms in the language, though which order this is may differ from form class to form class. Other rule pairs will be such that no natural orders are defined, and the grammar must contain a specification if they are to apply correctly. In the case where a natural order is defined only for some of the forms in a language, however, it is necessary on the one hand to specify an order for the forms in which this is not so, and on the other hand, it is natural to expect that the rules would apply in the natural order where there is one. There is no particular reason to expect a priori that the specified order in the one case would be the same as the natural order in the other, and a contingent ordering restriction therefore has the same status (for the forms to which it is applicable) as any other language particular restriction.

In resolving such problems by the device of contingent ordering restrictions, the theory should be seen as making a claim of sorts about phonological structure. We could instead have introduced a notion of an ordering restriction which is limited to a specified (arbitrary) class of forms. The Kasem problem would then be resolved by stating that 'metathesis precedes truncation' in a class of forms including /pia+i/, and 'truncation precedes metathesis' in a class of forms including /pia+a/. The difference between these two theoretical moves is that the introduction of (absolute) ordering restrictions relative to a class of (arbitrarily specified) forms would implicitly claim that whatever property defines the relevant class is unrelated to any other property of the class, and in particular is unrelated to any general properties of the ordering of phonological rules. By defining contingent ordering restrictions in the way this was done above, however, we extend the claim that where rules apply in different orders in different classes of forms, the relevant classes are defined in terms of the independent properties of natural rule ordering. This distinction would be somewhat blurred if it is necessary to introduce a notion of exception features for rule orderings, as has sometimes been proposed; however, the fact remains that we would like to maintain as far as possible the claim that the principles of natural ordering define the classes which serve as the domains of particular orders of rule application.

Another instance of a contingent ordering restriction can be found in the phonology of an Alaskan Eskimo dialect.[11] In discussing this dialect, Underhill (1970) argues for several rules which affect combinations of noun bases with suffixes. The first of these is related to the division of suffixes into deleting and nondeleting suffixes. All treatments of Eskimo morphophonemics distinguish at least these two classes, though more are probably necessary. Some suffixes seem to be deleting in some combinations but not in others, determined in complex ways. Other class divisions of suffixes have been based on the operation of other rules

---

[11] The dialect in question is that described by Krauss, Miyaoka, and Reed (1970). It should be emphasized that these facts are not identical with those of other dialects, particularly the better known West Greenlandic dialects. The analysis below is essentially that of Underhill (1971), though it has been altered in ways Underhill might not agree with. I am grateful to Michael Krauss, Robert Underhill, and Jørgen Rischel for sharing their knowledge of Eskimo with me, although it is especially clear in this case that they are not to be blamed for the use I have made of the facts that have pointed out to me.

which do not concern us here, though it may be noted that both arbitrary features of morphological structure and straightforward phonological conditioning are relevant.

The basis of the deleting / nondeleting (/partially deleting) distinction is the effect a suffix has on the final consonant of a root to which it is attached. We see in (27a–c) that a nondeleting suffix such as /put/ 'our' has no effect on the final of the preceding root; while (27d, e) show that a deleting suffix like /li/ 'to make a . . . ' results in the deletion of a root final consonant:

(27)[12]   a.   *nunaput*   'our land'   (/nuna+put/)
          b.   *aŋeyarput*   'our boat'   (/aŋeyar+put/)
          c.   *ačagput*   'our aunt'   (/ačag+put/)
          d.   *aŋeyali*   'to make a boat'   (/aŋeyar+li/)
          e.   *kameguli*   'to make a boot'   (/kamegug+li/)

Whether a given suffix is of the deleting or the nondeleting type seems to be unrelated to its segmental structure. Thus, /put/ 'our (singular)' is nondeleting, while /put/ 'our (plural)' is deleting, though identical in segmental structure. Underhill and others represent this distinction in terms of the boundary element preceding the suffix: deleting suffixes are written with preceding = boundary, while nondeleting suffixes are written with preceding +. The two suffixes for 'our', then, could be represented as /+put/ and /=put/. Given this convention, we could write the truncation rule as applying simply before =.

No systematic importance should be attached to this convention, however. The complexity of the facts of deletion, and the existence of partially deleting suffixes, make it impossible to associate the difference in boundary elements with different lexical items in general; and there is no possible basis for positing a difference in syntactic structure between deleting and nondeleting suffixes, which would justify representing the boundary differently in the two cases. There is, furthermore, no other property of phonological behavior which is correlated with the deleting / nondeleting distinction. If there were some other process that occurred in certain definable environments, such as at word end, and also before deleting suffixes, that would justify our representing deleting suffixes by some distinctive property (that also characterizes, in the example chosen, word end). No such process or property appears to exist,

---

[12] In the representation of these forms from the Alaskan dialect, *g* and *r* represent voiced velar and uvular spirants, respectively; *q* is a voiceless uvular stop; and *ł* is a voiceless lateral spirant. I also follow Krauss, Miyaoka, and Reed (1970) in using *e* for schwa.

however. It is simply the case that certain suffixes cause truncation (sometimes with all roots; sometimes only in certain combinations). There is no basis for coding this behavior into the representation otherwise than by a minor rule feature (a sort of morphological mark). We will continue to write = and + for purely expository purposes to distinguish the two kinds of suffix behavior; these should both be interpreted as formative boundary, however, with and without a rule feature attached to the following morpheme. The rule is thus as in (28), and is a minor rule (in the sense of Lightner, 1968):

(28) $$[-\text{syll}] \longrightarrow \emptyset / \underline{\hspace{1cm}} =$$

$$(= [-\text{syll}] \longrightarrow \emptyset / \underline{\hspace{1cm}} + [+\text{DELETING}])$$

Processes of epenthesis and/or vowel deletion interact with truncation. First, stem-final *t* is not deleted; instead, epenthetic schwa appears, as in the alternation *čiut* 'ear' *čiutema* 'my ear' with the deleting suffix /=ma/ 'my (singular)'. This vowel appears before both deleting and non-deleting suffixes, and could be treated in either of two ways: either as part of the root, or as inserted by an epenthesis rule. In the first case, there is no interaction with truncation to be explained: *t* never appears in root final position (in nouns), and hence never needs to be truncated. The vowel following it is lost only in word-final position, where truncation cannot, of course, apply. If we choose to insert the vowel in nonfinal position, however, we must impose the ordering 'epenthesis precedes truncation', since this is a bleeding order. Neither of these solutions seems entirely satisfying; while there is convincing evidence in West Greenlandic for treating these vowels as underlying rather than epenthetic, we do not know of such evidence for the dialect in question. Since the choice does not affect the part of the analysis with which we are concerned, we leave it open.

Another set of vowel / ∅ alternations is of more interest, however, and seems securely to be the result of an epenthesis rule. There appears to be a distinction between stems ending in the sequence CVC, where V may be schwa, and stems ending in underlying CC, although the latter always occur phonetically as CeC. Compare, for example, (29a, b) with (29c, d):

(29)   a.   *aseveq* 'walrus';   *asevera* 'his walrus'
       b.   *qayaq* 'kayak';   *qayapik* 'real kayak'   (/qayaq=pik/);
            qayapiga 'his real kayak'

c. *ateq* 'name'; *aqqa* 'his name'[13]
d. *qimugte* 'dog'; *qimugteɬeq* 'the former dog'; *qimugteɬra* 'his former dog'

When the stems in (29c, d) come to stand before a vocalic ending, they do not show a vowel between their last two consonants; but elsewhere they do. The stems in (29a, b), on the other hand, preserve their vowels under all conditions. It is natural to assume that the stems in (29c, d) end in a cluster, while those in (29a, b) end in the sequence CVC. A rule then applies to break up the clusters when the stem is followed by end of word or by a consonant initial suffix (either deleting or nondeleting), as in *ateq* 'name' and *aterma* 'my name':

$$(30) \qquad \qquad \emptyset \longrightarrow e \ / \ C \ \underline{\qquad} \ C + \left\{ \begin{matrix} \# \\ C \end{matrix} \right\}$$

In fact, this rule is even more general in this dialect (though not in Greenlandic), and applies in cases other than those of stem-final clusters. If the following suffix begins with a cluster, even stems which end in only one consonant show epenthesis. From /tanegurraq/ 'boy' plus /nka/ 'my (plural)', we get /tanegurraqe+nka/ by epenthesis. Other rules delete certain intervocalic uvulars, and assimilate schwa to an adjacent vowel to give the surface form *tanegurraanka* 'my boys'. Clusters of three or more consonants never arise within a single morpheme, and we cannot tell what would happen in that event. It is clear from *tanegurraanka,* however, that epenthesis occurs regardless of where the morpheme boundary is in a three consonant cluster, and so we are justified in removing it altogether from (30). On the basis of reasonable assumptions about syllabification in Eskimo, in fact, we could observe that word final clusters and internal three-consonant clusters are both characterized as the cases in which syllable-final clusters would result, contrary to Eskimo phonetic principles. If we were to allow the use of syllable boundary (written '.') in rules, as we will argue is necessary in Chapter 14, we could then state the epenthesis rule as (31):

$$(31) \qquad \qquad \emptyset \longrightarrow e \ / \ C \ \underline{\qquad} \ C.$$

---

[13] A rule not discussed here assimilates *t* to a following consonant; other rules specify the distribution of the feature [± continuant] in clusters. Thus, *qq* in (29c) and *ɬr* in (29d) represent deeper /tq/ and /ɬq/.

Now let us consider the interaction between the rules of truncation as in (28) and epenthesis as in (31). From the stem /atq/ 'name', plus the deleting suffix /=ma/, we get *atema* 'of my names'. In order for this to happen, we should first apply epenthesis to /atq = ma/ (giving /ateq = ma/) and then truncation (giving *atema*). If truncation were to apply first, the environment for epenthesis will no longer be satisfied, and *e* would not be inserted.[14] Notice that the order which is required here is neutral, as opposed to a bleeding order, and hence natural for this form. Thus this ordering need not be imposed by the grammar.

In the form *tanegurramta* 'of our boys', from /tanegurraq=mta/, we see a different interaction of the rules, however. If we apply first epenthesis and then truncation as in the derivation of *atema,* we would expect (after uvular deletion and schwa assimilation) **tanegurraamta.* If we apply truncation first, on the other hand, epenthesis cannot apply, and we get the correct *tanegurramta.* Note that for this form both orders are bleeding: if epenthesis applies first, it will bleed truncation by inserting a vowel to 'protect' the stem-final consonant, whereas if truncation applies first, it will block epenthesis by eliminating the triconsonantal cluster. Since there is no natural order defined for this form, and the order truncation–epenthesis is desired, we can impose this as a contingent ordering restriction. That will allow both this derivation, and the correct derivation of *atema* where a natural ordering was defined.

In this chapter, we have suggested that the view generally held on the character of the ordering relation in phonology should be replaced by a different one, which does not involve linear ordering relations. In our proposed substitute, the theory of local ordering, ordering relations are stated between certain pairs of rules in the grammar of a language. Such stated restrictions are independent of one another, and they may in addition be either absolute or contingent in their applicability. To determine the order in which the set of rules should apply to a given form, we assume that any pair of rules applies in the natural order for the form in question (if one is defined), unless this is overruled by an absolute ordering restriction. In the event that neither order of a pair of rules is natural for this form, the grammar must contain a restriction (either absolute or contingent, depending on the existence of a subclass of forms for which a natural ordering does exist, and on whether the natural situation in fact obtains there). Such a restriction specifies the order in which

---

[14] Even if we chose to resolve the problem about stem final *t* raised above by an epenthesis rule, rather than by having *t* followed by *e* in underlying forms, this rule could not be the one responsible for the *e* in *atema.* In a form such as *qimugtelema* 'of my former dogs', from /qimugt(e)+ʎq = ma/, epenthesis must precede truncation even after ʎ.

rules apply, where this is significant and unpredictable or language-particular. Where two rules are completely unrelated, the grammar need contain no statement since the rules can equally well be applied in either order (or indeed simultaneously). Where the correct ordering is specified by the principles of natural ordering, it is also unnecessary to include a statement of it in the grammar of the individual language. In the next chapter, we will examine further examples which are inconsistent with the theory of linear ordering, but which are expressed naturally in terms of the theory just outlined. A number of derivations will also be given in connection with these examples, from which some of the details of the theory will perhaps become clearer.

CHAPTER 11

More Violations
of Linear Ordering

In the previous chapter we discussed several cases in which the application of a pair of rules violated the antisymmetry condition (10.2c), in that the ordering required in one class of derivations was not the same as the ordering required for the derivation of other forms. We proposed to resolve this problem by allowing the order of application of at least some rules in the grammar of a language to be determined by general principles of natural ordering, after observing that such principles can give exactly the result that the order which is natural for some forms may not be for others. In this chapter we will explore further consequences of allowing rules to apply in this way.

The final requirement on our list for an ordering relation that is to be linear is that it be transitive (10.2d). If, as has traditionally been the case, the ordering relation in a grammar is conceived of as nonlocal, defining the interrelations of all of the rules of the grammar simultaneously, this seems a natural condition to expect; but once we shift to a conception of the ordering relation as a pairwise condition on the interaction of rules, we see that there is no reason to expect it to be met. Given derivations in which A precedes B, and derivations in which B precedes C, these rules need provide no information whatever about the interaction of A and C in derivations in which B does not apply, and there is no necessity that A precede C in such derivations.

A case that directly contradicts that assumption (of transitivity) can be found in Faroese, a West Scandinavian language related to Icelandic.[1] This language displays a consonantal alternation which we refer to as VERSCHÄRFUNG, by analogy with the corresponding sound change(s) in early Germanic, also known as Holtzmann's Law. The change in question is posited to account for the correspondence between glides in certain WGmc forms and clusters of velar or palatal plus glide in NGmc and EGmc. Thus [j] in WGmc often corresponds to [ǰ] (=*ddj* or *ggj*), while [w] often corresponds to [gw] (= *ggw*). As pointed out in a recent study of the Faroese *Verschärfung* (Roe, 1965), parallels with similar sound changes in other than Germanic languages have often been left out of account in discussions of the phenomenon. Romance, for instance, shows many instances: Ital. *maggiore* 'greater', from Lat. *māior;* Prov., etc. *guardar* from Gmc. *wardon* 'to ward off'; Span. *guadanar* 'to mow' from Gmc. *waidanjan,* from *waida* 'meadow'; elsewhere, Gujarati *-ija-* ([ija]) 'future', is from *-iyya-*, which, in turn, is from *-iya-* (cf. Skt.), etc. Examples could be multiplied from a variety of languages. In each case, the first step in the change is apparently a development of lengthened (or geminate) glides under some or other circumstances; these long glides then undergo a dissimilation of continuance, by which the first element becomes a stop. The process is further analyzed below; it is necessary at this point to note only that it is of a relatively common and natural sort.

Such an alternation between glides and velar / palatal clusters is found in a very productive form in Faroese. For instance, most verbs that show the clusters *ggj* (=[j]) and *gv* (=[gv]) before a vocalic ending such as /-a/ 'infinitive' show simply a glide which is the second part of a diphthong before a consonantal ending such as /-r/ '3sg. pres.'. Similarly, nouns that show these clusters before /-ur/ 'nom. sg.' show only the glide (in most cases) before /-s/ 'genitive sg.'. These alternations can be seen in the forms in (1), where an additional (morpholexical) Umlaut rule has affected some of the 3sg. forms. This perfectly regular Umlaut alternation, which is motivated by large numbers of forms not involved in the Verschärfung alternation, relates basic *ó* (= [ɛw] or [öw]) to *ø* (= [ö]), and basic *u* (= [iw] or [üw]) to *ý* (= [uj]), among others:

(1) a. *búgva* [bɪgva] 'to dwell'; *býr* [bujr] 'id., 3sg. pres.'
     b. *grógva* [grɛgva] 'to grow'; *grør* [grör] 'id. 3sg. pres.'
     c. *doyggja* [doja] 'to die'; *doyr* [dojr] 'id., 3sg. pres.'

---

[1] The analysis to follow can be found, with further supporting detail, in Anderson (1972d); an earlier version appears as Anderson (1968). Many phonetic details, especially regarding the vowels written as *ó, ú, í, ý*, have been arbitrarily simplified below. See the sources just mentioned for a fuller treatment.

d. *spýggja* [spuˑja] 'to   vomit';   *spýr* [spujr] 'id.,   3sg. pres.'

e. *skógvur* [skɛgvur] 'shoe', 'nom. sg.';   *skós* [skɛws] *or* [sköws] 'id., gen. sg.'

The endings /-a/ 'infinitive', /-r/ '3sg. pres.', /-ur/ 'nom. sg.', and /-s/ 'gen. sg.' are well established from many other forms. On the basis of analogies with other forms, we would expect the roots to be /bú-/, /gró-/, /doj-/, /spí-/,[2] and /skó-/, respectively. After the operation of the morpholexical rule of Umlaut, and the rules which spell out underlying tense vowels as diphthongs, we arrive at the forms in (2):

(2)   a. /biw+a/   /buj+r/
       b. /grew+a/   /grö+r/
       c. /doj+a/   /doj+r/
       d. /spuj+a/   /spuj+r/
       e. /skew+ur/   /skew+s/

It is in terms of these forms that we must explain the Verschärfung alternation. The forms in the second column, preceding consonantal endings, are essentially correct as they stand, and the problem is to account for the presence of a velar / palatal element in the surface forms corresponding to those of the first column, where the root precedes a vowel. If we recall the glide formation rule in Faroese, which was discussed above in Chapter 8, we immediately see one difference between the two classes. This rule was formulated as (8.14), and is reproduced here:

(3) $\emptyset \longrightarrow \begin{bmatrix} -\text{syll} \\ -\text{obst} \\ -\text{cons} \\ +\text{high} \\ \alpha\text{back} \end{bmatrix} \% \begin{bmatrix} -\text{cons} \\ +\text{high} \\ \alpha\text{back} \end{bmatrix} + \underline{\hspace{1cm}} [-\text{cons}]$

The rule inserts a glide at a morpheme boundary between two vowels or glides, provided at least one of them is [+high]. Its conditions are met in the forms in the first column (and in the other forms where we find velars or palatals in Verschärfung alternations) but not in the forms of

---

[2] Note that orthographic *ý* and *í* are both [uj], phonetically. It is not clear that two sources for this diphthong need be kept distinct, except that *ý* often is the result of the i-Umlaut of *ú*.

the second column of (2). The result of applying glide formation, then, will be the forms in (4):

(4) a. /biw+wa/   /buj+r/
     b. /grew+wa/   /grö+r/
     c. /doj+ja/   /doj+r/
     d. /spuj+ja/   /spuj+r/
     e. /skew+wur/   /skew+s/

We have apparently found the basis for the rule creating the velars or palatals: wherever a geminate glide arises [by the operation of (3)], its first element is converted into a velar. The Verschärfung rule, then, should apparently convert / · · · w+w · · · / into / · · · g+v · · · /, and / · · · j+j · · · / into / · · · ǰ+ · · · /.

These changes can be analyzed further, however. There is in the grammar of Faroese a rule which converts a sequence of velar plus (front vowel or) glide into [j], which is required to account for alternations such as *stingur* [stɪŋgʊr] 'pain, nom. sg.' versus *stingi* [stɪnǰi] 'id., dat. sg.' and *liggur* [lɪggʊr] '(he) lies' versus *liggja* ⌐lɪǰa] 'to lie' (underlying /ligg+j+a/, where /ligg/ is the root, /+j+/ is a weak verb formative, and /+a/ is the infinitive marker). We can thus reduce the change / · · · j+j · · · / → / · · · ǰ+ · · · / to a change / · · · j+j · · · / → / · · · g+j · · · /, and make use of the palatalization rule to account for the rest of the change.

Similarly, in the sequence / · · · g+v · · · /, the /v/ can be taken to be basic /w/. As was pointed out in Chapter 8, in the discussion of the glide formation rule, /w/ in Faroese is replaced by /v/ generally except after a high vowel. This rule will allow us to state this part of the alternation as / · · · w+w · · · / → / · · · g+w · · · /. We now see that the Verschärfung rule simply turns the first element of a geminate glide into a velar stop.

The choice of a velar stop is perfectly natural, of course, on phonetic grounds. If we examine the feature configurations corresponding to the glides [j], and [w], we see that their position features are the same as those of stops in the fronted velar and plain velar categories, respectively. If, then, we simply change the major class and manner features in the first element of a geminate glide from those appropriate to a glide into those appropriate for a stop, the correct result is obtained. The change in question is then seen as a simple dissimilation of continuance, and we will refer to the rule involved (without attempting to formulate it) as the DISSIMILATION rule.

Although it is not essential to the thrust of the argument here, it can be pointed out that this dissimilation rule is by no means isolated, either within Faroese or within Scandinavian. All of the West Scandinavian dialects have rules that affect sequences of consonantal sonorants (usually identical ones) such as *ll, nn, mm, rn, ln*, etc. The effect of the rule is precisely to turn such a sequence of homorganic sonorants into a sequence of stop plus sonorant, under conditions which vary widely from one dialect to another (see Chapman, 1962, for some descriptive details). In Faroese, for instance, such a rule converts *ll* into [dl] in all positions, and some other clusters of dental sonorant plus *n* into [dn] after long vowels or diphthongs. This rule is responsible for alternations such as *seinur* [sajnʊr] 'late' versus *seinni* [sajdni] 'later'; *morgun* [mɔrgʊn] 'morning, nom. sg.' versus *morni* [mɔdni] 'id., dat. sg.', among others. The dissimilation rule which affects glides, then, can be regarded simply as a generalization of another rule so that it affects nonconsonantal as well as consonantal sonorants. In any event, the complete derivation of the forms in (1) with consonants is now clear. Let us take *spýggja* and *skógvur* as typical:

(5)	underlying:	/spí+a/	/skó+ur/
	diphthongization:	/spuj+a/	/skew+ur/
	glide-formation:	/spuj+ja/	/skew+wur/
	dissimilation:	/spug+ja/	/skeg+wur/
	palatalization:	/spuǰ+a/	
	w ⟶ v		/skeg+vur/
	(later vowel quality rules give as output):	[spuǰa]	[skɛgvʊr]

This derivation is completely unproblematic, and the only thing to note about it is that it requires the rule of glide formation to apply before the dissimilation rule, since it is the inserted glide which is dissimilated.

We have so far accounted for the forms in which Verschärfung is found in terms of a natural set of rules of the language. We must now turn to a set of forms which appears to contradict the account just given. These forms appear to satisfy the conditions for the formation of the long glides which gave rise to velars in derivations such as (5). In fact long glides are found phonetically in the forms in question, but these are not dissimilated as in (5). Such forms are exemplified in (6):

(6) a. *víga* [vʊǰja] 'dedicate'
   b. *júgur* [jɪwwʊr] 'udder'
   c. *síga* [sʊǰja] 'lower (v. tr.)'
   d. *blíður* [blʊǰjʊr] 'friendly'
   e. _ *týða* [tʊǰja] 'translate'

These long glides do not dissimilate, and some explanation for this fact must be found. It is not sufficient to mark these forms as exceptions: they are too numerous, and clearly constitute a regularity of their own. Some basis must be found for distinguishing between long glides that dissimilate [as in the forms in (1)], and those that do not.

The orthography gives a clue to the solution here. In every case in which a long glide does not dissimilate, the glide sequence was formed as a result of the juxtaposition of two vowels that are separated in the orthographic representation by a consonant which does not appear phonetically. Of course, this might be simply an orthographic convention (in fact, the segments in question appear orthographically for somewhat extraneous etymological reasons, rather like the *b* in English *doubt*), but there is considerable evidence that the consonants in question are, nonetheless, present in the underlying phonological representation. The forms (6a–c), for instance, involve the deletion of intervocalic /-g-/. In these and many other forms, it can be seen that underlying /g/ is preserved next to a consonant or word boundary, but deleted intervocalically, resulting in alternations such as those in (7):

(7) a. *víga* [vʊjja] 'dedicate';   *vígdi* [vʊjgdi] 'dedicated'
    b. *júgur* [jɪwwʊr] 'udder (nom.)';   *júgs* [jɪwks] 'id., gen.'
    c. *síga* [sʊjja] 'lower';   *sígdi* [sujgdi] 'lowered'
    d. *øga* [öːa] 'increase';   *øgdi* [ögdi] 'increased'
    e. *siga* [sija] 'say';   *sagdi* [sagdi] 'said (participle)'
    f. *fagur* [fæa̭vʊr] 'beautiful';   *fagran* [fagran] 'id., acc. sg. masc.'

Forms like (6d, e), on the other hand, result from the deletion of intervocalic single /-d-/. This is shown in alternations such as (8):

(8) a. stríða [strʊjja] 'struggle';   *stríddi* [strujddi] 'struggled'
    b. tyða [tʊjja] 'translate';   *týddi* [tʊjddi] 'translated'
    c. blíður [blʊjjʊr] 'friendly';   *blítt* [blujʰt] 'id., neuter'[3]
    d. heiðin [hajjɪn] 'heathen';   *heidnan* [hajdnan] 'id., acc.'
    e. soðin [soːjɪn] 'cooked';   *sodnan* [sɔdnan] 'id., acc.'

Orthographic ð generally represents intervocalic /-d-/, but not always: some forms with an etymological dental have been restructured so as to

---

[3] In Faroese, as in Icelandic, geminate voiceless stops are realized as preaspirated stops. The final [ʰt] in (8c), then, represents / · · · tt/.

conform to the (slightly more transparent) pattern with intervocalic /-g-/:

(9) a. *tr-iður* [trɔavʊr] 'thread';   *traðri* [træagri] 'id., dat.'
     b. *veður* [ve:vʊr] 'weather';   *vegri* [vɛgri] 'id., dat.'
     c. *suður* [su:wʊr] 'south';   *syðri* [sɪgrɪ] 'more southerly'

Nonetheless, we can assume that a rule deletes intervocalic voiced dental and velar obstruents[4]:

(10) $$\begin{bmatrix} +\text{obst} \\ +\text{voice} \\ -\text{labial} \end{bmatrix} \longrightarrow \emptyset\ /\ V \underline{\hspace{1.5em}} V$$

Our analysis involves the deletion of intervocalic voiced dental and velar stops by rule (10), and their subsequent replacement by glides through the operation of glide-formation. We claim, that is, that the glides which appear in (7)–(9) in the position of underlying voiced stops are a consequence of the same rule that produces glides in other forms to break up underlying vowel sequences. The conclusions which will be drawn from this below could be avoided by another analysis of forms such as (7)–(9), but only at a prohibitive cost. The alternative to our analysis is to replace rule (10) by a rule which converts /-d-/ and /-g-/ directly into glides in intervocalic position. Such a rule, however, would have to exactly duplicate the statement of glide-formation. As (7)–(9) show, the glide which replaces intervocalic voiced stops is determined by the quality of the surrounding vowels, and according to exactly the same principles which determined the glide to be inserted by glide-formation: if the preceding vowel element is [+high], the glide produced is homorganic with it; while if the preceding vowel element is [−high], but the following one is [+high], the glide produced is homorganic with this following element. This analysis would therefore have to duplicate exactly the statement of glide-formation in the form of a new rule of stop-replacement. Furthermore, this move would still not be sufficient to replace rule (10): forms like *øga* / *øgdi* 'to increase' / 'increased' ([ö:a] / [ögdi]), *plaga* / *plagdi* 'to be wont to' / 'was wont to' ([plæ:a] / [plagdi]), *ráða* / *ráddi* 'to advise' / 'advised' ([rɔ:a] / [rɔddi]) and others show that intervocalic voiced stops, when between two nonhigh vowels, must still be deleted. Thus, intervocalic stops not af-

---

[4] This analysis thus differs slightly from that in the sources cited in footnote 1, page 167, in which the deleted segments were treated as spirants. This modification is of no consequence for the argument here.

fected by the posited rule of stop replacement must still be deleted, and rule (10) will be necessary in any case. Rule (10) by itself has the effect of creating the conditions for glide formation in all of the forms above with voiced dental or velar stops between two vowels, one of which is high. There is no motivation whatsoever for the rule of stop-conversion, which simply duplicates exactly the statement of the independently needed rule of glide-formation. We conclude, therefore, that rule (10) by itself is the correct way of accounting for the loss of intervocalic voiced stops.

Obviously, the operation of rule (10) creates new vowel sequences, to which the rule of glide formation can (and does) apply. But now a problem arises: why is it that when these inserted glides result in a geminate glide [as in the forms in (6)], they do not undergo dissimilation? That is, why is the infinitive of e.g., 'to translate' *týða* [tUjja], rather than **týggja* [tUĵa]? We saw above that dissimilation, the rule which was used to create the Verschärfung forms, must follow glide insertion in derivations such as those in (5), and we would expect it to apply here as well.

Let us examine the ordering relations we have established above. In (5), we saw that glide formation precedes dissimilation. This is a FEEDING ORDER, as opposed to a NONFEEDING ORDER, hence it is natural. It is not, therefore, stated in the grammar of Faroese. Similarly, in the forms in (6), rule (10) (obstruent deletion) precedes glide formation. This, too, is a feeding order, as opposed to a neutral order and hence natural. Thus, neither of these orders need be stated in the grammar. If the requirement of transitivity of ordering restrictions were correct, we could deduce from these two statements that rule (10) precedes dissimilation. However, suppose we include in the grammar of Faroese an absolute restriction to the effect that dissimilation precedes rule (10), and make this the only stated ordering among the rules just considered. What will be its effect? In derivations such as those in (5), the forms contain no intervocalic voiced stops that could undergo rule (10), and so that rule does not come into play. The only applicable rules are glide formation and dissimilation, and since the grammar contains no statement to the contrary, these apply in the natural feeding order glide insertion–dissimilation. In the case of a form such as underlying /tíd+a/, however, the only rule that can apply to this form is (10), giving /tí+a/ (or rather /tuj+a/, after diphthongization). To this form, the only applicable rule is glide formation, and as there is no ordering restriction to prevent it, this rule can now apply, giving /tuj+ja/. At this point, the SD of dissimilation is met; but if it were to apply, this would violate the ordering restriction which we have stated in the grammar: 'dissimilation precedes rule (10)'.

Accordingly, dissimilation is prevented from applying to this form, and the problem we set out to deal with is resolved.

The content of the ordering restriction is that deleted stops cannot give rise to dissimilated clusters. This is exactly the generalization we would like: long glides fall into two classes, depending on whether they arose from the deletion of an intervocalic stop or not. Failure to undergo dissimilation is correlated with this fact. This is brought out perfectly by the ordering restriction, and therefore the solution just proposed to the problem of differentiating the forms in (1) from those in (6) is a reasonable one. This solution would not be available, however, if we accepted the requirement of transitivity of ordering relations, since the other orderings that have been observed above would require the opposite (feeding) order to obtain between these two rules, an incorrect result. As has just been illustrated above, such violations of transitivity are handled perfectly naturally in the theory of local ordering, and this theory is correspondingly confirmed by the discovery that such cases exist in natural languages.

Examples of similar structure are found in a variety of other languages. One of these is the Gitksan dialect of Tsimshian. Early anthropological investigators in the Pacific Northwest referred to speakers of several related dialects as Tsimshians, but linguistic research revealed that two distinct dialect groups were involved. The great differences between the two are evident from Boas' (1911) parallel treatment of Nass River Tsimshian and Coast Tsimshian, or Tsimshian proper. Rigsby (1967) indicates that there are enough differences involved to make it reasonable to speak of two languages, rather than simply of different dialects. One of these languages is Coast Tsimshian, and the other is Nass-Gitksan, uniting two clusters of mutually intelligible dialects. We are concerned here only with the facts cited by Rigsby for the Gitksan dialects of Nass-Gitksan.

Gitksan displays a typical Northwest coast phonological system with distinct glottalized and plain sonorants ($\acute{m}$, $\acute{n}$, $\acute{l}$, $\acute{w}$, and $\acute{y}$ versus m, n, l, w, y) and obstruents (ejective versus plain p, c, t, k, k^w, and q), a lateral affricate (ejective $\acute{Ł}$) and a set of spirants (s, l, x, x^w, and uvular x), plus h and glottal stop. There are five underlying long vowels (*aa*, *ee*, *ii*, *oo*, and *uu*) and three short vowels (*a*, *i*, *u*). Consonant clusters can be quite complex, though there do not appear to be underlying uninterrupted clusters of different vowels. The stops are aspirated in final position, and voiced before sonorants; the glottalized segments are frequently realized as sequences of glottal stop plus plain consonant; and in the same circumstances the (underlying glottalized) sonorants tend to be vocalized. Thus, /ý/ in final position is [· · · ?^{i}], etc.

An important rule of Gitksan phonology shortens underlying long vowels before plain sonorant consonants. Thus, the stem /tʼaa/ 'to sit' forms an imperative by the addition of /-n/ (a second person mark), giving [tʼan], with short vowel; examples of shortened vowels before other sonorants include [gum] 'ashes' (from /kʷoom/); [ʔamm̓al] 'cottonwood tree' (from am m̓aal/); [daw] 'freeze (intr.)' (from /taaw/); and [dayks] 'concoction of snow and grease' (from /taayks/). A few exceptions exist, perhaps borrowed from Nass dialects where shortening is much more restricted: e.g., [ẙeen] 'fog' (but with shortening in [miʔin] 'smoke', from /mi+ẙeen/). In general however (with exceptions noted below due to the operation of other processes), long vowels do not stand before plain sonorants, and they are shortened when morphological processes would give rise to sequences of long vowel plus sonorant. The rule does not apply before glottalized sonorants, as shown by such forms as [jiljooltxʷ] 'wrinkles' (from /čil+čool+tkʷ/), [m̓aam̓axs] 'pairs of pants' (from /m̓aa+m̓ax̣+s/); [ganaaʔu] 'toad' (from /qanaaw̓/); this restriction also excludes shortening before glottal stop, as shown by [ʔił̓eeʔe] 'blood' and other forms. We might therefore formulate the shortening rule as (11):

(11) $$[+\text{syll}] \longrightarrow [-\text{long}] \ / \ \underline{\hspace{2em}} \begin{bmatrix} -\text{syll} \\ -\text{obst} \\ -\text{gl. const.} \end{bmatrix}$$

In discussing the sonorants above, we have ignored the segment *h*. Underlying *h* does not appear as the first member of clusters or finally (although *h* is inserted finally after short vowels in some circumstances), and intervocalic *h* is deleted (as will be discussed below). Some *h*'s do arise after long vowels, however, by a process which turns the uvular spirant *x̣* into *h* intervocalically. Thus, the paradigm of /haseex̣/ 'shaman's rattle' is as follows:

(12) a. /haseex̣+y/ ⟶ [haseheʔⁱ] 'my rattle'
      b. /haseex̣+n/ ⟶ [hasehen] 'your rattle'
      c. /haseex̣+t/ ⟶ [haseex̣tʰ] 'his rattle'

Accordingly, we can write a rule, which is schematically shown in (13):

(13) $$x̣ \longrightarrow h \ / \ V \ \underline{\hspace{2em}} \ V$$

As we see from (12a, b), the *h*'s produced by rule (13) have the effect of shortening a preceding vowel. Since *h* is a sonorant which does not have glottal constriction, this effect is predicted if rule (13) applies before rule (11).

In addition to the conversion of uvular spirants to *h* by rule (13), Gitksan has another process which makes spirants into glides. In the environment after a vowel and before another sonorant, the front velar continuant *x* becomes *y*, while the rounded velar x^w becomes *w*. Since *x* is generally said to be articulated well forward of the back velars, we will assume it is palatal, and accordingly that *y* and *w* are glides corresponding in position to the spirants *x* and x^w; the rule can then be given as (14):

$$(14) \qquad \begin{bmatrix} +\text{high} \\ +\text{cont} \end{bmatrix} \longrightarrow \begin{bmatrix} -\text{obst} \\ +\text{voice} \end{bmatrix} / \; [+\text{syll}] \underline{\qquad} [-\text{obst}]$$

This rule results in paradigms such as those in (15):

(15)   a.   /waax/ 'paddle'
          i.   /waax+y̓/ ⟶ [waayiʔⁱ] 'my paddle'
          ii.   /waax+n/ ⟶ [waayn] 'your paddle'
          iii. /waax+t/ ⟶ [waaxtʰ] 'his paddle'

    b.   /ixʷ/ 'fish with a line'
          i.   /yukʷɬ ixʷ+y̓/ ⟶ [yukʷɬ ʔiwiʔⁱ] 'I fish with a line'
          ii.   /yukʷɬ ixʷ+n/ ⟶ [yukʷɬ ʔiwn] 'you fish with a line'
          iii. /yukʷɬ ixʷ+t/ ⟶ [yukʷɬ ʔixʷtʰ] 'he fishes with a line'

Forms such as (15a, i–iii) and [laawiʔⁱ] 'my trout' (from /laaxʷ+y̓/) show a difference between the effects of rule (14) and those of rule (13): The glides produced by (14), while plain sonorants, do not have the effect of shortening a preceding vowel, as do those produced by (13). We would therefore want (14) to follow shortening [(11)], while (13) precedes it. It is interesting to note that this ordering difference is correlated with the fact that the changes of (13) and (14), while very similar, apparently cannot be collapsed completely, since (13) is formally a more complex change than (14).

In forms cited above we have seen the operation of a process of epenthesis, which serves to break up impermissible clusters of obstruents and sonorants. Rigsby does not formulate the rule for this, nor do his vocabularies contain enough data to clarify all details of its formulation. The inserted vowel has the quality *a* after the uvulars *q* and *q'* (e.g., [c̆éegan], from /céeqn/ 'you licked it') unless the stop is preceded by a rounded vowel, in which case the inserted vowel becomes *o* (e.g., [yúk^{w}ɫ wógon], from /yúk^{w}ɫ wúgn/ 'you were sleeping'). After *x* the inserted vowel is a copy of the preceding vowel, (e.g., [yúk^{w}ɫ báhan], from /yúk^{w}l paxn/ 'you were running) but the *x*'s in question are always converted to *h* by rule (13), so we can regard this as another subsequent assimilation, by the extremely common process which assimilates vowels across *h* in many languages. After nonuvulars, the epenthetic vowel is *i*. There is nothing else to note about this rule except the facts that its operation provides the intervocalic environment for rules such as (13), and that stops also voice before these vowels. Therefore, presumably, they are inserted before such processes operate.

The last process which we must note is the loss of intervocalic /h/. This is seen in such reduplications as the formation of the plural of /hanaq'/ 'woman', which is /ha+hanaq'/ → [haanaʔq^{h}]. Similarly, in [gooks] / [looks] 'float (sg., pl.)', we find the root /hooks/ preceded by the elements /ki-/, /li-/ which also appear in [gip^{h}ayk^{wh}], [lip^{h}ayk^{wh}] from the stem /phaayk^{w}/ 'fly (intrans.)'. Other instances of palatalized (front) velars before back vowels also arise from sequences of *kihV* by loss of *h* and subsequent elision of *i* before another vowel. In some forms, the elision of intervocalic *h* is apparently optional, since we have both [miin] and [mihin] in free variation, representing /mihin/ 'foot, base, bottom'. Apparently, then, we have a rule like (16):

(16) $$ h \longrightarrow \emptyset \,/\, V \underline{\quad\quad} V $$

It is the relative ordering of (16) and the other rules discussed in Gitksan that is of interest here. Rule (16) gives rise to long vowels, which are apparently just like any other long vowels. As forms like [haanaʔq^{h}] 'women' and [miin] 'foot, etc.' show, however, these secondary long vowels do not shorten before plain sonorants. It must be the case, then, that rule (16) applies only after shortening [rule (11)]. But, on the other hand, we saw that secondary *h* from *x* by rule (13) *did* cause shortening, and so (13) had to precede (11). The problem is that secondary *h* from *x* by (13) is not deleted, though it is of course intervocalic. The natural explanation of this would be to say that (13) follows *h*-deletion [rule (16)], but that is not available to us if we accept the requirement that orderings be transitive.

Let us examine the status of the orderings we have deduced. Rule (13) creates new instances of long vowel plus sonorant, and thus feeds shortening [rule (11)]. The observed ordering, with (13) preceding (11), is

thus a natural one, since the opposite order would be neutral. The rule of
h-deletion, on the other hand, could feed shortening, but does not; the
observed order of (16) after (11) is thus an unnatural order and must be
noted in the grammar. Similarly, the creation of *h* from /x/ could feed *h*-
deletion, but does not, and so the ordering of (16) before (13) is also
unnatural[5] and is noted in the grammar. Within the theory of local ordering, then, a grammar of Gitksan will contain two absolute ordering
restrictions involving rule (16), but no statement relating rules (11) and
(13) directly.

This will result in the following derivations: starting from a form such
as /ha+haneq'/, the only (relevant) rule which can apply is (16) (*h*-dele-
tion), which yields /ha+aneq'/. The structural description of rule (11)
(shortening) is satisfied at this point, but the rule cannot apply because
of the ordering restriction '(11) precedes (16)', which would be violated
now that (16) has applied if (11) were to be applied also. Rules for the
final stop give phonetic [haaneʔqʰ]. If we start with, e.g., /haseex+n/, on
the other hand, the only rule which can apply is epenthesis, giving
/haseex+an/. At this point, the only applicable rule is (13), which yields
/haseeh+an/; now (11) (shortening) can apply, since its environment is
satisfied and there is no ordering restriction to prevent it. This yields
/haseh+an/, which becomes (by vowel assimilation over *h*) the phonetic
[hasehen]. While the environment for rule (16) (*h*-deletion) is satisfied,
this rule cannot apply because of the ordering restriction '(16) precedes
(13)'. Whereas this set of orderings and derivations violates the principle
of transitivity, it is naturally expressed in terms of the theory proposed
here.

Another example of the failure of transitivity, this time involving a
longer chain of ordering relations, is found in the phonology of Greenlandic Eskimo.[6] In this dialect, as in the Alaskan dialect discussed in

---

[5] Actually, this pair of rules exemplifies a situation that ought to be provided for in the
principles of natural ordering. Whenever a process $A \to B \mid C \underline{\quad} D$ creates new *B*'s in
some environment, and another process $B \to E \mid C \underline{\quad} D$ converts (original) *B*'s into
something else in the same environment, it is clear that if they were allowed to apply in
this order, the first rule could be dispensed with entirely by generalizing the second to
$\{A,B\} \to E \mid C \underline{\quad} D$. Accordingly, the first rule could only exist in the grammar, given
the presence of the second, if (1) some third rule intervenes between them crucially; or (2)
the first rule in fact applies only after the second. The situation exemplified by /h/ in
Gitksan is, then, a sort of 'drag-chain' effect (in terms of structuralist discussions of historical change), which ought to be regarded as natural. A related modification to the principles
of natural ordering is discussed in Chapter 12.

[6] The analysis given below is again based on Underhill (1970). I would like to thank
Robert Underhill and Jørgen Rischel for discussion of this material, though neither of them
altogether agrees with me. They should be absolved from blame for any misuse I may have
made of facts they brought to my attention.

Chapter 10, there is a process of epenthesis which breaks up certain clusters of three consonants word-internally or two consonants word-finally. A difference from the Alaskan dialect is found in the identity of the inserted vowel: in Alaska, the quality of this vowel as schwa is generally preserved, while in Greenlandic schwa always becomes *a* (before vocalic suffixes), *u* (before *p*) or *i* (elsewhere). The *i*'s from schwa can be distinguished from underlying *i*'s by their morphophonemic behavior, however, and it is usual in treatments of the language to posit a fourth vowel (which we might represent as *ɨ*) to account for the difference. We will thus represent the epenthetic vowels, and certain other vowels that show the same morphophonemic behavior as *ɨ*.

In Greenlandic, epenthesis applies before a suffix consisting of a single consonant (e.g., /t/ 'plural', /p/ 'relative case', as in *irnirit* 'sons', *irnirup* 'son (rel.)', from /irnɨr+t/, /irnɨr+p/; *assinit* 'pictures', from /assɨn+t/; *inuit* 'people', from /inuk+t/; *surqait* 'whalebones', from /surqaq+t/, etc.[7]). Epenthesis also applies before a consonant followed by word boundary or a morpheme initial consonant in a class of stems for which we posit an underlying final cluster, as in *atiq* 'name', *atirma* 'of my name' from a root /atq/ (note the preservation of the cluster in *arqa* 'his name', with assimilation of *t* to a following consonant by a regular rule; this pattern is opposed to that of *savik* 'knife', *savia* 'his knife', for which we assume underlying /savik/). We might formulate the epenthesis rule as (17):

$$(17) \qquad \emptyset \longrightarrow \textit{ɨ} \,/\, C \underline{\qquad} C \begin{Bmatrix} \# \\ +C \end{Bmatrix}$$

Plurals such as *arqit* 'names', *kaŋmit* 'boots' (from /atq+t/ and /kamg+t/) show that epenthesis before word boundary takes precedence over (and bleeds) epenthesis in three consonant sequences.

Uvular consonants at the end of stems (in the singular absolutive form) show three sorts of behavior. In some stems, the final *q* disappears in all forms where it is followed by any affix at all, and it is reasonable in these cases to treat it as a separate 'singular' morpheme (some speakers, for instance, extend this to forms such as *iniq* 'cabin', *matuq* 'door', with plurals *init*, *matut*, in place of 'standard' singulars *ini*, *matu*); the crucial point here is that the final uvular is neither preserved (perhaps only as a

---

[7] Recall that *k* and *q* represent velar and uvular stops, and *g* and *r* velar and uvular fricatives, respectively. Forms such as *inuit*, *surqait*, etc. show the effects of a rule deleting intervocalic velars and uvulars except after *ɨ*. We have ignored here the treatment of alternations between *k* and *g*, *q* and *r*. These are described in standard sources. A further fact which should be noted is that *-ss-* is the standard Greenlandic orthographic representation of (phonetic and underlying) [š].

ghost) as in *irniq | irnirit* 'son / sons' nor dropped with gemination, as in *nuluq | nullut* 'buttock / buttocks', but simply lost altogether. In cases where final *q* is undeniably part of the stem, however, two sorts of behavior must be distinguished. In one class of words, *q* is preserved and conditions epenthesis before appropriate endings: this is the behavior of *irniq | irnirit* 'son / sons' and (with subsequent deletion of intervocalic *q*) *surqaq | surqait* 'whalebone / whalebones' from the roots /irniq/ and /surqaq/. Before a suffix causing neither epenthesis nor intervocalic *q*-deletion, this *q* is simply preserved: *killiq* 'westernmost', loc. *killirmi*.

In another class of forms, however, *q* is lost before almost any suffix. Before a vowel, this follows from intervocalic *q*-deletion, but before a consonant a distinct rule is required. Thus, from *arnaq* 'mother', we have the plural *arnat,* locative *arnami*. The only traces of the *q* are in the fact that an initial *g* of a suffix is replaced by *r*, as is regular after a uvular (but not after a vowel-final stem, as we would be required to say if we treated *q* in this case as the separable singular marker mentioned above); and also in the fact that it is preserved before a very few suffixes: e.g., *arnartaq* 'mother belonging there'. If the preceding medial consonant is not a geminate or part of a cluster, it undergoes gemination[8]: *atuwagaq* 'book', *atuwakkat* 'books', etc. Since most of the stems with 'deleting' final *q* undergo this gemination, it might be claimed that the distinction between deleting and nondeleting *q* is eliminable (perhaps phonologically) in terms of the gemination environment; but the inclusion of stems like *arnaq* (which could not undergo gemination, but which have 'deleting' final *q*) in the deleting class shows this is not possible in general. Underhill (1970) represents this contrast notationally as a difference between stem-final /q/ and /r/, where /q/ deletes, but /r/ is preserved. There is no basis for distinguishing the two classes on the basis of any phonetic feature, however, and we will therefore represent both *arnaq* 'mother' and *surqaq* 'whalebone' with final /q/. We assume the existence of a rule like (18),[9] to which stems like *surqaq* are

---

[8] There is a substantial controversy over the question of whether this gemination is in fact the consequence of a sequence of metathesis plus assimilation: on that analysis, /nuluq+t/ 'buttocks' becomes /nulqu+t/, which in turn becomes /nullu+t/. For a summary of the arguments, and (to my mind) a conclusive demonstration that this analysis is untenable, see Rischel (1972), who argues that the gemination involved is a sort of compensatory lengthening.

[9] It might be suggested that (18) could be abolished, given the fact that the rule of truncation (mentioned in the previous chapter for the Alaskan dialect) already exists to delete stem final consonants before consonantal endings. We reject this solution, however, on the grounds that (1) truncation is otherwise a property associated primarily with certain end-

exceptional[10]:

(18)
$$q \longrightarrow \emptyset / \underline{\quad} + [+\text{cons}]$$

There are also, as noted above, a few suffixes which are exceptional with respect to (18).

We must now deal with the behavior of stem-final q before the suffix /ga/. This suffix is in fact the only nondeleting[11] suffix in the nominal paradigm that begins with g, and there is no reason not to take its behavior as typical of suffix-initial g. Stem final velars and uvulars merge with this g to give g and r, respectively (as in *arnara* 'my mother', from /arnaq+ga/, and *agsaga* 'my finger', from /agsak+ga/). In the verbal paradigm, a similar effect can be seen in the merger of the imperative suffix /gi/ with stem final velars and uvulars (cf. *tusarit* 'hear!', from /tusaq+gi+t/). We might suggest that these mergers are performed directly by a rule schematically like (19):

(19)
$$\begin{Bmatrix} k \\ q \end{Bmatrix} + g \longrightarrow \begin{Bmatrix} g \\ r \end{Bmatrix}$$

Since stem-final (deleting) q takes part in this merger, it must obviously be present when (19) applies. This means, of course, that rule (18) (q-deletion) must follow (19). The rule of epenthesis (17) must in turn follow q-deletion, in order for epenthesis to apply in *surqait* (with nondeleting q), but not in *arnat* (with deleting q). The rule of merger of final velar / uvular with g (19), in turn, must follow epenthesis: given /atq+ga/, the application of (19) would eliminate the three conso-

---

ings: that is, some endings are truncating, some are nontruncating, and some are sometimes truncating. In order to extend this process to cover uvular deletion, however, we would have to establish a class of deleting *stems,* which undergo truncation even before nontruncating affixes. (2) To do so would then miss the generalization that all of the members of the class of truncating stems end in q, while no parallel phonological generalizations are possible concerning the class of truncating affixes. It seems much better to say that the deletion of q before any consonantal affix with some roots is a separate process from the truncation of any stem final consonant before certain other affixes.

[10] This is in accord with Underhill's claim that stems like *surqaq* are members of a small and exceptional class.

[11] Recall the discussion of the deleting / nondeleting distinction above in Chapter 10 for Alaskan Eskimo. Greenlandic deletion is essentially the same, except that the class of deleting suffixes is different, and there seems to be more irregularity in the form of 'sometimes deleting' suffixes.

nant cluster, making epenthesis impossible, and we would have no way
to derive *atira* 'my name'. In a theory with transitive orderings of rules,
the facts that (18) precedes (17) and (17) precedes (19) imply that (18)
should precede (19), which is the opposite of what we want. The only
obvious way to remove this difficulty within the framework of transitive
ordering restrictions would be as Underhill (1970) does: by restricting
q-deletion so that it does not apply before *g*. However this move is obviously both ad hoc and unfortunate: it misses the fact that exactly
where (it is claimed) *q* is preserved, it is in fact deleted by another rule
(the merger rule).

Before proceeding to suggest a resolution of this problem, let us look
more closely at the process of merger. We could say that rule (19) actually performs two operations: it assimilates *g* to a preceding uvular, and
then simplifies the resulting geminate uvular (or a geminate velar, after a
velar-final stem). Suppose that we separate these two, then: the assimilation rule assimilates *g* to a preceding uvular.

$$(20) \quad \begin{bmatrix} -\text{syll} \\ +\text{back} \\ +\text{cont} \end{bmatrix} \longrightarrow [-\text{high}] \ / \ \begin{bmatrix} -\text{syll} \\ +\text{back} \\ -\text{high} \end{bmatrix} \underline{\quad\quad}$$

This rule receives some slight additional support from the isolated form
nigiq / *nirrit* 'south wind (sg. / pl.)'. The shape of the singular and the
vowel / Ø alternation suggest that this stem is a member of the class with
stem-final clusters, and that its shape is /nigq/. In the singular,
epenthesis applies, as in *atiq* 'name'. In the plural, /nigq+t/ becomes
/nigq+it/ by epenthesis. A metathesis rule, which is well attested elsewhere in the language adjusts the shapes of many internal clusters, and
would apply to this form to give /niqg+it/. Such a rule also applies to
metathesize the cluster in the root /kamg/ 'boot' where this is preserved:
this gives rise to the alternation *kamik* 'boot' / *kaŋma* 'his boot'. Rule
(20) can then apply to /niqg+it/, giving /niqr+it/ from which *nirrit*
follows naturally. The rule of geminate simplification is also needed independently: from underlying /tikit+gi+t/, we get /tikik+gi+t/ by the
independent rule assimilating *t* to the position of a following consonant;
geminate reduction is then required to reduce this to the surface form
tikigit 'come!'[12]

---

[12] There are several bits of complexity which should be mentioned in connection with
this geminate reduction rule. First, in the verb paradigm, /gi/ 'imperative' is not the only
suffix that begins with g. There are also /ga/, /gu/, and /gi/ (all nondeleting) of the subordinate moods. These suffixes assimilate to a stem-final uvular, and the resultant geminate
simplifies: *tusarama* 'I hear (conj)', from /tusaq+ga+ma/. After stem-final velars, however,

The methathesis rule which gives /niqg̣it/ from /nigq̇it/ must precede velar assimilation [rule (20)], since the environment of the latter is not satisfied in this form until after metathesis. Metathesis, further, must follow epenthesis, in order to prevent its occurrence in the singular form *nigiq*. The rule of *q*-deletion [rule (18)], in addition, must apply before epenthesis as we noted before, in order to distinguish *arnat* (with *q*-deletion, and consequently no epenthesis) from *surqait* (without *q*-deletion, and thus with epenthesis). From this chain of facts, transitivity of ordering relations would require that *q*-deletion precede velar assimilation, which is not the correct result and leaves us right where we were.

Now let us examine these ordering relations in terms of local ordering:

1. The ordering of epenthesis before metathesis prevents metathesis from applying in *nigiq,* and is therefore bleeding. Since it is opposed to a neutral order, it is unnatural, and must be stated in the grammar.

2. The ordering of *q*-deletion before epenthesis is also bleeding (cf. *arnat*), as opposed to neutral, and hence unnatural. This, too, must be listed in the grammar.

3. The ordering of metathesis before velar assimilation, on the other hand, is feeding as opposed to neutral, and hence natural. It does not appear in the grammar.

4. The relation between velar assimilation and *q*-deletion which we want, whereby velar assimilation precedes, is neutral as opposed to a bleeding order, and so this too is natural. It is accordingly not listed in the grammar.

Of the four, then, only (1) and (2) need be stated as absolute ordering restrictions in Greenlandic.

This grammar, now, will allow all of the correct derivations. In /nigq/, either epenthesis or metathesis could apply, but ordering restriction (1) above gives priority to epenthesis, and no other rules apply to give *nigiq*. In /nigq+t/, on the other hand, epenthesis again precedes, by the same restriction, but in this form the end-of-word environment predominates

---

the geminate does not reduce: from /naalak+ga+ma/, we get *naalakkama,* not *naalagama.* A further fact concerns geminate dentals: from /tikit+tit/ we get *tikitit* 'let come' with simplification, but from /sinik+tit/ we get (by assimilation) *sinittit* 'let sleep' without simplification. Furthermore, with some suffixes reduction does not even occur if the *t + t* cluster is underlying: from /tikit+tuq/ we get *tikittuq* 'come (participle)'. It is clear that the rule of geminate simplification exists, and that it is not restricted to combinations of stem-final velar or uvular with *g*, or even to velars and uvulars. It is not clear what should be done to incorporate these facts into the rule, however.

and bleeds the word-internal environment. The environment for metathesis is still satisfied in /nigqɨt/, so this applies to give /niqgɨt/. Velar
assimilation can now apply and there is no restriction to prevent it, and
the result is ultimately *nirrit*. In the case of /arnaq+t/, either *q*-deletion
or epenthesis could apply, and restriction (2) gives priority to *q*-deletion.
The result is no longer subject to epenthesis, and we get *arnat*. In the
case of /arnaq+ga/, only *q*-deletion and velar assimilation can apply. In
this form, *q*-deletion would bleed velar assimilation, and since there is no
ordering stated, this would be unnatural, and hence does not occur. We
thus apply first velar assimilation, and then *q*-deletion (or degemination;
the result is the same in either case) to get *arnara*. The total set of orderings that can be seen to obtain would give rise to a paradox if taken
to be transitive, but in terms of the view taken in this work of the ordering relation, this is not so.

The examples discussed in Chapter 10 showed the untenable character of the requirement of antisymmetry of rule orderings; the examples
discussed thus far in this chapter have demonstrated that transitivity
cannot be maintained either, when larger numbers of rules than two at a
time are considered. It is worthwhile, at this point, to return to the first
of the 'important' criteria for a linear ordering—irreflexivity—and to
reexamine our conclusions with respect to that requirement. It will be
remembered that the arguments of Chapter 9 showed that rules must in
some cases be allowed to reapply to their own outputs, and that this constitutes a violation of the requirement of irreflexivity, since some derivations will now contain instances of rule *A* preceding rule *A*. This was not
taken to be a serious objection to the requirement of linear ordering,
since (if reapplication of a rule to its own output were the only exception
to irreflexivity) it would be largely a matter of terminology whether the
requirement was in fact being violated. We might perfectly well group all
of the consecutive reapplications of a given rule together into a block,
and call this block the 'application' of the rule, and then discuss ordering
restrictions between such blocks. In this way, the requirement of irreflexivity might still be maintained.

We have seen examples, however, which show that the reapplication
of a rule to its own (immediate) output is not the only violation of irreflexivity that exists in natural languages. In the case of Sundanese
nasalization, discussed in the previous chapter, there was a much more
'pernicious' or significant violation of irreflexivity. Recall the derivation
of a form like [nãriʔĩs]: the underlying representation we took to
be /ar#ni(ʔ)is/[13]; this underwent nasalization, giving /ar#nĩʔĩs/, to

---

[13] The parentheses around [ʔ] in this form are there because this element is epenthetic,
and hence does not properly belong in an 'underlying' form.

which infixation applied, giving /narĩ?ĩs/. A rule of nasalization was then required to apply again, affecting the first vowel; denasalization of the second vowel gave the final form [nãri?ĩs]. Notice that this derivation involves two applications of the nasalization rule, one preceding the other, but these two cannot be grouped together into a block because they are separated by the application of infixation. Here, then, we have a more significant violation of linear ordering than reapplication of rules to their own immediate output: the rule of nasalization precedes itself in a way which is not as easily resolved. Incidentally, we can note that such a derivation makes another point: other examples have violated antisymmetry by providing some derivations in which rule *A* precedes rule *B*, and other derivations in which rule *A* follows rule *B*. In this case, however, rule *A* (nasalization) both precedes and follows rule *B* (infixation) in the same derivation, based on the fact that the order which is natural in one portion of the form is the opposite of that which is natural in the other portion of the form.

This conclusion might be avoided in the following way: suppose we claim that, in Sundanese, the application of nasalization within the root alone is a distinct rule (a morpheme structure rule) from the application of nasalization within the whole word, including its infixes. The fact that the two processes would be identical would certainly discourage us from this analysis, but we might adopt it in order to avoid the ordering problem.[14] In that case, the nasalization rule which precedes the infixation would no longer be identical with that which follows it, and neither irreflexivity nor antisymmetry would be violated. This solution is not generalizable to other examples above (such as those of Kasem, Eskimo, Modern Greek, etc.), but it is worth presenting an example whose structure is similar to that of the Sundanese one, but where it is definitely not available.

In Chapter 10, we saw examples of the operation of a rule of *u*-UMLAUT in Icelandic, which produced an alternation between basic /a/ and *ö*, when the /a/ was followed by /u/ in the next syllable. We must now note that this is not the only alternation which the presence of a following /u/ can produce. In forms like *jeg kalla* / *við köllum* 'I / we call', *jaki* / *jökull*, 'piece of ice / glacier', etc., we have *a* alternating with *ö*;

---

[14] In fact, this proposal is untenable because the same ordering problems discussed above arise in cases where the nasalization is not inherent in the root, but is rather imported into it by a prefix which coalesces with the underlyingly oral root initial. Thus, in a form such as [ɲãraĩãn] 'to wet' (underlying /ar+ŋ#čai+an/), the prefix /ŋ/ first coalesces with the root initial č, then nasalization affects the result, then /ar/ is infixed, then nasalization reapplies. Since the nasality of the root initial is not present in the underlying form, it could not have affected the remainder of the root by the operation of a 'morpheme structure rule', nor could it have affected the vowel of the suffix /-an/.

but in e.g. *dómari / dómurum* 'judge (nsg. / dpl.), *héraδ / héruδum* 'region (nsg. / dpl.)', the alternation is between *a* and *u*. The difference between the two plainly depends on stress: when the /a/ in question is in the stressed initial syllable of the word, it alternates with *ö* (without exception); but when it is in an unstressed syllable later in the word, it generally alternates with *u* instead. One approach to this complementarity, of course, would be to write two rules of *u*-Umlaut:

(21)　　　　　　　　a.　$a \longrightarrow \ddot{o}$ / $\left[\underline{} \atop +\text{STRESS} \right] C_0 u$

　　　　　　　　　　b.　$a \longrightarrow u$ / $\left[\underline{} \atop -\text{STRESS} \right] C_0 u$

This would be a most undesirable solution, however; rather, we would prefer to relate the difference between (21a) and (21b) to some other difference between stressed and unstressed syllables, so as to preserve the unity of the alternation.

Such an alternative is readily available to us. As argued in Anderson (1969a), the rich vowel system of stressed syllables is related to the reduced system of unstressed syllables (basically only *a*, *i*, and *u*) by a rule of vowel reduction, which converts non-low vowels into the corresponding high vowels. As argued there and in Anderson (1972b), the effect of this on the product of the rule of *u*-Umlaut (assuming this rule produced only the *a* / *ö* alternation directly) would be to convert *ö* to *u*. We can therefore eliminate rule (21b) and the condition of (21a) that the vowel be stressed, and assign the difference to the operation of the vowel reduction rule.

We can now examine forms such as *bakari / bökurum* 'baker, (nsg. / dpl.);, *fatnaδ / fötnuδum* 'suit of clothes (nsg. / dpl.)'. In these forms, we see both the *a/ö* and *a/u* alternations in the same form. We might suggest, then, that *u*-Umlaut should be formulated to apply before an *u* two syllables away as well as one in the next syllable; but a form such as *akkeri / akkerum* 'anchor (nsg. / dpl.)' shows that this relaxation of the conditions on Umlaut would be incorrect. In fact, Umlaut can only affect a vowel two syllables away from the conditioning *u* if the intervening vowel is Umlauted as well. In terms of Chomsky and Halle's device of simultaneous infinite schemata, we could formulate this as (22):

(22)　　　　　　　　$a \longrightarrow \ddot{o}$ / $\underline{}$ $(C_0 a)^* C_0 u$

Such a rule will affect both of the vowels in, e.g., /fatnaδ+um/, giving

/fötnöð+um/; this latter will then undergo vowel reduction to give *fötnuðum.* In Chapter 9, however, we argued that the device of simultaneous infinite schemata ought to be excluded from phonological theory, and replaced by the possibility that some rules reapply to their own outputs. In these terms, the rule is somewhat harder to formulate; we must now extend Umlaut so as to apply before either *u* (underlying) or *ö* (derived by a previous application of the rule):

$$(23) \qquad\qquad a \longrightarrow ö \mathbin{/} \underline{} \; C_0 \begin{Bmatrix} u \\ ö \end{Bmatrix}$$

This rule will apply to /fatnað+um/ once, giving /fatnöð+um/, and then again, giving /fötnöð+um/. Once again, vowel reduction gives the desired form *fötnuðum.*

It is not hard to see that this is not yet the whole story. There are some words in Icelandic (a substantial class, in fact), in which vowel reduction does not apply. Most of these are foreign words, including the names of various foreign countries, but some are original Germanic words with a long history in the language. The word *akkeri,* for example, shows the operation of a very early Old Norse sound change (almost entirely lexicalized by now) by which nasals were totally assimilated to a following voiceless stop. Its native character is thus assured; but the *e* in the second syllable shows that it belongs to the nonreducing class. Some other nonreducing words, such as *meðal / meðölum* 'medicine (nsg. / dpl.)' contain the vowel *a* in their unstressed syllable, and in this case, the result of Umlaut remains *ö,* rather than being raised to *u.* The most interesting cases are words in which two consecutive vowels (or more) are /a/, and the word does not undergo reduction. When we consider forms like *akarn / akörnum* 'acorn (nsg. / dpl.)', *japani / japönum* 'Japanese (nsg. / dpl.)', *almanak / almanökum* 'calendar (nsg. / dpl.), etc., we see that this exceptionality with respect to vowel reduction is also correlated with another kind of exceptionality: if a vowel does not reduce, Umlaut cannot be propagated past it. Thus, we would have to revise either (22) or (23) to reflect this fact:

$$(24) \quad \text{a.} \quad a \longrightarrow ö \mathbin{/} \underline{} \left(C_0 \begin{bmatrix} a \\ +\text{VOWEL REDUCTION} \end{bmatrix} \right)^{\!*} C_0 u$$

$$\text{b.} \quad a \longrightarrow ö \mathbin{/} \underline{} \; C_0 \begin{Bmatrix} u \\ ö \\ \begin{bmatrix} +\text{VOWEL REDUCTION} \end{bmatrix} \end{Bmatrix}$$

The rule feature '[+VOWEL REDUCTION]' might be replaced with some other diacritic, such as a hypothetical secondary stress (which does not occur phonetically, but which prevents vowel reduction), but the essence of the revision which is necessary is the incorporation into the environment of a restriction that only vowels which are subject to reduction can be in the environment for *u*-Umlaut. The final blow to such an attempt comes when we consider words in which vowel reduction is optional. From *fargan* 'racket' we can have either *fargönum* or *förgunum* as dative plural. Clearly umlaut in the first syllable here is a direct consequence of vowel reduction in the second, since we cannot have **förgönum*.

As soon as we have put the problem in such terms, however, we can see that such a restriction is the wrong way to go about it. There is, of course, something else that we know about syllables containing *a* which intervene between a given *a* and the next *u*, which are, furthermore, subject to reduction; or about syllables containing *ö*'s subject to reduction: they are going to become *u* by the operation of reduction. But, in fact, the basic environment which produces *u*-Umlaut is just 'before *u*'; it is blatant that a generalization is being missed by either of the formulations in (24). The generalization that is missed is, furthermore, exactly the sort of generalization we were concerned to capture in chapter 9, when we discussed the device of allowing rules to apply to their own output. In Icelandic, *u*-Umlaut is produced by the vowel *u*; the point of the restrictions in (24) is to say exactly that, and to allow the Umlaut to be produced by *u*'s which are secondary as well as underlying *u*'s. This would, obviously, be better served by returning to the original form of the *u*-Umlaut rule as (25), and allowing this to apply after all of the relevant secondary *u*'s have been produced:

(25) $a \longrightarrow ö \ / \ \underline{\hspace{1cm}} \ C_0 u$

But there is an obvious problem here: some of the *u*'s which cause Umlaut are produced by the vowel-reduction rule, applying to vowels which were derived by the Umlaut rule itself. No simple solution is possible here, on the usual assumptions about the ordering relation. Let us assume, in the framework adopted here, that the rules of *u*-Umlaut (rule (25)) and vowel reduction are not related by any overt ordering restriction in the grammar of Icelandic. Then the following derivation can result:

(26)   underlying form: /fatnað+um/

               Umlaut   ö
               Vowel reduction   u
               Umlaut   ö

               output: [fötnuðum]

In the underlying form, only Umlaut is applicable, and it applies; to this intermediate form, only vowel reduction is applicable, and it applies. But now, a new possibility for the application of Umlaut has been created, and the rule can apply again. This way, the only possibility for the application of the rule to the first syllable vowel automatically incorporates the restriction that the second syllable vowel must undergo reduction, because it is only if it does that it will supply the conditions for the original Umlaut rule to reapply. In this way, the generality of the condition on Umlaut is preserved.

This solution is possible only if one abandons the usual restrictions on the ordering relation between rules. It is clear, furthermore, that no device of morpheme structure rules, cycles, or such principles can produce derivation (26). This is because the conditions for both applications of Umlaut are created at the same level of syntactic structure, and there are no higher levels of structure which could be motivated for this form. In the theory of local ordering, it is assumed that the conditions which may result in the ordering of a pair of rules differing from one derivation to another are fundamentally phonological, rather than syntactic, in nature. We have seen, in Chapters 10 and 11, a number of examples of rules which must be applied in ways that violate the assumptions of linearity of rule ordering. In each case, phonological conditions, as defined by the principles of natural ordering, were able to deal with the 'paradox'. We assume, therefore, that a grammar need only contain a few ordering statements, some of which may be absolute and some contingent. When two rules interact, but no ordering statement appears in the grammar to relate them, they are to be applied in the natural order. This will occasionally give rise to 'paradoxes' of the sort we have been concerned with, but these are perfectly consistent with the organization of the grammar as we envision it.

CHAPTER 12

Further Aspects
of Local Ordering

In Chapters 10 and 11, we have given examples which show that the requirements of linear ordering cannot be met by the ordering relation among phonological rules in a variety of languages. We have suggested that these cases can be resolved by replacing the notion of specifying rule order in a linear list of the entire set of rules in a language by a conception in which orderings relate only two rules at a time. Furthermore, and most importantly, we suggested that some rules might not be related by an explicit ordering statement in the grammar, and that in these cases the interaction of the rules in question is to be specified by the principles of natural ordering. In these cases, the ordering specified for a pair of rules might differ from one form to another, or it might be that the total set of orderings that results is not transitive. Our examples demonstrate that some replacement for linear ordering is necessary, and we have shown the theory of local ordering to be sufficient, but we have not demonstrated that there is no other logically possible theory that would fit the facts. Obviously this is impossible, unless the capacity of linguists to construct radically ingenious new theories is sharply curtailed in the near future, but we can at least argue against some alternatives that have been or might be proposed to deal with these and similar cases.[1]

---

[1] Recall that we have already argued, in the preceding chapter, against a view that would take the 'reapplication' of rules at more than one point in the derivation to be a consequence simply of the existence of two versions of the same rule, one of them a 'morpheme structure condition'.

190

One possibility that comes readily to mind can be sketched as follows: suppose we say that the rules of a grammar are of two types. First, there is a set of phonological rules of the ordinary sort, whose relative ordering is specified in the form of the standard linear list. Thus, the ordering relations among these rules conform to the requirements of linear orderings. In addition, another set of rules could be defined, and given the property of applying at any point in a derivation where their structural description is met. These rules would not satisfy the conditions of linear ordering, and therefore this theory would be a departure from the standard, linearly ordered, view of the ordering relation; but this is in some sense a minimal deviation from linear ordering, in that it restricts nonlinearity to a subset of the rules, and specifies fully the alternative ordering which is associated with this subset. Let us call this the theory of ANYWHERE RULES, after similar proposals which have been made in syntax.[2]

How are we to distinguish the theory of local ordering from the theory of anywhere rules, on empirical grounds? It is clear that the main difference between them is the following: while the theory of local ordering claims that the order obtaining between a pair of rules is in principle independent of any orderings obtaining between either of them and other rules, the theory of anywhere rules would claim that if a rule applies 'paradoxically' with respect to one other rule of the grammar, it must be capable of applying in similar fashion with respect to all the others. In other words, 'once an anywhere rule, always an anywhere rule'. A counterexample to this claim could be found, then, if we exhibited an example in which some rule A must be able to apply both before and after some other rule B; but where there is a third rule C such that A must apply only before (or perhaps only after) C. By virtue of the relation between A and B, A would have to be an 'anywhere rule', but by virtue of its relation with C, it could not. If such an example were still consistent with the theory of local ordering, it would furnish conclusive evidence favoring that theory over the theory of 'anywhere rules'.

Such an example is not hard to find, in a case that we have already discussed in some depth. In Chapters 10 and 11 we discussed the rule of u-Umlaut in Modern Icelandic, and we showed that it must be allowed both before and after syncope, and also that it must be allowed to apply both before and after vowel reduction. By virtue of these facts, it is clear that the theory of anywhere rules would take Icelandic u-Umlaut to be

---

[2] E.g., by Lakoff and Ross, in unpublished lectures. It will be seen that the theory of 'anywhere rules' in phonology would be a language-particular variant of the theory of marking conventions as linking rules, proposed by Chomsky and Halle (1968) and discussed briefly in Chapter 15.

an example of an anywhere rule. There is, however, at least one other rule in the phonology of Modern Icelandic with respect to which *u*-Umlaut cannot be allowed to apply freely.

We mentioned above that there are some instances of the vowel *u* in surface forms before which *a* does not become *ö* (or *u*, if unstressed). These non-Umlauting *u*'s are all found before *r*, most commonly in the endings of the nom. sg. of many strong nouns, and the masc. nom. sg. of the strong adjective declension:

(1)   a.   *hattur / hatt / höttum*   'hat (nsg. / asg. / dpl.)'
      b.   *dalur / dal / dölum*   'valley (nsg. / asg. / dpl.)'
      c.   *staður / stað / stöðum*   'place (nsg. / asg. / dpl.)'
      d.   *harður / hörðum*   'hard (M. nsg. / M. dsg.)'
      e.   *snarpur / snörpum*   'rough (M. nsg. / M. dsg.)'
      f.   *ryðga / ryðgaður / ryðguðum*   'to rust / rusted (M. nsg. / M. dsg.)'
      g.   *kalla / kallaður / kölluðum*   'to call / called (M. nsg. / M. dsg.)'

These nouns, adjectives and participles all display the ending *-ur*, with no Umlaut of a preceding *a*. The words of this class (which includes a great many nouns, and all adjectives and participles with the vowel *a*) cannot be treated as exceptions to *u*-Umlaut, since all of them show Umlaut before such other endings as *-um* (dative plural of nouns and strong adjectives), *-um* (masculine dative singular of strong adjectives), *-u* (neuter dative singular of strong adjectives), *-u* (oblique cases, singular, feminine of weak adjective declension), *-u* (all genders and cases, plural of weak adjective declension), *-u* (oblique cases, feminine singular; and npl., apl. neuter, weak noun declension). It must be the ending *-ur* itself that is responsible for the failure of Umlaut.

One possibility would be to represent the *u* of *-ur* as some other underlying vowel (let us say /o/), which becomes *u* only after the operation of the *u*-Umlaut rule (perhaps by the vowel reduction rule). Such a line would lead to a loss of generality with the ending *-ur*, however. After nouns whose stems end in vowels, the ending in question takes the shape *-r*, with the vowel *u* lost. This would be unusual since the usual result of adding a vowel-initial ending to a vowel-final stem is either the preservation of both vowels (if the stem vowel is tense) or the loss of the first (if lax and unstressed):

(2)   a.   *mór / mó / móum*   'peat, heath (nsg. / asg. / dpl.)'

    b.   *snjór / snjó / snjóum* 'snow(fall) (nsg. / asg. / dpl.)'

    c.   *læknir / lækni / læknum* 'doctor (nsg. / asg. / dpl.)'

The vowel-loss rule which would have to apply in the nominative singular (but not, e.g., in the dative plural) of the forms in (2) would thus be restricted to this one ending. But we can see that the vowel of the ending would have to be dropped in other environments as well, where the positing of such a loss is even harder to explain:

(3)   a.   *humar / humar* 'lobster (nsg. / asg.)'

        b.   *djöfull / djöful* 'devil (nsg. / asg.)'

        c.   *jötunn / jötun* 'giant (nsg. / asg.)'

        d.   *steinn / stein* 'stone (nsg. / asg.)'

        e.   *bíll / bíl* 'car (nsg. / asg.)'

        f.   *ís / ís* 'ice (nsg. / asg.)'

        g.   *lax / lax* (=[laks]) 'salmon (nsg. / asg.)'

The ending thus appears as $\emptyset$, *l*, or *n* after stems ending in *r*, *s*, *l*, or *n*. When the full range of facts is considered, it appears that the ending assimilates to one of these consonants; then word-final *r + r*, *s + s* are reduced to a single consonant. The assimilation does not take place after a stressed short syllable [cf., e.g., *dalur / dal* 'valley (nsg. / asg.)']. In addition, *l + l*, *n + n* are also reduced after a consonant (as in, e.g., *hrafn / hrafn* 'raven (nsg. / asg.)', and monomorphemic *rr* is retained (as in, e.g., *verr* 'worse').

    This pattern of assimilations is paralleled in the adjective declension, when stems ending in a dental sonorant come to stand before the ending /-ri/ 'F. dsg.':

(4)   a.   *seinn / seinan / seinni* 'late (M. nsg. / M. asg. / F. dsg.)'

        b.   *gamall / gamlan / gamalli* 'old   (M.   nsg. / M.   asg. / F. dsg.)'

        c.   *gulur / gulan / gulri* 'yellow (M. nsg. / M. asg. / F. dsg.)'

        d.   *hertur / hertan / hertri* 'dried hard (M. nsg. / M. asg. / F. dsg.)'

Similar facts obtain with the adjectival endings /-rar/, /-ra/ 'gen. sg.; gen. pl.'. In (4), the declension of *seinn* and *gamall,* etc. is parallel to that of *steinn* 'stone', *djöfull* 'devil', etc. in (3); while *gulur* is just like *dalur* 'valley'. In the case of the adjectival endings, it is clear that no vowel is present, and we are dealing with the assimilation of *r* to a preceding dental sonorant. If we are to explain the nsg. ending *-ur | -r | -Ø | -l | -n* in the same way, it is clear that we must eliminate the vowel *u* from the ending after a vowel, *l, n, r,* or *s,* but not after, e.g., *l* preceded by a short syllable. This rule would obviously be missing the generalization that the vowel is lost exactly where the resultant cluster will undergo assimilation, and it cannot thus be maintained.

A much more plausible analysis would assume that the ending *-ur* is underlyingly simply /+r/; this then assimilates and/or simplifies where it can, and an epenthesis rule then applies to resultant final clusters of $C + r$:

(5) $$\emptyset \longrightarrow u \mathbin{/} C \underline{} r\#$$

We can now ask whether rule (5)[3] is simply a property of the single nominal and adjectival ending *-ur,* or whether it explains other facts in the language. In fact, even if one chooses to identify the noun ending *-ur* with the adjective ending, it is clear that there are other endings in the language which cannot be the same, but which show the same behavior. In the active present indicative of verbs, the following are typical:

(6)   a.   *kalla*   'to call';   *kalla | kallar | köllum*   (1sg. | 3sg. | 1pl.)
      b.   *vaka*   'to be awake'; *vaki | vakir | vökum*   (1sg. | 3sg. | 1pl.)
      c.   *tala*   'to count';   *tel | telur | tölum*   (1sg. | 3sg. | 1pl.)
      d.   *gafa*   'to give';   *gef | gefur | göfum*   (1sg. | 3sg. | 1pl.)

The verbs *kalla* and *vaka* are typical of the weak verbs of classes 2–4, in that the stem is followed by a thematic vowel (*a* with *kalla, i* from underlying /e/ with *vaka*). The endings are /Ø/ for 1sg., /-r(ð)/ for 2sg., and /-r/ for 3 sg. (as well as, e.g., /-um/ for 1pl.; etc.). Strong verbs, such as *gafa,* and weak verbs of the first class, such as *tala,* do not show a theme vowel,[4] and the endings here are /Ø/, /-ur(ð)/, and /-ur/ for 1sg., 2sg., and 3sg., respectively. Obviously, if we assume the operation of rule (5), the same endings can be assumed for all verbs, and the *-r | -ur* alternation accounted for in the same way as for nouns and adjectives.

---

[3] This rule should probably be generalized to account for the *u* (or *o*), which appears in the zero grade of strong verb stems of shape *CrC;* see Anderson (1969a, b) for some discussion. It must also be restricted to prevent epenthesis in *verr* 'worse' and other words ending in unreduced monomorphemic *rr.*

[4] Actually, the root is followed in both cases by underlying lax /i/, which causes *i*-Umlaut of the stem vowel and is then deleted. See Anderson (1969a, b) for discussion.

In addition to the inflections we have seen thus far, there are a certain number of nouns and adjectives which show an alternation of *r* with *ur*, where the *r* is preserved in all cases and must thus be taken to be part of the stem:

(7) a. *akur | akri | ökrum* 'field (nsg. | dsg. | dpl.)'
    b. *aldur | aldri | öldrum* 'age (nsg. | dsg. | dpl.)'
    c. *fagur | fagran | fögru* 'beautiful (M. nsg. | M. asg. | N. dsg.)'
    d. *magur | magran | mögru* 'thin (M. nsg. | M. asg. | N. dsg.)'

The alternation of *r* with -*ur* here is completely parallel to that which appears in inflectional endings, and it seems reasonable to set up these roots as /akr/, /aldr/, /fagr/, /magr/, etc. The nsg. ending /+r/ is, of course, reduced to Ø after these, by the degemination discussed above. The *r* which occurs, whether after *u* or not, is thus a part of the stem.

On the basis of this evidence, it seems secure to posit rule (5) as a phonological rule of Modern Icelandic. We can now examine its ordering with respect to other rules. The primary point is its ordering with respect to *u*-Umlaut. As we have seen in the examples above, epenthetic *u*'s created by rule (5) in all categories (i.e., whether before *r* in a noun ending, an adjective ending, a verb ending, or in a root) have the property of not producing Umlaut. In fact, the class of non-Umlauting *u*'s is probably exactly coextensive with the class of *u*'s created by rule (5). The natural way to capture this fact is to state an (absolute) ordering restriction to that effect: *u*-Umlaut never follows epenthesis. This is, of course, a NONFEEDING ORDER, as opposed to a feeding order; thus it is unnatural. We have found here an example of the sort proposed above: *u*-Umlaut would have to be treated as an anywhere rule (because of the arguments in Chapters 10 and 11) in a theory that distinguishes anywhere rules from linearly ordered rules; but it cannot be an anywhere rule. It must be prevented from applying to the output of epenthesis. The positing of a class of anywhere rules in addition to a class of linearly ordered rules, therefore, cannot account for the full range of facts concerning nonlinear ordering relations.

The demonstration that one rule which must apply 'paradoxically' cannot be treated as an anywhere rule, obviously, also argues against an even stronger version of the anywhere-rule position that has been discussed in some recent work. This is the view that all extrinsic, or language-particular ordering relations are superfluous, and that a correct view of phonology (and syntax, as well) would predict by general principle all of the ordering relations actually found in the languages of the world.[5] Of course, it is always possible that a principle will be found that predicts that *u*-Umlaut in Icelandic cannot apply to the output of epenthesis, but in the absence of such a proposal expressed in concrete terms, one must remain skeptical. The best evidence we have concerning what is and what is not natural strongly suggests that the maximization of feeding orders is an important principle, and its failure to apply in this case suggests equally strongly that language-particular ordering restrictions can, in fact, be part of a grammar. This is a conclusion that is already strongly suggested by many other facts cited above in other connections, and indeed could come as no surprise to any investigator familiar with the wealth of boring and language-particular detail in the phonology of any natural language.

Another form of the theory of anywhere rules has been proposed by Chafe (1968). Chafe presents some examples (the most important of which we will reproduce below) in order to suggest the need for a revision of the standard theory of linearly ordered rules. His proposal to deal with these examples is approximately as follows. The rules of a grammar are organized in several sets or DEPTHS. The underlying forms are operated on by all of the forms of the greatest depth, applying simultaneously. The resultant representation is then operated on by all of the rules of the next depth (simultaneously, again); and so on, until the rules of depth 1 are reached, which give the output form. In Chafe's examples, all of the rules at any given depth are rules which do not significantly interact with one another. For the structure of the theory it is an

---

[5] This is, more or less, the position of Vennemann (1971) and Koutsoudas, Sanders, and Noll (1971), as well as several recent syntax papers influenced by these and similar works. A considerably more sophisticated variant of the claim that there are no language-particular ordering restrictions in phonology could be constructed along the following lines: we could note that a restriction '*A* precedes *B*' actually has two consequences. First, it requires that rule *A* applies before rule *B*, and hence that rule *B* applies to the output of rule *A*. Second, it requires that rule *A* does not apply to the output of rule *B*. If we separate these two consequences of such a statement, it is clear that the Icelandic example presented in the text only demonstrates the need for the second type, that is, for statements of a language particular restriction that rule *A* does not apply to the output of rule *B*. Many examples exist in the literature of orderings of the type 'Rule *B* must apply to the output of rule *A*' (and not to some other level), however. For example, Postal (1968, 1969) discusses various rules that interact with a rule of penultimate stress assignment in Mohawk. He demonstrates that the stress rule must apply before and not after many of these, in ways that could not be predicted in terms of any known principles of natural ordering. Since we believe both sorts of ordering statement may be necessary in phonology, and the relation PRECEDES expresses both, we will continue to assume that the grammar of a language contains only language-particular statements of the type '*A* precedes *B*', and not statements of the type '*A* does not follow *B*', which would be a type of (arbitrary) disjunctive order.

important question whether this requirement is to be imposed on grammars, or whether any arbitrary set of rules (some of which potentially might interact with one another) can be organized into a single 'depth'. If the requirement of mutual irrelevance is imposed on the rules at any given depth, the theory thus far is nothing but a notational variant of the standard theory, with some of the vacuous orderings eliminated. It is worth noting that a requirement which is very close to this one will be proposed below in Chapter 13 to govern the interaction of several applications of the same rule to the same string; it is not, therefore, simply a 'straw man'. If this requirement is not imposed, it is important to ask what sort of empirical evidence exists for the claim that arbitrary pairs of rules may be organized either sequentially or simultaneously, depending on the grammar. Further research would be needed to determine the amount of added power this gives to grammars.

Where Chafe's proposal explicitly departs from the requirements of linear ordering, however, is in the notion of PERSISTENT RULES. Chafe proposes that a certain subset of the rules at depth 1 are specially marked as 'persistent', and that a persistent rule can apply not only at depth 1, but also at any other depth. In these terms, we might give an account of the example of Sundanese nasalization in Chapter 10 as follows: the rule of nasalization itself is persistent, and thus appears at depth 4 as well as at depth 1. The arrangement of the rules would then be as follows:

(8) depth 4: nasalization
depth 3: metathesis
depth 2: denasalization
depth 1: nasalization

Similar accounts could be given of some of the other examples that have been discussed above.

The first example Chafe gives to support this proposal is from the American Indian language Caddo. He cites a rule (which we designate as rule *C1*) the effect of which is to stress a vowel before a resonant (i.e., a nasal or glide) followed by a stressed vowel:

(9) (*C1*) $[+\text{syll}] \longrightarrow [+\text{stress}] / \underline{\hspace{1cm}} \begin{bmatrix} -\text{syll} \\ \alpha\text{nas} \\ \alpha\text{cons} \end{bmatrix} \begin{bmatrix} +\text{syll} \\ +\text{stress} \end{bmatrix}$

A second rule is not specified in detail, but Chafe describes a process (rule *C2*) which deletes certain internal unstressed vowels. When these two apply to a form like /cihawáynikah/ 'we have run away', rule *C1* applies first to stress the second vowel, with the result that rule *C2* is now inapplicable to this vowel. We obtain, therefore, [ciháwáynikah]. This shows that, for a given vowel, *C1* must precede *C2*.

Another rule of Caddo phonology which interacts with *C1* and *C2* converts a sequence of vowel plus *h* into a stressed vowel in the position before two nonsyllabic segments. Let us call this rule *C3*:

(10)   (*C3*)   [+syll] *h* [−syll][−syll]

$$\begin{array}{cccc} 1 & 2 & 3 & 4 \end{array} \longrightarrow \left[\begin{array}{c} 1 \\ \text{+STRESS} \end{array}\right] 3\ 4$$

Given a form like /hanahyaʔah/ 'there are many', the vowel dropping rule (*C2*) applies to the third vowel, yielding /hanahyʔah/; this, in turn, undergoes *C3* [rule (10)] to give /hanáyʔah/, which undergoes *C1* to give the final [hánáyʔah]. Thus, although for any given vowel, *C1* must precede *C2*, there are derivations in which *C2* precedes *C3*, which, in turn, precedes *C1*. It will be seen that either ordering of *C1* and *C2* is BLEEDING (in isolation); if *C1* applies first, some vowels that would otherwise be deleted become stressed, and hence are preserved; while if *C2* applies first, some vowels that would otherwise be stressed are deleted. There is therefore no natural ordering of these two rules, and in the terms of the theory of ordering suggested here, we would have to en- sure the derivation of the correct form [ciháwáynikah] rather than the incorrect *[cihwáynikah] by an explicit (contingent) ordering restriction '*C1* precedes *C2*'.

In a form like /hanahyaʔah/, the application of *C2* produces new forms for *C3* to apply to that would not be affected if *C3* applied first. '*C2* precedes *C3*' is thus a feeding order, and natural; it would not be stated in a locally ordered grammar. Rule C3, in turn, creates stressed vowels that allow *C1* to apply (where it could not otherwise), and so the or- dering *C3*–*C1* is also feeding and natural. The fact that *C2* precedes C1 in such a derivation, then, follows from an ordering defined in terms of natural relations, and thus overrides the contingent statement '*C1* precedes *C2*'. The case is formally similar to the Kasem example dis- cussed in Chapter 10.

Chafe's other set of rules is attributed to Schane, and applies in French. The rules in question are the following:

(11)   a. $\emptyset \longrightarrow \text{ə} / C \left[\begin{array}{c} \text{+cons} \\ \text{+son} \end{array}\right]$ _____

b. $C \longrightarrow \emptyset / \underline{\quad} + C$

c.[6] $[+syll] \longrightarrow \emptyset / + \underline{\quad} +$

Given the underlying form /ekriv+r/, both (11a) and (11b) could apply, but the application of (11b) would make (11a) inapplicable. The order (11b)–(11a) would thus be a bleeding order, and the opposed (neutral) order (11a)–(11b) is natural. The natural order obtains, and yields [ekrirə]. In a form such as /viv+e+r/, the *e* is lost, but the *v* is not; hence, rule (11c) must apply only after (11b). This is an unnatural ordering, and hence must be stated in the grammar. After (11c) does apply, however, the environment for (11a) is satisfied, and this rule can apply. The order (11c)–(11a) is natural, and the rules apply in that way to give [vivrə]. Despite the fact that (11a) precedes (11b) in some forms (such as /ekriv+r/), and follows it in others (such as /viv+e+r/), both of these orderings are natural for the forms in question, and the example can be accommodated within the theory we propose by simply stating the ordering restriction '(11b) precedes (11c)'.

Chafe's analysis of these cases in terms of persistent rules is easy to construct. In the Caddo case, the rule *C1* (the rule which spreads stress) is treated as persistent; the rules are arranged as in (12):

(12)   depth 4: *C1*
              depth 3: *C2* (vowel deletion)
              depth 2: *C3* (V+h $\longrightarrow \acute{V}$ / $\underline{\quad}$ CC)
              depth 1: *C1*

In the French case, the rule of schwa-insertion is the persistent one; the set of rules (11) is arranged as (13):

(13)   depth 4: (11a) (schwa insertion)
              depth 3: (11b) (truncation)
              depth 2: (11c) (thematic vowel dropping)
              depth 1: (11a)

It is easy to confirm that these arrangements give the right results in these two cases.

It is clear that on some assumptions, Chafe's theory is equivalent to the theory of anywhere rules. If we impose the requirement that all of

---

[6] The environmental statement '+ $\underline{\quad}$ +' is my notational interpretation of Chafe's use of the cover symbol 'V_t' for thematic vowels; it is undoubtedly inadequate.

the rules applying at any given depth be independent of one another (i.e., that their simultaneous, as opposed to sequential, application has no important consequences), then Chafe's theory is exactly that of anywhere rules, with an added limitation on the class of anywhere rules that a grammar can contain (i.e., all of the anywhere rules must be mutually irrelevant, since they must all apply at level 1) and some potential incoherencies (e.g., since each of the anywhere rules has to be able to apply at any level, it would seem that it would have to be mutually irrelevant with every other rule of the grammar, unless the requirement is explicitly waived for the 'persistent' rules). As such, it would be falsified by the example we have just adduced against anywhere-rule theories in general. Let us assume, then, that the requirement of mutual irrelevance at each depth is not imposed, and the class of rules applying simultaneously at each depth is therefore arbitrary.

In this case, the facts discussed thus far in this chapter would not falsify the theory. In the case of Icelandic, it is clearly the rule of *u*-Umlaut which must be persistent; we can give the following account of its interaction with other rules:

(14)   depth 3: syncope; *u*-Umlaut
              depth 2: vowel reduction
              depth 1: *u*-epenthesis; *u*-Umlaut

This rule system will allow all of the derivations we have seen so far: since *u*-Umlaut is simultaneous with syncope, we will be able to operate on /jak+ul+e/ to give *jökli;* since another instance of *u*-Umlaut follows syncope, we will be able to operate correctly on /katil+um/ to give *kötlum;* since *u*-Umlaut both precedes and follows vowel reduction, we will be able to operate correctly on /fatnað+um/ to derive *fötnuðum;* and since *u*-epenthesis is simultaneous with the *last* application of *u*-Umlaut, epenthetic vowels will never be able to produce Umlaut. Note that in this last case we are using the possibility of simultaneity crucially.

In fact, this example is typical of one class of cases for which nonlinear orderings are required: cases in which some rule (e.g., *u*-Umlaut) must be allowed to apply both before and after other rules, and where there are few if any other limitations on it of the sort 'rule *A* must not apply before (some other) rule *B*.' This is, of course, the sort of case that would suggest the plausibility of an anywhere rule hypothesis. Because of the possibility of simultaneous application, it is not sufficient to provide a single instance of a restriction of the type 'rule *A* must not apply before (some) rule *B*' to falsify it; the ordering in (14) gives an example which is perfectly consistent with such a fact in this framework.

Notice, however, the sort of fact which would falsify (14) as an adequate account: if we can provide some other rule which must be allowed to apply to the output of *u*-epenthesis, then there must be at least one more depth, and *u*-epenthesis must in fact be at depth 2 (with all of the other rules also being pushed down one depth). But then, since persistent rules can apply at any depth and (especially) at depth 1, *u*-Umlaut will also be able to apply at this new depth 1; and in consequence will be able to operate on the output of *u*-epenthesis, which, of course, we have seen to be incorrect.

In fact, there are at least two rules which must operate on the output of epenthesis. One of these specifies the distribution of phonetic length in the language: vowels are long if (stressed and) followed by a vowel, a single consonant, or a single voiceless obstruent followed by *j*, *r*, or *v* (= underlying /w/). This lengthening is independent of whether there is another vowel after the consonant(s) in question. Otherwise vowels are short. In forms prior to the operation of epenthesis, many clusters of consonant plus *r* exist that would give rise to short vowels in the preceding syllable. Because epenthesis breaks up these clusters, the preceding syllable comes to be open, and the resulting vowels are lengthened. Thus, we have clusters such as ðr, fr (= [vr] after a sonorant), and many others which shorten vowels when preserved (as seen, for instance, in comparatives and other adjective forms whose inflections begin with *r*: *efri* [ɛvrɪ] 'upper'; *neðri* [nɛðrɪ] 'lower', etc.); but which yield long vowels when broken up by epenthesis (e.g., *maður* [ma:ðür] 'man (nsg.)',[7] *stafur* [sta:vür] 'letter (of the alphabet)', etc.). The vowel length rule, then, must clearly follow epenthesis, and so would constitute a later 'depth' than epenthesis. This would then give *u*-Umlaut a chance to apply to the output of epenthesis, incorrectly.

Another process, which also gives the same conclusion, is the simplification of many clusters of three or more consonants. These are often simplified by the loss of either the first or the second (but never the last) member of the cluster. The clusters which undergo simplification, however, are those which remain after *u*-epenthesis has broken up final *Cr*; thus we get alternations such as *hálfur* [haulvür] 'half, M. nsg.' versus

---

[7] This is a particularly interesting form. The underlying form is /mann+r/, with the root /mann/ which shows up in the other declensional forms of the word. /nn/ becomes /ð/ before /r/ (as shown by the paradigm of *annar* 'second': F. asg. *aðra*, M. dsg. *öðrum*, etc. *ann-* appears before the root *a* when this is unsyncopated, but *að-* before the root *r* when the second vowel of /annar-/ is lost). Epenthesis then applies, to give [ma:ðür]. This is another argument for the epenthesis rule, since without it, the /nn/ of /mann/ would not stand before *r* in *maður* and hence could not be converted into /ð/. The distribution of vowel length clearly must follow both *nn* → ð and epenthesis.

halfri [haulrı] 'F. dsg.', where the medial /v/ in the cluster
/ · · · lvr · · · / can be dropped only after it is determined that the cluster will not be broken up by epenthesis. The root here is /hálf/, followed by /+r/ and /+ri/.

We see, therefore, that the theory of persistent rules including the most liberal view of the possibility of simultaneous ordering cannot accommodate an example like that of Icelandic *u*-Umlaut. The reason, of course, is the fact that *u*-Umlaut behaves differently in its relation to different rules: with respect to some, *u*-Umlaut applies freely either before or after, according to the principles of natural order. With respect to others, however (e.g., *u*-epenthesis), *u*-Umlaut is restricted, and cannot apply to their output. A theory such as Chafe's, which divides rules into fully linear and fully 'anywhere' cannot accommodate these facts; even the use of simultaneity does not help, if the rule with respect to which a putatively persistent rule is restricted cannot be ordered last among the linear rules. Since both vowel length and cluster simplification must follow epenthesis in Icelandic, this example provides conclusive evidence against such a theory.

Another class of cases exists for which nonlinear orderings are required, and these also provide a counterargument to a theory such as Chafe's. In cases like Icelandic Umlaut, Sundanese nasalization, etc., the nonlinearity arises because some rule must apply on either side of some other rule; but in other cases, the nonlinearity arises from the fact that rule *A* is allowed to precede rule *B* in some derivations, but required to follow it in others. In such a case, an order of application like *A–B–A*, given by the theory of persistent rules, will give incorrect results since it will allow *A* to precede *B* in all derivations. Such an example will be presented below in the discussion of Grassmann's and Bartholomae's laws in Sanskrit.

From examples of the sort we have been discussing, we can see that the correct solution to cases which violate linear ordering is not to establish a special class of nonlinear rules. It seems that the move of considering the ordering relations between any given pair of rules as independent of other ordering relations is nearer to the truth. Some of these orderings will of course be consistent with linearity, but others will not; however, a rule which is nonlinear with respect to some of the rules may well be strictly linear with respect to others.

We have so far assumed that the ordering principles which may be relevant to the operation of rules are limited (in addition to explicitly given orderings) to the maximization of feeding orders and the minimization of bleeding orders; but it is important to ask whether this is the case. Since P. Kiparsky (1968a) originally noted that some orders seemed to be more natural than others, several other proposals have been made about orderings that are natural, as opposed to their opposites, but which are not covered by Kiparsky's proposals. Unfortunately, in many cases the initial plausibility of the suggestions is not supported by evidence of the sort Kiparsky provided for his original proposal. When we see that rules have shifted, as a result of historical change, from one order into another, we can take this as evidence for the naturalness of the innovated ordering (assuming we believe in the principle that historical change is in the direction of more natural grammars). Similarly, in the cases we have been discussing thus far, we find the concepts of bleeding and feeding orders substantiated synchronically by the fact that they enable us to give an account of ordering relationships which are literally indescribably in terms of absolute statements 'rule *A* precedes rule *B*.' The fact that the two lines converge on the same set of orderings as natural provides substantial confirmation of the claims that feeding orders are natural and bleeding orders unnatural. Not all proposals that have been made are supported in such ways, however. For example, Kisseberth and Kenstowicz (1971) discuss several instances of bleeding orders in a variety of languages, and argue that these cases are in fact instances of natural, rather than unnatural orderings. They then relate this set of cases to generalizations about rules that affect syllable structure. While their suggestions are in several cases attractive, it is hard to evaluate their claims, because evidence is not presented that it is *necessary* to consider these orderings as natural. It might conceivably be the case that all of their examples are in fact instances of language-particular unnatural orders. This seems unlikely, from the actual cases; but without further evidence, it is impossible to evaluate their specific proposals about naturalness. Once the class of necessarily natural orderings in their domain has been established, it might well be that some totally different hypothesis will be suggested. It does seem likely that additional hypotheses of the sort Kisseberth and Kenstowicz suggest will prove to be necessary, however, and that some instances of bleeding orders will actually turn out to be natural.

A different sort of example from those given by Kisseberth and Kenstowicz, in which it seems to be necessary to say that a bleeding order is more natural than a possible neutral alternative, is provided by the rules specifying the behavior of aspirates in Classical Sanskrit. In Chapter 3 we discussed some phenomena related to Grassmann's law in this language. It will be recalled that two related facts suggested the existence of a rule which deaspirated a root initial consonant when another aspirate followed in the root: (a) reduplicated forms from roots with initial aspirates reduplicate this segment as a nonaspirate; and (b) for many roots, the loss of aspiration on the final entails the appearance of aspiration in the initial. We suggested that reduplication be preserved as a general process copying the root initial, and that the roots with an apparently 'mobile' aspirate be treated as containing two aspirates. The deaspiration rule, then, will treat these two classes as aspects of the same fact. That the rule should be formulated so as to require the second aspirate in its structural description to be part of the root is clear, since an aspirate in an ending does not cause the root to lose its aspiration. These points are illustrated by the following alternations:

(15) a. /phal/ 'burst': pres. *phalati,* perf. *paphala*
      b. /ḍhauk/ 'approach': pres. *ḍhaukati,* perf. *ḍuḍhauka*
      c. /bhudh/ 'awake': pres. *bodhati,* perf. *bubodha,* fut. *bhotsyati*
      d. /dhugh/ 'milk': pres. *duhati,* perf. *duduha,* fut. *dhokṣyati*
      e. /bhṛ/ 'bear': 2pl. act. pres. *bibhṛtha*
      f. /dhā/ 'put': 2du. mid. pres. *dadhāte*

We suggest, then, that the synchronic form of Grassmann's law be given as (16),[8] below (referred to in subsequent discussion as '*GL*'):

$$(16) \qquad [+\text{cons}] \longrightarrow [-\text{spr. gl.}] \,/ \underline{\quad\quad} [+\text{seg}]_0 \begin{bmatrix} +\text{cons} \\ +\text{spr. gl.} \\ +\text{ROOT} \end{bmatrix}$$

[8] The feature '[+ROOT]' in this rule is ad hoc, but the existence in several other languages of rules whose application depends on whether or not a given segment belongs to the root suggests that this is an important distinction, access to which should be permitted to phonological rules. An example of such a rule is the Umlaut rule in Takelma, discussed above in Chapter 9; several others are known to us. The feature distinguishing aspirates from plain stops is taken to be [+spread glottis], in accord with Kim (1970). Ladefoged's (1972) recent claim that voiced aspirates and voiceless aspirates do not form a single category is nearly incomprehensible to us. He claims that voiceless aspirates are characterized solely by the delay in onset of voicing, while voiced aspirates are characterized by the 'murmured' character of the following vowel. In these terms, there is nothing in common. Very little literature exists on the precise character of the voiced aspirates, but Ladefoged presents some observations reportedly made by fiber-optics techniques. Without access to the data alluded to, it is impossible to be sure; but Ladefoged himself shows that the voiced aspirate is characterized by a glottal configuration substantially open at one end, with an irregular mode of vibration affecting only part of the length of the vocal cords. Voiceless aspirates, on the other hand (cf. Kim, 1970) are characterized by a widened glottal aperture and no vibration, as well as extra tension in the vocal cords which results in stiffness which actively hinders the subsequent onset of vibration. These results are entirely consistent with a characterization of 'aspiration' as 'spread vocal cords' and of 'voicing' (in at least some cases) as 'slackened vocal cords'. Unless one intends totally to abjure physiological interpretation of acoustic phenomena, it seems needlessly obscure to claim that voiced aspirates are not in fact aspirated at all, but rather 'murmured'. I see no reason whatever to deny the unitary character of a deaspiration rule such as (16).

In addition to *GL*, Sanskrit contained a rule which assimilates the voicing of an obstruent to that of a following obstruent, and deaspirates stops before obstruents. In final position, obstruents are devoiced and deaspirated. Other assimilations and related processes are also performed by this complex of rules, but we can isolate the phenomenon of deaspiration from the others without apparent loss of generality:

$$(17) \qquad [+\text{cons}] \longrightarrow [-\text{spr. gl.}] / \underline{\hspace{1em}} \left\{ \begin{array}{l} [+\text{obst}] \\ \# \end{array} \right\}$$

The operation of this process (together with devoicing) is illustrated before *s* by (15c, d) above; before *bh* and finally it can be seen in such sets as *vṛt / vṛdham / vṛdbhis* 'increasing (nsg. / asg. / inst. pl.)', *bhut / budham / bhudbhis* 'awakening (nsg. / asg. / inst. pl.)', and *pat / patham* 'road (nsg. / asg.)'. We can see from these forms that when the root is of the *ChVCh* class, rule (17), which we will henceforth refer to as *DaC*, must precede *GL*, since the loss of an aspirate by *DaC* results in the preservation of the initial.

We have discussed above the loss of aspiration before *s*, *-bh*, and finally. Inflectional morphemes that might be juxtaposed with a root-final consonant are limited in their phonetic structure; in fact, they can only begin with one of the above, with *dh*, with *t* or with *th*. In the case of endings beginning with *dh*, such as the 2pl. middle desinences, both primary and secondary (*-dhve, -dhvam*), the behavior is the same as with those just mentioned: from /dhogh/ 'milk' we get, e.g., *adhugdhvam* (2pl. imperf. mid.). Before endings beginning with voiceless dental stops, however, Sanskrit was subject to a process known as Bartholomae's law [which some Indo-Europeanists have claimed has traces in other non-Indic dialects; see Puhvel (1971)]. By this rule, a cluster consisting of voiced aspirate followed by voiceless dental stop becomes voiced unaspirate followed by voiced aspirate. The rule applies to voiced-aspirate-final stems when followed by desinences such as *-ta* (past participle), *-tas* (3du. act.), *-tva* (gerund), *-tha* (2pl. act.), *-thas* (2du. act.), among others:

(18) a. /rundh+tas/ $\longrightarrow$ runddhas
      b. /rundh+thas/ $\longrightarrow$ runddhas
      c. /labh+ta/ $\longrightarrow$ labdha

If Bartholomae's law did not apply in these forms, we would expect the root-final stop to be devoiced and deaspirated, yielding clusters such as *-tt-*, *-tth-*, *-pth-*, etc., instead of the observed *-ddh-*, *-bdh-*, etc. Of the observed effects of the rule, the deaspiration of the root final is clearly a

special case of the operation of *DaC*, and the synchronic form of Bartholomae's law need only affect the following stop:

(19)
$$\begin{bmatrix} -\text{cont} \\ -\text{voi} \end{bmatrix} \longrightarrow \begin{bmatrix} +\text{spr. gl.} \\ +\text{voi} \end{bmatrix} / \begin{bmatrix} +\text{spr. gl.} \\ +\text{voi} \end{bmatrix} \underline{\qquad}$$

In fact, there is one element which is an exception to rule (19) (henceforth *BL*): this is the reduplicated stem /dhadh-/, from /dhā/ 'put'. When
this stem is followed by the voiceless dental stop endings, we find forms
such as *dhattas, dhatthas, dhatte,* etc., with the expected devoicing and
deaspiration of the final. Many other such forms, with *BL* failing to
apply where it would be expected, are found in early texts such as the
Vedas.

When we consider the *ChVCh* roots before endings to which *BL*
would apply, we find forms such as *buddha* (from /bhudh+ta/) 'understanding', *banddhas* (from /bhandh+thas/) 'bind', etc. The root initial in
these cases is deaspirated, as is the root final. The deaspiration of the
initial must, however, precede the deaspiration of the final, since the
only other aspirate that could provide the environment for *GL* is in an
ending, and we have seen that aspirates in endings do not cause *GL* to
apply. Furthermore, *BL* must also apply before the root final is deaspirated, since root-final nonaspirates do not cause *BL* to apply: cf. *atti*
'eats' from /ad+ti/. These facts lead to an ordering problem, of course:
we observed above that in order to derive, e.g., *bhotsi*, it was necessary
to apply *DaC* before *GL*, while we have just seen that it is necessary to
apply *GL* before *DaC* in order to derive *buddha*.

In Anderson (1970), some attempts to deal with this problem by
reformulating the rules *GL, DaC,* and *BL* are discussed and shown to be
inadequate. Since the appearance of that paper, several other alternative
solutions have been proposed, but none of these seem to deal with the
ordering difficulty while preserving the generality of the phenomena. We
can note in particular that it will not do to ascribe the ordering peculiarities of forms like *buddha* to the nature of the cluster produced, such as
by saying that the orthographic representation *-ddh-* represents a cluster
which is aspirated throughout. Aside from the fact that there is no support whatever for this in the ample phonetic testimony of the Indian
grammarians, such a move totally misses the essence of the problem.
Exactly the same clusters which are produced by *BL* can also arise by
the juxtaposition of a root-final stop and a desinence-initial voiced aspirate, and here the required ordering is the same as for, e.g., *bhotsi*.[9] We

---

[9] A problem here is the 2sg. imperative ending *-hi/-dhi*. Before this ending, diaspirate
roots behave in the same way as before the endings that undergo *BL*: thus we get, e.g.,
dugdhi 'milk!' from /dhugh/. The only way we could be certain of whether *BL* is involved

have, in fact, a virtual minimal pair from the root /bhudh/: *buddha,*
before the desinence /+ta/, but *abhuddhve* before the desinence
/+dhve/. Thus it cannot be the phonetic nature of the cluster that is at
issue. The point is that not the phonetic character, but the derivational
history of the cluster is relevant: if it is derived by *BL*, it provokes loss
of root-initial aspiration by *GL*, but otherwise it does not. Attempts to
reformulate the rules given here, such as that by Brame and Phelps
(1973), do not seem any more successful. At least for early Classical
Sanskrit, where the unity of *GL* is best supported, we can only say that
the rule reformulations that we have seen appear to abandon important
generalizations with no basis except to avoid our theoretical conclusions.

   Let us consider the ordering relations that can be defined among the
three rules *GL*, *BL*, and *DaC*. We can note first that the ordering of *BL*
with respect to *DaC* is natural: if *DaC* preceded *BL*, it would wipe out
the environment for the application of that rule. In fact, if the order were
not *BL–DaC*, *BL* could never apply at all, and would presumably not be
part of the grammar. This neutral as opposed to bleeding (indeed, hem-
orrhaging) order is thus natural. *BL* and *GL* do not, however, interact
in a way that would define any ordering between them as natural. It is
clear that the applicability of *BL* does, in fact, affect the operation of
GL; an order therefore must be specified for them. Let us specify the
order '*GL* precedes *BL*'. Now, in forms to which *BL* applies, the rules
will apply in the order *GL–BL–DaC,* and the correct relative ordering of
GL and *DaC* will also obtain. From underlying /bhudh+ta/, then, the
first rule to apply will be *GL*, giving /budh+ta/ (because of the ordering
restriction); *BL* can then apply, giving /budh+dha/, to which *DaC*
applies to give the final form *buddha.*

   Now consider a form like /bhodh+si/. Since the ending does not begin
with a voiceless stop, *BL* cannot apply, and only *GL* and *DaC* are relevant. Both of the orderings we discussed before involved *BL*, so neither
of them are relevant. Now it would appear that the order '*GL* precedes
DaC' is natural: this is a neutral order, while '*DaC* precedes *GL*' is
bleeding. The observed order for this form, *DaC* before *GL*, looks
unnatural. We cannot state an ordering restriction to that effect, how-

---

here or not is by examining the one root that is systematically exceptional with respect to
BL, /dhā/. Unfortunately, the imperative from this root does not show the reduplication
characteristic of other forms: the imperative is simply *dhehi,* which tells us nothing. In any
case, the imperative ending *-hi/-dhi* is peculiar in other ways. The alternation of *VhV* with
CdhV is essentially isolated in Classical Sanskrit, and suggests that the segment in question is not simply underlying /dh/. It is perhaps also noteworthy that the cognate of this
suffix in Greek, $-\theta\iota$, is subject to a sort of reverse Grassmann's law, becoming $-\tau\iota$ *after*
another *suffix* containing an aspirate.

ever, since any such ordering restriction would prevent the correct derivation of *buddha*.

Let us look more closely at the ordering '*GL* precedes *DaC*', however; in fact, if this ordering were to obtain, the result would be that the initial aspiration of roots like /bhudh/ would be removed by Grassmann's law in every single form built on them. But in that case, Grassmann's law would no longer account for an alternation: the same effect could be obtained by simply entering these roots in the lexicon as, e.g., /budh/, and by eliminating *GL* from the grammar (while incorporating the remaining part of its effect into the morpholexical reduplication rule). We can say, therefore, that the order '*GL* precedes *DaC*' would result in the elimination of *GL* from the grammar. Accordingly, if *GL* is in fact a part of the grammar of Classical Sanskrit (which we have argued is the case), it must follow *DaC* in at least some derivations.

We have seen above that *GL* precedes *DaC* in derivations in which *BL* also applies, but that fact was attributed to the interaction of the two rules *GL* and *DaC* with *BL*. Accordingly, when only *GL* and *DaC* apply in a derivation, it would be reasonable to say that their natural order is *DaC–GL*; for only in this way is *GL* preserved as a rule in the grammar. The resulting natural order is bleeding, but a principle which we can call the principle of SELF-PRESERVATION overrides the principle of minimizing bleeding orders where necessary. We suggest, therefore, that this principle be incorporated into the theory of ordering relations along with those of feeding and bleeding orders. In some cases, the principle of self-preservation will argue for the same ordering as will the others: this was, for instance, the case above with the interaction of *BL* and *DaC*. The ordering *BL–DaC* is not only neutral (as opposed to bleeding); it is also the only order which can preserve *BL* as a rule of the grammar. In other cases, however, as in the one we are concerned with here, the two principles give different results, and we must assume self-preservation to take precedence in such a case. This principle is essentially the same as that referred to above (page 178) by which the subrules of a 'drag chain' apply in 'dragging' order, rather than in the order which would merge all of the affected elements in a single result. The Sanskrit example just discussed, then, may not be as isolated as it appears initially. We should also note that the principle of self-preservation is only intended to apply to SYNCHRONIC grammars: it states that, given that rule *A* is part of the grammar of a natural language, it must have some work to do. This by no means precludes a change by which rule *A* is in fact lost from the grammar of a subsequent stage of the language.

If, then, there are indeed natural bleeding orders, it is clear that modifications must be made to the theory of natural ordering as it has been developed up to this point. One such modification has just been suggested (and it is also possible that the examples of Kisseberth and Kenstowicz referred to above will have similar consequences when they are sufficiently well understood). Another sort of modification to this theory has been proposed by Harris (1972). Harris would like to rehabilitate the concept of paradigm uniformity, and he provides examples from Spanish which suggest that this is correct. The cases in question consist of sets of inflectional forms of the same root ('paradigms') which have the property that if the rules applied in the same order to all forms in the set, the root would show different shapes for different forms. In fact, what appears to happen is that the rules apply in different orders to different forms in just such a way as to ensure that the root has a constant shape throughout the paradigm. Harris' examples are quite convincing, and we are quite sure that an adequate account of natural ordering will have to include the consideration of paradigmatic uniformity. We will not discuss this further here, however, because we do not have any further examples to add to Harris', and we do not know how to incorporate his observations formally. It is also unclear whether such factors are ever operative generally in a language, or whether they are restricted to certain paradigms or groups of paradigms. The interaction of paradigmatic uniformity with the principles of feeding and bleeding is also in need of further explication.

A further modification of the principles of natural order (which is somewhat allied to Harris' ideas) has recently been suggested by P. Kiparsky (1971b). He suggests that rules tend to apply in such a way as to maximize the TRANSPARENCY of their operation. Transparency is the extent to which the applications of a given rule to a given form can be seen in the phonetic output at the end of the derivation of the form. Kiparsky suggests that, if we have a rule of the form '$A \longrightarrow B \mid C$ _____ D', the following factors reduce a rule's transparency: any instances of A in the environment C _____ D in surface forms; any instances of B in environments other than C _____ D; or instances of B in C _____ D which do not derive from $/A/$. Like the notion of paradigmatic uniformity, the notion of transparency is a reasonably familiar one, and has been invoked overtly or implicitly in many contexts in other studies. Kiparsky gives examples, however, in which historical change can be seen to operate on nontransparent (or OPAQUE) rules so as to make them more transparent or to eliminate them from the grammar.

An example in which we can see such a principle at work in the organization of a synchronic grammar is found in the rule(s) of vowel harmony in some dialects of Turkish. This is surely one of the best known phonological rules in any language, because of its very general applicability and clear phonetic character. Descriptions in traditional grammars (such as Swift, 1963; Lewis, 1968) are often quite sketchy, consisting of a list of the possible sequences of vowels found within morphemes and within words, together with some classes of exceptions. Lees (1961, 1967) has discussed the problem within the framework of generative phonology, and a recent treatment by Foster (1968) has organized most of the relevant facts. These works form the basis of the following discussion. We are concerned here with the operation of the rules of harmony, and not with some of the other issues which have been raised in connection with the process: we do not, for instance, take a stand on the question of whether or not vowels in suffixal morphemes should be fully specified, which is tangential to our concerns.

The facts are as follows, in outline. Turkish words consist of a stem and a sequence of suffixes, which can be quite long. A word generally can contain only vowels with the same value for the feature [±back]. Furthermore, a high vowel in the second syllable or later has the same value of the feature [±round] as that of the preceding syllable. As is reasonably common in Altaic languages, [−high] vowels after the first syllable are all [−round]. In addition, the consonants /k, g, l/ have two phonetic shapes: [+back, +high] in words with [+back] vowels, and [−back, +high] in words with [−back] vowels. The lateral is thus 'dark *l*' in back vowel words and 'palatal *l*' in front vowel words. Where necessary to indicate this distinction, we will write the [−back] forms of these segments as k_1, g_1, and l_1. The result of these facts, in any event, is that most suffixes containing either vowels or /k, g, l/ have at least two alternate forms, depending on the word in which they appear and the harmonizing features of other elements of that word.

A first issue to be resolved is the question of whether 'consonant harmony' (i.e., the alternations in shape of /k, g, l/) is to be treated as part of the same rule as VOWEL HARMONY. Since consonant harmony involves the same feature ([±back]) as does vowel harmony, there is a strong temptation to seek a single formulation of the class of segments which are affected by BACKNESS HARMONY. Foster (1968), however, argues that the two should not be treated by the same rule. His first argument for the separation is from universal phonetics: the assimilation of backness in velars to that in adjacent vowels is extremely common, if not universal, while the assimilation of backness in vowels is much more restricted. Since the two are frequently found separately, they should not be collapsed in Turkish. The argument by itself has little if any force. For one thing, the assimilation of /l/ is linked to that of the velars, but this is surely a more restricted process (in terms of the languages of the world). As we will note in Chapter 15, language-particular instantiations of universal rules often have very idiosyncratic details associated with them, which are inseparable from the general rule. There is no a priori reason for or against combining vowel and consonant harmony in any particular language.

More important facts are also adduced by Foster for the separation of the two processes, however. He notes that there are words like [k₁ar] 'job, profit' in which the velars exceptionally do not agree in backness with the adjacent vowels, but in which vowel harmony behaves normally. Thus, from this root we get [k₁ardan] 'because of profit', with a back vowel in the suffix, just like [kardan] 'because of snow', from the regular [kar] 'snow'. Furthermore, there are words like [dak₁ika] 'moment', [hak₁ikat] 'truth', [šeftal₁i] 'peach', etc., in which the vowels are exceptional, in that they do not agree with one another; but in which harmonic consonants are regularly in agreement with the backness of the adjacent vowels.

Since vowel harmony and consonant harmony have distinct classes of exceptions, we conclude that they are distinct rules. Consonant harmony is generally conditioned by a following vowel (as we see from the exceptional forms just cited); if the consonant is not followed by a vowel, the preceding vowel determines its backness. We could formulate this process as the mirror-image schema (20), which applies disjunctively (as argued in Chapter 8):

$$(20) \qquad [+\text{cons}] \longrightarrow [\alpha\text{back}] \; \% \; \left[\begin{array}{c} \underline{} \\ -\text{strident} \\ +\text{high} \end{array} \right] \left[\begin{array}{c} +\text{syll} \\ \alpha\text{back} \end{array} \right]$$

The feature [−strident] is included in this rule so as to exclude the segments [š, ž, č, ǰ] from its application. These, we presume, are always [−back]. It may be the case, however, that these segments are actually velarized in the environment of back vowels, in which case this feature could simply be eliminated from the formulation of the rule. We do not have sufficient detailed information about Turkish phonetics to decide this issue. It can be noted that the mirror-image nature of consonant harmony is part of the reason some authors (e.g., Lightner, 1965) have been led to the radical claim that this kind of process is not phonological at all, but rather represents the distribution of an arbitrary morpheme feature over the whole word. This morpheme feature is then given phonetic realization in individual segments as the feature [±back]. The development of a theory of processes which are simultaneously progressive and regressive, as described in Chapter 8, makes this conclusion unnecessary.

Having accounted for backness harmony in consonants, we can return to the vowels. As we noted above, the backness of the stem vowel(s) in regular Turkish roots determines the backness of the suffix vowels. The backness of vowels is uniform within the stems of such words as well. There are many other roots, however, in which the vowels of the stem itself do not agree, due to the word's belonging to the (rather large) class of loans from Arabic, Persian, and other languages, which have not yet been completely assimilated to the Turkish phonological pattern (and could, in fact, be said to constitute quasi-autonomous subsystems). In these nonharmonic stems, the backness of the suffixes is generally determined by the backness of the last vowel of the stem:

(21)   a.   *ziyaret* 'visit';   *ziyaretinizden*
              'because of your (pl.) visit'
        b.   *kitap* 'book';   *kitaplar* 'books'
        c.   *eşya* 'collection of items';   *eşyalar*
              'collections of items'
        d.   *şeftali* 'peach';   *şeftalilerin* 'peaches (gpl.)'

Since the backness harmony rule apparently does not apply within these roots to make them harmonically regular, but does apply between their last vowels and the vowels of suffixes, we conclude that suffix harmony is a process distinct from internal root harmony. We could effect this by having harmony appear as a morpheme structure condition (which the incompletely assimilated words violate) and also as a phonological rule. This rule would then be restricted to vowels which are [−ROOT].

We note further that there are some suffixes which contain vowels not subject to harmony. The most common example is the suffix /(ı)yor/[10] found in progressive tenses. In this suffix, the vowel *o* is not subject to harmony, and is thus invariant (giving rise to most of the instances of non-high rounded vowels outside of the initial syllables of words, other than those in exceptional stems), though the /ı/ is affected by harmony. When the suffix appears with a front vowel stem, the initial vowel harmonizes with the stem; the *o* remains unaffected; and the vowels of subsequent suffixes harmonize with the *o*. From the root /gel-/ 'come', for instance, we can make the word [g₁el₁iyorum] 'I am coming' (from

---

[10] The practice of representing harmonizing suffix vowels by capital letters, common in the literature on Altaic languages, is adopted here. /ı/, therefore, represents a vowel which is [+high], but whose backness and rounding are determined by the operation of the harmony rules. We do not mean this 'archiphonemic' representation to be a serious claim about the underlying structure of affixes; in particular, we do not mean to claim that suffix vowels are left unspecified for harmonic features. As mentioned above, we take no position on this issue here. Similarly, /A/ represents a vowel which is [−high], but whose backness and rounding are determined ultimately by the harmony rules.

/gel+ɪyor+ɪm/). The backness of a vowel affects only those that follow it, so we can assume vowel harmony operates only progressively. Furthermore, this sort of example makes it clear that each vowel harmonizes (if it harmonizes at all) exactly with the preceding vowel. Aside from the fact that this provides another basis for distinguishing vowel from consonant harmony (the predominantly regressive character of the latter as opposed to the exclusively progressive character of the former), this process also provides a further argument for the position of Chapter 9 that processes with potentially unbounded domains should be formulated in terms of iterative reapplication, rather than in terms of simultaneous application. A simultaneous rule would have to divide the word into harmonic domains, independent of one another, and restrict the operation of the rule to 'within a harmonic domain'. These harmonic domains would be bounded by (the ends of words and) vowels which are exceptional with respect to the harmony rule itself; thus the fact that each vowel in fact harmonizes with the preceding one, except for those which are invariant, would be unexpressed. The reason that any given vowel harmonizes (on this analysis) with another vowel from which it is separated only by nonexceptional syllables is precisely that all of these intervening syllables will also have harmonized with it. The range of the harmonic effect of a given vowel is automatically expressed if we write the rule as (22) below, and simply allow vowels like the /o/ of /ɪyor/[11] to be marked [−rule (22)]:

$$(22) \qquad [+\text{syll}] \longrightarrow [\alpha\text{back}] / \begin{bmatrix} +\text{syll} \\ \alpha\text{back} \end{bmatrix} C_0 \begin{bmatrix} \underline{} \\ -\text{ROOT} \end{bmatrix}$$

Rule (22) applies iteratively, of course.[12]

---

[11] Notice that this contradicts the claim which is sometimes made that the scope of an exception or other morphological feature is always an entire morpheme, rather than an individual segment. There seems to be no way to avoid this conclusion, for the suffix /−ɪyor/; its first vowel harmonizes and its second vowel does not, and there seems to be no synchronic basis for putting a morpheme boundary between them.

[12] A complete account of backness harmony must provide for those words like *helal*₁ 'legitimate property', *kalp* 'heart', *harf* 'letter of the alphabet', *kabahat* 'fault', *imsak* 'fasting', and others where the suffixes do not in fact harmonize to the last vowel of the stem. Many of these words end in exceptional palatal consonants, and this has often been thought to be the cause. As this list shows, however, this is not always the case, and virtually any consonant *can* end an exceptional word. It is the case that all of the exceptions except one (*Utarid* 'the planet Mercury') are words with back vowels in their final syllables, which take front vowel affixes. This suggests that in fact affixes contain underlyingly front vowels, and the words in question are simply exceptions to the harmony rule, which allow the suffix vowels to appear in their underlying shape. This analysis cannot cope with *Utarid*, however, and we are trying to remain neutral on the question of underlying specification of suffix vowels for harmonic features.

The remaining harmonic process to be accounted for is that involving the feature [±round]. It will be recalled that only high vowels participate directly in this harmony, since nonhigh vowels after the first syllable are all [−round] (except for cases like /+ɪyor/). We can assume that this is due to a morpheme structure or other constraint that [−high, +round] vowels do not occur in suffixes (or in roots after the first syllable). Since the roundness of high vowels agrees with that of the preceding vowel (whether this is [−round] because [−high], [−round] because of another application of harmony, [+round] because of an application of rounding harmony, or [+round] because exceptional), there is again need to consider the process as iterative, affecting one vowel at a time:

$$(23) \qquad [+\text{syll}] \longrightarrow [\alpha\text{round}] \; / \begin{bmatrix} +\text{syll} \\ \alpha\text{round} \end{bmatrix} C_0 \begin{bmatrix} \underline{} \\ +\text{high} \\ -\text{ROOT} \end{bmatrix}$$

Rules (22) and (23) could be collapsed into one, but there is no obvious reason to do so. We will, nonetheless, refer to the complex of both rules together as 'vowel harmony'.

There are two classes of exception to rounding harmony as just formulated. The first is relatively trivial: a group of words violate the morpheme structure restriction which realizes rounding harmony within the root, in that they contain the vowel *u* in their second syllable. Words like *cabuk* 'quick', *hamul* 'patient', *maymun* 'monkey' *samsun* 'mastiff' *havruz* 'chamberpot', etc. illustrate the nature of this subregularity: if the first vowel of the word is *a*, the second is high, and the intervening consonant (cluster) involves at least one labial, then the second vowel is [+round]. This is presumably another morpheme structure condition (since it does not apply across morpheme boundaries) and can be disregarded. It is necessary to mention it simply to point out another way in which [+round] vowels can arise in the second syllable, and thus induce rounding later in the word by harmony.

A more interesting and difficult set of exceptions to rounding harmony than those produced by the so-called LABIAL ATTRACTION process just described, however, is the result of the process of PALATAL UMLAUT. This phenomenon varies somewhat from dialect to dialect; however,

The essence of the palatal umlaut of the Istanbul dialect is the following: a short vowel is unrounded immediately before a palatal /y, ş, j, ç, c/ within word boundaries if morpheme final or not in the first syllable of the word and it is, moreover, also raised if that palatal is followed immediately by a vowel. Thus, we would have the following pronunciations:

/ye+yen/	[yiyen]
/oku+muş/	[okumış]
/üşü+yüş/	[üşiyiş]
/üşü+me+yiş/	[üşümiyiş]
/gümüş+tür/	[gümiştir]

From the last example we see that the regular vowel harmony rules assimilate vowels to a preceding vowel after the latter has already undergone the palatal assimilation, and therefore that the rule for rounding must follow the palatal umlaut rule (Lees, 1967, pp. 289–290).

The segments that produce the application of the palatal Umlaut rule are all [+high, −back]; unfortunately, so are k_1, g_1, and l_1, which apparently do not. The inelegance of the following rule therefore leaves something to be desired, but seems dictated by the phenomenon:

(24)

$$[+\text{syll}] \longrightarrow \begin{bmatrix} -\text{round} \\ _d\langle +\text{high}\rangle \end{bmatrix} / \, _a\langle\#\rangle C_0 \underline{\hspace{1cm}} _b\langle + \rangle \begin{bmatrix} +\text{high} \\ -\text{back} \\ +\text{grad. rel.} \\ -\text{lateral} \end{bmatrix} \, _c\langle[+\text{syll}]\rangle$$

conditions: if *a*, then *b*
if *c*, then *d*

Recall Lees' statement to the effect that rule (24) must precede rounding harmony [rule (23)], because the unrounding of vowels by (24) results in unrounded suffix vowels where rounded ones would otherwise be expected. This could not simply be incorporated as a condition on rounding harmony (23), to the effect that its operation is blocked in certain environments. This is because rule (24) above is needed in the grammar in any event, to account for the unrounding of basic vowels such as that of [üşiyiş], which would otherwise be [+round]. To impose an extra condition on (23) would require that the environment of (24) be entirely restated as part of (23) also, and would result in the loss of the generalization that vowels after a palatal umlauted vowel are [−round] because that vowel has itself been made [−round] [by (24)]. In addition, there are dialects such as one discussed by Foster (1968) in which the palatal umlaut rule does not unround the vowel, but only raises it; in such dialects, suffixes following palatal umlauted vowels are still round if the basic (pre-Umlaut) vowel was round. In this case, basic

/üşü+me+yiş/ gives [üşümüyüş], rather than the [üşümiyiş] described by Lees for Istanbul. If the restriction on rounding harmony were really distinct from the presence in the grammar of rule (24), we would expect grammars to contain one but not the other; instead we find either both (Istanbul : Lees) or neither (North Anatolian : Foster). We must therefore assume that the [−round] quality of vowels after a palatal umlauted vowel, cited by Lees, is a direct consequence of the fact that harmony applies (regularly) after these vowels in terms of their derived values.

If rounding harmony simply operates on the output of palatal umlaut, however, we will still get the wrong results. The vowel which was unrounded by palatal umlaut will simply be rounded again by harmony, and the following suffixes will be rounded as well. The North Anatolian dialect will thus be the only one describable. It seems impossible to order (23) and (24) in either order—if they apply in the order (23)–(24), /gümüş+tır/ will become /gümüş+tür/, and then the incorrect *[gümiştür], while if we order them as (24)–(23), /üşü+me+yiş/ will become /üşü+mi+yiş/ and then the equally incorrect *[üşümüyüş].

Lees (1967) solved this ordering problem by applying the rules in the order (umlaut)–(harmony), and having the umlaut rule introduce the ad hoc diacritic [−rounding harmony] on the vowel it affects. If we allow rules to introduce diacritical features in this way, the result is of course even more powerful than allowing any arbitrary pair of rules to be ordered disjunctively—of which this proposal is a variant. Chomsky and Halle (1968) suggested that it might be possible for rules to introduce a feature '[−next rule]', but this device has little if any substantive support, and can easily be questioned as too powerful. In any case, the feature [−next rule] would have to be assigned in this example not to the entire word (as Chomsky and Halle suggest), but only to the segment affected. A solution not involving rule features should be found, if possible.

Notice the derivation which we would like to achieve for a form such as [okumıştınız], from underlying /oku+mış+t+ın+ız/: we would like to apply harmony to the first suffix vowel (the third vowel of the word), giving /oku+muş+t+ın+ız/, then apply palatal Umlaut, giving /oku+mış+t+ın+ız/, and then apply harmony to the rest of the word, giving [okumıştınız]. The order we want, assuming as we do that harmony applies iteratively, is harmony–Umlaut–harmony–harmony. Umlaut must, therefore, both precede and follow harmony. Why should this be the case? It is clear that the principles of feeding and bleeding are of no help to us here, for no matter how the rules apply, both harmony and Umlaut will both be allowed to operate.

Let us decompose the orderings a bit more. First, in reference to the first suffix vowel, the rules are to apply in the order harmony–Umlaut. This neutral order is paralleled by the neutrality of the opposite ordering, in terms of feeding and bleeding, but principles like those of self-preservation and transparency allow a decision here: if Umlaut applied first, and then harmony, the effects of unrounding by the Umlaut rule would never be visible in the surface form, since they would always be concealed by the operation of harmony. For a vowel affected by Umlaut, then, the Umlaut rule must clearly apply after the harmony rule, if it is to unround any vowels that would otherwise be round. This must be the natural order for the rules as they affect an 'umlautable' vowel.

Passing on to the next vowel, we see again that whether the Umlaut rule affects the preceding vowel before or after harmony affects this one (now the second suffix vowel, or the fourth of the word) makes no difference to the applicability of the two rules, since both will get to apply no matter which order is chosen. However, if harmony precedes Umlaut, the result will be that this vowel violates the harmony rule in the resultant surface form. If harmony follows Umlaut, however, the harmony rule will be satisfied on the surface for this vowel, since it will in fact harmonize in rounding with the vowel preceding it. The ordering by which palatal Umlaut of the third vowel precedes harmony in the fourth vowel, then, is transparent, while the opposite order would be opaque. If we incorporate something like transparency into the principles of natural ordering, we can use this to obtain the correct derivation in this case. The fact that such a principle plays a role in the organization of synchronic phonology, then, is confirmation of Kiparsky's suggestion that it also plays a role in explaining the direction of historical change.

We can note a sort of hierarchy among the principles that have been discussed this far. The principle of self-preservation, we saw from the Sanskrit example, takes priority over that of feeding and bleeding, since it was necessary for the self-preserving order of rules to obtain even where this was bleeding (given that the rules in question are, in fact, part of the language). Transparency, however, would seem to be subordinate to that of feeding and bleeding. In several cases we have discussed above, it was necessary for the natural order to be the nonbleeding one (in, e.g., the ordering of *u*-Umlaut before syncope rather than after it in such Icelandic forms as /jak+ul+e/). It is immediately obvious, however, that such nonbleeding orders are nontransparent, as well. That is, in the Icelandic form, the result of applying the rules in the nonbleeding order is to produce an instance of *ö* which is inexplicable in terms of its surface environment: there is no following *u*. Yet here, and elsewhere, it is the nonbleeding order, rather than the transparent one, which must obtain. In the only cases we know of where transparency must be invoked as an aspect of natural ordering, the principles of feeding and bleeding do not apply, since both orders are equivalent in these terms. It appears, therefore, that the principle of transparency is one which serves to decide only those cases which feeding and bleeding cannot resolve.

The principles of natural order, which we have invoked in this and the preceding chapters, are all based on consideration of the interrelation of two rules at a time. This is to some extent a consequence of our decision to construct an ordering theory based on pairwise ordering relations. There is no reason to exclude, however, principles of ordering that *relate* only two rules at a time, but take into consideration the interaction of the rules in question with other rules. Examples of this sort have in fact been suggested recently: both Robertson (1970) and Thomas (1971) have presented examples in support of such a claim. These are again cases in which feeding and bleeding do not give unambiguous results; but where the ordering of rules *A* and *B* is determined by the fact that if *A* precedes *B*, some other rule or rules (*C*, *D*, etc.) will be allowed to apply, while if *B* precedes *A*, then *C*, *D*, etc. will be blocked. These examples are highly complex, and cannot really be said to be well understood at present. Some such principles are undoubtedly correct, however, and their exploration should form another area for further research into the character of the ordering relation.

PART IV

SOME PROBLEM AREAS
FOR THE FUTURE

CHAPTER 13

How to Apply
a Rule to a Form

In the chapters of Parts II and III, we have assumed that it was clear what was meant by 'applying' a rule to a given form. Our concern up to this point has been with the interaction of different rules, or with the same rule as it applies at different stages in a derivation, and not with the application of a single rule to a single form. Indeed, while there are problems in formalizing this notion, the vast majority of cases are entirely unproblematic. Given a string which contains an instance of the element A in the proper environment, say $WXAYZ$, it is clear what should be done to effect an application of a rule such as '$A \rightarrow B \mid X \underline{\quad} Y$' to this string, giving as output '$WXBYZ$'.

Problems of a substantive nature begin to arise, however, when we consider the application of a rule to a string which contains several instances of substrings satisfying the rule's structural description. When several potential applications of a rule exist in a single string, how is the change specified by the rule to be carried out? Numerous alternatives can be imagined: apply the rule simultaneously everywhere; apply the rule in one place at a time, in random sequence; apply the rule in only one place, making the choice either randomly or on some universal or language particular basis; etc. These alternatives of course have concrete empirical consequences for the analyses of specific languages, and it is necessary to obtain evidence in order to decide among them. The relevant cases are by no means easy to find, however, and it is not surprising that this issue has only arisen in rather recent work.

Chomsky and Halle (1968) saw the existence of this issue, though they had no cases at hand to allow them to make a principled decision. Accordingly, the algorithm for rule application which they propose was intended simply to make as strong as possible a hypothesis about linguistic structure. Their choice was the simultaneous application of a rule at every possible place in the string:

> To apply a rule, the entire string is scanned for segments that satisfy the environmental constraints of the rule. After all such segments have been identified in the string, the changes required by the rule are applied simultaneously (Chomsky & Halle, 1968, p. 344).

This principle makes the claim that information about the application of the rule at one point in the string cannot be relevant to the application of the same rule at another point in the same string. It thus minimizes the extent of the interaction between different applications of the same rule. In order to maintain this principle completely, Chomsky and Halle were led to propose the device of simultaneously applied infinite schemata of rules [the ( )* notation] for the description of processes with potentially unlimited scope. In Chapter 9, we examined this device and found it to lead to the loss of generalizations in many cases. We proposed there that some rules should be allowed to reapply to their own outputs, thus introducing a certain amount of interaction among applications of the same rule in the same derivation.

Interactions of the sort discussed in Chapter 9, however, do not exhaust the range of cases that must be considered. Cases in which one application creates other potential applications are allowed in this way, but no decision has yet been reached on the matter of what to do when several potential applications exist in the same string. To make the problem concrete, consider a hypothetical language with a rule which applies stress to a vowel preceding and following an unstressed vowel:

$$(1) \quad [+\text{syll}] \longrightarrow [+\text{stress}] \ / \begin{bmatrix} +\text{syll} \\ -\text{stress} \end{bmatrix} C_0 \underline{\hspace{1cm}} C_0 \begin{bmatrix} +\text{syll} \\ -\text{stress} \end{bmatrix}$$

Now consider the way this rule might apply to a form such as /CVCVCVCVCV/. We might choose to apply (1) in accord with the simultaneous principle suggested by Chomsky and Halle, in which case we would stress all but the first and the last of the vowels in this form. If, on the other hand, we should choose to apply the rule in one place at a time, proceeding from left to right, we would obtain an alternating pattern of stress, with the second and fourth but not the first, third, fifth, or sixth vowel stressed. This is because the application of the rule to the second vowel (the leftmost vowel that meets its structural description) removes the environment for its application to the third vowel, and the next vowel that can be affected is the fourth vowel. After the rule applies to the fourth vowel, it can no longer apply to either the fifth or the sixth. If we proceeded one step at a time from right to left in the same form, however, we would again obtain two stressed vowels, but this time these would be the third and the fifth.

If we can find cases, then, in which the application of a rule is possible in several different places, but in which some of these applications would have the effect of removing the environment for others, we can confirm or deny the predictions made by Chomsky and Halle. A case of this sort is discussed by Dell (1970), who deals with the rules affecting the vowel ə in French. Dell demonstrates the existence of a number of rules producing and deleting this vowel, including the two rules abbreviated by the schema (2):

(2) $$\text{ə} \longrightarrow \emptyset \ / \ [+\text{syll}] \ (\#) \ C \underline{\hspace{2em}}$$

This rule, which deletes schwa if it is preceded by just one consonant which is in turn preceded by a vowel, is optional in its application across word boundaries, though obligatory within words. Given a form such as *tu devenais* (/tü # dəvənɛ/) the rule could potentially apply to either of the two schwas. Application to the first schwa would destroy the context for the application of the rule to the second schwa. In fact, this form has two alternative pronunciations: either [tüdvənɛ], or [tüdəvnɛ], but not *[tüdvnɛ], with both schwas elided. In this case, a principle exists which allows us to obtain the correct results without regard to the application algorithm employed. Rule (2), as we noted, is an abbreviation for the two rules in (3):

(3)   a. $\text{ə} \longrightarrow \emptyset \ / \ [+\text{syll}] \ \# \ C \underline{\hspace{2em}}$

            b. $\text{ə} \longrightarrow \emptyset \ / \ [+\text{syll}] \ C \underline{\hspace{2em}}$

It is only (3a) which is applicable to the first schwa in *tu devenais,* while it is only (3b) which is applicable to the second. Rule (3a) is optional, and precedes (3b); if we choose to apply (3a), it makes (3b) inapplicable, and we get [tüdvənɛ]. If we choose not to apply (3a), however, rule (3b) will then apply (obligatorily, as we noted), yielding [tüdəvnɛ]. There is thus no way we would expect to obtain the incorrect form *[tüdvnɛ].

What of cases where several schwas are all affected by the same subrule of (2), however? Numerous such examples arise from sequences of clitics, complementizers, and such items, which in French frequently have the form *Cə* (e.g., *me, te, se, ce, que, le,* etc.). When several of these items are concatenated, interesting results are seen. Consider, for example, the pronunciation of the sequence '. . . *voudrais que ce que le bedeau . . .*'. We can give the underlying form of this sequence as (4), in which the vowels which could potentially be affected by (3a) are numbered:

(4)   /· · · vudrɛ #kə #sə# kə #lə #bədo · · · /
                     1   2   3   4   5

A form such as this has a large number of possible alternative pronunciations, owing to the fact that the rule's application to any given vowel is optional. We summarize these in the following table, where deletion is symbolized by 'Ø', and nondeletion by 'ə':

(5)   vowel: 1   2   3   4   5

1	2	3	4	5
Ø	ə	ə	ə	ə
ə	Ø	ə	ə	ə
ə	ə	Ø	ə	ə
ə	ə	ə	Ø	ə
ə	ə	ə	ə	Ø
Ø	ə	Ø	ə	ə
Ø	ə	ə	Ø	ə
Ø	ə	ə	ə	Ø
ə	Ø	ə	Ø	ə
ə	Ø	ə	ə	Ø
ə	ə	Ø	ə	Ø
Ø	ə	Ø	ə	Ø
ə	ə	ə	ə	ə

There are a number of possibilities for deleting no vowels, one vowel, two vowels, or three, depending on such factors as emphasis, speed of speech, etc. No possibilities other than those in the tabular example (5), however, are grammatical. The generalization underlying (5) is clear: the rule can apply freely, as long as it does not apply in two adjacent syllables. All of the excluded possibilities involve the deletion of two consecutive schwas, in violation of the well-known 'three-consonant law' of French. Some of the possibilities allowed by (5) would certainly be most unusual, but all can be characterized as potentially grammatical.

It is clear that the simultaneous application algorithm is not capable, by itself, of dealing with this set of facts. While the optionality of the rule will allow all of the outputs in (5) to be derived, it will also allow the derivation of all of the incorrect possibilities. Dell shows that it is not possible to explain this fact in terms simply of a constraint on the consonant clusters that can arise in French; a cluster such as / . . . kskl . . . / is well formed, as shown by words such as *exclusif,* but the schwa elision rule must still be prevented from operating on (4) to give *[· · · vudrɛksklǝb(ǝ)do · · ·], etc. Some principle must be found either to supplement or to replace the simultaneous application algorithm. It is always possible that there is simply a complex, language particular restriction involved in such a case. It would be much better, however, if we could make this behaviour follow from the general principles of rule application.

One principle that has been suggested which is capable of dealing with the facts of schwa elision in French is that of LINEAR RULES, proposed by Johnson (1970). Johnson proposed that, instead of applying simultaneously, a rule should be applied in one place at a time, proceeding either from right to left or from left to right. The direction to be followed in any particular case is treated as an additional property of the rule, to be specified in each case.[1] In the case of French schwa, we can give rule (2) as above, and specify it as applying from left to right. In this framework, the fact that the rule never applies to two consecutive syllables follows naturally. When the rule applies to any given syllable, it will create a consonant cluster; this consonant cluster will then precede the following syllable, so that when the rule comes to this syllable, the environment of the rule is no longer satisfied, and it cannot apply there. The optionality of the rule at any step will allow it to produce all of the outputs in (5), whereas its left-to-right stepwise character will prevent it from producing any of the incorrect outputs.

The reasoning behind Johnson's suggestion of linear rules is not particularly persuasive in itself. He argues on formal grounds, by analogy to the arguments often given in syntactic studies, that a grammar incorporating simultaneously applying rules has a greater strong generative

---

[1] A further discussion of this principle of application is found in Howard (1972), where some of the problems of formalism are dealt with. Howard observes that the theory of linear (or 'directional') rules would be more attractive if it were possible to predict the direction of application of a rule from its formal structure, thus removing the necessity of specifying it ad hoc for every rule. As Howard observes, the necessary direction is generally quite clear. It seems unlikely that such attempts to predict directionality can be successful, however, in light of the existence in different languages of formally identical rules which must, in these terms, be applied in different directions. The Slovak rhythmic law and the Gidabal vowel shortening rule to be discussed below constitute such a case.

226 Part IV Some Problem Areas for the Future

capacity (in the sense of Chomsky's studies of mathematical models of syntactic structure) than a grammar incorporating only linear rules. That is, he constructs a formal grammar using simultaneous application which generates a language which cannot be generated by any grammar including only linear rules. Whatever the merits of this line of reasoning in syntax, it is not immediately applicable to phonology. Any adequate theory of phonology will have to put very strong substantive constraints on the notion of 'possible rule' (as is suggested in Chapter 15), and these constraints will surely be much more restrictive than any formal constraint of the sort discussed by Johnson. Since the grammars constructed in Johnson's proof contain rules which seem highly implausible as part of the phonology of a natural language, they would undoubtedly be ruled out by substantive considerations, and not on formal grounds. In any case, the correct procedure in this area is surely not to establish such limitations a priori; rather, the structure of individual rules must be established from simple, noninteractive cases, and then the operation of the rule in more complex circumstances investigated. Only on such a basis can we decide what sort of principle should be followed in applying a rule. Johnson's argument from generative capacity for linear rules, then, must be rejected. In the case of French schwa elision, however, we have an argument of more than purely formal character which supports a revision of the theory of rule application such as that envisioned by Johnson. Although any other theory which also accounted for these facts in a natural way would be equally confirmed by them, the theory of linear rules is a perfectly plausible alternative, and clearly superior to the theory of simultaneous application.

We can now enquire as to whether it is possible to construct any other theory which is like the theory of linear rules in being able to deal with French schwa elision, and which is empirically distinct from that of Johnson. If so, we would then look for cases which would allow us to choose between the two. It is reasonably clear what gives the French rule of schwa elision its special character: the problem it raises is due to the fact that no application can be permitted to destroy the environment which was employed for another, simultaneous, application. The various applications of the rule which take place simultaneously, that is, must be independent of one another. This principle recalls the restriction we proposed above in Chapter 12 for Chafe's theory of persistent rules: recall that in that theory all of the rules at a given level were intended to apply simultaneously, and we suggested that it would be plausible to impose as a constraint on the construction of grammars that all members of a set of rules which apply simultaneously in this way must be independent of one another. We might suggest a modification of Chomsky and

Halle's simultaneous application principle, then, which is also subject to this restriction on the simultaneous application of interacting rules. We state such a principle semiformally in the following revision of Chomsky and Halle's principle quoted above:

(6)   *To apply a rule, the entire string is first scanned for segments which satisfy the environmental constraints of the rule. As many such segments are identified as can undergo the rule independently of each other, where independence consists in the fact that no segment requires, in the environment which allows it to undergo the rule, the presence of a segment which is itself to be altered by undergoing the rule. After all such segments have been identified in the string, the changes required by the rule are applied simultaneously.*

The notion of independence in this formulation should perhaps be clarified in the following way: if the structural change of the rule is such that it could not introduce a feature specification into an environment segment that contradicts the requirements of the structural description, overlapping applications could be considered independent even if segments undergoing the rule served simultaneously as environments. Suppose, for example, we had a rule which assigns high pitch to a vowel which is neither initial nor final in the word, i.e., in the environment $VC_0 \_\_\_ C_0V$. The structural description of the rule requires only that vowels be present on both sides, and not that they be low pitched; while the rule introduces only the feature of high pitch, and does not alter the status of a segment as a vowel. The modification proposed would allow all of the possible applications of the rule to a string such as $C_0VC_0VC_0VC_0VC_0VC_0$ (i.e., the applications of the rule to the second, third, and fourth vowels of the form) to be considered independent. Without this change, however, the application of the rule to the third vowel would be dependent on the applications to both the second and the fourth vowels. We have no empirical evidence to confirm or deny this conjecture, but it seems a plausible refinement of (6) as stated.

Further substance can be given to principle (6) in the form of an algorithm for application of a rule to a given string:

(7)   *To apply a rule to a string*

        a.   *Identify all of the segments which satisfy the conditions for the application of the rule, and circle them. For each such segment, identify the minimal substring of*

> *the form which provides the environment allowing the segment to undergo the rule. Each such environment is associated with a particular segment which is to undergo the rule.*
>
> b. *If the rule is optional,[2] eliminate from consideration any or all of the segments which could undergo the rule, together with their associated environments.*
>
> c. *If, in the resultant string, any environment contains a circled segment other than the one with which that environment is associated, eliminate the minimal number of segments and associated environments from consideration so as to remove all such violations [of principle (6)].*
>
> d. *Apply the change of the rule simultaneously to all of the remaining circled segments.*

Observe the way in which the rule applies to the string in (4). Step (7a) results in the following partitioning of the string, with potential applications encircled and associated environments underlined. Violations of principle (6) are indicated with '*':

(8)   /· · ·v u d r ε # k ə # s ə # k ə # l ə # b ə d o · · · /

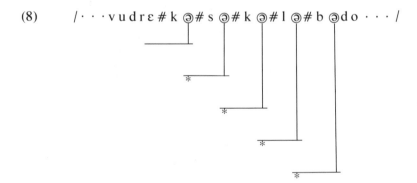

By (7b), we could optionally eliminate any of these circles and their associated underlines. In order to determine the adequacy of the algorithm, however, let us attempt to apply the rule everywhere. At this

---

[2] Howard (1972) has suggested examples which appear to show that rules may differ as to whether they are optional separately with respect to each potential position of application, or only optional globally (i.e., with respect to application to the whole string or to none of it). Much more study needs to be devoted to the subject of rule optionality, but this topic seems orthogonal to our present concern.

point, when (7c) applies, there are four violations of principle (6). The minimal number of applications which can be disregarded in order to remove these violations is exactly two: the application to the second schwa, and to the fourth schwa. The reader can confirm for himself that if any other application is disregarded instead of one of these two, at least three will have to be disregarded in total in order to eliminate all of the violations of (6). The resultant string, with no remaining violations, is

(9)   /· · · v u d r ɛ # k ⓞ # s ə # k ⓞ # l ə # b ⓞ d o · · ·/

By (7d), then, the three schwas which remain with circles are deleted simultaneously, giving rise to the output [· · · vudrɛksəkləbdo · · ·], a possible pronunciation of the phrase in question. The remaining possibilities can all be generated by various eliminations of schwas [on grounds of optionality, by (7b)], together with the application of (7c) to force the elimination of others. The reader can readily confirm that all of the possible forms, and none of the impossible ones, can be derived in this way.

After rule (2) has been applied to the string in this way, it cannot of course be allowed to reapply to its own output, since that might permit the deletion of undeletable schwas. Suppose for example that on a first application, we decided to eliminate the first and second schwa from consideration, on grounds of optionality. Two violations of principle (6) would remain, both of which could be removed by eliminating the fourth schwa from consideration. The rule would then apply to delete only the third and fifth schwas, yielding /· · · vudrɛ#kə#sə#k#lə#bdo · · ·/. If the rule were then allowed to reapply, there would be nothing to stop it from applying to delete the second schwa, giving the impermissible /· · · vudrɛ#kə#s#k#lə#bdo · · ·/. It is clear that some rules must be prevented from reapplication to their own outputs, however, so that this property of the schwa-elision rule in French is not a novelty.

It is also clear that cases may arise in which the set of segments which should be eliminated from consideration at stage (7c) will not be uniquely determined by the requirement that the minimal number be disregarded that eliminates all of the violations of (6). Suppose, for example, that we chose to eliminate the first schwa from consideration in (8) on optionality grounds. The three violations of (6) that would still remain could then be removed in two equally minimal ways: by disregarding the second and fourth schwas, applying the rule only to the third and fifth ones; or by disregarding the third and fifth schwas, applying the rule only to the second and fourth ones. In this case, both outputs are possible, and we might take the theory to predict free variation in such circumstances.

In the case of other, nonoptional, rules we will see that such free variation is not generally allowed. We suggest, however, that choices can be made in most (and perhaps all) such cases by means of the principles we have established already in Chapters 10–12 for the interaction of pairs of rules. Recall that these included the principle of self-preservation; the principle of maximizing feeding (and minimizing bleeding) orders; and the principle of transparency. The three can be arranged in a hierarchy, ordered in just this way; so that each one applies just in case no higher one does. The principle of self-preservation does not, so far as we know, play any role in connection with the application of a single rule [and so in connection with resolving indeterminacies at the stage of (7c)], but the other two do. We will see in examples below that, when a rule is allowed to apply to its own output, an indeterminacy is resolved in favor of the way that will allow one application to feed another rather than to bleed it; while in the case of rules that are not allowed to apply to their own output, and hence could not feed themselves, the indeterminacy is resolved in the direction of maximizing transparency. This use of the same principles of natural order which determine the interaction of a pair of rules to determine the method of application of a single rule is an important result. It allows the principles of natural ordering (and the associated theory of local ordering of pairs of rules) and the revised simultaneous application convention to provide support for one another.

Thus far, we have simply attempted to expound the revised simultaneous application convention, and to demonstrate that it provides a viable alternative to the theory of directional rules in that it can deal with a type of example which the original simultaneous application convention was unable to account for. We have not yet tried to show that there are empirical differences between the revised simultaneous theory and the directional theory. An example which appears to illustrate such differences, and to provide evidence in favor of the revised simultaneous theory, is found in the complex accentual system of Acoma (see Miller, 1965). In this language there are three accents which can appear on a given vowel: a high pitch (marked with an acute accent); a falling pitch (marked with a circumflex); and a 'glottal' falling pitch contour (marked with a glottal stop). The rules for the distribution of these accents are extremely complex, and it is often difficult to determine where accents should be expected to fall, but in a large group of forms, we can be sure of a particular basic accentual distribution. This is the set of forms which contain suffixes conditioning what Miller calls 'accent ablaut'. A group of approximately twelve suffixes[3] induce this change, which consists in the assignment of the high accent to every syllable of the word (together, in some cases, with the lengthening of the final vowel), except for certain final syllables. Examples of forms with accent ablaut are given in (10)[4]:

(10)   a.   *ʔúyáasbáani* 'grinding stone';   cf. *ʔúyåaspaani* 'to grind'

           b.   *káizúwiita* 'taxpayer';   cf. *kåizúwiita* 'he is paying'

           c.   *sdyə́ríiná* 'bells worn by dancers';   cf. *sdə́ri-* 'dangling, jingling'

           d.   *táaṁawá* 'five times';   cf. *táaṁa* 'five'

           e.   *ṁáidyáanáwá gáaná* 'by sevens';   cf. *ṁåidyaana* 'seven'

           f.   *háanámí* 'the east';   cf. *hâa* 'east'

           g.   *rúuníšíizé* 'on Monday';   cf. *rûuniši* 'Monday'

           h.   *héemíšíici* 'Jemez Pueblo';   cf. *héemiši* 'Jemez Indian'

           i.   *rúuníšíiṁa* 'every Monday';   cf. *rûuniši* 'Monday'

           j.   *šíizáačúwání* 'when I woke him up' (suffix *í* + Ablaut)

           k.   *súwágə́ní* 'when I got dressed';   *suwagə́ni* 'I got dressed'

There are two principle circumstances in which high accents assigned by the accent ablaut rule are lost: one is in short syllables adjacent to a glottalized sonorant, as discussed in Chapter 8 [see also (10d)]. The other condition under which such accents are lost is in a short syllable

---

[3] It is very difficult to determine what, if any, generalizations can be made about the properties of suffixes causing accent ablaut. While Miller's description is a model of completeness, he frequently goes out of his way to avoid making generalizations. For instance, in discussing the fact that stem final consonants in verbs are preserved before vowels but lost finally and before consonants, he makes it clear that the stem-final consonant will be preserved before any suffix beginning with a vowel. Nonetheless, in discussing the individual consonants which can appear, he makes a point of saying for each that it is preserved before each of a list of suffixes, where this list contains all and only the vowel initial suffixes with which the roots in question are attested. It is only in a footnote that he suggests that there is a principle to these lists (the statement of which would make them unnecessary). He is also quite willing to make use of totally abstract 'process morphophonemes' as the conditioning factor for alternations whose conditioning is not phonetically transparent. It is thus extremely difficult to see how far one could go in explaining accent ablaut in terms of the underlying phonological shape of suffixes which condition it.

[4] Note that the accent on a long vowel or vowel sequence is marked only on the first element.

between obstruents, when followed by another accented syllable. The following examples illustrate this process; each is from a category in which accent ablaut is regular. The vowels whose accent is lost are capitalized:

(11)   a. *kUbə́ní* 'at sunset'
         b. *šISíusdyáni* 'when I roped him'
         c. *ʔúubək'áak'áci* 'nail'
         d. *síukAčáni* 'when I saw him'
         e. *séinúust'Uzími* 'when I put the fire out'

We could write this rule as (12) below:

$$(12) \quad V \longrightarrow [-accent] \ / \ [+obst] \ \underline{\hspace{2em}} \ [+obst] \ C_0 \begin{bmatrix} +syll \\ +accent \end{bmatrix}$$

Now if two consecutive vowels meet the conditions for the application of this rule, both may be deaccented, as in the forms in (13).

(13)   a. *k'APIšúm̓a* 'every night'; cf. (10i) and *k'ápišu* 'it is night'
         b. *šAPəgám̓a* 'every evening';   cf. *šápəka* 'it is evening'
         c. *šIpəkáawáni* 'when I chopped wood'
         d. *k'Acəkáñi* 'his cigarettes'

How are we to apply (12) to the forms in (13) in order to obtain this result? Let us see how a form such as /k'ápíšúm̓a/ would be analyzed by step (7a) of the revised simultaneous application procedure:

(14)   / k' (á) p (í) š ú m̓ a /

In (14), there is one violation of principle (6) above. Since the rule (12) is not optional, step (7b) is not relevant, and (7c) must resolve this violation. This can be done by removing either of the two potential applications of the rule from consideration. If we assume that rule (12) is allowed to affect its own output, however, this ambiguity is resolved: if we ignore the second of the two possible applications in (14), the rule will not bleed itself, in that another application will still be possible in the resultant form; while if we ignored the first of the two, the rule would bleed itself, and another application would not be possible. This is illustrated below in two alternate derivations, showing the way rule (12) analyzes the form at each step:

(15)　　　　a.　(7a)　/ k' â p í š ú m̊ a /

(7c)　/ k' â p í š ú m̊ a /

(12)　/ k' a p í š ú m̊ a /
reapplication:
(7a)　/ k' a p í š ú m̊ a /

(7c)　no violations; inapplicable
(12)　[k' a p i š ú m̊ a]

　　　　b.　(7a)　/ k' â p í š ú m̊ a /

(7c)　/ k' á p í š ú m̊ a /

(12)　/ k' á p i š ú m̊ a /
(no reapplication possible)
*[k' á p i š ú m̊ a]

Derivation (15a), in which (12) is allowed to reapply, obtains because the principles of natural order require a bleeding order to be avoided. As mentioned above, the theory of (revised) simultaneous application assumes that this principle applies as well to the resolution of indeterminacies in the application [by (7)] of a single rule as it does to the determination of the relative order of two rules.

The principle under consideration, then, is able to accommodate the examples in (13), on the assumption that (12) is an iterative rule. The theory of linear rules is also able to accommodate these examples, on the assumption that (12) applies from left to right. That is, given /k'ápíšúm̊a/, the first (leftmost) application of the rule yields /k'apíšúm̊a/; then the second (next to the right) application yields [k'apišúm̊a], correctly. We therefore have no way, as yet, of distinguishing between the two theories. It is only when we consider the more complex forms, in which three consecutive vowels meet the conditions for the application of rule (12), that a difference emerges:

(16)　　　　a.　*kəzáçəkáni*　'your cigarettes'
　　　　b.　*kagə́cədíní*　'when it was in bloom'
　　　　c.　*sučítistáaní*　'when I was thinking'

Here we see that rule (12) has deleted the first and the third of the three accents which satisfy its structural description, but not the second. Now observe that this is exactly what is predicted by (7). That is, given an input form like /súčítístáaní/, rule (12) will analyze this as (17), at the stage (7a):

(17)   / s ⓤ č ⓘ t ⓘ s t á a n í /

There are two violations for (7c) to eliminate. Both of these can be eliminated if the second possible application of (12) is dropped from consideration, while if either the first or the third is dropped, one of the remaining two will have to be dropped as well. Since (7c) requires that the minimal number of applications be removed from consideration to eliminate the violations of (6), it is clear that only the second possible application should be dropped. However, rule (12) will then affect the first and third vowels, to the exclusion of the second vowel. This gives the correct result, [sučítistáaní], to which the rule cannot reapply. The revised simultaneous application procedure, then, is capable of dealing with forms such as those in (16) satisfactorily.

The theory of linear rules is also capable of dealing with the forms in (16), by assuming that rule (12) applies from right to left. In the input form /súčítístáaní/, the rightmost application of (12) is to the third vowel in the form, giving /súčítistáaní/; in this form, the second vowel no longer satisfies the structural description of (12), and the next possible application to the left is to the first vowel, giving the correct output [sučítistáaní]. Thus, the correct output can be generated by means of linear rules. The difficulty is that the rule (12) must apply from left to right in order to generate the forms in (13), but from right to left in order to generate the forms in (16). This result is inconsistent, and no obvious reformulation of the rules allows it to be avoided. We must conclude, therefore, that the theory of linear rules does not allow for a correct and coherent description of the facts of Acoma accent loss, while the revised simultaneous application theory does. Since both theories account equally well for cases such as schwa elision in French, and there is no other substantive argument in favor of the theory of linear rules, it is probable that we should reject the theory of linear rules in favor of some such device as principle (7).

The revised simultaneous application principle is capable of accounting for patterns such as French and Acoma, and also (as will be discussed below) for simple alternating patterns, in cases where a number of potential applications of a rule overlap in the way we have been considering. One pattern that could not be produced by the algorithm in (7) without additional principles, however, is exactly the pattern that the original simultaneous algorithm was limited to: application of the rule to every possible segment. It is therefore important to inquire as to whether such cases exist in natural languages. There are four cases presently known to us of rules which might appear to present this character. Further examination reveals in each case that an alternative account is at least as adequate, and in some cases to be preferred, in each example. While such primarily destructive discussion is perhaps a bit tedious, each example raises some other issues of interest.

One such example is the behavior of the third tone in Mandarin Chinese, discussed recently by Cheng (1968) and Browne (1972). The surface tones of Mandarin, in isolation forms, are approximately as follows, where contours are given in Chao's tone letters[5]: Tone 1 is phonetically high level ([˥]); tone 2 is mid–rising ([˧]); tone 3 is falling–rising ([˩]); and tone 4 is high–falling ([˥˩]). The interesting problems arise in connection with the behavior of sequences of tone-bearing syllables, where rules of tone sandhi apply. Sandhi affecting tone 3 is of particular interest: when followed by another instance of tone 3, tone 3 is replaced by tone 2; and when followed by another tone other than tone 3, tone 3 is replaced by a mid-falling contour, the so-called 'half–third' tone ([˧˩]).

The important fact to observe is the behavior of several consecutive instances of tone 3. Cheng (1968) discusses the influence of syntactic structure on the realization of such sequences; we can assume that processes determined by the interaction of syntactic structure with speed of speech and other stylistic concerns delimit stretches of the utterances within which sandhi can occur, and at the ends of which the tones display their isolation, or word-final values. Within such a sandhi-domain, all consecutive instances of tone 3 except the last are converted into tone 2, as required by the above sandhi rule. Thus, a sequence *3–3–3–3–3#* becomes *2–2–2–2–3#*. The obvious suggestion is that the sandhi rule is something like the following:

(18)   [tone 3] ⟶ [tone 2] / ____ [tone 3]

---

[5] There is some question as to the exact phonetic values in some cases; it is unclear, for example, whether the final high pitch in the isolation form of tone 3 is to be identified with the level of tone 1 and/or the final high of the isolation form of tone 2, or is to be marked lower. These details are irrelevant to our analysis, and we will assume that the contours can be adequately specified in terms of high, mid, and low pitch.

If (18) is, in fact, the correct form of the rule, it is necessary to apply it in a way which violates principle (6) above, since some of the instances of tone 3 before which sandhi of other tone 3 syllables is to apply are themselves being converted into tone 2 by the same rule at the same point in the derivation. Since each instance of tone 3 is altered to tone 2 under the influence of a following instance of *tone 3,* which may itself be changed, it is difficult to see how the independence of all of the consecutive applications can be maintained. Notice that the simultaneous application principle of Chomsky and Halle can handle this situation perfectly well (indeed, this is the only possible behavior, on the basis of that algorithm); the linear rules theory can also handle this rule, by declaring it left to right.

Upon further analysis of the tone system, however, this problem disappears. As will be discussed below in Chapter 14, several writers have recently argued that a single syllable can contain several separate tone elements, realized in sequence, and that the so-called contour tones are not elementary units, but rather sequences of level tones. The Mandarin 'mid–rising' tone, for example, is not to be treated as an unanalyzable unit, but rather as a sequence '*m–h*' (*l* = low, *m* = mid, and *h* = high). Similar treatment should also be given to the other contour tones. Let us assume now that the tone contours for Mandarin syllables are specified in terms of two tone levels per syllable, in sequence: tone 2, mid-rising, is as just noted represented as [*m–h*]; tone 4, high-falling, is represented as [*h–l*]; and tone 1 (high level) is agreed to be simply [*h–h*]. In the case of tone 3, however, several investigators have argued (completely independently of the issues we are concerned with here) that this tone has an underlying representation which is distinct from any of its surface shapes. Both Cheng (1968) and Woo (1969) have argued on other grounds that tone 3 should be treated as underlyingly a low level tone ([⌟] or [*l–l*]). In that case, we would need rules quite distinct from (18) to predict the phonetic forms. Let us assume now that (at least in tone representations) syllable boundaries are marked, so that a rule can determine whether two adjacent tone elements belong to the same syllable or to different syllables. We will mark syllable boundaries in the derivations below with a period (.).

In tone 3 syllables, we can note that the first tone element is realized not as the underlying low, but as mid in all cases. To account for this, we need a rule such as (19):

(19) $$[l] \longrightarrow [m] \ / \ . \ \underline{\quad}$$

This formulation is adequate, since tone 3 is the only tone in the system which begins with *l* in the underlying form. Taken by itself, rule (19) will correctly generate the 'half–third' contour ([꜔꜕]), though if no other rules appeared, it would incorrectly assign this value to all instances of tone 3 in all positions. We need, in addition, principles by which the other contours can be produced.

The isolation value of the tone is easy to deal with. What is necessary is to assume (with other recent authors, as will be discussed in Chapter 14) that some syllables in a language may come to have a different number of sequentially realized tone elements assigned to them than others. In that case, we can say that the isolation (or final) form of tone 3, mid–falling–rising ([꜔꜖꜕]), is to be represented as $[m–l–h]$, and that syllables bearing this tone contain three tone elements, rather than two. The rule which produces this contour, then, is simply a process which inserts an extra tone element ($[h]$) into a tone 3 syllable followed by the boundary of the phrase (i.e., when not followed in the phrase by another tone):

(20) $\emptyset \longrightarrow [h] \ / \ .[-h][l] \ \_\_\_\_ \ .\#\#$

The term '$[-h]$' in this rule means either mid or low, and is a perfectly natural one in a system of features such as that of Halle and Stevens (1971), where it would be expressed more accurately as '[−stiff vocal cords]'.

We have ignored here the problem of a small class of fixed compounds with an initial syllable of tone 3 and a second syllable having the 'neutral' tone. Tone 3 is always said to be realized in its isolation form ([꜔꜖꜕]) in these compounds. It is interesting to note, however, that where the complex (or three element) realization of the third tone is followed by a neutral tone syllable, the neutral tone is realized as high, and the tone 3 syllable is in fact realized as $m–l$. What is clearly going on in this case is that the contour is spread out over more than one syllable if it contains more tone elements than usually can fall on one syllable (in Mandarin, two) and an extra syllable is available to accomodate the surplus. This is exactly analogous to phenomena in African and other tone systems which are discussed in Chapter 14.

Rules (19) and (20), then, will correctly derive the third and half-third contours, which phonetically realize the underlying low-level tone. But what of our original problem, the generation of a second tone from a third followed by another third? For this, we need simply specify a rule which converts the second l of a syllable to h when it is followed by another syllable-initial l:

(21) $[l] \longrightarrow [h] \ / \ .[l] \ \_\_\_\_ \ .[l]$

Rule (21) applies before rule (19) converts the first element of a low level tone to [*m*]; this ordering follows from the fact that (19) would otherwise bleed (21). Now given a sequence of several third tone syllables, we propose the following derivation:

(22)   underlying form: / . *l   l* . *l   l* . *l   l* . *l   l* . *l   l* . # /
       rule (21):   / . *l   h* . *l   h* . *l   h* . *l   h* . *l   l* . # /
       rule (19):   / . *m h* . *m h* . *m h* . *m h* . *m l* . # /
       rule (20):   / . *m h* . *m h* . *m h* . *m h* . *m l h* # /
       phonetic output: [˦   ˦   ˦   ˦   ˧˩   #]

Now observe that in connection with this system of rules, the problem of the application of the third-tone sandhi rule has disappeared. It is true that several instances of third tone are converted into second tone, but the crucial difference between rule (18) and rule (21) is the following: in (21), the element which undergoes the rule is a syllable-final tone element; the elements which furnish the environment for the operation of the rule are all syllable-initial elements. Thus, the rule is never required to make use of an item in satisfying its structural description which is to be affected by the structural change of the rule. In terms of the algorithm (7) above, rule (21) analyzes the underlying form in (22) as follows:

(23)   / . 1①. 1①. 1①. 1①. 11 . /

Since no circled element appears in an underlined environment which is associated with any other circled element, the rule can (and must) be applied to all of the circled elements simultaneously. This example is thus seen not to be inconsistent with principle (6) and its realization as the algorithm (7), as might be suggested by a rule such as (18) which is not based on a complete analysis of the internal structure of tones.

   Another example which appears to contradict principle (6) is discussed by Browne (1970, 1972) in Slovak. In Browne (1970), it is demonstrated that Slovak is in general subject to a 'rhythmic law', by which a long vowel is shortened following another long vowel:

(24) $[+\text{syll}] \longrightarrow [-\text{long}] / \begin{bmatrix} +\text{syll} \\ +\text{long} \end{bmatrix} C_0 \underline{\quad\quad}$

This rule applies to, e.g., underlying /čīt+ām/ to give [čītam] 'I read (pres.)' (for the length of /+ām/, cf. [volām] 'I call', with a short root vowel). In general, only two long vowels in succession can arise in Slovak, but there is an exception in forms which contain the iterative marker /+āv+/. This can appear, for example, in the first singular from the root /čīt/, giving underlying /čīt+āv+ām/, with three consecutive long vowels. Rule (24) applies to shorten both of the vowels which meet its environment, giving [čītavam] 'I read (pres. iterative)'. Thus far, this case is parallel to that of the accent-loss rule in Acoma, and we can conclude that rule (24) is allowed to apply to its own output. The simultaneous theory of Chomsky and Halle (1968) can also handle these data, as can the theory of linear rules [which would characterize (24) as applying from right to left].

The problem arises from the fact that there is one possible source for a sequence of four or more consecutive long vowel syllables in Slovak: the iterative marker can itself appear several times, indicating an increased notion of iteration in forms such as /čīt+āv+āv+āv+ām/ 'I read and read and read and read (pres.). The difficulty for principle (6) is that all of the long vowels (except, of course, the first) in this form are shortened, giving the output [čītavavavam]. This result is consistent with either the simultaneous or linear theories, but not, apparently, with principle (6). The algorithm (7) should give something like [čītavāvavam], with an alternating pattern of length.

As long as forms with multiple instances of the iterative marker are the only instances of four or more long vowels, however, the Slovak rhythmic law cannot be considered a critical case. As is evident from the gloss of [čītavavavam], 'I read and read and read and read (pres.)', English, too, has a device for forming intensified iteratives: copy the verb several times. This device has some very interesting properties, as has been pointed out by Browne (in personal communications and class discussions in 1967). There are some verbs in English for which two past tense forms exist in free variation for many speakers: the past of *dive* can be either *dived* or *dove,* the past of *leap* can be either *leaped* or *leapt* (i.e., with or without shortening of the stem vowel), etc. Any of the forms in free variation can be the basis of an iterated formation, so we can have either 'he leapt and leapt and leapt' or 'he leaped and leaped and leaped'; but the two cannot be intermixed, so we cannot have *'he leapt and leaped and leapt', etc. This suggests that the formation of iteratives does not take place freely within the syntax, but rather takes place only after inflectional elements have received their phonological realization, in order to insure that all of the iterated elements will have the same phonetic shape. If we extend this constraint analogously to the case of Slovak repeated iteratives, we might suggest that parallel facts obtain there. Suppose that /čīt+āv+āv+āv+ām/ is not the underlying form of [čítavavavam], but rather /čīt+āv+ām/ is. Rule (24) applies (and reapplies) to this representation, giving /čīt+av+am/. If the repetition of the iterative element is carried out only at this point, then the element which is copied will be not /+āv+/, but /+av+/. Thus, if an intensified iterative is formed by copying an element whose phonetic shape has already been determined, as is suggested by the formation in English, forms such as *čítavavavam* can be derived without any violation of principle (6).

Another case that appears to contradict principle (6), brought to our attention by Paul Kiparsky, is the rule of consonant gradation in Finnish. It will be remembered from Chapter 6 above that this rule affects stops at the beginning of a short, closed syllable, simplifying geminates and converting single stops into 'weaker' segments. Since the presence of a geminate closes the preceding syllable, this raises the possibility that an element which is providing the environment for one application of the rule may itself be subject to another application. Recall that the environment for the gradation rule was stated as[6]

$$(25) \qquad \begin{bmatrix} -\text{cont} \\ \alpha\text{cor} \end{bmatrix} \begin{bmatrix} \underline{\qquad} \\ \alpha\text{cor} \end{bmatrix} [+\text{syll}][-\text{syll}] \left\{ \begin{matrix} [-\text{syll}] \\ \# \end{matrix} \right\}$$

The last element of a geminate, then, might be analyzable both as the affected segment in one application of the rule, and as the final segment of the environment in some other application. Owing to the extensive possibilities of suffixation in Finnish, such cases are not too hard to come by. From the word *rokko* 'infectious disease, esp. one producing skin pustules', we can form a verb *rokottaa* 'to inoculate' by adding the suffixes /+tta+/ 'to fix up with something' (cf. *vero* 'tax', *verottaa* 'to tax') and /+ta/ 'infinitive marker' (which loses its *t* after a short vowel). The first person singular of this verb is *rokotan*, showing gradation both of the root and of the suffix. From *rokottaa* we can further form a causative *rokotuttaa* 'to cause to be inoculated' with the suffix /+utta+/ (cf. *kirjoittaa* 'to write' versus *kirjoituttaa* 'to cause to be written'; /+utta+/ causes the loss of an immediately preceding vowel by regular processes). The underlying structure is /rokko+tta+utta+ta/. The second person plural of this verb then shows four consecutive geminates, each separated by a short vowel: /rokko+tta+utta+tte/ gives *rokotutatte*, with the first three of these geminates undergoing gradation.

---

[6] We confine our attention here to the portion of gradation which affects geminates. The problem being dealt with could not possibly arise in the case of gradation of single stops.

Forms like *rokotuttaa,* with two overlapping instances of gradation, can be reconciled with any of the theories we have considered. The theory of simultaneous application obviously needs no modification for this example; the linear rule theory deals with it by characterizing gradation as left-to-right; and the revised simultaneous theory incorporating principle (7) describes the rule as one which reapplies to its own output.[7] A case like *rokotutatte,* however, is different. The simultaneous and linear theories need no modification, but the example is inconsistent with principle (6) if (25) is the correct formulation of the environment. Algorithm (7), that is, would analyze this form in terms of the gradation rule (which follows the loss of *a* before *u*) as (26):

(26) $/ \text{r o k} \textcircled{k} \text{o} + \text{t} \textcircled{t} + \text{u t} \textcircled{t} \text{a} + \text{t t e} /$

There are, as we see, two violations of (6) in (25), which (7c) would eliminate by disregarding the second of the two possible environments for gradation. This would result in the incorrect form **rokottutatte,* with only the first and third geminates reduced.

It is not hard to argue, however, that (25) is incorrect as the statement of the environment for gradation. The rule, as is generally agreed, applies at the beginning of a short closed syllable; this is formulated as (25) simply because there is at present no device available in phonology to permit rules to refer directly to syllable structure. There is an increasing body of evidence, however, that syllables must be delimited in phonological representations. This matter is discussed below; an example of a rule making reference to syllable boundaries is the Mandarin tone process discussed previously, and other such rules are suggested in Chapter 14 and by Hooper (1972). The term '$\{^C_\#\}$' is present in rule (25) simply in order to encode the principles of syllabification in Finnish into the gradation rule. This last element of the structural description is necessary not because of any property it has itself, but simply because its

---

[7] It is of course true that single stops produced by gradation must not be further weakened by the gradation rule. Thus, *rokottaa* must not be further converted to **roottaa.* This is perfectly consistent with the provision that the rule applies to its own output, however; recall that in Chapter 9 we imposed the general limitation that rules never reapply in the same position as a previous application. Furthermore, as we argued in Chapter 6, gradation of single stops is a distinct rule from gradation of geminates, and regardless of the behavior of degemination, the single stop rule precedes the geminate rule (by the principle suggested above in Chapter 11, in connection with the Gitksan rules converting *x* into *h* and *h* into Ø intervocalically, if that principle can be formally founded).

presence will cause a syllable boundary to fall after, and not before, the consonant preceding it, thus closing the syllable. The rule should really be formulated in such a way as to refer to a short syllable ending in a consonant, and should not have to duplicate the statement of the conditions under which this will be the case:

$$(27)^8 \qquad \begin{bmatrix} -\text{cont} \\ \alpha\text{cor} \end{bmatrix} \begin{bmatrix} \\ \alpha\text{cor} \end{bmatrix} [+\text{syll}][-\text{syll}].$$

If the environment of gradation is given as (27), however, the problem this example would pose for principle (6) disappears. In this case the three separate examples of degemination in *rokotutatte* are independent in the relevant respect. The revised gradation rule now analyzes the form not as (26) but as (28):

(28) $\qquad$ / . r o k . ⓚ o + t . ⓣ + u t . ⓣ a + t . t e . /

Although the environments overlap in (28), principle (6) is not violated, since no segment which is affected (i.e., no circled segment) is used in an environment other than the one it determines. Accordingly, (7c) is inapplicable, and the rule applies so as to delete all three consonants which are circled. Subsequent resyllabification will relocate the syllable boundaries in front of the remaining members of the original double stops, giving [ro.ko.tu.tat.te] as the output. We see, however, that Finnish consonant gradation is not in fact a counterexample to principle (6).

A fourth and final example, which appears to contradict (6), is provided by the rule(s) of Slavic phonology known as Havlík's law. Common Slavic possessed two lax high vowels ь and ъ, known as the

---

[8] The symbol '.' in this rule represents syllable boundary, as above. Rule (27) is essentially the formulation of the environmental specification for Finnish gradation which is suggested independently by Hooper (1972). Both Hooper's discussion and the present one ignore the fact that problems are presented for any analysis of gradation by postvocalic [j], since some occurrences of this segment close a syllable, others do not, and others (while they do not close the syllable) do not make the syllable long, either. These problems, which have not been completely resolved, are probably irrelevant to the present concerns; if anything, they seem to suggest that it may be even more important to recognize the reality of syllables in formulating the rule. It can be noted that Hooper's formulation of the environment without use of syllable boundaries is a bewilderingly complex one, that makes the difference between (25) and (27) look greater than it has to be.

JERS. In all of the modern Slavic languages, however, these vowels have been replaced phonetically. The conditions for this replacement were first formulated (for Czech) by Havlík, in a way that appears to be valid for early West Slavic in general. The jers can be divided into two classes: weak jers are those that are final or followed by a non-jer vowel. Other jers (i.e., those followed by another jer) are strong. Havlík's law states that weak jers were lost, and strong jers lowered to *e* and *o*, depending both on the original backness of the jer in question and on the following consonant.

Isačenko (1970) provides an excellent and comprehensive discussion of the history of these phenomena in Russian. He first disposes of the claim that Ь was uniformly lowered to *e*, and Ъ to *o*, and that *e* was later backed to *o* in forms like[9] /p,os/ (from *pЬsЪ*). He formulates the following as the treatment of the strong jers:

(29)   /Ь/ ⟶ /e/ before soft consonants only
         /Ь/ ⟶ /o/ in all other cases
         /Ъ/ ⟶ /o/

We will refer to the process in (29) as simply 'jer → [−high]' without attempting to express it in formal terms. We will also follow Isačenko in representing both jers indifferently as *, ignoring (incorrectly) the difference between them in general.

From the etymologies of forms that do not show alternations, and from attested forms shortly after the period to which the 'jer-shift' is assigned (late twelfth to early thirteenth century), it appears that Havlík's law was a valid synchronic rule at that time, in essentially the form outlined above. The rule is stated by V. Kiparsky (1963; cited by Isačenko, 1970) as follows: "starting with the end of the word, or with the last full vowel, every odd Ъ, Ь is dropped, while every even Ъ, Ь is vocalized" (or lowered). The rule is illustrated with such forms as

(30) a. /l Ь s t Ь ts Ь / ⟶ /l (Ь) c t e ts / (R) 'flatterer'
             1   2   3

      b. /r Ъ p Ъ t Ъ / ⟶ /r p o t (Ъ) / (OR) 'murmer, grumble'
             1   2   3

      c. / s Ъ n Ь m Ъ / ⟶ /s n e m (Ъ) / 'meeting, gathering'
             1   2   3

---

[9] In accordance with Slavistic practice, we use a following comma to indicate the palatalized ('soft') consonants in transcriptions. In addition, the sign Ь indicates the front jer, and Ъ the back jer.

In these cases, odd-numbered jers (from the end of the word) are dropped, though sometimes preserved orthographically to represent the quality of a preceding consonant; and even numbered jers are lowered. This process could be formulated in either of two ways:

(31)   a. jer $\longrightarrow$ $\emptyset$ / ____ C_0 $\left\{ \begin{matrix} \# \\ \left[\begin{matrix} +\text{syll} \\ \left\{ \begin{matrix} -\text{high} \\ +\text{tense} \end{matrix} \right\} \end{matrix} \right] \end{matrix} \right\}$

    b. jer $\longrightarrow$ [$-$high]

(32)   a. jer $\longrightarrow$ [$-$high] / ____ C_0 $\begin{bmatrix} +\text{syll} \\ +\text{high} \\ -\text{tense} \end{bmatrix}$

    b. jer $\longrightarrow$ $\emptyset$

The difference between (32) and (31) rests on the choice of which process to treat as the 'elsewhere' case. If the lowering of jers is treated as the elsewhere case (i.e., as specifying the fate of residual jers after the operation of jer-loss), (31) is the formulation; if the loss of (nonlowered) jers is treated as the elsewhere case, (32) results. The principal difficulty in providing a solution to this example comes from the fact that there is apparently no evidence that points to a choice between (32) and (31). From historical sources, it appears that weak jers were lost in certain positions before other aspects of the jer-shift occured, which would favor (31) slightly, but this evidence is virtually impossible to interpret unambiguously. The derivations in (30), however, would suggest that (assuming no other factor, such as intonation, differentiated between strong and weak jers) (32) is correct, given our assumptions thus far about the application of rules in forms to which they can apply in several places. On the theory of linear rules, (32a) applying from right to left (as suggested by V. Kiparsky) followed by (32b) gives the correct result; while on the revised simultaneous theory, (32a) prevented from reapplying to its own output, followed by (32b), will also generate the required alternating pattern in a fashion analogous to other examples discussed in this chapter. There is no obvious way the original simultaneous theory can provide this result from either system of rules, nor is there any obvious way (31) can be applied correctly on any theory.

In Modern Russian, however, the facts are somewhat different. As first proposed by Lightner (1965a), later discussed by Worth (1967), and supported by Isačenko (1970), the 'Havlík's law' rule now applies quite differently. Worth's formulation was that the rule should now be treated as applying from left to right, rather than from right to left, as originally. Isačenko phrases this as follows: 'In stems not divided by a prefix / preposition boundary (=) and containing more than one vowel / zero alternation (i.e., more than one underlying jer: *sra*), only the last of these alternations is preserved; all other vowel / zero alternations are vocalized.' The import of this is as follows: any jer followed by another jer within the stem is lowered. Only the stem final jer alternates, being either dropped or lowered depending on the following desinence. This can be illustrated by forms such as the following:

(33)   a. from /v,etr/, by epenthesis in stem-final *TR* clusters:

/v,et,∗r/ from which /v,et,∗r+∗k+∗/ gives *v,et,erok* and /v,et,∗r+∗k+a/ gives *v,et,erká* from which further, /v,et,∗r,+∗č+∗k+∗/ gives *v,et,eróček* and /v,et,∗r,+∗č+∗k+a/ gives *v,et,eróčka*

b. from /st∗kl/, by epenthesis, /st∗k∗l/; from this /st,∗k∗l,+∗n+ɨj/ gives *st, ekól, nɨj*

This result could be obtained by applying rules (31) on the simultaneous theory; or by applying (32) from left to right, on the linear rules theory. It could also be obtained by applying rules (31) on the revised simultaneous theory. The change from the original alternating pattern of jer loss to the Modern Russian one of the preservation of all but the last jer would thus be viewed on the linear theory as a change in the direction of the jer-lowering rule; while on the revised simultaneous theory it would be viewed as the change from (32) to (31). Either change could be motivated by the fact that (as Isačenko notes) it results in greater uniformity of the forms within a single inflectional paradigm, since the alternation between vowel and zero is now confined to the last syllable of the stem. These facts, then, do not pose any particular problem for either of the theories under consideration. The reason for citing them is that the rule is often taken in works on Slavic to be (32), and in that case the Modern Russian rule would present a problem for the revised simultaneous theory. There do not appear to be any facts, however, which require (32) as the formulation, and (31) (which is the form assumed by Halle, 1971) is just as adequate. (31), as we saw, removes the problem for the revised simultaneous theory: the rule which must apply in several places on this analysis (31b, jer-lowering) is unconditioned, and hence the question of violations of (6) cannot arise.

Other facts show that this analysis is at least incomplete. The formulation given above covers only cases of stems not containing the boundary $=$; when forms with this boundary are considered, a different pattern emerges. If a jer precedes this boundary, and is followed by another jer after it, the preservation of the first jer is determined by the fate of the second. Thus, we have alternations such as (34):

(34)　　a.　/s*=ž*g+*/ gives *sžog;*　/s*=ž*g+la/ gives *sožgla*
　　　　b.　/ot*=p,*r+*/ gives *otp,er;*　/ot*=p,*r+ū/ gives
　　　　　　otopru
　　　　c.　/v* = r*t+*/ gives *v rot;*　/v* = r*t+ū/ gives *vo rtu*

The alternating patterns here are like those of the original Havlík's law cases. They could be provided for in several ways, none of which are satisfactory. The simplest, and least insightful way to provide for such cases is simply to introduce another rule which precedes (31) [or (32)], which drops a jer followed immediately by prefix / preposition boundary exactly when the next two syllables contain jers:

(35)　　　　　　　　　　JER $\longrightarrow$ ∅ / ____ $= C_0 JER C_0 JER$

This brute force method will work, but hardly explains anything. Another unpleasantly brutal solution would be to say that, on the linear theory, rule (32a) applies from left to right within a stem, but (simultaneously) from right to left across a $=$ boundary. Yet another alternative which surely must be rejected is to say, on the revised simultaneous theory, that rules (31) apply within the stem, but rules (32) apply across $=$.

　　Clearly, if there is a generalization to be captured here it is the following: if the following vowel is or becomes a full vowel, the prefix or preposition vowel is lost, as any jer is lost before a full vowel. If the jer of the stem is not turned into a full vowel, however, the jer in the prefix or preposition is lowered, as any jer is lowered before another jer. This fact cannot be obtained by any simple application of the rules and theories discussed above, and it is necessary either to lose it [by adopting rule (35) or something like it] or to modify our theories somewhat. The most attractive modification would seem to be the following: suppose we adopt a version of the theory of cyclic rules, according to which integral lexical items (i.e., stems plus derivational affixes and inflectional affixes but not clitic elements such as prepositions) undergo a subset of the rules of the phonology as lexical items, in the dictionary as it were. Then the full word, with inflectional and clitic elements attached, undergoes all of the rules of the phonology. This position can perhaps be supported by some other observations of Halle's (1973) about stress in Russian, though these would have to be formalized more completely before their import could be properly assessed. On this analysis, the rule of jer-lowering (32a) would apply both at the lexical item level and at the level of the full phonological word. In that way, the quality of the stem jer could be determined before that of the prefix or preposition, as seems to be indicated. This theory would thus capture the relevant generalization, but only at the cost of a major theoretical innovation which cannot be said to have important support elsewhere. Until such support is forthcoming, the unpleasantly ad hoc rule (35) would seem to be unavoidable. In any case, this problem is unconnected with the other problems discussed above, and whatever solution is adopted for it can be incorporated equally well into the grammar with either linear rules (32) or with rules (31) applying under the revised simultaneous convention.

We have seen, therefore, that none of the examples which have been discussed in the literature are, in fact, counterexamples to principle (6). In each case, an alternative analysis is available, for which some evidence can usually be given, such that principle (6) is satisfied. This absence of counterevidence furnishes definite evidence in favor of principle (6), for it makes it clearer that adjacent applications of a rule are possible exactly when they can be treated as independent, as principle (6) requires. No alternative analysis exists, however, for the stress-loss rule in Acoma in terms of either the simultaneous or the linear application theories. We should, accordingly, prefer the revised simultaneous application principle to any of these.

This theory produces cases such as that of Mandarin, etc., where the rule in fact applies everywhere it could simultaneously, and also cases such as French, where the rule applies only in alternate positions, depending on whether adjacent applications are independent [in terms of (6)] or not. By allowing the rule to apply to its own output, and then invoking the natural ordering principle of minimizing bleeding application, it can also accommodate cases like that of Acoma, where two adjacent applications are possible, but where three possible applications result in an alternating pattern. Other cases also exist, in which three possible overlapping applications give rise to alternating patterns, as in Acoma, but where two overlapping applications also give rise to such a pattern, unlike the Acoma case. It is to such an example that we now turn.

In the Australian language Gidabal,[10] there is a process of vowel

---

[10] The data below on Gidabal are from Geytenbeek and Geytenbeek (1971), as cited by Kenstowicz and Kisseberth (1972).

shortening which is formally just like that of the Slovak rhythmic law: it
applies to long vowels that follow other long vowels:

(36) $$[+\text{syll}] \longrightarrow [-\text{long}] \ / \ \begin{bmatrix} +\text{syll} \\ +\text{long} \end{bmatrix} C_0 \underline{\qquad}$$

The following alternations attest to the operation of this rule in the language:

(37) a. *badi+ya:* 'should hit';   *badi+ye* 'may hit'
   b. *yaga:+ya* 'should be fixing';   *yaga:+ye* 'may be fixing'
   c. *ga:da+ya:* 'should chase';   *ga:da+ye* 'may chase'
   d. *mani+ya:gan* 'to get wallaby';   *muru:n+dagan* 'to get firewood'

Clearly, we have to do here with roots such as /badi/ 'hit', /yaga:/ 'be
fixing', /ga:da/ 'chase', /mani/ 'wallaby', and /muru:n/ 'firewood'; and
suffixes such as /+ya:/, /+ye/, /+Ca:gan/. Long vowels in the affixes are
shortened when possible by rule (36). There are also cases in the language of affixes which cause the lengthening of a preceding vowel (along
with the lowering of /i/ to /e/). When the preceding vowel is already
long, it stays that way; but when it is preceded by another long vowel, it
is not lengthened:

(38) a. *badi+ye* 'may hit';   *bade:+nj* 'will hit';   *bade:+n*
      'hit (past)'
   b. *yaga:+ye* 'may be fixing';   *yaga:+nj* 'will be fixing';
      yaga:+n 'was fixing'
   c. *ga:da+ye* 'may chase';   *ga:da+nj* 'will chase';
      ga:da+n 'chased'

The difference between (38c) and the others is also predicted by rule
(36).
   For cases in which four consecutive long vowels arise, the last three
of these can potentially undergo the rule. Consider, for example, the underlying form /gunu:m+ya:+da:ŋ+be:/, consisting of the root /gunu:m/
'(on the) stump', with the suffixes -ya: (seen also, with assimilation of the
/y/ to preceding nasal consonants, in *bala+ya:* 'is under' *ba:m+ba* 'is
halfway'), -da:ŋ [also found in *njule+da:ŋ* 'he (emph.)', *yu:+daŋ* 'much
later'], and -*be:* (also seen in *gadi+be:* 'right here', *buřu:ř+be* 'is certainly
two'). This form gives the surface *gunu:m+ba+da:ŋ+be* 'is certainly
right on the stump', with the shortening of the second and fourth, but not

the third, of the long vowels in the underlying form. This is just what we would expect: rule (36) gives an analysis of this form as (39) after step (7a) of the algorithm for applying a rule applies:

(39)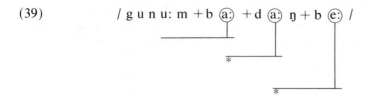

In (39), there are two violations of (6), which are eliminated by (7c) by disregarding the second of the three possible applications. This is the minimal way to eliminate both violations, as was the case in previous examples. The rule then applies to the remaining circled vowels (the third and fifth of the entire form), giving the correct result *gunu:m+ba+da:ŋ+be*. This alternating pattern is consistent with either (7) or with the theory of linear rules (which characterizes (36) as left to right in Gidabal, while the same rule operates right to left in Slovak), but not with the original simultaneous application theory.

Consider what happens when three (and not four) consecutive long vowels occur. This arises when we consider a formation just like that of (39), with a root whose last vowel is basically short: /djalum+ba:+da:ŋ+be:/, which gives rise to *djalum+ba:+daŋ+be:* 'is certainly right on the fish'. Note that here only the middle one of the three vowels that are underlyingly long is shortened. Similarly, the present tense suffix *-la* requires a preceding vowel to be long (as did *-nj* and *-n* considered above), and can be added to bases which have already been suffixed with *-le* 'repetitive'. When these two are added to a stem with final short vowel, the repetitive affix is long and the present affix is short; but if the last vowel of the stem is long, the distribution of length in the affixes is reversed:

(40) a. *nama+le:+la* 'is holding';   *badi+le:+la* 'is hitting'
      b. *yaga:+le+la:* 'is fixing';   *ginjalga:+le+la:* 'is coughing'

These facts obviously suggest that *-la* itself has an underlying long vowel, as well as a lengthening effect on the preceding vowel; and that the length in /-la:/ only shows up in cases where the induced length in the preceding vowel is canceled. The underlying form of 'is fixing', then, is /yaga:+le:+la:/ (after operation of the morphological lengthening rule). The vowel shortening rule then has two overlapping possibilities, but only the first of these is actually applied, just as was the case in *djalum+ba:+daŋ+be:*.

This result is inconsistent with the original simultaneous theory, just as in the case with more than two overlapping applications; it is consistent with the linear theory (since the same left-to-right application of (36) will give the right results in all cases). In terms of the revised simultaneous application convention, a form like /djalum+ba:+da:ŋ+be:/ is analyzed as (41):

(41)   / dj a l u m + b a: + d ⓐː ŋ + b ⓔː /

There is one violation of (6) in this form at the point (7c) applies, which can be eliminated by disregarding either of the two possible applications. If we assume that the rule applies to its own output, the first will be disregarded, and the rule will apply only to the fifth vowel; it will then reapply, shortening the fourth vowel and yielding the incorrect form *djalum+ba:+daŋ+be*. Let us suppose that the rule is not permitted to apply to its own output: in that case, the principle of maximizing the possibility of reapplication (minimizing bleeding) is irrelevant, and we are left with a choice of ways for eliminating the violation of (6) in (41). In that event, however, the principle of minimizing opacity allows us to make a decision: if we disregard the first of the two possible applications, we will derive *djalum+ba:+da:ŋ+be*, which is opaque in that it contains an instance of a long vowel following another long vowel, which should be eliminated by (36). However, if we disregard the second possible application instead, we derive *djalum+ba:+daŋ+be:*, which is not opaque because the long vowels are not adjacent. The minimizing of opacity, then, requires us to disregard the second possibility, and this results in the correct form. This example too, then, is consistent with the revised simultaneous application convention. Whereas the linear theory characterizes the difference between the vowel shortening rules in Slovak and in Gidabal in terms of the ad hoc parameter of right-to-left versus left-to-right application, the revised simultaneous theory characterizes this as the difference between rules that can and rules that cannot reapply to their own output, a distinction which must be made in any event.

Of the theories that have been considered in this chapter, the simultaneous theory adopted by Chomsky and Halle (1968) is clearly the least adequate, since it cannot deal with several of the cases above. The linear theory is a distinct improvement, since it can deal with all of them except the accent loss in Acoma. The revision of the simultaneous application theory [incorporating (6) and (7)] must, however, be considered the most nearly adequate on the basis of evidence presently available, since it can also accommodate the Acoma example, which provides rather striking confirmation of its claims. It has the important merit of making use of the same principles that govern the interaction of pairs of rules to control the interrelation of applications of the same rule. The desirability of such a solution has been pointed out by Kenstowicz and Kisserberth (1972) (who do not really claim, however, to provide a satisfactory one). The issue cannot be considered completely closed, (if any phonological issue ever can), due to the paucity of critical examples. Although interesting, the Acoma example is isolated; and the absence of cases in which four, five, and more applications of a rule can impinge on one another (and where the rule can reapply to its own output) leaves room for doubt. At present, however, it is safe to say that there is no positive evidence for the theory of linear rules, and a certain amount of evidence against it, favoring a revision of the simultaneous application principle along the lines of (6).

CHAPTER 14

Syllables,
Segments, and More

We have assumed thus far that representations of phonological and phonetic structure have the character proposed in Chapter 1: each is regarded as a string of segments, perhaps divided into morphological elements by nonsegmental boundaries, where each segment is specified by values for each of the descriptive phonetic parameters provided by a theory of universal phonetics. The important thing to note about this type of representation is that it makes the implicit claim that no further structure can be relevant to the statement of phonological generalizations, that is, that each segment is structurally just like every other segment in the string, and (at least within the scope of 'phonetically relevant' boundaries, such as #) there are no necessary units with their own structure which are either larger or smaller in size than the segment. A fair amount of evidence has accumulated that this assumption is untenable, and that our notion of a representation is in need of revision.

The first phonologically relevant unit other than the segment for which an argument can be given is the syllable. Syllables have of course played a tremendously important role in traditional phonetics, though a satisfactory definition is still lacking. Articulatorily, it is often tantalizingly close to the truth to associate the syllable with individual chest pulses, or units of activity of the musculature controlling the flow of air from the lungs. Unfortunately for this view, Ladefoged (1967) has shown that there are cases where (at least on the basis of neural activity) two chest pulses may be associated with a single syllable, and others in which a single chest pulse may span two syllables. There is clearly a sense in which syllables are articulatory units, however, as shown by a host of observations over a long period. Recent psycholinguistic evidence confirms this, in suggesting the importance of the syllable as a unit in perception and production [see, for example, Kozhevnikov and Chistovich (1965), and Fromkin (1971)].

The consistent attempt in generative phonological studies to ignore the syllable as a structural unit has not been based generally on a refusal to recognize the existence and potential articulatory and psychological integrity of such elements. A case against the inclusion of syllables in phonological representations has never been made in any detail in print, but it has generally been assumed that the sort of facts associated with syllable structure can in fact be attributed to the strictly segmental representation, and do not require additional elements. Instead of saying 'vowels lengthen in open syllables', for instance, it has generally been assumed that it is possible to say 'vowels lengthen when not followed by a cluster (or word-final consonant)'. In this latter formulation, the syllable boundary is unnecessary, and a purely segmental statement is possible.

If it were generally true that phenomena associated with the syllable as a structural unit could be recoded satisfactorily without reference to elements other than segments and morphological/syntactic boundaries, this would be an interesting result. Just as many (although not all) of the facts traditionally ascribed to phonotactics turn out on further examination to be the mechanical consequences of independently motivated phonological rules, so it would be of some importance if facts of syllable structure were to turn out to be mechanical consequences of other aspects of the phonological representation. This does not, however, appear to be the case, and some revision of our attitude toward the syllable seems called for.

In Chapter 1, we suggested that an adequate theory of universal phonetics would have to include any feature in terms of which two languages could systematically differ. Thus, even though the parameter of RELEASED / UNRELEASED never seems to function distinctively within a single language, languages differ considerably in the principles by which release is determined, and so this parameter must be included in phonetic representations. On these grounds, it is clear that phonetic representations must also specify a division into syllables, for the same segmental elements may be syllabified differently in different languages. This is independent of the fact that the presence of a syntactic or morphological boundary may result in the fact that a syllable boundary coincides with it, rather than falling in the place that would be expected on purely phonetic grounds. Even in cases where no such boundaries are involved, different languages can show different principles of syllabification. For example, most languages divide a string of the shape VCV with the syllable boundary preceding the consonant (assuming there is no syntactic boundary following it). A group of Australian dialects described by Sommer (1970), however, differ significantly from this. The canonical syllable shape in these dialects is not CV, but VC_0 and in VCV strings, the syllable boundary falls after, rather than before, the consonant: cf. such forms as *iy.ar.am.an* 'horse', etc. Even where more than one consonant appears in intervocalic position, the syllable boundary comes before the second vowel, rather than somewhere in between: cf. *elw.an udn.an.am* 'from sleeping', *egŋ oygŋg.orḡ.an* 'bitter onion', etc.[1] It is clear that the dialects in question (identified by Sommer as Oykangand, Olgol, Okunjan, and Kawarrangg) have a principle of syllabification which differs significantly from the usual one, and hence it must be possible to represent such facts somehow.

Just as languages can differ in the placement of syllable boundaries where consonants are concerned, so vowels can also be treated differently. A problem which recurs in many languages is that of the representation of diphthongs, or sequences of vowels belonging to the same syllable. In some languages, sequences of vowels are divided into different syllables, whereas others allow more than one vowel element to appear in a single syllable. In order to account for the first class of languages mechanically, it is necessary to assume a principle of syllabification that inserts syllable boundaries between adjacent syllabic segments, but this makes it difficult to avoid inserting such an element between the parts of a diphthong. Insofar as this problem has been recognized, it is generally treated by marking the second element of the diphthong [−syllabic], but this in turn makes it difficult to distinguish the diphthong [ai] from the VC sequence [aj]. Since there are articulatory differences (in particular a difference of height) between [i] as the second element of a diphthong and [j], this is unfortunate. The matter is made even worse by the existence of languages with triphthongs. In Pame (see Gibson, 1956)

---

[1] Dixon (1970) has pointed out, no doubt correctly, that the clusters of obstruent and nasal in forms such as these are probably to be treated as single segments: prenasalized (or postnasalized) stops. His further claim that this syllabification is not correct because of the fact that consonants have fortis variants before, rather than after, a stressed vowel is not as cogent, however. The existence of a phonetic rule which crosses syllable boundaries hardly shows that these are not present, and Sommers' report on syllabification is presumably based on observed syllabification, not simply on syllabification as inferred from phonological processes. As such, it could only be disproved by demonstrating that speakers in fact place syllable divisions elsewhere than as claimed.

three vowel elements can appear without a syllabic division: thus ŋgwâoi 'her (two) daughters-in-law' is monosyllabic. Any principles of syllable division which are adequate for languages (like many Malayo-Polynesian ones) where long sequences of vowels can arise which are always divided into several syllables, will fail in this case. We can only conclude that syllable boundaries are independently variable, even though the principles of syllabification in any given language are quite fixed, and indeed are much the same in most languages.

The demonstration that syllable boundaries should be specified in the final phonetic representation still leaves open the possibility that this is the only level of representation at which they appear. This possibility cannot be seriously maintained, however, in light of evidence for the structural importance of the syllable at other levels. Haugen (1956), for example, gives an argument that shows the necessity of including syllables as units in underlying representations. He shows that in Kutenai, the constraints on medial clusters are by no means arbitrary: a possible medial cluster is essentially a possible (syllable-) final cluster followed by a possible (syllable-) initial cluster. Obviously this argument could be extended to numerous other languages, and suggests that constraints on medial clusters will often fall out automatically in terms of independently needed constraints on other positions, if syllables are available, and that it is in that case only necessary to state the ranges of possible syllable initial and syllable final elements. More important than mere economy, however, is the fact that the use of syllables as structural elements allows us to capture a generalization about medial clusters in underlying forms that would otherwise be missed.

In addition to underlying and superficial representations, it can also be shown that syllables must be delimited in intermediate representations. This follows from the fact that syllable boundaries play a part in the operation of phonological rules. Recall, for example, the rule of glide insertion in Faroese, discussed above in Chapters 8 and 11: according to that rule, a glide is inserted between two adjacent nonconsonants, if one of them is [+high]. The backness of the inserted glide is then determined by that of the high segment in question. A problem with this rule is the following: it is reasonable to believe that the diphthongs represented orthographically as *í* / *ý* and *ú* are in fact /ui̯/ and /iu̯/ through much of the derivation. It is necessary, however, to prevent a glide from being inserted in such sequences. This cannot be done by a prohibition in the *SD* of glide insertion against both vowels being high, as shown by words like *blíður* [blujjʊr]. In the formulation of the rule above, this difficulty was largely circumvented by requiring a morpheme boundary to be present at the point between the two vowels where the glide is to be inserted. This expedient will not work in general, however, since vowel sequences which must be broken up sometimes arise entirely within a morpheme. We do not refer here to vowel sequences that occur in every instance of a given form, and which could therefore be treated by requiring a glide to be present in underlying forms wherever two vowels would otherwise come together. There are also intramorphemic vowel sequences, which arise by the operation of rules, and which could therefore only be broken up by a phonological rule. In the forms *veður* / *veðri* 'weather (nsg / dsg)' (phonetically [ve:vʊr] / [vɛgrɪ]), the stem is /vegur/, as shown by the fact that the dative singular *veðri* preserves its *g* and its *r* (before which the underlying quality of the medial element appears). In the dative, the second vowel is syncopated, and nothing else of interest happens; but in the nominative, the medial voiced stop is deleted (as discussed in Chapter 11), which gives rise to a vowel sequence · · · *eu* · · · . This sequence is broken up by the regular insertion of a *w* glide, which then becomes *v* in the position after a segment which is not a high vowel. Note that the vowel sequence · · · *eu* · · · in which insertion must take place is entirely morpheme-internal. If we allow insertion in all morpheme internal vowel sequences, however, the diphthongs of the language will be destroyed. The difference between vowel sequences which should be broken up, and those which should not, is not at all difficult to state, however: it is precisely heterosyllabic vowel sequences in which a glide should be inserted. Glide insertion can be formulated satisfactorily as in (1) if syllable boundaries are available, but not otherwise:

$$(1) \qquad \emptyset \longrightarrow \begin{bmatrix} -\text{syll} \\ +\text{son} \\ -\text{cons} \\ +\text{high} \\ \alpha\text{back} \end{bmatrix} \% \begin{bmatrix} -\text{cons} \\ +\text{high} \\ \alpha\text{back} \end{bmatrix} . \underline{\quad\quad} [-\text{cons}]$$

Hooper (1972) has presented other cases of rules which apparently must refer to syllable boundaries in order to operate correctly, although her analyses have been questioned by J. Harris (personal communication).

We conclude from the above that syllable boundaries are an important aspect of the structure of phonological representation at all levels. But does this mean simply that, in addition to the segments and boundary elements that mark morphological divisions, a new class of boundary element appears in the string to mark syllable division? That is, is the sort of quasi-segmental representation usually given to morphological boundaries appropriate as a device for marking syllables? A negative answer to this question would be suggested if there were phonetic (or phonological) features which took as their domain not the segment, but the syllable. If the syllable functions as a unit for the assignment of some property, analogously to the way segments are generally taken as the unit for assignment of features, this would suggest that syllabification has a status more like that of the division of the string into segments than that of division into morphemes.

It is generally agreed (see Lehiste, 1970) that the feature of stress takes the syllable rather than the segment as its domain: that is, that phonetic stress cannot appear on units smaller than the syllable. It is also the case that stress rules often have the property of operating in terms of an environment stated in syllables: an antepenultimate stress rule can be formulated as operating in the environment / ____ $C_0VC_0VC_0$, but clearly the vowels and consonants have nothing to do with the rule, in themselves. The rule skips over two syllables, not over a collection of vowels and consonants satisfying the description above. Accordingly, we might suggest that stress rules analyze strings not in terms of segments, but simply in terms of syllables, and that all of the material between segmental syllable boundaries is treated as a unit S by such rules. This is immediately shown to be too restrictive, however: stress rules must be able to refer not only to the syllables of words, but also to their segmental composition. Stress rules may skip over only syllables with a short vowel, for instance, or may stress only syllables containing a vowel which is followed by two consonants, or may stress the last nasal vowel of a word,[2] etc. From this we can see that the segment is not excluded from the structural descriptions of stress rules, and it is better to consider the division of the string into syllables as coordinate with the division of the same string into segments. The analogy made earlier between phonetic representation and a musical score becomes closer here: if segments are taken to correspond to the notes of a score, syllables correspond to measures. We suggest that the unit S representing a syllable (or all of the segmental material contained in a given syllable) might appropriately be available for the statement of phonological rules, in order to make clear those generalizations that appear to depend on syllabic structure. In these terms, the familiar stress rule of Latin would appear as (2):

(2) $$S \longrightarrow [+\text{stress}] / \_\_\_ ((C_0\breve{V}.)S)\#$$

[2] This somewhat unusual rule is attested in some South American languages.

We know of no evidence showing the necessity of this mild formal innovation, but it seems appropriate.

We can consider then that the feature [+stress] can be assigned to the unit *S*, and any segmental element of the syllable can be considered to 'partake of' this stress. It would be nice if we could restrict rules introducing this feature so as to require them to assign it to an entire syllable at a time, but it is not clear that this is possible. An example of stress assignment in a mora-counting language (the St. Lawrence dialect of Eskimo) where it appears that a single mora can bear the stress, at least abstractly, is discussed below.

Besides stress, however, are there any other features which it is appropriate to associate with syllables, rather than with segments? Another obvious candidate is pitch, which is quite often described as 'suprasegmental' like stress. Although it is obvious that pitch, unlike stress, can be carried distinctively by a single segment within a syllable (see Lehiste, 1970), it might still be the case that a correct description of pitch would be in terms of pitch patterns which are realized over an entire syllable, so that a single pitch level realized on a single segment would simply be a sort of limiting case.

In a discussion of the phonological features which should be added to the universal feature inventory to account for pitch phenomena, Wang (1967) claims explicitly that the syllable is the domain of such features. In addition to features for the description of five distinct tone levels, Wang also posits features for the description of contour tones. In this system, then, a tone such as [∖] (high–falling) is treated as a unit, with the features [+high] and [+falling]. In these terms, any of the complex tonal patterns that have been observed in natural languages within the scope of a single syllable can be described as a unit. The fact that these contours may then be realized either on a single segment (in some languages) or on a sequence of elements within the syllable (in others) suggests that tones are associated with syllables, rather than with segments individually.

Wang's proposal thus treats contour tones as units; but Woo (1969) has suggested that this is incorrect. Some contour tones, of course, are simply the phonetic realizations of basically level tones, specified as gliding by low level rules of no particular interest. Whenever contour tones are contrastive, however, Woo suggested that there must be at least as many tone-bearing elements available to carry them as there are distinct levels in the contour. She presents several examples which suggest that, in general, the more complex a (contrastive) tone pattern is, the more segmental material is involved in its realization. For example, she discovered that Mandarin Chinese syllables with tone 3 in isolation ([∨], which would require three levels to specify) are on the average about 50% longer than syllables bearing other tones (which would only require two levels to specify). This in turn suggests the strong hypothesis that contour tones as units do not exist: that wherever a contour tone is found, it should be treated as the realization of a sequence of level tones. The tone [\] (high–falling), then, would be treated not as a unit with the features [+high] and [+falling], but rather as a sequence of units: [+high] followed by [+low] (or perhaps [+mid]). Besides reducing the set of tone features, this proposal makes a very strong claim about the situations in which contour tones can be present, because it treats tone patterns not as syllabic entities, but as segmental.

Unfortunately, the strong claims of Woo's proposal do not seem to be borne out when we examine tone systems in African languages. Recent papers by McCawley (1970b) and Leben (1971) have presented examples in which it is clear that a contrastive contour tone is carried by a syllable containing only one vowel mora. This would appear to support Wang's contention: tone patterns cannot be reduced to segmental pitch levels. Where McCawley and Leben provide dramatic confirmation of Woo's proposals, however, is in the decomposition of contour tones. Leben, for example, demonstrates the existence of a tone-copying rule in Mende, which copies the last tone of the first member of certain compounds onto the first syllable of the second member of the compound. The interesting feature of this rule is that a falling tone is copied as low, and a rising tone as high. This fact follows naturally if a falling tone is represented as high followed by low—the last tone element, which is the copied one, will then be (correctly) low. In Wang's system, however, the tone in question would be [+high], [+falling]—which has no obvious natural relation to a level low. The same is true for the rising tone, which gives the right results if specified as a sequence low–high.

Leben and McCawley also demonstrate that important generalizations can be obtained in several languages by positing the existence of rules which delete or add individual level-tone elements. Such rules affect contours in ways that are only specifiable in terms of sequences of levels, and therefore provide further support for the decomposition of contours. The most dramatic proof of the necessity of decomposing contour-tone patterns into sequences of levels, however, comes from systems such as that described by McCawley for Tiv, where a given tone pattern is associated with a grammatical category. The realization of such pattern then depends on the number of syllables in the form: if a given pattern contains n tone elements, and the form in question contains at least n syllables, the pattern is realized as a sequence of level toned syllables. When the form contains fewer than n syllables, however, the same pattern is realized by contour tones corresponding to the same sequence. Thus, a pattern low–high–low will be realized as that sequence in a trisyllabic word, but as rising–low on a bisyllabic word. Clearly, what is going on is that the same elements are distributed equally across syllables where possible, but where there are not enough syllables available, some patterns have to be squeezed together on a single syllable.

An example of such a system can be given from the Ekoid Bantu language Etung, described by Edmondson and Bendor-Samuel (1966). They give several patterns of tones, and show that the contour patterns can all be analyzed as variants of sequences when these are realized on fewer syllables than there are elements in the pattern. The confirmation of this analysis comes from the fact that certain grammatical categories are associated with constant tone patterns. In the remote past tense, for example, all verbs have either all high or all low tones on the sequence of pre-root prefix elements, and the pattern high–low(–low) over the root. When the root is at least bisyllabic, we get a form such as *à gbómè* 'he met'; in the same tense, with a monosyllabic root, we get a pattern such as *m̀ mân* 'I finished', where $\acute{V}$ marks high tone, $\grave{V}$ marks low, and $\hat{V}$ marks falling tone. We see that the falling tone corresponds to the sequence of a high tone and a low tone when these must both be realized on the same syllable.

A similar situation can be illustrated from outside Africa[3] by the development of tones in some Punjabi dialects described by Bailey (1920).[4] Tones in Punjabi arose in stressed syllables when original voiced aspirates were devoiced and deaspirated. If the stressed syllable originally began with a voiced aspirate, the result was a rising tone; if it originally ended with a voiced aspirate, the result was a falling tone; and if it originally both began and ended with a voiced aspirate, the result was a rising–falling tone. Otherwise, stressed syllables acquired high tone. These facts can clearly be described most easily in terms of sequences of level tone elements: assume that a stressed syllable had a basic high tone, and that the loss of voiced aspiration on either side left a low tone element as a 'residue'. Then the following developments would have occurred:

$$\begin{array}{ccc} & \text{h} & \text{l–h} \\ (3) \qquad \text{a.} \quad {}^*\text{dhVt} & \longrightarrow & \text{t V t} \end{array}$$

---

[3] Another such example is of course provided by Mandarin Chinese, as discussed in Chapter 13.

[4] This situation is largely obscured by later developments and simplifications in most modern Punjabi dialects.

$$
\begin{array}{ccc}
& \text{h} & \text{h--l} \\
\text{b.} & \text{*tVdh} & \longrightarrow \text{t V t}
\end{array}
$$

$$
\begin{array}{ccc}
& \text{h} & \text{l--h--l} \\
\text{c.} & \text{*dhVdh} & \longrightarrow \text{t V t}
\end{array}
$$

$$
\begin{array}{ccc}
& \text{h} & \text{h} \\
\text{d.} & \text{*t V t} & \longrightarrow \text{t V t}
\end{array}
$$

The interesting fact about this development was the point that it only operated in just this way in *final* stressed syllables. If the stressed syllable was followed by another (unstressed) syllable, the rising contour was realized as low tone on the stressed syllable followed by high tone on the unstressed syllable; the falling contour as high tone on the stressed syllable and low tone on the following unstressed syllable; the rising–falling tone as a rising tone on the stressed vowel, and a low tone on the following vowel. Clearly what is taking place here is that where more than one tone element is to be realized on a syllable, the last element of the sequence is moved off to the following syllable if there is one. Such a description is taken for granted in many works on African and Asian languages by adherents of the London school of prosodic analysis, but within generative phonology it is an important novelty.

These systems provide important confirmation for Woo's claim that contour tones are to be analyzed as sequences of level tones, for they are completely incoherent if contours are analyzed as indivisible units. On the other hand, they also disconfirm the claim that tone units are associated one for one with segments, for they involve the realization of several tone elements on the same segment. Thus, even though tone contours are sequences of elements, the scope of a tone pattern may be a syllable, as claimed by Wang. It is important to note that the syllable is indeed the relevant unit here, and not the word. This is suggested by examples such as McCawley's treatment of Tiv. In this case, if a tone pattern associated with some tense category contains, say, two elements, these are both realized on the same syllable (as a contour tone) if the verb is monosyllabic, and separately on two syllables if bisyllabic. If the word were the unit of tone assignment, we would then expect a pattern such as 'low–high' to be realized on a four-syllable word as low–low–high–high, with the break exactly in the middle of the word. A trisyllabic word might be expected to appear with the pattern low–rising–high. The fact that such tone systems are not attested confirms the claim that the syllable is the unit of tone assignment. 'Tone *Ablaut*' processes assign tone elements on a one (or more)-per-syllable basis. The utility of the syllable in such examples is confirmed, rather than denied, by the existence of such whole-word patterns.

We assume, therefore, that a tone pattern specified as a sequence of levels is associated with a syllable, and is then realized on the syllabic elements of the syllable (perhaps including sonorant consonants, as in Lithuanian where a sonorant consonant is functionally the same as the second element of a diphthong). In some cases, this may involve a subdivision of the segment, resulting in a contour tone. Some languages allow this situation to arise; others impose a constraint that the number of segments that can bear tone be the same (or at least as great) as the number of tone elements. Still others impose this constraint on underlying forms, but not on surface forms: in this case, contour tones can arise only by the deletion of elements that would otherwise bear tone, with a resultant shift of the associated tone element onto another segment. The degree to which tone elements can be lined up with segmental elements is an important aspect of the typology of tone languages.

If the primitives of tone specification are level pitches, we can now ask what the inventory of features associated with them is. It has usually been assumed that tone features are largely independent of the features that specify the 'segmental' content of phonetic elements, though a certain amount of interaction has often been noted. Phonetic investigation has revealed (see Lehiste, 1970) a relationship between certain articulatory configurations in the supraglottal region and certain pitch phenomena (e.g., the fact that different vowels have different 'intrinsic pitches'), and mechanical explanations can be suggested for some of these. The most interesting relations, however, are between segmental features such as voicing, aspiration, etc. and pitch. It is generally agreed that it is the action of the larynx that is responsible for both classes of phenomena, though details of the range of gestures and articulatory controls available for this organ are among the most elusive targets in phonetics. It is therefore difficult to give empirical evidence of a direct sort for the nature of the relation between voicing, etc., on the one hand, and pitch variations on the other. That some such relation exists is clear: instrumental studies of a number of languages show a characteristic of voiceless consonants to be an increase in pitch in the adjacent portion of a vowel, and for voiced consonants, a lowering of pitch. This relation has also provided the basis for numerous far-reaching changes in the tonal systems of Asian languages (for a survey of several such cases, see Haudricourt, 1961). Typically, voicing distinctions in syllable-initial or syllable-final consonants are lost, with concomitant alterations in the tone patterns of adjacent vowels: vowels after an originally voiceless obstruent begin on a higher pitch than vowels after an originally voiced obstruent.

Since the same organ (the larynx) is involved in both cases, it would obviously be desirable to employ the same set of features for both, if this is not inconsistent with the facts. This is analogous to the move made by Jakobson, Fant, and Halle (1956) (after Jakobson) in suggesting a feature system in which tongue position in vowels and in consonants was controlled by the same features. To that end, Halle and Stevens (1971) have recently suggested a system of four laryngeal features (describing two doubly privative dimensions of possible laryngeal activity): [±stiff vocal cords] versus [±slack vocal cords]; [±spread glottis] versus [±constricted glottis]. A brief description of the phenomena covered by these features (after Halle and Stevens) can be found in the Appendix.

To identify the features of voicing, etc. with pitch features makes a very strong claim, both about the structure of linguistic processes and about the structure of the larynx. This claim has in fact already been challenged by Fromkin (1972), whose principal argument is the following: it is very natural for languages to contain rules voicing obstruents intervocalically. This is usually considered an assimilation of voicing. If voicing corresponds to absence of tension in the vocal cords, however, it is hard to see how this could be the case in a language with distinctive high tones, which are also controlled by tension in the vocal cords. For such a language, the natural looking rule (4a) would have to be replaced with (4b), where the assimilatory nature of the process is obscured:

(4)   a.   [+obst] $\longrightarrow$ [+voice] / [+voice] ____ [+voice]

       b.   [+obst] $\longrightarrow$ [−stiff] / [+syll] ____ [+syll]

It is certainly true that (4b) is less appropriate than (4a). It can be questioned, however, whether Fromkin's argument is cogent. It is noteworthy first of all that Fromkin does not actually provide an example of a language in which voicing is a matter of vocal cord stiffness, distinctive high tones are distributed essentially freely, and a voicing assimilation process applies to all intervocalic obstruents. She relies, instead, on our linguists' intuition that such processes are common. This may, however, be an example of a case in which linguists construct their intuitions on the basis of considerations other than exposure to the facts of numerous languages, and it is important to look at actual cases of attested voicing assimilation rules for intervocalic obstruents.

In claiming that a relation can exist between pitch phenomena and voicing phenomena, Halle and Stevens are clearly on reasonably firm ground. Perhaps the most famous intervocalic voicing rule in any language is Verner's law, which operated in (at least most dialect areas of) early Germanic. According to this rule, intervocalic spirants (including *f*, þ, and [x], from PIE $*p$, $*t$, and $*k$, as well as original s) were voiced if they did not follow the syllable bearing the IE accent. In Fromkin's terms, this might look like (5):

(5) $\quad$ [+cont] $\longrightarrow$ [+voice] / $\begin{bmatrix} +\text{voice} \\ -\text{accent} \end{bmatrix}$ ____ [+voice]

It is generally agreed, however, that the IE accent was not one of stress (as in later Germanic) but rather one of pitch. Accordingly, the environment expressed in Verner's law was 'between vowels except after high pitch'. High pitch thus served to inhibit voicing intervocalically, just as Halle and Stevens would predict. The rule for Verner's law might have looked rather like (6), making reasonable assumptions about the nature of early Germanic segments:

(6) $\quad$ [+cont] $\longrightarrow$ $\begin{bmatrix} -\text{spread} \\ -\text{stiff} \end{bmatrix}$ / $\begin{bmatrix} -\text{spread} \\ -\text{stiff} \end{bmatrix}$ ____ [−spread]

This appears to be a noticeable improvement on (5), in supplying more of a basis for explaining the restriction of Verner's law to spirants that did not follow the IE accent.

This example brings up another point: while 'stiff' is said to be the primary determinant of high pitch, and 'slack' the primary determinant of low pitch, vowels do not generally involve configurations other than [−spread, −constricted] for the other features. These other features serve to describe glottalized (or laryngealized) vowels, voiceless (or breathy-voiced) vowels, etc. Consonants, on the other hand, generally involve all four features crucially in an interaction. Absence of voicing can be achieved by a variety of laryngeal configurations, as can presence of voicing, and it is not necessary in Halle and Stevens' terms that 'stiff' versus 'slack' be the primary feature of the voicing dimension in any given language. 'Spread' versus 'nonspread' will do as well, given appropriate values for other features, and this possibility must be considered. If the voiceless obstruents in a language are those with the feature [+spread], then the voicing assimilation rule in intervocalic position might look like (7), in which vowel pitch plays no role:

(7) $\quad$ [+obst] $\longrightarrow$ [−spread] / [−spread] ____ [−spread]

Such a formulation would explain another fact: many languages have intervocalic voicing processes which are restricted to spirants. Studies of the glottis show that voiceless spirants are generally articulated with spread glottis, for the obvious reason that this increases airflow, and hence the possibility of audible turbulence at the spirant's point of constriction. Many early Germanic dialects (e.g., Old English) had a rule (of 'allophonic distribution'), independent of Verner's law, by which spirants (and not stops) were voiced intervocalically. We can assume that the voiceless stops were heavily aspirated (on the evidence of most of Germanic), and hence [+spread, +stiff]. Spirants, on the other hand, while [+spread], were not, we assume, [+stiff]: compare the fact that it is precisely after a spirant that voiceless stops are less aspirated. Vowels were presumably [−spread, −constricted, −stiff, −slack]. The spirant voicing rule might have looked like this, then:

$$(8) \qquad [-\text{stiff}] \longrightarrow [-\text{spread}] \ / \ \begin{bmatrix} -\text{stiff} \\ -\text{spread} \end{bmatrix} \underline{\hspace{1cm}} \begin{bmatrix} -\text{stiff} \\ -\text{spread} \end{bmatrix}$$

The assimilatory nature of the process, as well as the motivation for its restriction to continuants, comes out better in this formulation than in one in which the feature [+continuant] appears directly.

Other sorts of processes could also be adduced to show that the feature system provided by Halle and Stevens for the larynx is adequate (though there are without doubt areas in which it is in need of refinement), and in many cases it is superior to a system separating pitch phenomena from those of voicing, etc. We do not, therefore, share Fromkin's reservations about this system. But in any event, the features of voicing, aspiration, etc. are certainly most closely allied to those of pitch; and if we are to find facts similar to those discussed above for tone systems, arguing for the relevance of domains of specification of features other than the segment, it is clearly in this area that we should look first.

While we know of no examples in which units larger than the segment serve as the domain of specification of aspiration, voicing, etc. (unless one chooses to see voicing assimilation in clusters in these terms, as we suspect is correct), there is one phenomenon in this area which suggests the relevance of domains smaller than the segment. Although some phonetic descriptive frameworks have tended to ignore them, several of the world's languages contain preaspirated stops (of the type [ʰp], [ʰt], [ʰk], etc.), in addition to the usual postaspirated ones. These are often the surface realizations of long or geminate consonants, and so do not appear distinctively in underlying representations in any language we know of, but they are a real and distinctive phenomenon in phonetic representations, and some descriptive device must be available to account for them.

Preaspirated stops in fact have quite an interesting realization. For many speakers of Icelandic and those Faroese dialects where these segments appear, preaspiration depends on the character of the preceding vowel. If this is long (or diphthongal), preaspiration consists in the devoicing of the second element of the vowel. Icelandic *háttur* 'mode, manner', for example, is for most speakers phonetically [hau̯tur], with the second element of the usual diphthong [au̯] devoiced. When the preceding vowel is short, however, we do not get either a short voiced vowel or a short voiceless vowel or a short vowel followed by a period of 'aspiration': rather, we get a very short voiceless vowel preceded by a very short voiced vowel. Thus *hattur* 'hat' is phonetically [hăḁ̆tür]. It is clear what the generalization is here: a preaspirated consonant has the effect of devoicing exactly one-half of the preceding syllabic element. If there are two moras in that element, one is devoiced; if there is only one, half of it is devoiced.[5] This is exactly analogous to the cases of contour tones discussed above: when two tone elements are to be realized on a form, and two syllabic moras are available, one tone element is realized on each mora. When only one mora is available, however, each tone element is realized on half of it.

From these facts, it is apparent that glottal features may be related to segmental (or oral–articulatory) features in a different way from the way these segmental features are related to one another. We presume (though this may eventually require revision) that the segment is an integral unit, as far as these oral articulatory features are concerned, and that each such feature is specified over a domain which is coextensive with the specification of all of the other features. Thus, in, e.g., a [t], the feature [+coronal] refers to the same stretch of the speech event as the coordinate features [−high], [−back], [+anterior], [−distributed], etc. The features describing the configuration of the glottis, however, may not exactly 'line up' with these. Thus, a single feature specification for the glottis may line up with two or more articulatory configurations of the other organs (in the case of a level tone realized over a long vowel or diphthong); or it may refer to only a part of the portion of the speech event characterized by one such configuration (in the case of one element of a complex tone realized on a short vowel, or of preaspiration realized on a short vowel). In the majority of cases, laryngeal configurations probably correspond one to one with configurations of the supraglottal organs (thus forming unitary segments), but the results just dis-

---

[5] Ken Hale informs me that exactly the same facts obtain for the preaspirated series in Papago, though some recent instrumental studies show that this description is not accurate for all speakers of Icelandic.

cussed show that this is only a frequent (and perhaps natural) result, rather than a necessary aspect of phonetic representation.

It is presumably the case that further structure could be given to the laryngeal component of a phonetic description. It seems likely that the natural CVCVCV rhythm of speech articulation is reflected here, as well as in the alternating closed and open positions of the vocal tract; and hence that the laryngeal configuration for a given syllable can be divided into two or three portions: syllable-initial consonantism, syllable peak, and a possible syllable final consonantism. The feature [±syllabic], then, would correspond not directly to a property of individual segments, but rather to the location of the peak / margin boundaries, or the distribution of syllabic energy across the syllable. The initial-margin glottal configuration would be realized on those segmental articulations that precede the peak; the peak elements in the glottal specification would then be realized on vowels, sonorants, or other elements falling within the domain of [+syllabic], and any postpeak articulations would be accompanied by the postpeak portion of the glottal specification of the syllable. In this case, syllable boundaries in the laryngeal and in the supraglottal representations will coincide, but perhaps not 'segment' boundaries. This sort of representation, in terms of parallel components whose alignment must be given, is similar in ways to the sort of phonetic representation used in many places in such works as Pike (1943), where the position of each articulatory organ is specified separately over time.

We do not, however, mean to introduce a dimension of timing directly into the laryngeal component of a phonetic representation, as has recently been advocated by Lisker and Abramson (1972) and Ladefoged (1972). These scholars go too far, we feel, in advocating a virtual abandonment of the specification of distinctive laryngeal postures corresponding to different sorts of consonant, in favor of a simple temporal specification of some such parameter as delay in voicing onset time (negative or zero for voiced consonants, small for voiceless plain consonants, large for voiceless aspirated consonants, etc.). It seems entirely worthwhile and productive to attempt to explain these time differences in terms of differences of laryngeal configuration, and hence to preserve as far as possible the 'timeless' character of phonetic and phonological representation. The introduction of noncoinciding domains for feature specifications is not to be construed, therefore, as the introduction of real-time parameters. The fact that one event (the shift from one laryngeal configuration to another) takes place "in the middle" of another is not at all the same as saying that it takes place 57 milliseconds (rather than 31 or 109) after the beginning of the second event.

We have suggested that supraglottal and laryngeal features may not be

perfectly aligned in some cases. In fact, there is some reason to believe
that even articulatory features generally taken to have an unimpeachably
'segmental' character may have this property as well. In numerous
South American languages of the Gé, Tupi-Guaraní, Panoan, Arawakan,
Tucanoan, and other families, we find treatments of nasality that are
very different from that in more familiar languages. It is in these languages, for example, that the sort of nasalization process exemplified
above in Sundanese is most widely found: many have processes that
spread nasality either progressively or regressively until they come to
some element that serves to block further propagation. In some cases
this is any supraglottally articulated consonant, as in Sundanese; in some
cases, any obstruent; in some cases a voiceless obstruent, and in some
cases the main stress or some syntactic boundary. More interesting than
the processes affecting nasality in vowels (and glides and continuant obstruents, in some cases), however, are the rules which determine nasality
in stops.

A typical underlying system in such languages contains, in addition to
liquids and perhaps some continuant obstruents, two basic series of
stops. One is usually voiceless unaspirated in most positions, and the
other varies among voiced oral, voiced nasal, voiced prenasalized, and
voiced prestopped nasal. Typologically, then, these systems are rather
similar to two-symmetrical-series systems common in Australia (where
voiceless stops are opposed to voiced nasals) and New Guinea (where
voiceless stops are frequently opposed to prenasalized voiced stops).
The differences among the oral, nasal, prenasal, and postnasal realizations of these segments are controlled by the nasality of the surrounding
vowels, which generally distinguish oral and nasal.

A good example of such a system is found in Maxakalí[6] (cf. Gudschinsky, Popovich, & Popovich, 1970). In this language, the obstruents
consist of voiceless /p, t, c, k/ and voiced /m, n, ñ, ŋ/. /c/ varies between
stop, spirant, and affricate in various positions, but otherwise the voiceless series is straightforward. The voiced series appears least problemat-
ically in syllable-initial position: there /m, n, ñ/ are realized by nasals [m,

---

[6] The main interest of this language for phonological theory rests in the fact that under
certain conditions, syllable final stops develop vocalic onglides, after which the stops themselves may disappear. This leads to a situation in which stops have VOWEL ALLOPHONES
in some positions. The description to follow does not take this situation into account, and
is primarily based on forms to which it does not apply. This is simply to base the discussion on forms whose analysis is reasonably clear; a discussion of the admirably lucid and
insightful analysis of these complex phenomena which is presented in the paper in question
would lead us too far afield and would not contribute materially to our point.

n, ñ] before nasal vowels. /m, n, ñ, ŋ/ are realized as prenasalized stops [m͡b, n͡d, ñ͡j, ŋ͡g] before oral vowels (and, in the case of [ŋ͡g] for /ŋ/, before nasal vowels as well). The prenasalized stops may be denasalized to fully oral voiced stops optionally in word-initial position, and always after an immediately preceding oral consonant. Except across boundaries, nasal vowels are almost always followed by nasal consonants, and oral vowels by oral consonants.

In syllable-final position, the facts are as given in (9) below. A syllable final C may be preceded by either an oral vowel (V) or a nasal vowel (Ṿ), and may be followed by either an oral consonant (T), a nasal consonant (N), or end of word (#):

(9) a. After V:

      i. V ____ .T

          /p/ = [p] (cf. /ce+pïtïc/ > /ceptïc/ = [šæptïɣi] 'heavy hair')

          /m/ does not occur

      ii. V ____ .N

          /p/ = [b͡m][7] (cf. /cokcop ñịcïc/ = [šokšob͡m ñịšïɣiị] 'yellow animal')

          /m/ = [bm] (cf. /ce+mịnnị/ > /cemnị/ = [šæb͡mnị] 'black hair')

      iii. V ____ .#

          /p/ = [p] (cf. /teptep/ = [tɛptæëp] 'araponga bird')

          /m/ does not occur

  b. After Ṿ:

      i. Ṿ ____ .T

          /p/ = [m͡p] (cf. /ị+pïtïc/ = /ịptïc/ = [ʔịm͡ptïɣi] 'it is heavy')

          /m/ = [m͡p] (cf. /mịmkoc/ = [mịm͡pkoy] 'canoe')

      ii. Ṿ ____ .N

          /p/ does not occur

          /m/ = [m] (cf. /mạhạm ñịcïc/ [mạhæẽm ñịšïɣiị] 'yellow fish')

      iii. Ṿ ____ .#

          /p/ does not occur

          /m/ = [m] (cf. /mạhạm/ [mạhæẽm] 'fish')

---

[7] Voiceless stops in this position either assimilate in voicing to the following segment, as in this example, or remain unchanged. We assume here the assimilation is the primary variant, as Gudschinsky, Popovich, and Popovich assert (1970, p. 85).

The first problem we face is the simple one of description: what features differentiate the nasal, prenasal, postnasal, and oral stops? It is clear that all are obstruents, and from other languages which distinguish [n] from [ð] phonetically (such as Cubeo, an Eastern Tucanoan language described by Salzer, 1971), in addition to [n͡d], we can see that continuance cannot be the relevant feature. Phonetically, in Maxakalí as in other languages with prenasalized and postnasalized segments, all variants are voiced stops: the difference is simply in how much of the articulation is accompanied by lowered velum. The same mechanism, distributed in different ways, is at work in all of these segments: a lowered velum. The lowering of the velum is generally described by the feature [+nasal], and while it is no doubt perfectly adequate to describe all of these segments as underlyingly [±nasal], this is obviously insufficient to distinguish their surface forms.

One possible move would be to distinguish two features, [±nasal] and [±prenasal].[8] Segments that are [+nasal] could be described as having lowered velum during the period of stop closure; [+prenasal] segments could be said to have lowered velum during the formation of a stop closure. In these terms [m] is [+nasal, +prenasal]; [d] is [−nasal, −prenasal]; [n͡d] is [−nasal, +prenasal]; and [d͡n] is [+nasal, −prenasal]. This pair of features at least allows us to describe the facts, but it is still necessary to see if they allow us to express the correct generalizations. As is clear from (9), the primary place where interesting things happen in the description of syllable-final nasality in Maxakalí is in the position between a vowel and a following syllable initial consonant when these disagree in nasality. Here both /p/ and /m/ appear as [b͡m] if preceded by oral syllabic and followed by syllable initial nasal; and as [m͡p] if preceded by nasal syllabic and followed by syllable-initial oral consonant. These facts could be described by the rules (10):

$$(10) \quad [-\text{cont}] \longrightarrow \begin{bmatrix} +\text{prenasal} \\ -\text{nasal} \end{bmatrix} / \begin{bmatrix} +\text{syll} \\ +\text{nasal} \end{bmatrix} \underline{\quad} . [-\text{nasal}]$$

$$\longrightarrow \begin{bmatrix} -\text{prenasal} \\ +\text{nasal} \end{bmatrix} / \begin{bmatrix} +\text{syll} \\ -\text{nasal} \end{bmatrix} \underline{\quad} . [+\text{nasal}]$$

These rules describe the facts, on the assumption that the nasal (pre-

---

[8] This move is made by Ladefoged (1972), though without considering the existence of postnasalized stops. The present author has also taught these features for several years in phonetics classes.

nasal, etc.) series are underlyingly fully nasal, and the others fully oral, as well as that the other facts described above have already been specified.

While these rules operate correctly, they are not fully satisfying, in that they do not bring out fully the assimilatory nature of the rule. There is no obvious reason why [+prenasal] should be intimately associated with a preceding nasal vowel, and [+nasal] only with a following one, nor is there a clear indication of how nasality in stops is related to the specification of nasality in continuants (including vowels). There are numerous languages in the world in which fully nasal consonants nasalize a following vowel, but apparently none in which the nasalization of a vowel results from the presence of a preceding prenasalized stop; yet the articulatory mechanism (lowered velum) is the same in both cases. Further, in these terms the feature [+nasal] might have to arise in some cases by assimilation to a following prenasalized segment. In Guarani (the dialect of Paraguay; cf. Lunt, 1972, for a description of nasalization in this dialect), prenasalized stops have fully nasal variants if the next syllable in the word begins with a prenasalized stop. This is also typical of other Tupi-Guaraní languages, and reflects the following process: a prenasalized stop nasalizes the preceding vowel; prenasalized stops become fully nasal before nasal vowels; and then nasality is optionally lost in unstressed vowels (the further from the stress, the more oral the vowel is likely to be). This sort of assimilation shows clearly that the mechanisms of nasality in vowels, prenasalization, and postnasalization are the same, and we should therefore abandon the feature [±prenasal], and try to make do with just [±nasal].

A final push in this direction comes from a consideration of Kaingang (see Wiesemann, 1972). This language also has the three series of prenasalized, postnasalized, and fully nasal variants of underlying nasals. These are distributed as we might expect: fully nasal between two nasal vowels, prenasal between nasal vowel and following oral vowel and postnasal between oral vowel and following nasal vowel. In the position between two oral vowels, however, Kaingang has another series: 'medionasal' [b͡mb], [d͡nd], [d͡ñd̪], and [g͡ŋg]. In order to describe these segments as well, we would have to introduce a third feature: [±postnasal]. Then fully nasal segments would be [+nasal, +prenasal, +postnasal]; prenasalized stops would be [+prenasal, ±nasal, −postnasal], etc. This is obviously incorrect, since one mechanism (not three) is at work here.

If we are to use simply [±nasal] to describe all of these facts, it is clear that we will face a situation somewhat like that we encountered above in connection with pitch: a single segment may have to contain more than one specification for the feature. A natural account of the segment types we have just been considering would represent oral stops as [−nasal] throughout, and nasal stops as [+nasal] throughout, but prenasalized stops as a sequence [+nasal] [−nasal] realized on the same segment; postnasalized stops as [−nasal] [+nasal] in the same segment, and the Kaingang medionasal stops as [−nasal] [+nasal] [−nasal], all imposed on the same oral segmental articulation.

Given this possibility, we could describe the Maxakalí facts by saying that an extra nasal element is inserted in a syllable final consonant if it is oral and adjacent to a nasal, or an extra nonnasal element in a nasal consonant adjacent to an oral element. This would cover the facts, and seems a little more satisfying than rules (10). A better solution might be the following, however: the generalization which emerges from the facts in (9) is that a syllable final consonant has *no* distinctive value of nasality if followed by another consonant. Rather, the first part of the segment shows a continuation of the nasality (or nonnasality) of the preceding vowel, while the remainder of the segment shows an anticipation of the nasality (or nonnasality) of the following segment. Instead of saying that these prenasalized and postnasalized segments contain two specifications of nasality, therefore, it might be more appropriate to say that they contain no specification of nasality at all, and that the nasality of the segment in question is entirely due to the adjacent segments. For this to be possible, what we want is not features whose domain is less than a single segment, as was the case with the laryngeal features, but rather, features whose domain is greater than a single segment. What we propose, that is, is that the phonetic representations of the sequences [· · · V m͡p T · · ·] and [· · · V b͡m N · · ·] be approximately as in (11):

(11)   a.

	V	m͡p	:	T
syll	+	−	:	−
cons	−	+	:	+
nasal		+	: −	
cor	−	−	:	+

b.

	V	b͡m	:	N
syll	+	−	:	−
cons	−	+	:	+
nasal		−	: +	
cor	−	−	:	+

$\left(\begin{matrix} \cdot \\ \cdot \\ \cdot \end{matrix} = \text{syllable boundary} \right)$ $\left(\begin{matrix} \cdot \\ \cdot \\ \cdot \end{matrix} = \text{syllable boundary} \right)$

Representations like (11) might, then, be taken to arise through the operation of a rule like (12):

$$(12) \qquad [\pm\text{nasal}] \longrightarrow \emptyset \, / \left[\underline{} \atop -\text{syll} \right] . [-\text{syll}]$$

This rule must be interpreted as deleting only the specification '[±nasal]', rather than the entire segment; it is also necessary to assume the existence of a (possibly language-specific) convention that fills in the gap left by this deletion in the necessary way, rather than (say) extending the scope of the nasality of a preceding tautosyllabic segment all the way into the segment which is now unspecified, or some other alternative. The deletion problem arises in any event with the features of pitch already discussed, since pitch elements are sometimes lost without affecting segmental articulations; we could assume that no rule deletes an entire segment unless it requires the deletion of an oral articulation (i.e., unless it specifies that a feature which is associated one to one with articulatory moras, such as [±consonantal] or [±sonorant] or a feature which may be associated with segments on a one–many basis, as [±syllabic] is to be deleted). The second issue is more complex: languages will clearly require principles of alignment of different features to cover cases in which the numbers of specifications for some features are not equal. Whether these alignment rules can be given universally or must be specified on a language particular basis is a problem for future research. Presumably, this is related to issues such as that of the typology of languages based on whether they allow nonalignment of features in underlying representations, in surface representations, or nowhere at all.

A rule such as (12) seems the most satisfactory way to capture the facts of nasalization in syllable final consonants in Maxakalí, if it is taken to lead to representations like (11). An interesting further confirmation of the correctness of this formulation is furnished by facts concerning nasality in Apinayé (as described by Callow (1962)). Here, the following situations are typical of the nasality of the nonvoiceless stops between vowels of various sorts:

(13)

a.	V .b V	e.	V b.d V
b.	Ṿ .m̂ Ṿ	f.	V m.n Ṿ
c.	Ṿ .m̂b V	g.	Ṿ m.d V
d.	V .b̂m Ṿ	h.	V b.n Ṿ

Here, if there is a single intervocalic consonant, it is fully oral between oral vowels, fully nasal between nasal vowels, and partly nasal between vowels that differ in nasality. When there is a cluster, the same facts obtain; with the exception that where a single segment would be prenasalized or postnasalized, a cluster is represented by a fully nasal consonant preceded or followed by a fully oral one. A situation like this is extremely difficult to describe in terms of features like [±nasal] and [±prenasal], but it follows easily from a rule deleting nasality in non-syllabics at syllable boundary which are surrounded by segments on both sides. If the remaining nasality specifications (from the adjacent syllabics) each fill half of the resulting gap, this will be only part of a segment in (13a–d), but an entire segment in (13e–h).

We have suggested a model of phonetic representation, then, which is quite close to the traditional decomposition of articulations into an energy source, a laryngeal configuration, an oral articulation, and a nasal (or velum) articulation. It is possible that the oral articulation should be further decomposed into tongue articulation and lip articulation, though evidence for this is not presently known to us. Associated with the energy source is the feature [±syllabic], whose values control the structure of the syllable. Within a syllable, this feature may begin as [−], then changes to [+], and then may return to [−]. These are presumably the only possible combinations within a syllable: the feature serves simply to pick out some portion of the syllable and identify it as the syllable peak. Associated with the laryngeal position are the features [±stiff], [±slack], [±spread], and [±constricted], discussed above in connection with pitch. The oral articulation is specified in terms of degree of constriction (by the features [±sonorant] and [±consonantal]), position (by the tongue and lip features) and manner (by such features as [±continuant], [±lateral], [±gradual release], [±instantaneous release], etc.). The position of the velum is specified by the single feature [±nasal]. The most important aspect of such representations is the fact that, while the specifications for these four systems are generally synchronized, it is possible for this not to be the case, with the result that the boundaries of a specification in one system will not coincide with the boundaries of a specification in another. Thus, more than one laryngeal specification may be realized during a single oral articulation, while a single nasal specification may extend over more (or less) than one oral articulation. This presumably corresponds to the fact that the articulating organs of the different systems have differing response times.

The approach just outlined may also provide a start toward a solution of one of the perennial problems of phonology, the difference between long and short segments. The question of whether long vowels and consonants should be represented as single units with an added feature, or as sequences of two short segments, has been debated within structuralist theories of both American and European sorts, prosodic analysis, generative grammar, and others.[9] In some cases a distinctive quality is associated with 'long' sounds, as when in Icelandic long voiceless stops are preaspirated, or when 'long' vowels are distinctively tenser than 'short' vowels. The problem arises most acutely, however, in the case of languages which oppose long segments (either vowels or consonants) to short segments solely in temporal terms. In many cases, there are excellent reasons for considering the long elements as sequences: for instance, they may arise at morpheme boundaries, from the juxtaposition of an element ending in some segment with an element beginning with the same segment; they may arise from the deletion of a segment separating two identical short segments; or they may have the same function as two such elements separated by other material, as in the case of stress rules in a 'mora-counting' language, which treats two short vowel syllables and one long vowel syllable in the same way. In other cases, however, no such argument exists and the treatment of long segments as units or as sequences must be made on general grounds. This decision may have consequences, as for example in the formulation of rules that affect long segments uniformly (e.g., a rule altering the quality of a long vowel).

In some instances, phonetically long vowels of both sorts may exist in the same language. In Kasem, for example, we saw above that long vowels may arise either by juxtaposition of two vowels (as in *voo* 'leaf', from underlying /vua+u/) or by secondary lengthening (as in *vo:do* 'leaves', from /vua+du/). In a Honduran dialect of Island Carib, Taylor (1955) reports that long consonants derived from the syncope of an unstressed vowel between two identical consonants (as in *mátatti* 'he doesn't (or can't) drink', from /mátadi+ti/) are not homophonous with long consonants arising from lengthening of stops in poststress syllables (as in *mátat:i* 'he doesn't bleed' from /máta+ti/). It is clear, therefore, that we need a feature which specifies purely phonetic length, and which is distinct from gemination. This feature does not ever, as far as we know, have distinctive values in underlying representations, however, since underlying length contrasts seem always to be representable in terms of clusters versus single elements. We will therefore refer to this purely phonetic feature as [*n*long], rather than as a classificatory feature [±long].

---

[9] See, for example, Swadesh (1937), Trubetzkoy (1939), and Mitchell (1957), as well as a host of others in the nongenerative literature.

Positing both long sounds and geminate sounds does not eliminate the problem, however. In some languages, an element which must be treated as a cluster for the purpose of some rules must be treated as a single unit with the property of length for the purpose of other rules. Kenstowicz (1970) discusses cases of this sort: in Lithuanian, for example, long vowels are treated as two segments by accent rules, but as units by vowel-quality rules. He considers some possibilities for resolving this problem. One of these is to assume that long segments originate in underlying representation as clusters, but that at some point in the phonology, a rule converts sequences of identical elements into units with the feature of length. This alternative he rejects, since there are cases in which a rule treating long segments as clusters may follow a rule treating them as units. He proposes as an alternative that rules treat long segments either as clusters or as units, depending on the type of rule involved. Accent rules, for example, will analyze long segments as clusters, while rules affecting oral articulation ('quality features') will treat them as units. This position is disputed by Fidelholtz (1971), who presents examples which he argues show that quality changes may require the cluster representation, and accent rules the unit representation. He also argues that rules treating long segments as clusters and as units may be intermixed in the ordering, in ways that make it hopeless to imagine the two representations as related by a rule of coalescence. Fidelholtz' rejection of Kenstowicz's proposed distinction between accent rules and quality rules is entirely plausible, since counterexamples come easily to mind. Thus, any accent rule, such as penultimate stress, in a syllable-counting language with distinctive length, falsifies the proposition that long vowels are always equivalent to two short vowels for the purpose of accent rules; and the very frequent process by which long vowels are diphthongized is most naturally treated in terms of a quality change in a cluster representation of length.

Any attempt to relate the ambiguity of representation of vowel and consonant length to differences in rule type must fail in the face of examples in which the same rule must make use of both representations. A simple example is Latin, which treats the final syllable as a unit, but counts moras in the penult. Consider further in this connection the principle of assignment of stress in the St. Lawrence Island dialect of Eskimo.[10] In this dialect, there is a mora-counting alternating stress principle of the following sort: all long vowels receive stress, and a short

---

[10] I am indebted for these facts to Krauss (1971) and later correspondence with Michael Krauss.

vowel receives stress if it is separated by a short syllable from a preceding stressed vowel, either long or short, and is not word final. Short vowels are also stressed in the second syllable if the first syllable is short.[11] This might be formulated as the pair of rules (14):

(14)

$$[+\text{syll}] \longrightarrow [+\text{stress}]$$

$$/ \left\{ \begin{array}{l} \left[\begin{array}{c} \underline{} \\ +\text{long} \end{array} \right] \\ \left\{ \begin{array}{l} \# \\ \left[\begin{array}{c} +\text{syll} \\ +\text{stress} \end{array} \right] \end{array} \right\} C_0 \left[\begin{array}{c} +\text{syll} \\ -\text{long} \end{array} \right] C_0 \underline{} C_0[+\text{syll}] \end{array} \right\} \qquad \text{(iterative)}$$

This rule would, of course, violate the claim that long vowels are not units for the purpose of accent rules. There is a more important difficulty with this rule, however: long vowels are assigned a distinctively high tone if they are in an open syllable which is separated from the preceding stressed syllable by a short, unstressed syllable. This could be achieved by adding rule (15):

$$(15) \quad \left[\begin{array}{c} +\text{syll} \\ +\text{long} \\ +\text{stress} \end{array} \right] \longrightarrow [+\text{high tone}] / \left[\begin{array}{c} +\text{syll} \\ +\text{stress} \end{array} \right] C_0 \left[\begin{array}{c} +\text{syll} \\ -\text{stress} \end{array} \right] C_0 \underline{}$$

While rule (15) will operate correctly, it suggests that a generalization is being missed in rules (14). Note that the second part of (14) specifies an alternating stress principle: stress a vowel which is two vowel moras away from the beginning of the word or from another stressed vowel. Since long vowels contain two moras, all long vowels will satisfy this requirement automatically, and hence the stressing of long vowels by a separate rule [the first part of (14)] is not necessary. Furthermore, the distinction between syllables that get high tone and those that do not falls out naturally from this formulation: a long vowel preceded by an unstressed short vowel would be stressed on its first mora by the alternating stress principle, while a long vowel in the first syllable or immediately preceded by another stressed vowel would carry its stress on its

---

[11] All stressed short vowels are also assigned phonetic length, a complication which we ignore here. It is only the difference between underlying long and short vowels which is of interest to us here.

second mora. We could thus replace the rules (14) and (15) by (16):

$$
(16) \quad
\begin{aligned}
&[+\text{syll}] \longrightarrow [+\text{stress}] \Big/ \left\{ \begin{matrix} \# \\ \begin{bmatrix} +\text{syll} \\ +\text{stress} \end{bmatrix} \end{matrix} \right\} C_0 [+\text{syll}] \, C_0 \underline{\hspace{1cm}} C_0 [+\text{syll}] \\[2mm]
&[+\text{syll}] \longrightarrow [+\text{high tone}] \Big/ \begin{bmatrix} \underline{\hspace{1cm}} \\ +\text{stress} \end{bmatrix} [+\text{syll}]
\end{aligned}
$$

Given words with structures such as /tatataatataataata/ and /taatataa-taata/, the first part of this rule (applying iteratively) will place stress as follows: /tatátaátatáataáta/ and /taátatáataáta/. High tone will then be assigned (marked as *â*): [tatátaátatâataáta], [taátatâataáta]. The distinction between high tone syllables and non-high-tone stressed long vowels, then, is that high tone falls on vowels which have stress on their first part.

In order for this explanation to work, however, some refinement is necessary. The alternating stress principle operates in terms of stress falling two moras after a stressed vowel: if that vowel is long, it counts as stressed regardless of whether it is stressed on its first mora or on its second mora. The first portion of the environment then (the specification $\left[\begin{smallmatrix} +\text{syll} \\ +\text{stress} \end{smallmatrix}\right]$ treats long vowels as units. In order to make the alternating stress rule be mora counting, however, as is necessary if long syllables are not ever to be skipped, the second instance of [+syll] in the above rule must refer to a mora, treating long vowels as clusters. Further, the element to which stress is assigned should be a mora if the distinction between initially stressed long vowels and finally stressed long vowels is to serve as the basis for the pitch difference. For the purpose of this rule, then, long vowels must be ambiguous: they must be analyzable both as units and as two moras simultaneously.

In terms of the notion of phonetic representation which we have discussed above, this ambiguity can be achieved. The feature [+syllabic], as we have suggested, is really a mark of the boundary between margin and peak within the syllable. The peak of a long syllable is the sequence of two moras, and accordingly, a single feature specification '[+syllabic]' includes both moras in its scope. Each mora is, however, characterized as a sonorant articulation. A feature such as [+sonorant] is assigned separately to each oral articulation (or mora), and hence a reference to [+sonorant] will be restricted to a single mora. Even if two adjacent moras have identical specifications for this feature, they are assigned it separately. A long vowel can thus be referred to as a unit, by referring to a unit which is [+syllabic] (which may include more than one mora), or as a sequence, by referring to $\begin{bmatrix} +\text{sonorant} \\ +\text{syllabic} \end{bmatrix}$ elements (which are limited to one mora in length). Rules (16), then, should be reformulated as (17):

$$(17) \quad \begin{bmatrix} +\text{syll} \\ +\text{son} \end{bmatrix} \longrightarrow [+\text{stress}] \; / \; \left\{ \begin{matrix} \# \\ \begin{bmatrix} +\text{syll} \\ +\text{stress} \end{bmatrix} \end{matrix} \right\} C_0 \begin{bmatrix} +\text{syll} \\ +\text{son} \end{bmatrix} C_0 \underline{\quad\quad} C_0[+\text{syll}]$$

$$\begin{bmatrix} +\text{syll} \\ +\text{son} \end{bmatrix} \longrightarrow [+\text{high tone}] \; / \; \begin{bmatrix} \underline{\quad\quad} \\ +\text{stress} \end{bmatrix} \begin{bmatrix} +\text{syll} \\ +\text{son} \end{bmatrix}$$

The ambiguity of long vowels, which is seen to be necessary within the scope of a single rule, thus falls out from the conception of a phonetic representation as a combination of specifications in different 'registers', whose internal boundaries may not be the same.[12]

There are numerous aspects of this view which must be clarified before it can be accepted with any degree of assurance. If it is correct, however, it suggests that many examples of phonological rules might productively be viewed in a way different from that assumed previously. We have assumed that phonological rules consist of processes that replace feature specifications with other values, leaving the boundaries of the segment intact. If segment boundaries are not absolute, however, many such processes might be better seen as shifts in the boundary of some feature. Assimilation phenomena are an obvious candidate for such treatment: instead of replacing a specification for some feature with a specification identical with that of the same feature in a neighboring segment, assimilation might be viewed as a shift in the boundary of a feature, so as to include a segment that was not in the domain of the original specification. On this view, the fact that most assimilations are to the nearest neighboring elements relevantly specified for the feature in question (as suggested by Palacas, 1971) is a mechanical consequence of the formulation of such processes.

Rules other than assimilations can be thought of in this way, as well. In Icelandic, for example, there are three cases in which we would ex-

---

[12] Andersen (1972) discusses a number of examples of diphthongization processes which may be related to this aspect of phonetic representation as well. He assumes that diphthongization takes place by virtue of a shift in the position of the internal boundaries of different feature specifications, within the confines of a long segment. While the theory underlying his discussion is only made explicit in part, his examples may well point to the possibility of nonsynchronized specifications of features all belonging to the same register.

pect a sequence of *e* plus vowel to arise: in the present tense stem of strong verbs with the structure C*eu*C; in the case of breaking, where an *a* is inserted between stressed *e* and a following consonant, if the next syllable contains a back vowel (under some circumstances); and in the case of underlying long *é*, which might be expected to be bimoric and become a falling diphthong by analogy with the other underlying long vowels. In all of these cases, what we actually get is a sequence of *j* plus vowel: *ju* (or *jú* or *jó*, in some cases) in the strong verbs; *ja* (or *jö*, if *u*-Umlauted) from breaking; and *je* for the phonetic shape of underlying /*é*/. Anderson (1969a) treated this fact as the consequence of a rule of stress shift: in a sequence of *e* plus vowel, shift stress from the *e* to the following vowel. Later rules then convert unstressed *e* to *j* next to a vowel. We could, however, treat this as a shift in the syllabicity boundary, and give a rule such as the following:

(18)

syll	−	+				−	+
son		+	+			+	+
cons		−	−	⇒		−	−
high		−				−	
low		−				−	
back		−				−	

If stress is taken to be a property of the syllable, realized on the syllabic portion, the shift in syllabicity boundary will result automatically in a shift of stress, and /e/ will become *j* by later phonetic processes specifying all glides as high in Icelandic. Such a view of the rule creating rising diphthongs is not forced by the facts, of course, since a treatment in terms of purely replacive operations is possible. It seems interesting and suggestive, however, to explore the possibilities of viewing phonological processes in this way, which is suggested by the other considerations above which motivate the concept of nonsynchronized representations in phonetics. A similar account of other processes is often revealing. Consider, for example, the common phenomenon of the insertion of a stop-element between a nasal and a following voiceless spirant (as in [warmpθ] *warmth*). This can be seen as a sequence of two feature boundary shifts: first the extension of the nonnasal specification for the spirant back into the preceding segment (for reasons that are not hard to explain phonetically; cf. Ohala, 1971); and secondly voicing assimilation of the resultant interval, which has all of the features of a voiced stop. Such a development, summarized in (19), seems more satisfactory than the simple epenthesis of a voiceless stop:

(19)

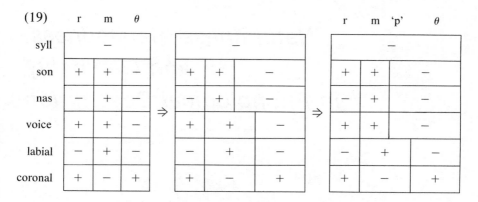

Other examples suggest themselves, and the formal properties of such operations deserve investigation.

CHAPTER 15

Naturalness, Relatedness, and Generality in Phonological Description

The discussion in this book since Chapter 3 has dealt primarily with the way a system of rules specifies the relation between an underlying (or phonemic) representation of an utterance and the more or less completely specified surface (phonetic) representation of the same stretch of speech. We have said very little about the way in which a grammar of language L characterizes the set of underlying representations of morphemes or utterances, and thus gives a formal account of the notion 'possible morpheme (or utterance) in L'. Such an account is obviously necessary, however, since decisions about the nature of underlying representations can have extensive consequences for the operation of the rules of the grammar.

For the theories known collectively as 'taxonomic' phonemics, the primary focus of attention was not the relation between forms, but the autonomous structure of each individual form.[1] Such theories were concerned to specify the regularities which obtain within the domain of the

[1] This concentration on individual forms rather than on relations between forms is perhaps another reason to prefer Postal's (1968) term 'autonomous phonemics' to Chomsky's (by now rather pejorative) 'taxonomic phonemics'. By 'autonomous' Postal refers to the fact that these theories were concerned to provide a phonological description that made little or no use of other sorts of information, such as that provided by the morphology and the syntax.

individual form, and to distinguish those aspects of the structure of forms that serve distinctively from those aspects of their structure that are due to regularities of the language. Regularities in the relation between, e.g., inflectionally or derivationally connected forms were not a primary concern, and had little role to play in the description of each form.

There are, of course, numerous regularities in any language that can be stated quite satisfactorily in terms of a characterization of (surface) forms, without taking into account a system of rules the primary concern of which is to specify the alternate shapes in which a morpheme occurs in different environments. It is interesting to note however that many of these intramorphemic regularities are expressed perfectly adequately within the system of rules, without the need of another set of statements. In Russian, for instance, we have noted that the feature of voicing is nondistinctive in all but the last member of a cluster of obstruents. This might be expressed in terms of a 'phonotactic' description of the class of possible obstruent clusters in Russian surface forms. Alternations such as [dat,l,i] versus [dad,bi], however, show that we need a rule in the grammar to assimilate the voicing of an obstruent to that of a following one. This rule of assimilation will state perfectly satisfactorily the fact that a cluster of obstruents disagreeing in the feature [±voice] cannot appear in Russian phonetic forms, and no additional 'phonotactic' statement is needed.

While this is true of a great many regularities that obtain entirely within the bounds of an underlying unit, it is not (unfortunately) true of all. It would be a result of the greatest interest if it were to turn out that every intramorphemic regularity was necessarily reflected in an alternation, and thus in a rule; but this position cannot seriously be maintained. Consider for example the well-known fact that the first member of an initial obstruent cluster in English must be *s*. It seems reasonable to say that there is a principle in English that the only obstruent that can occur in the environment '# ____ [+obstruent]' is a voiceless, coronal, distributed, anterior, etc. spirant. To reflect this in a rule, we might say that English contains (1):

$$(1) \qquad [\text{+obstruent}] \longrightarrow \begin{bmatrix} -\text{voice} \\ +\text{cor} \\ +\text{dist} \\ +\text{ant} \\ \cdot \\ \cdot \\ \cdot \end{bmatrix} / \# \underline{\quad} [\text{+obstruent}]$$

Rule (1) does not account for any alternations in English, however. There is no element, that is, which appears as *s* under the conditions of the structural description of (1), but as something else elsewhere. We have no motivation for positing (1) as a rule of English except an inductively arrived at generalization about the internal structure of each individual form in the language. There is, furthermore, no basis for the implication carried by rule (1) that the *s* in *spit,* for example, is basically something else, and only becomes *s* by the operation of (1).

It is clearly necessary therefore to supplement the rules which specify alternations with a set of principles specifying the regularities that obtain within individual morphemes. Early attempts to give such an account in a generative description, beginning with Halle (1959), were basically in the spirit of autonomous phonemic description. Just as the phonemic representation had been taken to be one specifying all and only the unpredictable features of a form, the morphophonemic representations that came to replace them were taken to include specifications only for features whose value was distinctive. In obstruent clusters in Russian morphemes, for instance, only the last member is distinctively voiced or voiceless, and so the other members of the cluster were given no specification at all for this feature. In English, if the initial obstruent is followed by another obstruent, only the feature '[+obstruent]' is distinctive, since all of the others are predictable. All of these other features, then, would be left completely blank or unspecified in the dictionary representation of *spit*. The grammar of the language then contained two sets of rules: one a set of phonological rules, which were responsible for describing alternations, and the other a set of *morpheme structure* rules, whose function was to fill in the blank (predictable, redundant) features in representations.

It soon became apparent, however, that this notion led to difficulties. A major formal problem was based on the fact that features are taken to be binarily distinctive. If a feature has two values, + and −, it should be the case that only two items can be distinguished solely in terms of the values they have for this feature, all other features being the same. The device of leaving some features unspecified, however, results in a violation of this principle. As first noted by Lightner, the problem arises when we ask how rules are to treat unspecified features. If a rule applies, that is, in the presence of a feature specification '$[+F_i]$', what is its effect on a matrix in which F_i is blank? There are two possibilities: one is to say that rules apply only if their structural description is explicitly satisfied (i.e., only if all required features are specified in the required way); and the other is to say that rules apply unless their structural description is contradicted (i.e., a requirement of $[+F_i]$ is satisfied by either $[+F_i]$ or blank, while $[-F_i]$ is satisfied by either $[-F_i]$ or blank). Either of these assumptions leads to a problem, since it is possible on either assumption to construct grammars in which three phonological matrices are distinguished phonemically only by the difference between $[+F_i]$, $[-F_i]$, and blank for F_i, but in which the three are distinctive in the phonetic output. On the assumption that rules apply only if explicitly satisfied, the rules in (2b) convert the three matrices in (2a) into the resultant (2c):

(2)   a. $F_1 : \begin{bmatrix} \ \ \end{bmatrix}\begin{bmatrix} + \end{bmatrix}\begin{bmatrix} - \end{bmatrix}$
            $F_2 : $

     b. $\begin{array}{l} [\ \ ] \longrightarrow [-F_2] \\ [+F_1] \longrightarrow [+F_2] \\ [-F_1] \longrightarrow [+F_2] \\ [-F_2] \longrightarrow [+F_1] \end{array}$ c. $\begin{bmatrix} +F_1 \\ -F_2 \end{bmatrix}\begin{bmatrix} +F_1 \\ +F_2 \end{bmatrix}\begin{bmatrix} -F_1 \\ +F_2 \end{bmatrix}$

On the assumption that rules apply unless their descriptions are contradicted, however, the rules in (3b) convert (3a) into (3c):

(3)   a. $\begin{matrix} F_1 \\ F_2 \\ F_3 \end{matrix} \begin{bmatrix} \ \ \end{bmatrix}\begin{bmatrix} + \end{bmatrix}\begin{bmatrix} - \end{bmatrix}$

     b. $\begin{array}{l} [\ \ ] \longrightarrow \begin{bmatrix} -F_2 \\ -F_3 \end{bmatrix} \\ [+F_1] \longrightarrow [+F_2] \\ [-F_1] \longrightarrow [+F_3] \\ \begin{bmatrix} +F_2 \\ +F_3 \end{bmatrix} \longrightarrow [+F_1] \end{array}$ c. $\begin{bmatrix} + \\ + \\ + \end{bmatrix}\begin{bmatrix} + \\ + \\ - \end{bmatrix}\begin{bmatrix} - \\ - \\ + \end{bmatrix}$

This effect of blank features is entirely contrary to the point of omitting some specifications: if a feature value is predictable (and hence omitted from the phonemic form) it should not at the same time be functioning distinctively.

In discussing this problem, Stanley (1967) concluded that no natural way exists to avoid this formal difficulty. He suggested, therefore, that an alternative to the formulation of phonological theory with blank features filled in by morpheme structure rules should be found. If we had some serious reason to wish to preserve unspecified features, we might be inclined to pursue further the possibility of finding a constraint on grammars that will make (2) and (3), and similar examples, impossible; but as pointed out in Chapter 3, there is no reason to require that phonemic representations contain specifications for all and only the unpredictable features. Once we take seriously the notion that a grammar contains rules, as well as representations, there is no reason to require that distinctiveness serve as a criterion for the features that are included in a given level of representation, so long as the grammar as a whole allows us to determine what values are commutable (in glossematic terms) and hence distinctive, and what values are dependent, or determined, and hence redundant.

In such terms, Stanley proposed (as accepted above in Chapter 3) that underlying representations, like phonetic representations, are specified for all members of the universal set of features. An additional set of morpheme structure constraints then provides, for any given language, a specification of the range of possible segments and morphemes, including dependencies that may exist between feature values. Since these constraints all apply to the same units (the underlying representation) they are simultaneous, rather than sequential (as morpheme structure rules were presumed to be), and do not have the effect of changing any feature specifications. Rather, they simply state what is and what is not a permissible feature combination. Stanley suggested that languages can contain morpheme structure constraints of three sorts. Positive conditions state that every morpheme in the language must meet some condition (such as CVCVCV · · · structure, monosyllabicity, etc.). Negative conditions state that no morpheme may meet some condition (such as containing a cluster of three or more consonants, or containing a nasal vowel, etc.). If–then conditions state that if a morpheme meets one condition, it must also meet another (for example, if it contains two obstruents initially, the first of these must be *s*). The formal independence of these three sorts of conditions is perhaps open to question, but since nothing seems to follow from it, we will not attempt to simplify Stanley's formal apparatus. The important point is that the phonemic representations of morphemes are specified for all features, and all must conform to the conditions established for the language.

In terms of matrices with some unspecified features, a natural procedure had been suggested for evaluating the complexity of a given representation (see Chomsky & Halle, 1965): simply count the number of feature specifications. This procedure was extended as is well known, into other areas of concern, to provide a measure of the relative complexity (in linguistic, rather than a priori formal terms) of various formulations of linguistic processes. If we grant that it makes sense to speak of the complexity of individual lexical items relative to one another, this device is not at all satisfactory in terms of the fully specified representations proposed by Stanley, since it would treat complexity as a simple linear function of length. Accordingly, Stanley proposed an alternative way of measuring the 'amount' of distinctiveness of morphemes: a procedure based on computing the number of features that could be changed without violating any of the morpheme structure conditions of the language gives essentially the same results as the counting of unspecified features in the earlier theory. It is thus possible to achieve all of the results of the theory of morpheme structure rules in a theory which posits fully specified underlying representations, without the attendant formal problems.

But Stanley's paper contains a further proposal, which is of great interest. He observed that in a great many cases, regularities that obtain within a morpheme (and hence are to be expressed as morpheme structure conditions) are also enforced across morpheme boundaries (and would thus have to be reflected in phonological rules). As an example, he notes that if a language has a morpheme structure condition which allows only short vowels to precede consonant clusters, it is likely that a morpheme ending in $V:C$, when followed by a consonant, will undergo a shortening process, so that $/\cdots V:C+C/ \rightarrow [\cdots VC+C]$. This is certainly a recurrent sort of situation, and it presents a problem for phonological theory. In such a case, the morpheme structure condition and the phonological rule are clearly different aspects of the same fact, and should not be treated as completely separate. If they are simply stated, each in its own component of the grammar, this will not be expressed, however: it will appear as an accidental fact that some of the phonological rules have the effect of ensuring that constraints on underlying structure are also imposed on derived structures.[2]

Stanley's proposal for dealing with this problem was to assign an additional function to the morpheme structure conditions. In addition to constraining the class of underlying representations, each of these would also have an interpretation as a quasi-rule. After the application of any given phonological rule, that is, we would examine the configuration produced in terms of the morpheme structure conditions, and then alter any necessary features so as to make the representation conform to the

---

[2] This point is pushed further by Kisseberth (1970), who notes that it is not only possible for a morpheme structure constraint and a rule to be related in this way (to form a CON-SPIRACY, in his terminology), but also for more than one rule to be related in terms of their effect. Thus, several rules reducing clusters, and a constraint against clusters of three consonants (internally; or two at boundary), form a conspiracy in the Yawelmani dialect of Yokuts. Kisseberth's point (for which he proposes no formal expression) is certainly correct, and constitutes an extension of the issue we discuss here. P. Kiparsky (1973) has recently shown that the problems raised by Kisseberth can be dealt with in terms of the motion of transparency.

morpheme structure conditions. In the language with a condition that only short vowels can occur before clusters, for instance, we might also have a rule that deletes a vowel (schwa, perhaps) in two-sided open syllable (VC ＿＿ CV). When such a rule applies to /V:CəCV/, it will produce /V:CCV/, which violates the morpheme structure condition. This form is thus altered to [VCCV], so as to conform to the requirement.

This is a very interesting theory, which deals with the relation between constraints on underlying and derived structures in terms of a very strong proposal. It would be of great interest if proven true. It is not hard to see, however, that it is much too strong as just stated: it is clearly impossible to impose all of the conditions on underlying representations on derived structure as well. If this were the case, numerous common situations in which new segment types or configurations are created by phonological rules would be unstable. Consider an early stage of Germanic, for example, in which the fronting of vowels by *i*-Umlaut was still completely phonological. In underlying forms, the only vowels are front unrounded, back rounded (and low back unrounded), long and short. There are no front rounded vowels in underlying forms, a fact which would be reflected by a morpheme structure constraint. If this constraint were imposed on derived structure as well, however, the Umlaut rule would create [ü], [ö], etc., only to have them revert to [u], [o] (or unround to [i], [e]) by the morpheme structure constraint interpreted as a rule. It is clearly necessary to prevent this constraint from reapplying to derived structure, and the same is true in numerous other cases. It is therefore clear that, within any given language, we will have to distinguish between those morpheme structure constraints that reapply to derived structure, and those that do not. Even in this restricted form, however, it is not hard to show that Stanley's theory (while highly suggestive) is both too strong and too weak.

One difficulty is the fact that Stanley assumes morpheme structure conditons reapply to the output of rules that create violations of them. In many circumstances, however, an alteration that has to be made in derived structure to enforce some constraint cannot naturally be associated with any particular application of a rule which creates the violation. English, for example, has a morpheme structure condition that requires vowels to be lax before (most) clusters in underlying forms (see Chomsky & Halle, 1968). This rule also applies across morpheme boundaries, as shown by alternations such as *convεne / convεntion, wɪde / wɪdth, descrɪbe / descrɪption,* etc. In these cases, however, there is no phonological rule which creates the clusters: they arise by the concatenation in underlying forms of consonant-final morphemes with consonant-initial morphemes. There is no natural place to impose shortening as a constraint on rule outputs, and we must therefore allow 'recurrent' morpheme structure conditions to apply to any representation, and not simply to violations produced by the operation of some rule.

The major problem rests in identifying a phonological rule with a constraint to which it is related, however. One class of counterexamples to this proposal is found in rules which, though obviously related to some constraint on underlying structures, must be formulated differently. Thus, English allows tense vowels before clusters if (and only if) the clusters consist entirely of dentals (see Chomsky & Halle, 1968), as in *wɪld, coʊnt, toʌst,* etc. The phonological rule which shortens vowels before clusters at boundaries, however, is not subject to this restriction, and shortens vowels even before dental clusters: cf. *retʌɪn / retɛntive, wɪde / wɪdth.* The two must, therefore, be stated differently, and cannot quite be identified.

A related problem concerns the treatment of exceptions. In Chapter 12, we discussed vowel harmony in Turkish. We pointed out that there are numerous forms which do not conform to vowel harmony stated as a morpheme structure condition, because they contain vowels which differ in backness: *ziyaret* 'visit', *kitap* 'book', etc. These words are not necessarily exceptions to vowel harmony as a rule applying across boundaries, however: their plurals (i.e., *ziyaretlɛr, kitaplʌr,* etc.) are perfectly regular. On the other hand, there are words which are exceptions to harmony across boundaries (e.g., *kabahat* 'fault', *kabahatɪ* 'his fault'), but which are perfectly regular internally. Since the morpheme structure condition and the phonological rule in this case have distinct classes of exceptions, it is clear that they cannot be identified.

Further evidence that constraints cannot be taken to specify completely a subset of the phonological rules of the language comes from the fact that the same constraint may be implemented in very different ways in different languages. Thus, all of Russian, English, and Swedish have constraints on underlying forms that prohibit obstruent clusters differing in voicing (with some limitations in each case; thus English allows a few words like *Aztec,* etc.). Each of these languages also has a rule of voicing assimilation across boundaries. In Russian, however, this rule applies regressively, assimilating an obstruent to the voicing of a following obstruent; in English, the rule which applies to inflections assimilates their voicing *pro*gressively to that of the preceding root-final consonant; while in Swedish (see Linnell *et al.,* 1971) the rule is a mirror-image one, and assimilates a voiced obstruent to a voiceless one in either direction. Each of these rules has the effect of converting clusters which are nonuniform in voicing into homogeneous voiced or voiceless clusters;

each is, furthermore, to be related to the requirement that heterogeneously voiced clusters are not possible in underlying forms. Since this latter fact is a fact about possible configurations, however, it cannot be the case that it alone determines these distinct realizations in the different languages, since all of these different processes result in the same range of allowable configurations.

Another problem that should be mentioned has to do with the point at which a rule related to a morpheme structure constraint can apply. In Finnish, for instance, there is both a morpheme-structure constraint of vowel harmony and a rule of vowel harmony (see P. Kiparsky, 1968b). If we identified them in the way Stanley suggests, we would allow vowel harmony to apply to any level of representation (as suggested above). But Finnish contains a rule which deletes the first member of certain sequences of vowels across boundaries. There are certain vowel initial affixes (see Rardin, 1970) which form derivatives, and which function for harmonic purposes as if they contained a back vowel. If no nonneutral vowel precedes such an affix, it appears with a back vowel, and following affixes also show back vowels. Now if such an affix follows a root whose only nonneutral vowel is front and in root final position, it will cause the truncation of this vowel. If vowel harmony applied before this truncation, we would expect the derivational affix and all following suffixes to appear as front, as is the case after other front harmonic roots. Instead, however, they all appear as back, which is only explicable if vowel harmony applies to the output (and not to the input) of truncation (as would be predicted by the principle of maximizing the transparency of rule application). Thus, vowel harmony does not apply freely, but only at certain levels of representation.

When the relevant cases are examined, in fact, it becomes clear that the rules which are related to morpheme-structure constraints have all of the properties of other phonological rules: independent, language-particular statements of their operation; idiosyncratic classes of exceptions; particular ordering relations, etc. Furthermore, their properties are not predictable simply in terms of configurational morpheme structure statements. It is clear, therefore, that the two sorts of rule cannot be identified. While it is clearly necessary for relatedness between rules and conditions to be expressed in some way, this cannot be done along the lines suggested by Stanley, by claiming that the two are in fact the same.

We can now note that one of the motivations for Stanley's proposal has already been disposed of earlier in this work. For various reasons, he wanted to have general processes such as voicing assimilation apply at several places, throughout the derivation. Such rules were to be seen as applying at any point at which their environmental conditions were satisfied. Since Stanley assumes a theory in which the rules of the phonology are arranged in a linear order, it is necessary for him to assume a special status for these rules. The class of rules that apply freely is thus taken to be exactly the class of those that can be identified with morpheme structure conditions (which have a unique status in the grammar in any event), while the other rules of the phonology apply in a linear order. We have seen above, however, that the property of applying at more than one point in a derivation is not a characteristic of some unique class of anywhere rules, but is simply the most general case of the normal ordering relation in phonology. The hypothesis we were led to adopt for ordinary rule ordering involved the claim that ordering relations are essentially independent of one another, and many are simply consequences of universal principles whose purpose is to ensure the most general possible application of rules. When a rule has no restrictions on its ordering with respect to other rules, it may apply anywhere in the derivation (as Stanley's morpheme structure conditions are assumed to); if it has some restricted orderings, it may still apply at several other points relative to other rules.

Chomsky and Halle (1968) propose a theory which is similar in important respects to Stanley's. They propose that the role of morpheme structure rules (or conditions) is to be filled by a set of MARKING CONVENTIONS, which have the effect of interpreting a matrix of features in terms of the naturalness of the configurations it contains. Instead of excluding certain combinations in a particular language, then, this theory only evaluates them as very unnatural, as opposed to the configurations which are acceptable (presumably because of their greater naturalness). These marking conventions also have an interpretation as rules (LINKING RULES), which apply to derived configurations to make them more natural by adjusting feature values. This position explicitly avoids some of the difficulties raised above; for example, the application of any particular marking convention as a linking rule can be prevented by complicating the rules of the grammar, since a marking convention cannot alter a feature which has just been explicitly mentioned in a rule. Others of the problems raised above remain, however. The motivation for this theory is essentially the same as Stanley's: to capture the relation between morpheme structure constraints and phonological processes by identifying them, and also to allow processes of considerable generality to apply at any point in a derivation. The major innovation is the elevation to universal status of the configurational statements that can appear both as conditions and as rules. The purpose of this move is primarily to remove the arbitrary and formal character of phonological theory, and to recognize the fact that different features behave differently in different rules because they all have an inherent content which is universal and not subject to language particular variation.

Despite the inherent correctness of these aims, at this point it should be clear that a theory like that of marking conventions (which in the relevant respects is simply a version of Stanley's, with universality posited in addition) is not the right way to go about achieving them. Surely a process like voicing assimilation in consonant clusters is the sort of thing that should be treated as a marking convention if anything should, since it is as widely distributed a phonological phenomenon as there is, and has a unified statement (in terms of the resultant configurations). Yet the facts noted above about the extent of variation in language-particular realization of this process show that, however universal the configurational statement of voicing assimilation may be, the processes involved are diverse and language particular. An even more dramatic example of the diversity of the processes which can realize a prohibition on clusters that differ in voicing is provided by a language like Mandan (see Kennard, 1936), in which such clusters are not assimilated, but rather broken up by epenthesis (in Mandan, of a copy of the following vowel). Clearly all of these realizations of voicing assimilation cannot be unified in terms of a single statement of a process.

The solution to this problem cannot, it seems, lie in equating some of the phonological rules in a language with constraints on underlying representations. Both the constraint and the rule require independent statement in the grammar, since each may have (independent) idiosyncracies. An attempt to elevate these into universality simply produces more trouble. Yet it is also the case, as Chomsky and Halle maintain, that there is a universal element in these connections. That is, the reason a language contains both a morpheme structure constraint of a given type and a phonological rule which results in much the same constraint applying to derived structures, though the two are distinct, is that both serve to enforce some natural constraint. Both the constraint and the rule, that is, have the same explanation, where an explanation in phonological terms is often provided by our substantive empirical knowledge of the physics and physiology (and perhaps eventually, neurology) of speech. In the present state of our knowledge of phonetics there seems no hope of providing a purely formal theory to express this sort of explanation, however; at least not of the sort envisioned by Chomsky and Halle. While attempting to incorporate the substantive aspect of phonological features and processes, their proposal actually has the effect of making purely formal description more entrenched.

As far as the formal apparatus of a description is concerned, then, we see no alternative to positing separate rules and conditions of morpheme structure. The attempt to unify a rule and a constraint (or two rules) is not, properly speaking, a job for phonological descriptions. If phonological representations and rules were in fact completely abstract formal entities, we could structure them in any way we wished. In particular, we could structure them (as was long proposed) in such a way that more natural processes have a formally simpler statement. Our experience in constructing concrete descriptions, however, shows us that representations and rules do not have the right character for this enterprise to succeed. As Chomsky and Halle rightly point out, representations and rules have an intrinsic content, which cannot be arbitrarily manipulated. Research in these areas has converged in an overwhelming number of cases (for completely independent reasons internal to particular analyses) on a class of features and processes that closely mirror the mechanisms of speech physiology insofar as we understand them.[3] If this is true, it is clear that there is a constraint imposed from the outside on our ingenuity in constructing formal accounts of phonological structure. The features and the processes, that is, have a sort of autonomous reality which must be reflected in descriptions. Explaining *why* a language has such and such a property, and not such and such another property, is in principle distinct from the business of describing just what properties it has, and the two projects must be kept separate. There is absolutely no a priori reason to imagine that the descriptively correct analysis of a given set of facts from natural language will also be the simplest formally, if the primes of the description are imposed for other reasons. One must start from the description and search for an explanation, rather than attempting to make the explanation shape the description.

A correct substantive theory of the issues alluded to in the title of this chapter, then, is not to be sought in a restructuring of phonological description as is implicit in the theory of marking conventions. There seem to be two aspects to this problem: one is the fact that certain configurations are natural, and the processes of a language are to be looked on as correspondingly natural insofar as they lead to them. The other aspect is the fact that, given particular unnatural configurations, some ways of rectifying them are more natural than others. There are natural configurations; and conversely, there are natural rules; and there are

---

[3] There are of course a wealth of sticky questions which are fundamentally unresolved in this area, concerning just what are the elementary units of control of the speech apparatus. As such, any assertions in detail are liable to instant disconfirmation from several sides. Nevertheless, it is probably fair to say that insofar as we have any inkling of what the physical basis of speech may be, research into the categories and processes of phonological structure shows that this basis is very directly reflected in linguistic structure. This is hardly startling, but it does have consequences that have not been fully explored.

connections between the two sets. The search for naturalness in phonological configurations is largely the attempt to find phonetic explanation (or rationalization) in phonology, an attempt with a long (and not always distinguished) past. Nonetheless, it is clear that there are some concatenations of phonetic elements which are more 'reasonable' than others on the basis of the mechanisms involved, and processes which limit a language to these where possible can thereby be said to have explanations. As we acquire more detailed knowledge about speech, the quality of these explanations is improved.

The role of surface structure in the search for such configurations should not be ignored, as has often been the case. While many of the regularities of surface structure are consequences more or less directly of individual rules, others (as suggested above) cannot be reduced to this form, and have a more autonomous status. Indeed, in some cases a prevailing pattern in surface structure, arising through a combination of factors, takes on a life of its own, and may become the motivation for other rules. A case of the sort is discussed by Kisseberth (1970) from Tunica, where a number of diverse rules are unified by the fact that together they result in a situation in which two adjacent syllables do not bear stress in surface forms. Presumably it is the fact that individual rules are related to generalizations about surface structures in this way that is at the basis of the tendency to make rules more transparent: the more transparent the rule, the more completely it can be related to a surface configuration. To increase a rule's transparency is thus to increase its phonetic basis.

Phonological configurations, then, may either be generally motivated, if they have a physical phonetic explanation, or language particular, if they arise as generalizations within a language and then acquire a sort of autonomy. Examples of the latter sort are to be found in the stress patterns of many languages: there is no general reason (on phonetic grounds) why a given language should have final stress, penultimate stress, or any other particular stress rule. Given the fact that a language has a particular stress rule, however, its other rules may well be structured so as to maintain it as far as possible. An example of such a situation is found in Breton (see Jackson, 1967). Of the major dialect areas of Breton, all but one (Vannetais) have generally penultimate stress. In these dialects, there is also an epenthesis process, which inserts a vowel in final clusters between a liquid and a following velar (schematically; many details vary from area to area). In Vannetais, however, the stress pattern is one of generally final stress; and there is no such epenthesis rule. In Vannetais, the absence of epenthesis can be related to the fact that it would have the effect of inserting a vowel after the stress, and thus of destroying the final stress pattern.[4] In the dialects of Tréguier, however, and much of Léon, we find penultimate stress, and an epenthesis rule with an important restriction: it only applies in monosyllables. Of course, it is precisely in monosyllables that epenthesis in a final cluster does not destroy a penultimate stress pattern, but rather reinforces it, by converting a word that would otherwise have final stress (for want of a nonfinal syllable) into a word with penultimate stress. In this case, too, the behavior of epenthesis can be related to the surface generalization about stress placement. Notice that here it is not possible to say that epenthesis CONSPIRES with stress placement to require penultimate stress everywhere, since some finally stressed words still exist (monosyllables not subject to epenthesis and some words with contraction of two vowels, as well as a few arbitrary exceptions). Still, the operation of epenthesis is organized so that the rule 'does what it can'.

In addition to a consideration of configurations whose naturalness is motivated on various grounds, the study of naturalness in phonology must also take into account the differences among various types of rules. Assimilation of voicing to a following voiceless stop is the most general form of voicing adjustment, but many other sorts occur. These can be arranged on a rough hierarchy. Nasal assimilation rules are generally regressive, most likely to affect *n*, most likely to assimilate the nasal to the obstruent; but other sorts occur. Thus, many (but not all) languages assimilate *m* as well; some languages assimilate progressively as well as regressively (e.g., Pame; see Gibson, 1956); some languages assimilate an obstruent to the nasal, rather than the other way around (e.g., Gidabal; see Geytenbeek & Geytenbeek, 1971). All of these possibilities are related to the desirability of having adjacent nasal and obstruent homorganic, and the various options can again be arranged into several hierarchically organized dimensions. Such a project should be undertaken for numerous kinds of rules, however, if the notion of 'possible rule in a natural language' is to be given an empirical foundation. An implicit typology of rules, dividing them into a number of different sorts each with its own range of possibilities, is apparent in the "Handbook of American Indian Languages" grammars, as well as in various phonetically motivated studies by European linguists. Indeed, Grammont (1939) is largely devoted to just this project, which needs to be extended in light of the great advances made both in phonetics and in our knowl-

---

[4] Since an important set of rules for quantity and quality of vowels depend on the placement of the stress, the alternative of ordering the stress rule after the epenthesis rule would have much more radical consequences for the structure of the language, since it would result in major changes in the shape of words subject to epenthesis.

edge of the languages of the world in recent years. The development of a more highly articulated theory of phonological rules is also facilitated by clarifying the distinction between phonological, phonetic, and morpho-lexical rules made earlier in this book. Presumably, phonological processes of these different sorts will show other typological differences. Some recent work has been directed toward a closer examination of the role played by universal rules in the structure of language particular processes (e.g., Stampe, 1972), but much more needs to be done in examining empirically the structure of individual processes in a variety of languages.

The matter of evaluation and naturalness, then, is a complex of these (and no doubt other) factors, rather than an engineering problem to be solved by a descriptive formalism. Some processes are in some languages, presumably, because their configurational motivation is so great that it would be unnatural (and 'costly') not to have them. Others are present because they have motivation, even though they are not necessary. Still others are present because of language particular factors not duplicated elsewhere. In each case, the shape taken by a particular process can be examined in terms of the alternatives available: just what sorts of nasal assimilation rules can languages have, and what are their relative likelihoods? If several processes in the same language are related, this is in many cases due not to a direct relation between the rules, but rather to the fact that all of them are explained by the same phonetically desirable configuration or similar factor. The exceptions are cases in which one rule establishes an arbitrary pattern which is so dominant in the language, that other rules are motivated largely by their contribution to establishing or preserving this pattern.

These remarks have been excessively diffuse and unsubstantiated by concrete facts and proposals. The purpose of offering them has been simply to underline the independence of description and explanation in phonology. On the basis of the theoretical framework developed in the first twelve chapters of this book, supplemented by answers to the speculative issues raised in Chapters 13 and 14, the project of description is clear at least in outline. By providing a substantial theory of the issues of explanation raised in this last chapter, however, important progress can be made in phonology, especially in relating it to the results of research in experimental phonetics. It is through such a connection with observable phonomena that phonology can best establish its claims to provide explanatory statements; conversely, experimental phonetics becomes most interesting when its results are related to other, more abstract, aspects of the total system of natural language.

A Set of
Phonetic Features

The features to be described below are essentially those of Chomsky and Halle (1968). Some modifications have been introduced since the appearance of that work, especially in the laryngeal features. Some further modifications are introduced below, though none of any great consequence. Brief articulatory descriptions of the positively characterized term of each opposition are given, except in those cases in which our present knowledge of speech physiology is inadequate. The definitions and indications below are intended as a guide for the reader of this work, rather than as a systematic presentation and defense of controversial points.

I. (Pulmonic) Source Features

1. [±SYLLABIC]: As discussed in Chapter 14, this feature serves to organize the syllable into an initial ([−syllabic]) margin, a ([+syllabic]) peak, and perhaps a final ([−syllabic]) margin. It serves categorically to distinguish vowels from homorganic glides, and sonorant consonants from their corresponding syllabic forms. It is probably the case that nearly any consonant, including stops, can serve as syllable peak in low-level phonetic representation (under conditions of syncope, etc.; see Bell, 1970).

297

2. [±STRESS]:   This feature, whose scope is basically the whole syllable, is put in this class on the basis of our belief that stress is largely a matter of increased expiratory energy, and is associated with the pulmonic mechanism that corresponds to the distribution of energy over the syllable.

II.   Manner Features

These features are associated with individual oral articulations, or segments. They control the degree and manner of the resultant closure and its release.

3. [±SONORANT]:   Sonorant sounds are articulated without sufficient constriction in the supraglottal tract to cause a significant rise in supraglottal pressure. Such an increase in supraglottal pressure, by reducing the pressure drop across the glottis, could have the effect of inhibiting spontaneous vocal-cord vibration. Vowels, glides, nasals, and liquids are [+sonorant]; obstruent consonants are [−sonorant]. The laryngeal glides *h* and ʔ have an unclear status; they have generally been treated as sonorants in this work, although we suspect that they are better described as nonsonorants.

At many points, the feature [±OBSTRUENT] has been employed instead; a sound which is [+obstruent] is the same as one which is [−sonorant], and vice versa. This interchange has no importance, and the two are simply inverse names for the same feature.

4. [±CONSONANTAL]:   Consonantal sounds are made with a radical (i.e., at least as extreme as in fricative consonants) approximation of the speech organs at some point in the mid-sagittal plane of the oral tract. Vowels and glides (including *h* and ʔ) are nonconsonantal; all other sounds are consonantal.

5. [±CONTINUANT]:   Noncontinuant sounds are made with a complete blockage of the oral tract. Stops, affricates, flaps, and nasals (except nasalized glides, fricatives, etc.) are noncontinuant. Spirants, trills, laterals, vowels, and glides (except ʔ) are continuant.

6. [±GRADUAL RELEASE]:   Sounds in which closure is incomplete, or in which the release is delayed during a period of fricative noise, are [+gradual release]. Affricates are thereby distinguished from plain stops. It is not clear whether this feature should be treated as specified at all in segments not involving a complete closure; the best case for such a specification is the fact that affricates and spirants might thereby form a class which is not otherwise easy to express.

7. [±INSTANTANEOUS RELEASE]: Instantaneous release can apply only to complete closures. If a sound is neither gradually released nor instantaneously released, it is unreleased.

8. [±LATERAL]: Lateral sounds are articulated with consonantal closure along the midline of the tongue at some point, but with a side channel for air flow created by lowering one or both sides of the tongue. Lateral sounds are generally made with the tongue blade, but they may be made with the tongue body (i.e., in the velar area), as in Zulu and some dialects of Arabic. They may be either continuant (liquid or spirant) or noncontinuant (affricate). Sounds which are [−continuant, +lateral, −gradual release] are lateral flaps.

9. [±DISTRIBUTED]: Distributed sounds are made with a relatively long constriction. Bilabial sounds are thus distinguished from labiodental; tongue blade from tongue tip; 'soft' palatals and alveopalatals from 'hard'. It is probable that the distinction of 'palatalized' versus 'nonpalatalized' palatals, velars, and uvulars in Northwest Caucasian languages such as Abaza and Ubykh is really a matter of distributed versus nondistributed sounds. There is some question whether all of these distinctions belong under a single head (and indeed whether this feature is a coherent one) but no superior alternatives have been proposed.

III. Features of Oral Articulation

A. LIP FEATURES

10. [±ROUND]: Round sounds are made with rounding and protrusion (usually) of the lips caused primarily by constriction of the orbicularis oris muscle. They may be either vowels or consonants.

11. [±LABIAL]: Labial sounds are produced by approximating the lower lip to either the upper lip or the upper teeth. The muscles involved are primarily the mentalis and the levator and depressor muscles of the lips, though some portions of the orbicularis oris are probably also involved. Some protrusion may result, as well as approximation. Basic labial consonants (which may or may not in addition be [+round]), as well as one closure of labiovelar ($\widehat{kp}$) and labialdental ($\widehat{pt}$) double stops are articulated by means of this mechanism. Vowels such as *u* are [+labial] rather than [+round] in some languages (e.g., Japanese). Swedish *u* and *ü* are probably both [+round], with *ü* being in addition [+labial] (a similar proposal is made by Fant in several publications).

Rounded vowels and glides in many languages are, however, [−labial]. Although these two features are quite distinct linguistically and physiologically, they are also closely interrelated in ways that remain to be explicated.

B. TONGUE FEATURES

1. TONGUE BLADE

12. [±CORONAL]: Coronal consonants are made with the blade of the tongue elevated from the neutral position for speech. Articulations from the interdental through the alveopalatal regions can be made in this way, involving either apical or laminal contact. Coronal vowels are retroflex.

13. [±ANTERIOR]: Anterior sounds are made with primary constrictions forward of the alveopalatal region. Labial, interdental, dental, and alveolar articulations are thus anterior; alveopalatal, retroflex (usually), palatal, velar, uvular, and pharyngeal articulations are [−anterior]. In double stops, either the front (labial) or back (alveopalatal or velar) closure can be designated as primary by this feature. Identical phonetic articulations are thus phonologically ambiguous. It is apparent that this feature does not really describe the tongue blade exclusively, but it is placed here since its principal use is to distinguish dental from alveopalatal articulations.

2. TONGUE BODY FEATURES

14. [±HIGH]: High sounds are made with the tongue body raised from the neutral position for speech. These include high vowels and glides, palatal, alveopalatal, velar, palatalized, and velarized consonants.

15. [±LOW]: Low sounds are made with the tongue body lowered from the neutral position for speech. These are primarily low vowels; we do not regard pharyngeal articulations as distinctively [+low], as do Chomsky and Halle (1968). If it were not for the fact that at least three degrees of height must be distinguished in front vowels in many languages, this feature could probably be dispensed with in favor of the tongue root features below.

16. [±BACK]: Back sounds are made with the tongue body retracted (and slightly raised) from the neutral position for speech. These include velar and uvular consonants, as well as velarized consonants and back vowels and glides.

17. [±VELAR SUCTION]: This feature is possible only if a [+high] closure and some forward closure (labial, dental, or alveopalatal) are both present. It refers to a retracting gesture of the tongue body, which creates a negative pressure between the two closures. The result is a click (if the forward closure is [+coronal]), or one of the possible air-stream articulations of a labiovelar stop.

18. [±SECONDARY GRADUAL RELEASE]: This feature refers to the manner in which the velar closure of a sound with velar suction is released. It is independent of the manner of release of the primary closure.

3. TONGUE ROOT FEATURES

19. [±ADVANCED TONGUE ROOT] and 20. [±RETRACTED TONGUE ROOT]: These two features describe the position of the tongue root, and thereby, the width of the pharynx. Retracted tongue root (narrow pharynx) is characteristic of pharyngeal and pharyngealized sounds. Pharyngeal width is an inadequately studied aspect of articulation, but these features are undoubtedly responsible for many of the phenomena subsumed under tenseness and laxness in traditional terms. Some discussion based on cineradiographic study can be found in Perkell (1972), but more research is needed before the status and function of these features will be clear.

IV. Nasopharyngeal Opening Feature

21. [±NASAL]: Nasal sounds are made with lowered velum, and consequent open passage through the nose. These include the usual nasal sonorants, nasalized glides, spirants and vowels, and prenasalized and postnasalized stops (the latter found in South American and in some Malayo-Polynesian and New Caledonian languages). The functioning of this feature in these classes of sounds is discussed in Chapter 14.

V. Laryngeal Features

22. [±SPREAD GLOTTIS]: Spreading or widening the glottal opening inhibits vocal cord vibration and increases airflow. In consonants, this is associated with voicelessness and especially with aspiration, whose

degree varies with the tension of the vocal cords. Voiceless and breathy voiced vowels are characterized by spread glottis, as are *h* and other voiceless glides. Voiced *h* is the glide whose laryngeal position corresponds to a voiced aspirate stop: [+spread glottis, +slack vocal cords].

23. [±CONSTRICTED GLOTTIS]:   An extreme degree of constriction or narrowing of the glottal opening results in glottalized or laryngealized sounds. In consonants, these are the ejective, implosive, and laryngealized types; in vowels, the creaky voiced type and the glottalized vowels associated with certain tonal accents in Vietnamese, Acoma, and Danish.

24. [±STIFF VOCAL CORDS]:   By stiffening the vocal cords, their resistance to vibration is increased. As an incidental effect of this gesture, a spread glottis is spread further open. In vowels, stiffness of the vocal cords is associated with raised pitch. In consonants, stiffness is associated with ejective varieties of sounds made with constricted glottis; heavily aspirated varieties of sounds made with spread glottis; and plain voiceless consonants made with moderate (low-turbulence) delay between release of obstruction and the onset of voicing in the following sound.

25. [±SLACK VOCAL CORDS]:   Slackening the vocal cords enhances their ability to maintain vibration under conditions which are otherwise somewhat unfavorable to voicing. With spread glottis, this results in voicing during the period of aspiration noise (as well, perhaps, as during the period of stop closure); with neutrally positioned glottis, this allows vibration to occur under the low airflow conditions of a stop closure.

VI. Ad Hoc Cover Features

Many other features occur in rules from one or another language in this book. Their interpretation in terms of the above is generally clear, except in a few cases in which the available phonetic data do not allow us to determine an interpretation. The feature [*n*LONG] may well be present in phonetic representations, but does not seem ever to adopt distinct categorial values. Where [+long] appears in rules, this is to be interpreted either as the distinction between one mora length and two, or as an abbreviation for a numeric value about which details are not available. Phonological length is thus treated as the distinction between two adjacent identical moras of oral articulation, and phonetic length (sometimes) as such gemination, sometimes varying specifications of [*n*long], and sometimes as a combination of the two.

The feature [±VOICE] occurs in a large number of rules, and its interpretation varies from language to language. It provides a parameter distinguishing 'more voiced' from 'less voiced' sounds in any given language. In some cases this is implemented as the distinction between slack vocal cords and neutral or stiff vocal cords, or as neutral vocal cords versus stiff vocal cords; in other cases as the distinction between neutral or constricted glottis and spread glottis, or between constricted and neutral glottis. Thus, the voiceless series of one language may be essentially the same as the voiced series of another. Generally some combination of glottal width and vocal-cord stiffness is involved, and some configurations are certainly typical of voiced sounds while others are typical of voiceless sounds. By 'voice', is meant a relative rather than an absolute parameter, and it is not possible to tell what interpretation should be given it in any particular case in the absence of detailed phonetic descriptions and/or inferential evidence from the operation of phonological rules.

The feature [±STRIDENT] is based on an acoustic distinction between sounds with high degrees of turbulence generated at their principal constriction and sounds without such high turbulence. It is generally recodable in terms of [±gradual release] and [±distributed].

With the exception of [*n*long], features of the sort discussed in this section (i.e., features not appearing on the preceding numbered list) should not be interpreted as having any systematic status. In a correct phonetic description, they would be replaced by combinations of features from the above list. Their use is simply to clarify exposition by removing some irrelevant details from considerations. As such, they have the same status as phonetic symbols for segments, which should be interpreted as abbreviations for complexes of features.

References

ANDERSEN, HENNING (1969). The phonological status of the Russian labial fricatives. *Journal of Linguistics* **5**, 121–128.

ANDERSEN, HENNING (1972). Diphthongization. *Language* **48**, 11–50.

ANDERSON, STEPHEN R. (1968). The Faroese vowel system and the Faroese *Verschärfung*. *MIT Quarterly Progress Report* **90**, 228–240.

ANDERSON, STEPHEN R. (1969a). An outline of the phonology of Modern Icelandic vowels. *Foundations of Language* **5**, 53–72.

ANDERSON, STEPHEN R. (1969b). *West Scandinavian vowel systems and the ordering of phonological rules.* Doctoral dissertation, Cambridge, Massachusetts: Massachusetts Institute of Technology.

ANDERSON, STEPHEN R. (1970). On Grassmann's law in Sanskrit. *Linguistic Inquiry* **1**, 387–396.

ANDERSON, STEPHEN R. (1972a). On nasalization in Sundanese. *Linguistic Inquiry* **3**, 253–268.

ANDERSON, STEPHEN R. (1972b). Icelandic *U*-Umlaut and breaking in a generative grammar. In E. Firchow, K. Grimstad, N. Hasselmo, & W. O'Neil (Eds.), *Studies for Einar Haugen.* The Hague: Mouton.

ANDERSON, STEPHEN R. (1972c). *U*-Umlaut and skaldic verse. In S. Anderson & P. Kiparsky (Eds.), *A Festschrift for Morris Halle.* New York: Holt, Rinehart, & Winston.

ANDERSON, STEPHEN R. (1972d). The vowel system of Faroese and the Faroese *Verschärfung*. In M. Brame (Ed.), *Contributions to generative phonology.* Austin: University of Texas Press.

ANDERSON, STEPHEN R. (1973). Remarks on the phonology of English inflection. *Language and Literature* **I**, 4: 33–52.

ANDERSON, STEPHEN R., & WAYLES BROWNE (1973). On keeping exchange rules in Czech. *Papers in Linguistics* **VI**, 4.

304

BACH, EMMON (1968). Two proposals concerning the simplicity metric in phonology. *Glossa* **2**, 128–149.

BAILEY, T. GRAHAME (1920). *Linguistic studies from the Himalayas.* London: Royal Asiatic Society.

BELL, ALAN (1970). Syllabic consonants. *Stanford University Working Papers in Language Universals,* **4**.

BEVER, THOMAS (1967). *Leonard Bloomfield and the phonology of the Menomini language.* Doctoral dissertation, Cambridge, Massachusetts: Massachusetts Institute of Technology.

BLOCH, BERNARD (1941). Phonemic overlapping. Reprinted in M. Joos (Ed.) *Readings in linguistics.* New York: American Council of Learned Societies.

BLOOMFIELD, LEONARD (1922). Reprinted in C. Hockett (Ed.), *A Leonard Bloomfield anthology.* Bloomington: University of Indiana Press. (A review of Edward Sapir, *Language.*)

BLOOMFIELD, LEONARD (1933). *Language.* New York: Holt, Rinehart, & Winston.

BLOOMFIELD, LEONARD (1939). Menomini morphophonemics. *Travaux du cercle linguistique de Prague* **8**, 105–115.

BLOOMFIELD, LEONARD (1962). *The Menomini language.* New Haven, Connecticut: Yale University Press.

BOAS, FRANZ (1911). Tsimshian. In F. Boas (Ed.), *Handbook of American Indian Languages. Bulletin of the Bureau of American Ethnology* **40**(1).

BOAS, FRANZ, & ELLA DELORIA (1939). Dakota grammar. *Memoir XXIII-2 of the National Academy of Sciences.*

BRAME, MICHAEL D. (1970). *Arabic phonology: implications for phonological theory and general Semitic.* Doctoral dissertation, Cambridge, Massachusetts: Massachusetts Institute of Technology.

BRAME, MICHAEL D., & ELAINE PHELPS (1973). On local ordering of rules in Sanskrit. *Linguistic Inquiry* **4**, 387–400.

BRESNAN, JOAN (1971). Sentence stress and syntactic transformations. *Language* **47**, 257–281.

BROWNE, E. WAYLES III (1970). The Slovak rhythmic law and phonological theory. *Slavica Slovaca* **5**, 253–256.

BROWNE, E. WAYLES, III (1972). How to apply phonological rules. *MIT Quarterly Progress Report* **105**, 143–146.

BRUNNER, KARL (1963). *An outline of Middle English grammar.* Cambridge, Massachusetts: Harvard University Press.

BUCK, CARL D. (1904). *A grammar of Oscan and Umbrian.* Boston: Ginn. & Co.

CALLOW, J. C. (1962). *The Apinayé language.* Doctoral dissertation, University of London.

CALLOW, J. C. (1965). Kasem nominals — A study in analyses. *Journal of West African Languages* **2**, 29–36.

CALLOW, J. C. (1968). A hierarchical study of nominalization in Kasem. *Journal of Linguistics* **4**, 33–46.

CHAFE, WALLACE (1968). The ordering of phonological rules. *International Journal of American Linguistics* **34**, 115–136.

CHAPMAN, KENNETH (1962). *Icelandic-Norwegian linguistic relationships. Norsk tidskrift for sprogvidenskap* Suppl. Blind **VII.**

CHENG, CHIN-CHUAN (1971). A synchronic phonology of Mandarin Chinese. *POLA University of California at Berkeley Report 14.*

CHOMSKY, NOAM (1964). *Current issues in linguistic theory.* The Hague: Mouton.

CHOMSKY, NOAM (1967). Some general properties of phonological rules. *Language* **43**, 102–128.

CHOMSKY, NOAM, & MORRIS HALLE (1965). Some controversial questions in phonological theory. *Journal of Linguistics* **1**, 97–138.

CHOMSKY, NOAM, & MORRIS HALLE (1968). *The sound pattern of English.* New York: Harper & Row.

CHOMSKY, NOAM, MORRIS HALLE, & FRED LUKOFF (1956). On accent and juncture in English. In M. Halle, H. Lunt, & H. MacLean (Eds.), *For Roman Jakobson.* The Hague: Mouton.

DELL, FRANÇOIS (1970). *Les règles phonologiques tardives et la morphologie dérivationelle du francais.* Doctoral dissertation, Cambridge, Massachusetts: Massachusetts Institute of Technology.

DIXON, R. M. W. (1970). Olgolo syllable structure and what they are doing about it. *Linguistic Inquiry* **1**, 273–276.

DOBSON, E. J. (1962). Middle English lengthening in open syllables. *Transactions of the Philological Society* **1962**, 124–148.

EDMONDSON, T., & J. T. BENDOR-SAMUEL (1966). Tone patterns of Etung. *Journal of African Languages* **5**, 1–6.

EINARSSON, STEFAN (1945). *Icelandic.* Baltimore: Johns Hopkins Press.

ELCOCK, W. D. (1960). *The Romance languages.* London: Faber & Faber.

FABRA, P. (1912). *Grammatica de la llengua Catalana.* Barcelona: Imprenta y libreria l'Avenc.

FABRA, P. (1914). Els mots atons en el parler de Barcelona. *Bulletí de Dialectología Catalana* **I**, 7–17.

FALC'HUN, FRANÇOIS (1951). *Le systeme consonantique du breton.* Rennes: Plihon.

FIDELHOLTZ, JAMES L. (1971). On the indeterminacy of the representation of vowel length. *Papers in Linguistics* **4**, 577–594.

FLEURIOT, LEON (1964). *Le vieux breton: éléments d'une grammaire.* Paris: Klincksieck.

FOSTER, JOSEPH (1968). On vowel harmony and concomitant phenomena is Osman Turkish. Unpublished manuscript, University of Illinois.

FROMKIN, VICTORIA A. (1971). The non-anomalous nature of anomalous utterances. *Language* **47**, 27–52.

FROMKIN, VICTORIA A. (1972). Tone features and tone rules. *UCLA Studies in African Linguistics,* March 1972.

FROMM, H., & M. SADENIEMI (1956). *Finnisches Elementarbuch I: Grammatik.* Heidelberg: Carl Winter.

GEYTENBEEK, B., & H. GEYTENBEEK (1971). *Gidabal grammar and dictionary.* Canberra: Australian Institute of Aboriginal Studies.

GIBSON, LORNA F. (1956). Pame (Otomí) phonemics and morphophonemics. *International Journal of American Linguistics* **22**, 242–265.

GODDARD, R. H. IVES, III (1972). *W*-Umlaut in Menomini. Paper read at meeting of Harvard University Linguistics Group.

GRAMMONT, MAURICE (1939). *Traite de phonétique.* Paris: Delagrave.

GREGERSEN, EDGAR (1972). Consonant polarity in Nilotic. Paper presented at Third Annual Conference on African Linguistics, Indiana University.

GUDSCHINSKY, SARAH, HAROLD POPOVITCH, & FRANCES POPVITCH (1970). Native reaction and phonetic similarity in Maxakalí phonology. *Language* **46**, 77–88.

GUTENBRUNNER, SIEGFRIED (1951). *Historische Laut- und Formenlehre des Islandischen.* Heidelberg: Carl Winter.

HALLBERG, STAFFAN (1972). Ordering relations in the phonology of Swedish adjectives. *Gothenburg papers in Theoretical Linguistics* **13.**

HALLE, MORRIS (1957). On the phonetic rules of Russian. Paper Read at LSA Annual Meeting, Chicago.

HALLE, MORRIS (1958). On the bases of phonology. Reprinted in J. Fodor & J. Katz (Eds.), *The structure of language*. Englewood Cliffs, New Jersey: Prentice-Hall.

HALLE, MORRIS (1959). *The sound pattern of Russian*. The Hague: Mouton.

HALLE, MORRIS (1962). Phonology in generative grammar. *Word* **18,** 54–72.

HALLE, MORRIS (1971a). Theoretical issues in phonology in the 1970's. Paper read at Seventh International Congress of Phonetic Sciences, Montreal.

HALLE, MORRIS (1971b). On meter and prosody. In Beirwisch & Heidolph (Eds.), *Progress in linguistics*. The Hague: Mouton.

HALLE, MORRIS (1971c). Remarks on Slavic accentology. *Linguistic Inquiry* **2,** 1–19.

HALLE, MORRIS (1973). The accentuation of Russian words. *Language* **49,** 312–348.

HALLE, MORRIS, & S. JAY KEYSER (1971). *The evolution of English stress*. New York: Harper & Row.

HALLE, MORRIS, & KENNETH STEVENS (1962). Speech recognition: a model and a program for research. *IRE Transactions on Information Theory* **IT8,** 155–159.

HALLE, MORRIS, & KENNETH STEVENS (1971). A note on laryngeal features. *MIT Quarterly Progress Report* **101,** 198–213.

HALLE, MORRIS, & VALDIS J. ZEPS (1966). A survey of Latvian morphophonemics. *MIT Quarterly Progress Report* **83,** 105–113.

HAMP, ERIC (1951). The morphophonemics of the Keltic mutations. *Language* **27,** 230–247.

HARRIS, JAMES W. (1969). *Spanish phonology*. Cambridge, Massachusetts: MIT Press.

HARRIS, JAMES W. (1972). On the ordering of certain phonological rules in Spanish. In S. Anderson & P. Kiparsky (Eds.), *A Festschrift for Morris Halle*. New York: Holt, Rinehart, & Winston.

HARRIS, ZELLIG (1951). Review of *Selected writings of Edward Sapir*. *Language* **27,** 288–333.

HAUDRICOURT, A. G. (1961). Bipartition et tripartition dans les systèmes des tons. *Bulletin de la Société Linguistique de Paris* **56,** 163–180.

HAUGEN, EINAR (1956). Syllabification in Kutenai. *Language* **22,** 196–201.

HOCKETT, CHARLES F. (1970). *A Leonard Bloomfield anthology*. Bloomington: Indiana University Press.

HOOPER, JOAN B. (1972). The syllable in phonological theory. *Language* **48,** 524–540.

HOUSEHOLDER, FRED W. (1965). On some recent claims in phonological theory. *Journal of Linguistics* **1,** 13–34.

HOWARD, IRWIN (1969). Kasem nominals revisited. *University of Hawaii Working Papers in Linguistics* **1**(10), 63–99.

HOWARD, IRWIN (1970). Kasem nominals and the ordering of phonological rules. *University of Hawaii Working Papers in Linguistics* **2**(3), 113–129.

HOWARD, IRWIN (1972). *A directional theory of rule application in phonology*. Doctoral dissertation, Cambridge, Massachusetts: Massachusetts Institute of Technology.

ISAČENKO, ALEXANDER V. (1970). East Slavic morphophonemics and the treatment of the jers in Russian: A revision of Havlík's law. *International Journal of Slavic Linguistics and Poetics* **13,** 73–124.

JACKSON, KENNETH H. (1961). The phonology of the Breton dialect of Plougrescant. *Études Celtiques* **9,** 327–404.

JACKSON, KENNETH H. (1967). *A historical phonology of Breton*. Dublin: Dublin Institute of Advanced Studies.

JAKOBSON, ROMAN (1971). The Kazan' school of Polish linguistics and its place in the international development of phonology (translation of Polish original). In R. Jakobson, *Selected writings*. Vol. II. The Hague: Mouton.

JAKOBSON, ROMAN, GUNNAR FANT, & MORRIS HALLE (1952). *Preliminaries to speech analysis*. Cambridge, Massachusetts: MIT Press.

JAKOBSON, ROMAN, & MORRIS HALLE (1956). *Fundamentals of language*. The Hague: Mouton.

JOHNSON, C. DOUGLAS (1970). *Formal aspects of phonological description. POLA University of California at Berkeley, Report 11*.

KARTTUNEN, FRANCES (1970). *Problems in Finnish phonology*. Doctoral dissertation, Bloomington: Indiana University.

KELLER, KATHRYN (1959). The phonemes of Chontal (Mayan). *International Journal of American Linguistics, 25* 44–53.

KENNARD, EDWARD (1936). Mandan Grammar. *International Journal of American Linguistics 9,* 1–43.

KENSTOWICZ, MICHAEL (1970). On the notation of vowel length in Lithuanian. *Papers in Linguistics 3,* 73–113.

KENSTOWICZ, MICHAEL, & CHARLES KISSEBERTH (1972). The multiple application problem in phonology. Unpublished manuscript, Bloomington: University of Illinois.

KEYSER, S. JAY (1963). Review of H. Kurath & R. McDavid, *The pronunciation of English in the Atlantic states. Language 39,* 303–316.

KIM, CHIN-WU (1970). A theory of aspiration. *Phonetica 21,* 107–116.

KIPARSKY, PAUL (1968a). Linguistic universals and linguistic change. In E. Bach & R. Harms (Eds.), *Universals in linguistic theory*. New York: Holt, Rinehart, & Winston.

KIPARSKY, PAUL (1968b). How abstract is phonology? Unpublished manuscript, Cambridge, Massachusetts: Massachusetts Institute of Technology.

KIPARSKY, PAUL (1971a). Metrics and morphophonemics in the Rigveda. In M. Brame (Ed.), *Contributions to generative phonology*. Austin: University of Texas Press.

KIPARSKY, PAUL (1971b). Historical linguistics. In W. Dingwall (Ed.), *A survey of linguistic science*. College Park, Maryland: University of Maryland Press.

KIPARSKY, PAUL (1972). 'Elsewhere' in phonology. In S. Anderson & P. Kiparsky (Eds.), *A Festschrift for Morris Halle*. New York: Holt, Rinehart, & Winston.

KIPARSKY, PAUL (1973). Phonological representations. In O. Fujimura (Ed.), *Three dimensions of linguistic theory*. Tokyo: TEC Co., Ltd.

KIPARSKY, PAUL, & M. JOSHI (1971). On Pāṇini's morphophonemic principles. Unpublished manuscript, Cambridge, Massachusetts: Massachusetts Institute of Technology.

KIPARSKY, VALENTIN (1963). *Russische historische Grammatik I*. Heidelberg: Carl Winter.

KISSEBERTH, CHARLES (1970a). On the functional unity of phonological rules. *Linguistic Inquiry 1,* 290–306.

KISSEBERTH, CHARLES (1970b). The Tunica stress conspiracy. Unpublished manuscript, Urbana: University of Illinois.

KISSEBERTH, CHARLES (1971). A global rule in Klamath phonology. To appear in B. Kachru (Ed.), *Papers in linguistics in honor of Henry and Renée Kahane*. Edmonton, Alberta: Linguistic Research.

KISSEBERTH, CHARLES (1972a). Cyclical rules in Klamath phonology. *Linguistic Inquiry 3,* 3–33.

KISSEBERTH, CHARLES (1972b). An argument against the simultaneous application of phonological rules. *Linguistic Inquiry* **3**, 393–396.

KISSEBERTH, CHARLES, & M. J. KENSTOWICZ (1971). Unmarked bleeding orders. *University of Illinois Studies in the linguistic sciences* (1).

KOUTSOUDAS, ANDREAS, G. SANDERS, & C. NOLL (1971). On the application of phonological rules. Unpublished manuscript, Bloomington: Indiana University.

KOZHEVNIKOV, V., & L. CHISTOVICH (1965). *Speech: articulation and perception*. Joint publications research service **30**, 5443.

KRAUSS, MICHAEL E. (1971). St. Lawrence Island Eskimo phonology. Paper read at AAA Meeting.

KRAUSS, MICHAEL E, E. REED, & O. MIYAOKA (1970). Yupik Eskimo teaching grammar. Unpublished manuscript, University of Alaska.

LABOV, WILLIAM (1972). The uses of the present to explain the past. Paper read at XIth International Congress of Linguists, Bologna.

LADEFOGED, PETER (1967). *Three areas of experimental phonetics*. London and New York: Oxford University Press.

LADEFOGED, PETER (1968). *A phonetic Study of West African Languages*. London and New York: Cambridge University Press.

LADEFOGED, PETER (1972). *Preliminaries to linguistic phonetics*. Chicago: University of Chicago Press.

LANGACKER, RONALD (1969). Mirror-image rules II: Lexicon and phonology. *Language* **45**, 844–862.

LANGENDOEN, D. TERENCE (1968). *The London school of linguistics*. Cambridge, Massachusetts: MIT Press.

LEBEN, WILLIAM R. (1971). Suprasegmental and segmental representation of tone. *UCLA Studies in African linguistics Suppl. 2*.

LEES, ROBERT B. (1961). *The phonology of Modern Standard Turkish*. The Hague: Mouton.

LEES, ROBERT B. (1967). Turkish harmony and phonological description of assimilation. *Turk dili avastırmaları yilligi-belletin 1966' dan ayrıbasım*. Ankara: Ankara universitesi basimevi.

LEHISTE, ILSE (1970). *Suprasegmentals*. Cambridge, Massachusetts: MIT Press.

LEWIS, D. (1967). *Turkish Grammar*. London and New York: Oxford University Press.

LIBERMAN, A. M., F. COOPER, K. HARRIS, AND P. MACNEILAGE (1963). A motor theory of speech perception. Paper D3 in *Proceedings of the Speech Communication Seminar, Stockholm, 1962* **II**.

LIBERMAN, A. M., F. COOPER, D. SHANKWEILER, AND M. STUDDERT-KENNEDY (1967). Perception of the speech code. *Psychological Review* **74**, 431–461.

LIGHTNER, THEODORE (1965a). *The segmental phonology of Modern Standard Russian*. Doctoral dissertation, Cambridge, Massachusetts: Massachusetts Institute of Technology.

LIGHTNER, THEODORE (1965b). On the description of vowel and consonant harmony. *Word* **21**, 244–250.

LIGHTNER, THEODORE (1968). On the use of minor rules in Russian phonology. *Journal of Linguistics* **4**, 69–72.

LIGHTNER, THEODORE (1970). On Swadesh and Voegelin's 'A problem in phonological alternation'. *Papers in Linguistics* **3**, 201–220.

LINNELL, P., B. SVENSSON, & S. ÖHMAN (1971). *Ljudstruktur: Inledning till fonologin och sardragsteorin*. Uppsala: Gleerups.

LISKER, LEIGH, & ARTHUR ABRAMSON (1971). Distinctive features and laryngeal control. *Language* **47**, 767–785.

LUICK, K. (1914–1921). *Historische Grammatik der englischen Sprache*. (republished) Cambridge, Massachusetts: Harvard University Press.

LUNT, HORACE (1972). Nasalization in Guaraní. In S. Anderson & P. Kiparsky (Eds.), *A Festschrift for Morris Halle*. New York: Holt, Rinehart, & Winston.

MATHEWS, PETER H. (1972). *Inflectional morphology*. London and New York: Cambridge University Press.

MCCAWLEY, JAMES D. (1964). Morphophonemics of the Finnish noun. Unpublished manuscript, Cambridge, Massachusetts: Massachusetts Institute of Technology.

MCCAWLEY, JAMES D. (1966). Revised version of the Finnish rules. Unpublished manuscript, Chicago: University of Chicago.

MCCAWLEY, JAMES D. (1967a). Further revisions of the Finnish rules. Unpublished manuscript, Chicago: University of Chicago.

MCCAWLEY, JAMES D. (1967b). Sapir's phonologic representation. *International Journal of American Linguistics* **33**, 106–111.

MCCAWLEY, JAMES D. (1970a). On the role of notation in generative phonology. Paper read at Conference on Formalization in Linguistics, Paris.

MCCAWLEY, JAMES D. (1970b). A note on tone in Tiv conjugation. *UCLA Studies in African Linguistics* **I**(2).

MILLER, WICK R. (1965). *Acoma grammar and texts*. (Univ. of California Publications in Linguistics Number 40.) Berkeley: University of California Press.

MITCHELL, T. F. (1957). Long consonants in phonology and phonetics. In *Studies in linguistic analysis* (special volume, Philological society). Oxford: Basil Blackwell.

MOORE, SAMUEL (1951). Historical outline of English sounds and inflections. Ann Arbor, Michigan: George Wahr.

NEBEL, P. A. (1948). *Dinka grammar*. Verona: Missioni africane.

NEWTON, BRIAN (1971a). Ordering paradoxes in phonology. *Journal of Linguistics* **7**, 31–53.

NEWTON, BRIAN (1971b). Modern Greek post-consonantal yod. *Lingua* **26**, 132–170.

OHALA, JOHN (1971). The role of physiological and acoustic models in explaining the direction of sound change. *POLA University of California at Berkeley Report 15* 25–40.

ÖHMAN, SVEN (1966a). Coarticulation in VCV utterances: Spectrographic measurements. *Journal of the Acoustic Society of America* **39**, 151–168.

ÖHMAN, SVEN (1966b). Word and sentence intonation: a quantitative model. *Quarterly progress report of the Speech Technology Laboratory, Stockholm*, **2–3**/1967, 20–54.

PALACAS, ARTHUR (1971). Simultaneous vs. iterative rules in phonology. Paper presented at LSA Annual Meeting, St. Louis, Missouri.

PERKELL, JOSEPH (1972). Physiology of speech production: A preliminary study of two suggested revisions of the features specifying vowels. *MIT Quarterly Progress Report* **102**, 123–137.

PIKE, KENNETH (1943). *Phonetics*. Ann Arbor, Michigan: University of Michigan Press.

PIKE, KENNETH (1947). Grammatical prerequisites to phonemic analysis. *Word* **3**, 155–172.

PIKE, KENNETH (1952). More on grammatical prerequisites. *Word* **8**, 106–121.

POPPE, NICHOLAS (1965). *Introduction to Altaic linguistics*. Wiesbaden: Otto Harrassowitz.

POSTAL, PAUL M. (1964). Boas and the development of phonology: Comments based on Iroquoian. *International Journal of American Linguistics* **30**, 269–280.

POSTAL, PAUL M. (1968). *Aspects of phonological theory.* New York: Harper & Row.

POSTAL, PAUL M. (1964). Mohawk vowel doubling. *International Journal of American Linguistics* **35**, 291–298.

PRITSAK, OMELJAN (1959). Das Neuuighurische. In J. Deny, K. Grønbech, H. Scheel, & Z. Togan (Eds.), *Philologiae turcicae fundamenta.* Wiesbaden: Steiner Verlag.

PUHVEL, JAAN (1971). Bartholomae's law in Hittite. *Zeitschrift für Vergleichende Sprachforschung* **86**, 11–15.

RARDIN, ROBERT (1970). A note on Finnish vowel harmony. *MIT Quarterly Progress Report* **94**, 226–231.

RIGSBY, BRUCE (1967). Tsimshian comparative vocabularies with notes on Nass-Gitksan systematic phonology. Unpublished manuscript, Albuquerque: University of New Mexico.

RISCHEL, JØRGEN (1972). Ever again on West Greenlandic gemination. Unpublished manuscript, Copenhagen: University of Copenhagen.

ROBERTSON, JOHN (1970). Some phonological rules in a French dialect of the Vendée. Unpublished manuscript, Cambridge, Massachusetts: Harvard University.

ROBINS, R. H. (1953a). The phonology of the nasalized verb forms in Sundanese. *Bulletin of the school of Oriental and African Studies* **15**, 138–145.

ROBINS, R. H. (1953b). Formal divisions in Sundanese. *Transactions of the Philological Society* **(1953)**, 125–132.

ROBINS, R. H. (1957). Vowel nasality in Sundanese: A phonological and grammatical study. In *Studies in linguistic analysis* (special volume, Philological society). Oxford: Basil Blackwell.

ROBINS, R. H. (1959). Nominal and verbal derivation in Sundanese. *Lingua* **8**, 337–369.

ROE, HARRY (1965). *Verschärfung in Faroese.* Doctoral dissertation, Cambridge, Massachusetts: Harvard University.

ROSS, JOHN R. (1969). A reanalysis of English word stress. In M. Brame (Ed.), *Contributions to generative phonology.* Austin: University of Texas Press.

SALSER, J. K., JR. (1971). Cubeo phonemics. *Linguistics* **75**, 74–79.

SAPIR, EDWARD (1922). The Takelma language of Southwestern Oregon. In F. Boas (Ed.), *Handbook of American Indian Languages (Bulletin of the Bureau of American Ethnology* **40**, II).

SAPIR, EDWARD (1925). Sound patterns in language. *Language* **1**, 37–51.

SAPIR, EDWARD (1930). Southern Paiute, a Shoshonean language. *Proceedings of the American Academy of Arts and Sciences* **65**, Nos. 1–3.

SAPIR, EDWARD (1949). The psychological reality of phonemes (transl. of French original). In *Selected writings of Edward Sapir.* Berkeley: University of California Press.

SAUSSURE, FERDINAND DE (1916). *Cours de linguistique générale.* Paris: Payot.

SAUVAGEOT, A. (1949). *Esquisse de la langue finnoise.* Paris: Klincksieck.

SHIBATANI, M. (1972). The phonological representation of English inflectional endings. *Glossa,* **6** 117–127.

SOMMER, BRUCE A. (1970). An Australian language without CV syllables. *International Journal of American Linguistics* **36**, 57–58.

STAAL, J. FRITS (1968). The ordering of rules in Pāṇini's grammar. Paper read at Annual Meeting of LSA, New York.

STAMPE, DAVID (1972). How I spent my summer vacation. Doctoral dissertation, Chicago: University of Chicago.

STANLEY, RICHARD (1967). Redundancy rules in phonology. *Language* **43**, 393–436.

STANLEY, RICHARD (1972). Boundary markers in phonology. In S. Anderson & P. Kiparsky (Eds.), *A Festschrift for Morris Halle.* New York: Holt, Rinehart, & Winston.

STEVENS, KENNETH N., & ARTHUR HOUSE (1970). Speech perception. In J. Tobias & E. Schubert (Eds.), *Foundations of modern auditory theory.* New York: Academic Press.

SWADESH, MARY HAAS, & MORRIS SWADESH (1932). A visit to the other world, a Nitinat text. *International Journal of American Linguistics* **7**, 195–208.

SWADESH, MORRIS (1937). The phonemic interpretation of long consonants. *Language* **13**, 1–10.

SWADESH, MORRIS, & C. F. VOEGELIN (1939). A problem in phonological alternation. *Language* **15**, 1–10.

SWIFT, LLOYD B. (1963). *A reference grammar of Modern Turkish.* The Hague: Mouton.

TAYLOR, DOUGLAS (1955). Phonemes of the Hopkins (British Honduras) dialect of Island Carib. *International Journal of American Linguistics* **21**, 242–265.

THOMAS, LINDA K. (1971). The pros and cons of local ordering. Paper read at Second Annual Meeting of Northeast Linguistic Society.

THURNEYSEN, RUDOLPH (1961). *A grammar of Old Irish.* Dublin: Dublin Institute of Advanced Studies.

TRUBETZKOY, N. S. (1939). Grundzüge der phonologie. *Travaux du cercle linguistique de Prague* **7**.

TRYON, DARRELL T. (1970). *Conversational Tahitian.* Berkeley and Los Angeles: University of California Press.

TWADDELL, W. F. (1935). *On defining the phoneme. Language Monogr.* 16.

ULTAN, RUSSELL (1970). Some sources of consonant gradation. *Stanford University Working Papers in Language Universals,* No. 2.

UNDERHILL, ROBERT (1971). Noun bases in two Eskimo dialects: A study in comparative morphophonemics. Unpublished manuscript, Cambridge, Massachusetts: Harvard University.

VENNEMANN, THEO (1971). Natural generative phonology. Paper Read at LSA Annual Meeting, St. Louis.

VERGUIN, J. (1955). L'accentuation en malagache-merina et en malais. *Orbis* **4**, 522–528.

VOEGELIN, C. F. (1935). Tübatulabal grammar. *University of California Publications in Archeology, Anthropology, and Ethnology* **34**(2), i–viii, 55–159.

VOGT, ERIC (1970). *Topics in Catalan phonology.* Unpublished BA essay, Cambridge, Massachusetts: Harvard University.

VOGT, HANS (1963). *Dictionnaire de la langue Oubykh.* Oslo: Universitetsforlaget.

WACKERNAGEL, JAKOB (ALBERT DEBRUNNER, & LOUIS RENOU) (1957). *Altindische Grammatik,* band I. Göttingen: Vandenhoeck & Ruprecht.

WANG, WILLIAM S.-Y. (1967). The phonological features of tone. *International Journal of American Linguistics* **33**, 93–105.

WHITNEY, WILLIAM D. (1889). *Sanskrit grammar* (republished 1964). Cambridge, Massachusetts: Harvard University Press.

WIESEMANN, URSULA (1972). *Die phonologische und grammatische Struktur der Kaingang-Sprache.* The Hague: Mouton.

WOLFE, PATRICIA (1970). Some theoretical questions on the historical English vowel shift. *Papers in Linguistics* **3**, 221–236.

WOO, NANCY (1969). *Prosody and phonology.* Doctoral dissertation, Cambridge, Massachusetts: Massachusetts Institute of Technology.

WORTH, DEAN S. (1967). On cyclical rules in derivational morphology. In *Phonologie der Gegenwart.* Graz-Wien-Küln: Böhlaus.

WRIGHT, JOSEPH (1928). *An elementary Middle English grammar.* London: Oxford University Press.

ZWICKY, ARNOLD (1970). Auxiliary reduction in English. *Linguistic Inquiry* **1**, 323–336.

Index of Languages Cited

Subject Index